Virtue and Action

Virtue and Action

Selected Papers

ROSALIND HURSTHOUSE
Edited by
JULIA ANNAS AND JEREMY REID

OXFORD
UNIVERSITY PRESS

Great Clarendon Street, Oxford, OX2 6DP,
United Kingdom

Oxford University Press is a department of the University of Oxford.
It furthers the University's objective of excellence in research, scholarship,
and education by publishing worldwide. Oxford is a registered trade mark of
Oxford University Press in the UK and in certain other countries

© Rosalind Hursthouse 2023

The moral rights of the author have been asserted

First Edition published in 2023

Impression: 1

All rights reserved. No part of this publication may be reproduced, stored in
a retrieval system, or transmitted, in any form or by any means, without the
prior permission in writing of Oxford University Press, or as expressly permitted
by law, by licence or under terms agreed with the appropriate reprographics
rights organization. Enquiries concerning reproduction outside the scope of the
above should be sent to the Rights Department, Oxford University Press, at the
address above

You must not circulate this work in any other form
and you must impose this same condition on any acquirer

Published in the United States of America by Oxford University Press
198 Madison Avenue, New York, NY 10016, United States of America

British Library Cataloguing in Publication Data
Data available

Library of Congress Control Number: 2022940615

ISBN 978–0–19–289584–4

DOI: 10.1093/oso/9780192895844.001.0001

Printed and bound in the UK by
Clays Ltd, Elcograf S.p.A.

Links to third party websites are provided by Oxford in good faith and
for information only. Oxford disclaims any responsibility for the materials
contained in any third party website referenced in this work.

Acknowledgements

The chapters were originally published as follows. Permissions, where appropriate, have been granted.

1. 'The Central Doctrine of the Mean', in Richard Kraut (ed.), *The Blackwell Companion to Aristotle's Ethics* (Oxford: Wiley-Blackwell, 2006): 96–115.
2. 'Practical Wisdom: A Mundane Account', *Proceedings of the Aristotelian Society* 106 (2000): 283–307.
3. 'What Does the Aristotelian *Phronimos* Know?', in Lawrence Jost and Julian Wuerth (eds), *Perfecting Virtue: New Essays on Kantian Ethics and Virtue Ethics* (New York: Cambridge University Press, 2011): 38–57.
4. 'Aristotle for Women Who Love Too Much', *Ethics* 117(2) (2007): 327–36.
5. 'Excessiveness and Our Natural Development', in Rachana Kamtekar (ed.), *Oxford Studies in Ancient Philosophy: Supplementary Volume in Honour of Julia Annas* (Oxford: Oxford University Press, 2012): 171–96.
6. 'Virtue Theory and Abortion', *Philosophy and Public Affairs* 20(3) (1991): 223–46.
7. 'Are the Virtues the Proper Starting-Point for Morality?', in James Dreier (ed.), *Contemporary Debates in Moral Theory* (Oxford: Wiley-Blackwell, 2006): 99–112.
8. 'Discussing Dilemmas', *Christian Bioethics* 14(2) (2008): 141–50.
9. 'Two Ways of Doing the Right Thing', in Colin Farrelly and Lawrence B. Solum (eds), *Virtue Jurisprudence* (Basingstoke: Palgrave Macmillan, 2008): 236–55.
10. 'Applying Virtue Ethics to Our Treatment of the Other Animals', in Jennifer Welchman (ed.), *The Practice of Virtue: Classic and Contemporary Readings in Virtue Ethics* (Indianapolis: Hackett, 2006): 136–55.
11. 'Environmental Virtue Ethics', in Rebecca L. Walker and Philip J. Ivanhoe (eds), *Working Virtue: Virtue Ethics and Contemporary Moral Problems* (New York: Oxford University Press, 2007): 155–71.
12. 'Virtuous Action', in Timothy O'Connor and Constantine Sandis (eds), *A Companion to the Philosophy of Action* (Oxford: Wiley-Blackwell, 2010): 317–23.

13. 'Arational Action', *Journal of Philosophy* 88(2) (1991): 57–68.
14. 'Hume on Justice', in Charles Pigden (ed.), *Hume on Motivation and Virtue* (Basingstoke: Palgrave Macmillan, 2009): 264–76.
15. 'After Hume's Justice', *Proceedings of the Aristotelian Society* 91 (1990–91): 229–45.
16. 'The Good and Bad Family', in Laurence Thomas (ed.), *Contemporary Debates in Social Philosophy* (Oxford: Wiley-Blackwell, 2007): 57–68.
17. 'On the Grounding of the Virtues in Human Nature', in Jan Szaif and Matthias Lutz-Bachmann (eds), *Was ist das für den Menschen Gute? Menschliche Natur und Gueterlehre/What is Good for a Human Being? Human Nature and Values* (Berlin and New York: De Gruyter, 2004): 263–75.
18. 'Human Nature and Aristotelian Virtue Ethics', in Constantine Sandis and Mark J. Cain (eds), *Human Nature* (New York: Cambridge University Press, 2012): 169–88.
19. 'The Grammar of Goodness in Foot's Ethical Naturalism', in John Hacker-Wright (ed.), *Philippa Foot on Goodness and Virtue* (Cham: Palgrave Macmillan, 2018): 25–46.

Contents

Introduction	1
Bibliography	16

PART I. ARISTOTLE AND ANCIENT VIRTUE ETHICS

1. The Central Doctrine of the Mean	23
2. Practical Wisdom: A Mundane Account	45
3. What Does the Aristotelian *Phronimos* Know?	66
4. Aristotle for Women Who Love Too Much	86
5. Excessiveness and Our Natural Development	94

PART II. NORMATIVE VIRTUE ETHICS

6. Virtue Theory and Abortion	121
7. Are the Virtues the Proper Starting Point for Morality?	144
8. Discussing Dilemmas	162
9. Two Ways of Doing the Right Thing	173
10. Applying Virtue Ethics to Our Treatment of the Other Animals	193
11. Environmental Virtue Ethics	210

PART III. ACTION THEORY, POLITICS, AND NATURALISM

12. Virtuous Action	233
13. Arational Actions	241
14. Hume on Justice	254
15. After Hume's Justice	269

16. The Good and Bad Family — 285
17. On the Grounding of the Virtues in Human Nature — 300
18. Human Nature and Aristotelian Virtue Ethics — 313
19. The Grammar of Goodness in Foot's Ethical Naturalism — 333

Index — 353

Introduction

Julia Annas and Jeremy Reid

Rosalind Hursthouse was born in Bristol, England on 10 November 1943. She was brought up in Wellington, New Zealand, and obtained her B.A. in Philosophy from the University of Auckland in 1964 and her M.A. the following year. She went to the University of Oxford for postgraduate study, being awarded her B.Phil. in 1968 and her D.Phil. in 1974. Her first academic position was as a Junior Lecturer in Philosophy at the University of Auckland from 1966, then she returned to Oxford as a College Lecturer at Corpus Christi from 1969–1975. Subsequently she taught at the Open University from 1975–2001, as Lecturer and then Senior Lecturer, also acting as Head of Department from 1991–1997. She moved back to New Zealand as a Professor of Philosophy at the University of Auckland in 2002, was Head of Department from 2002 to 2005, and retired in 2016. Hursthouse also held visiting positions at the University of California, Los Angeles (1981, 1983), the University of California, San Diego (1988, 1989), the University of Auckland (1991), the University of North Carolina, Chapel Hill (1993), Stanford (1996), and the University of California, Berkeley as Mills Distinguished Visiting Professor in Moral and Intellectual Philosophy and Civil Polity (2004). In 2016 she was elected a Fellow of the Royal Society of New Zealand.

Virtue Ethics and Right Action

When thinking about what to say about some philosophical issue, Rosalind Hursthouse would often suggest starting with Aristotle. Our interpretation of Aristotle, she said, should always end up saying something sensible—it could be wrong upon deeper philosophical inspection, of course, but it had to be sensible.[1] But because this is a volume about Hursthouse's thought, we might

---

[1] There was a rule in Rosalind's classroom that students were never to say 'Aristotle is wrong when he says X'; rather, they had to say, 'I find it puzzling that Aristotle says X, because it seems as though...'

well start by explaining how Hursthouse came to find Aristotle in the first place and why he came to exert such a large influence on her ethics.

It was not obvious that Aristotle and Hursthouse should have a meeting of the minds, and it wasn't until she was 26 that she said she had her 'epiphany' about Aristotle. Hursthouse was a student of both Philippa Foot and Elizabeth Anscombe, so it is easy to assume that *surely* they were talking about virtue ethics together back in the day. But while they noticed that something was amiss in the state of moral philosophy at Oxford (helped in large part by Anscombe's important article, 'Modern Moral Philosophy'), the way forward was less clear. So much of their attention was directed towards other philosophical issues, and Hursthouse's focus was primarily on action theory.

At the time Wittgenstein was influential in Oxford in a variety of ways: there were full-fledged Wittgensteinians, those who were quite hostile, and those, particularly Anscombe, who took his insights into their own work in a thoughtful and philosophically nuanced way. Hursthouse followed Anscombe and Foot in taking Wittgenstein's work to be important, and essential for philosophers in areas where there were confident pronouncements and debates which focused on examples defined ever more narrowly. But, although she occasionally taught graduate seminars on Wittgenstein at the University of Auckland later in her career, she did not sail by his star; she put his work to philosophical use in thinking slowly through her own ethical views. As a result, she distrusted ethical theories which built impressive academic structures and dismissed as less important their fit with the way people actually live. (One attraction of Aristotle turned out to be his anti-Platonic approach to ethics, starting from what works rather than aiming for theoretical perfection.) Hursthouse began from the way people live and talk, because that is where, literally, the action is. Like the ancient Greeks, even before studying them, she took an ethical theory to be one that has to be lived by. Actual human ways of life are not only the starting points of ethics, but something that ethics ought to respect, answer to, and explain.

The problem was that philosophical ethics in the mid-twentieth century was, to Hursthouse, uninspiring. At Oxford R. M. Hare's theory was studied while Hare was the Professor, and there were some efforts to define the term 'moral', but mainly ethics was constituted by two concerns. One concern was to see ethics entirely in terms of current theories about language; interest in the

---

Her point was that *you, dear student*, after reading perhaps a single passage once or twice, were unlikely to come up with a devastating objection to a philosopher that people much wiser than you have found deeply compelling for millennia.

content of moral judgements gave way to formal analysis of the language, a project generally regarded as completed. Philosophers were interested only in whether a moral judgement 'referred' to something, or, as the 'emotivist' theory had it, expressed a feeling or emotion. Later Hursthouse shared an insight that this latter approach might have been promising if accompanied by curiosity about emotions and how interestingly complex they are; but at the time it was routinely taken to be a childish 'boo/hurrah' theory, useless for understanding anyone's actual life and judgements. The other concern was a long-running debate as to whether the rightness of actions was determined by moral rules or by consequences. This debate had not really changed since the days of Ross, and the moves were very familiar. So despite the work of Anscombe and Foot, ethics at the time of Hursthouse's graduate work at Oxford was an unexciting and unattractive field. Moreover, as Foot noted, this kind of moral philosophy failed to respond in a serious way to the obvious horrors and wrongs of the Second World War. Thus the seeds of discontent were sown.

It wasn't until many years later when Hursthouse had to teach a course on Aristotle that something clicked. Part of this realization can be seen in one of Hursthouse's earliest articles, 'A False Doctrine of the Mean', updated in this volume as her revised 'The Central Doctrine of the Mean' (young scholars should be encouraged by the fact that the original article was met with cruel and unfair reviewer reports before being eventually accepted). Here Hursthouse noticed that Aristotle's doctrine of the mean was not a vacuous prescription amounting to the truism that we should be neither excessive nor deficient in our dispositions, but rather was providing a long list of dimensions along which an agent must *get it right*. Hursthouse thus emphasizes that the famous Aristotelian passage about the mean should not be understood quantitatively:

> Fearing the right objects with respect to courage, for example, is not a matter of fearing, say, three, some figure in a mean between two or less and four or more. I do not count as courageous if, as a 'fearless phobic', the three objects I fear are the dark, enclosed spaces, and mice, but only if they are death, pain, and physical damage—the *right* objects.[2]

On her reading of Aristotle, then, we were permitted to say—and *should* say—that while an action may in fact have been the right thing to do, it wasn't done

---

[2] 'The Central Doctrine of the Mean', 106 (34 in this volume).

at the right time, or with the right attitude, or directed at quite the right person, and so forth. This understanding of the Doctrine of the Mean, she noticed, was then supposed to apply to all of the virtues Aristotle lists. Thus, following Anscombe's suggestion, we can ask not only if an action is *right*, but whether it is just and kind and thoughtful, or callous and reckless and selfish, and then consider the further dimensions suggested by the mean: even if telling the truth here is honest, it's inconsiderate to say it like *that* and it could have waited until tomorrow when they're feeling better, and perhaps you weren't even the best person to say it, and... So we find ourselves with an enormous list of ways in which an action must be carefully calibrated in order to count as fully right—for it to get the two ticks of approval, as she would say.[3]

Hursthouse was drawn to Aristotle's ethics on this reading because it provided a veritable cornucopia of ethical resources in comparison to (what Wittgenstein would call) the one-sided diet of examples offered by consequentialists and deontologists of the period. For the consequentialists, an action was right or wrong depending on whether it maximized pleasure (or desire-satisfaction) or not, and for the deontologist, an action was either right or wrong depending on whether it was in accordance with the right moral rule or not. And that was the end of the discussion. So for Hursthouse, Aristotle was a breath of fresh air—finally there was a way of evaluating actions across a number of dimensions: in terms of the individual virtues and vices, in terms of the long list of criteria for hitting the mean, and in terms of the dispositions of the agent while performing those actions.[4] Once she saw that all of these modes of evaluation are at play in Aristotle, it was totally obvious why Aristotle doesn't provide a decision procedure or formula for acting rightly that any clever undergraduate might understand—how could you possibly say anything sufficiently general and sufficiently helpful to ensure that somebody gets it right in *all* of those ways?

It is with this background in mind that we should consider what Hursthouse is most well known for, namely her formulation that an action is right if and only if it is what a virtuous agent would characteristically do in the circumstances. If we think that Hursthouse is just providing a *tertium quid* or elegant alternative criterion of right action that cuts up the cases slightly differently to the consequentialist or deontologist, then we've missed the point entirely. As

---

[3] She would also grade student essays using this system.
[4] Her later thought arguably adds yet further evaluative dimensions, taking account of the institutional roles an agent might occupy and how sometimes an action can only be called right in the context of a diachronic *action plan* (see 'Two Ways of Doing the Right Thing' for an especially vivid example of this).

many commentators have noticed, it's not especially helpful to ask what a virtuous person would do in my circumstances, for I am not a virtuous person and a virtuous person likely wouldn't get into this mess in the first place. Indeed. But Hursthouse's point was that we should think about the virtuous person as a proxy for *someone who has the virtues* and is thus appropriately motivated by the right concerns—it is the virtues themselves doing the important theoretical work. While it might be unclear to me what a perfectly virtuous person would do in my circumstances, it's often utterly obvious that I can't do *that* because it would be dishonest, and that I shouldn't worry about *this* just because it might be painful for me, and that while it might be easier to do x I'd have to betray my friend, which is disloyal, so that leaves y and z. And so I start by thinking about what I can do that isn't prohibited by the vices and focus on what is required by the virtues.

With this framework established, we can see why, as Hursthouse emphasizes nicely in 'Are the Virtues the Proper Starting-Point for Morality?', the famous virtuous agent biconditional is in fact much less important—and much less helpful—than focusing on the individual virtues and what they require. We should be directing our attention to the huge range of considerations to which the virtue terms and the mean point us, rather than trying to ground right action in a single consideration, as 'no virtue ethicist remotely inspired by Aristotle aims for the reduction of significant moral concepts to others.'[5] This also explains why Hursthouse did not feel a pressing need to respond to the various articles attacking the virtue ethics biconditional: the biconditional was never meant to be the heart of the theory and the purported counter-examples others proposed did not undermine anything integral to her ethics, most especially the virtue- and vice-rules ('V-rules').

The virtues and vices themselves are thus a better starting point for ethical theorizing, Hursthouse claims, both because they provide a wealth of theoretical resources and because we all have a sufficiently firm grasp of virtue and vice concepts, deploying them regularly in our own lives. So even though Aristotle does not tell us what we should do, he also doesn't need to—we can work it out for ourselves most of the time. In a revealing passage from 'Applying Virtue Ethics' (in the Festschrift for Philippa Foot), Hursthouse writes:

---

[5] 'Are the Virtues the Proper Starting Point for Morality?', 101 (146 in this volume). See 'Environmental Virtue Ethics', 167 (225 in this volume), for further applications of this idea.

Perhaps what philosophers, as a body of professionals, tend to find uncomfortable about virtue ethics is that it makes all too explicit a fact we would like to think was not so; that we are not, *qua* philosophers, thereby fitted to say anything true or even enlightening on real moral issues. It requires that we give up the pretence that all we bring to bear on them is the expertise of our trade—our oft-claimed clarity and rigour of argument, our detachment, our skill in working out inconsistencies and dreaming up counter-examples. It reveals that, if we are to say anything true about them, we must also bring our knowledge of the correct application of the virtue-vice terms—about which actions are, say, charitable or dishonest—and, moreover, our knowledge of what is truly good and bad, of what is worthwhile, of what counts as a good, mature, developed human life and what as a wasted, perverted, or childish one.[6]

Philosophers, just because they are philosophers, have no better understanding of the virtue terms than any ordinary person. But this is an *advantage* of the theory—philosophers need not proclaim from on high what the right thing to do is; we just need to point ordinary people in the right direction, getting them to pay attention to the things that they knew all along and had been taught since they were children.[7] We suspect that this is why Hursthouse is perfectly happy to cite dictionaries (and even Amazon reviews!), as they show all too well that people often have a pretty solid grasp of the words that they use and of what's ethically significant.

But while she reminds us that it is obvious to most of us on a daily basis what the right thing to do is, much of Hursthouse's most insightful work is about those situations where the way out is less clear. In response to the objection that applying the virtue ethicist's rules are too difficult in complex moral situations, Hursthouse writes:

> Well of course it is difficult. Are you seriously suggesting that a condition of adequacy on a moral theory is that it should make life easy, that it should

---

[6] 'Applying Virtue Ethics', 74.

[7] 'You may complain that none of what I have said about our actions in relation to the other animals is exciting but all pretty obvious. I think myself that this is how it should be. Most of the results of applying virtue ethics *should* be pretty obvious, because, rather than constructing theoretical principles, virtue ethics just applies the everyday virtue and vice terms to our actions in the world as we find it. But what is there to be found, even right under our noses, is often not obvious until it is pointed out' ('Applying Virtue Ethics to our Treatment of Other Animals', 150–1 (206 in this volume)).

represent moral wisdom as something that any clever adolescent could acquire just by being taught the right rules?[8]

Thinking about moral dilemmas was a natural place for Hursthouse to try out the multidimensional mode of evaluation she found in Aristotle, but it also provided a space for her to make the equally important point that ethics should account for the complexity of our moral lives. On the one hand, consequentialists and deontologists made ethics too hard in obscuring the straightforward reasons for which we regularly act (and should act), but they also made ethics too easy in exactly those circumstances where good people find themselves torn apart and sleepless at night, and only make it out of such circumstances through creative strokes of moral brilliance—if at all.[9]

This sensitivity to ethical complexity and its implications for what we decree as 'the right thing to do' is perhaps why her application of virtue ethics to abortion has been so influential (see: 'Virtue Theory and Abortion' and *Beginning Lives*). Not only does Hursthouse draw our attention to the facts on the ground about what having an abortion involves, but she shows her characteristic sensitivity in pointing out the wide range of considerations that must figure in making such a decision (considerations that extend well beyond establishing that one is acting within one's rights) and how difficult it is to do justice to all the things that matter. Ethicists are thus making a mistake in thinking that they can provide from the armchair an exhaustive list of the relevant considerations, weigh them on behalf of a nameless person, and then pat themselves on the back once they've worked out what is the right thing to do. Ethical deliberation in these situations necessarily requires sensitivity to the particulars, contextual awareness, and practical wisdom. So philosophers shouldn't expect to be able to settle these kinds of dilemmas one way or the other at such a general level, even if there is a way out of them for the actual people who find themselves in such circumstances.

The fact that the individual virtues and vices are easily understood by pretty much everyone but that fully fledged, '24-carat' practical wisdom is rare and difficult may explain why Hursthouse devoted little time to the discussions of individual virtues in comparison to the increasing effort she put into specifying the operations of *phronēsis* later in her career (see: 'Practical Wisdom: A Mundane Account'; 'What Does the Aristotelian *Phronimos* Know?').

---

[8] 'Applying Virtue Ethics', 68.
[9] See especially her 'Fallacies and Moral Dilemmas', *Argumentation* 9(4), 1995: 617–632, and chapters 2 and 3 of *On Virtue Ethics*.

Hursthouse was particularly captured by the start of Book VI of the *Nicomachean Ethics* where Aristotle writes that though a virtuous action is done in accordance with right reason, this formulation isn't very helpful because we want to know what right reason *is*—and yet, it's deeply unclear *how* what Aristotle says in Book VI is supposed to be any more helpful than the original formulation. While she no doubt understands practical wisdom as involving a kind of moral perception, Hursthouse was also convinced that Aristotle was *somehow* providing us with more tools for working out the content and structure of practical wisdom.[10] Though it took her many difficult years to write, in 'Practical Wisdom: A Mundane Account' Hursthouse applied a similar strategy to what she had used in her much earlier work on the mean, showing the kinds of considerations practically wise agents paid attention to and characteristically got right, and what those lacking in experience— regardless of how clever or well-intentioned they might be—characteristically got wrong. These 'mundane' considerations, like knowing whether to accept the construal of some situation as a dilemma, knowing which courses of action are likely to be effective and which futile, or knowing whose testimony is likely to be obfuscating something relevant, provide *phronēsis* with a practical savvy that works in conjunction with the refined understanding of the virtue terms that fully virtuous agents have (a point developed in 'What does the Aristotelian *Phronimos* Know?'). These aspects of practical wisdom are what furnish the virtuous agent with ethical skill, common sense, valuable lessons from experience, perspective, and moral creativity—the latter being a feature of Anscombe's thought and teaching that had a lasting impact on Hursthouse.[11]

Thus those interested in Hursthouse's normative ethics would do well to pay closer attention to her work on these more exegetical Aristotelian topics, for it is there that we see that practical wisdom is not an ethical magic wand that conjures its way to the right solution, but is instead a very familiar faculty that takes a great deal of time, effort, and life experience to develop into an excellence. Hursthouse's *phronimos* is not a mystical ethical sage who somehow *just sees* what the right thing to do is; rather, she is somebody who has learned the way the world works and who has grasped the nuances of the virtue and vice terms of which we all have a basic understanding.

---

[10] The 'perceptual model' of practical reason is prominent in John McDowell's 'Virtue and Reason' (a paper Hursthouse always spoke very highly of) but can also be seen in, e.g., Martha Nussbaum's *Love's Knowledge*.

[11] See especially the wonderful application of this in 'Discussing Dilemmas', 142–3 (163–4 in this volume).

A particularly lovely example of this thinking in practice comes in Hursthouse's short piece, 'Aristotle for Women Who Love Too Much', which points out a common and painful error many of us make in assessing our friendships and romantic relationships—an error we can avoid with some good Aristotelian worldly wisdom. Nonetheless, Hursthouse would never claim to have fully characterized the content of practical wisdom; as she would surely remind us, there comes a point at which we, as philosophers, are *supposed* to stop answering questions ourselves and turn to people who have more experience in courage and compassion and justice than we do.

Naturalism and Eudaimonism

For Hursthouse, what makes a character trait a virtue is its relationship to eudaimonia or human flourishing. It is a mistake, however, to think that Hursthouse's normative virtue ethics is inextricably tied up with or ultimately depends on both Aristotelian eudaimonism (the view that happiness is the final end of one's actions and deliberations, and that virtuous activity has a large part to play in achieving happiness) and ethical naturalism (the view that our language for evaluating humans is continuous with our evaluation of other living things, and that the virtues are what make human beings good). There are many ways to ground the virtues, and Hursthouse never gave the impression that those with different theoretical frameworks, like Christine Swanton or Linda Zagzebski, were philosophical adversaries. Nonetheless, Hursthouse's thinking is systematic, and combining virtue ethics with both Aristotelian eudaimonism and ethical naturalism proved an attractive option to her insofar as the overall view promised to unify Aristotle, Foot, and Wittgenstein, and deliver an objective account of ethics in a satisfying way.

Hursthouse's naturalism is greatly indebted to Foot, and she proudly carries her teacher's baton in this regard. Hursthouse regularly taught graduate seminars that were entirely devoted to Foot, specifically to the short but rich book *Natural Goodness*. Hursthouse herself read slowly, carefully, and repeatedly—the book collection in her office was small but what she read she knew like the back of her hand. Given her admiration, it is easy to miss the ways in which Hursthouse developed Foot's own views. Firstly, Hursthouse highlighted the Wittgensteinian aspects of Foot and Michael Thompson, showing why objections based on evolutionary biology completely miss the mark, and clarified that the understanding of 'species' should be as 'form of life', rather than as a narrow biological category and thus at the mercy of scientific trends.¹² As Hursthouse puts the point at the very opening of 'The Grammar of Goodness in Foot's Ethical Naturalism':

> From her earliest years as a philosopher, under the guiding hand of Anscombe, Foot was always a Wittgensteinian, through and through. Hence she was anti-foundationalist and anti-reductionist on principle, and the most unlikely philosopher in the world to think that any of the natural sciences had any bearing on the philosopher's task, let alone if that were moral philosophy.¹³

The goal, then, was most certainly *not* to ground ethics in evolutionary biology, based on whatever theories the most up-to-date natural science delivered, but to investigate the logical structure of our language and ethical practices. Thus debates about the status of a 'species' in evolutionary biology have nothing to do with this kind of naturalism, and we certainly should not confuse 'flourishing' with 'fitness'. Foot's insight was that there is a pattern to the grammar of our evaluations of living things that applies to how we talk about and evaluate human beings and human action—this is the framework that Hursthouse thought was so promising for explaining why virtuous action is also *rational* action.

Building on Foot's project and taking it in new directions, Hursthouse did much to expand the number of Aristotelian categoricals that ethical naturalists should use in their theorizing, thus providing a richer conception of our ethical practices, and so the relevance of the virtues for our form of life. Aristotelian categoricals are what logicians now call 'generic generalizations' or simply 'generics'; these statements have a logical form that is difficult to express formally, but are commonplaces for describing ways of life; for example, 'bears hibernate during the winter' and 'in order to protect themselves from the cold Antarctic winds, emperor penguins huddle together and lean on each other, keeping the children warm on the inside of the huddle and taking turns on the harsh outside.' Aristotelian categoricals thus describe forms of life, both for human animals and non-human animals. For example, in 'The Good and Bad Family', Hursthouse uses the categorical 'the members of a good family live together well, for at least a period roughly determined by

---

¹² See 'On the Grounding of the Virtues in Human Nature' and 'The Grammar of Goodness in Foot's Ethical Naturalism'; Thompson, 'The Representation of Life', in R. Hursthouse, G. Lawrence, and W. Quinn (eds), *Virtues and Reasons: Philippa Foot and Moral Theory, Essays in Honor of Philippa Foot*, New York: Oxford University Press, 1995.
¹³ 'The Grammar of Goodness in Foot's Ethical Naturalism', 25 (333 in this volume).

the time it takes to produce, nurture, and socialize its younger members' as a basis for evaluating public policies with respect to infant mortality, homelessness, and education.[14] These rich descriptions of our human form of life greatly increase the explanatory power of Foot and Hursthouse's naturalism by providing a more substantial account of our natural human ends and how those ends are characteristically achieved by animals like us. In addition to Foot's specification of the natural ends as survival and reproduction, Hursthouse pointed out that all sentient animals have a natural end of freedom from pain, and that all social animals have a natural end of community and friendly interaction with others of their kind. Memorably, Hursthouse emphasized that reproduction in the characteristically human way is not just about *starting* a life but about raising children who can come to *have* a full human life.[15] Because this process involves many people over literal decades, it is a bad objection to say that naturalism condemns the celibate, people in same-sex relationships, or people who (like herself) choose not to have children.[16] Hursthouse understood herself to be contributing to reproduction in human life through her own teaching, and such examples show why we shouldn't understand human survival and reproduction in a simplistic or narrow way.

Hursthouse's naturalism gives a particular flavour to her eudaimonism that perhaps departs from her Aristotelian roots more than she realized. Because she had a rich view of what a good human life involves, Hursthouse came to the table with an objective conception of eudaimonia pretty fully worked out and it was one in which Aristotle's comment that eudaimonia requires virtue is sensible. But it was sensible because on Hursthouse's naturalism, our *fifth*

---

[14] 'The Good and Bad Family', 66–7 (292 in this volume).
[15] 'The Grammar of Goodness in Foot's Ethical Naturalism', 42 (348 in this volume).
[16] For further responses to these kinds of objections, including the objection that virtue ethics wrongly condemns homosexuality, see 'Virtue Ethics vs. Rule Consequentialism: A Reply to Brad Hooker', *Utilitas*, 14(1), 2002, 41–53. Hursthouse's summary of her view on this point, which emphasizes that it is *character traits* that are the focus of moral evaluation, is especially memorable: 'Let me revisit my thought that homosexuality, like heterosexuality, is not a character trait. The difficulty we encounter in trying to pin down the "certain ways" in which someone of the homosexual disposition is disposed to act and think and feel would come up again with respect to the heterosexual disposition, and I think this difficulty provides us with a clue. Sex is such a mysterious and powerful force in our lives, so (it seems) peculiarly hospitable to our individual and cultural projections, that there is just no knowing in which ways people are "disposed to act and think and feel" from their sexual orientation. Suppose I know that a man is heterosexual. I still do not know whether he loves having heterosexual sex or finds it disgusting or invests it with Lawrentian cosmic significance, loves women or hates them, is celibate or promiscuous or faithful to one woman, and whichever, for what reasons, what he thinks about Clinton and his cigar or Madonna and her book of photos or celibate priests or St Teresa D'Avila, how he reacts to other men's acts of rape, or self-castration or marriage or semen donation ... I just don't know—and couldn't even guess—*anything*, yet, about his character at all. And the same goes for homosexuality. So neither of them is a character trait and hence neither is up for assessment as a virtue or vice by my criterion' (46).

natural end—the characteristically human natural end—was rationality, and Hursthouse understood Foot's comment about rationality prompting a great 'sea change' to mean that once reason enters the scene, we can ask whether our current ways of achieving our other natural ends are *good* ways of achieving those ends.[17] Thus, while wolves cannot stop to ask whether hunting is the best way to provide sustenance or whether they should become farmers, we can. The addition of rationality changes the human animal life into something 'rich and strange'.

Notice, though, that this makes the conception of virtue on Hursthouse's account at least partly instrumental or productive—virtue is the *best way of achieving or bringing about our natural ends*. Hursthouse thus took the Aristotelian view about the relationship between virtue and eudaimonia to be akin to a doctor's advice about eating habits, smoking, and health: the doctor isn't wrong when he says 'if you want to be healthy when you get older, you should stop smoking and improve your diet' even if it isn't strictly necessary to do so.[18] Thus, as far as rationality goes, it is rational for us to be virtuous if we want to be happy—in her words, 'virtue is our only reliable bet.'[19] But because there is not a tight constitutive relationship between virtuous activity and eudaimonia for Hursthouse, happiness may well be a fragile thing, often beyond the grasp of virtuous people in demanding circumstances.[20]

Hursthouse did not get interested, until late in her career, in the question of whether virtue is ultimately necessary or (necessary and) sufficient for eudaimonia. Although Aristotle's own position on this is interesting and complex (and could be seen as inconsistent), the issue is one which defined ethical disagreement between philosophical schools for hundreds of years after Aristotle, once Aristotle's position was seen as needing clarification. Here

---

[17] Foot uses this phrase at the beginning of chapter 4 of *Natural Goodness*, and Hursthouse always made sure to read the passage to which this alludes (lamenting that philosophers don't read enough Shakespeare, and so miss Foot's point):

> Full fathom five thy father lies;
> Of his bones are coral made;
> Those are pearls that were his eyes;
> Nothing of him that doth fade,
> But doth suffer a sea-change
> Into something rich and strange.
> ('Ariel's Song', from *The Tempest*, Act 1, Scene 2)

[18] For this example, see 'Aristotle: *Nicomachean Ethics*', *Royal Institute of Philosophy Supplement* 20, 1986, 42.

[19] *On Virtue Ethics*, 172.

[20] See especially 'Environmental Virtue Ethics', 169–70 (227–9 in this volume).

Hursthouse's Wittgensteinian impulses led her to recoil from what she perhaps saw as an academic development going beyond a liveable and defensible position. In her most famous book, *On Virtue Ethics*, she considers the sufficiency thesis only in terms of McDowell's position that for the virtuous person virtue 'silences' other claims, a position which she criticizes for its lack of realism; only later did she consider the kind of arguments which enable the Stoics to hold the sufficiency thesis without going against our common sense. Hursthouse defended an Aristotelian position not in terms of virtue being necessary but not sufficient for eudaimonia, but in a broader way, as expressing what she saw as the obvious but harsh truth that some good, indeed, some outstandingly good people can have their lives ruined (or 'marred', as she put it) by factors that they are not responsible for and can do nothing about, however virtuously they live. Thus Hursthouse used ethical naturalism to show that it is rational to be virtuous, while acknowledging that virtue cannot guarantee a flourishing life.

Justice and Politics

Perhaps the least well known aspect of Hursthouse's thought is her work on justice and politics. Justice has always been a difficult virtue to account for, especially in an Aristotelian framework, and being unmoved by MacIntyre's communitarian proposals, Hursthouse turned to Hume for inspiration.

As with moral philosophy in the mid-twentieth century, Hursthouse thought throughout her career that there was something rotten in the state of contemporary political philosophy, but she was less sure about what exactly the solution should be. In the first place, she was utterly insistent that rights language is at best unhelpful and at worst corrupting for our ethical deliberation. In 'Virtue Theory and Abortion', Hursthouse jaw-droppingly sets aside rights-based considerations by writing simply that:

> Love and friendship do not survive their parties' constantly insisting on their rights, nor do people live well when they think that getting what they have a right to is of preeminent importance; they harm others, and they harm themselves. So whether women have a moral right to terminate their pregnancies is irrelevant within virtue theory.[21]

---

[21] 'Virtue Theory and Abortion', 235 (132 in this volume).

Elsewhere she writes that:

> It is charity, not justice, that requires that we stop to help the wounded stranger by the roadside and do for him all that the good Samaritan did; we would be 'quite within our rights', if not, perhaps, to pass by on the other side, at least to do a great deal less; and the predominant contemporary usage has lost its connection with Christian charity.[22]

So whatever role they play, rights massively underdetermine what the virtuous thing to do is, and Hursthouse did not give a central place to rights in her ethics.[23] (Contemporary readers should also note the conceptual drift in our understanding of 'charity', which—especially to American ears—now denotes primarily the giving of money, whereas Hursthouse makes clear that her meaning in the quoted passage is closer to what we might call compassion, benevolence, or kindness.)[24]

But Hursthouse also noticed that rights massively underdetermine what a good *society* is. Much of her frustration with contemporary political philosophy centred around what she referred to as 'the exceptionally pervasive—and deleterious—influence of Rawls's *A Theory of Justice* (1971)'.[25] In the first place, Hursthouse fought tirelessly against Rawls's claim that there are only two 'main concepts' or 'moral notions', the right and the good, which divide moral theories into *either* teleological *or* deontological in structure. Such a classification obviously does not work for virtue ethics, which in turn makes virtue ethics seem incoherent if your framework is Rawlsian. But aside from the moral philosophy, Hursthouse also spotted that there was something strange about Rawls's insistence on the priority of the right over the good, and its influence on mainstream liberal political philosophy.

---

[22] 'Human Dignity and Charity', 66.
[23] See also 'The Good and Bad Family', 57 (285 in this volume): 'Social philosophy is by definition about social issues, but it is not thereby coextensive with political philosophy. It is, for example, quite possible for a philosopher to discuss the rights and wrongs of abortion or euthanasia without committing herself to a single explicit thesis about what a, or any, just or good society would enact, endorse, enforce, promote, prohibit, or permit.'
[24] Similarly, when Foot talks about the contrasting demands of justice and charity in her famous article on euthanasia, she is not talking about giving sick people money; rather, 'charity is the virtue which attaches us to the good of others.' See also Foot's 1992 Oxfam Gilbert Murray Memorial Lecture, 'Justice and Charity'.
[25] 'Are the Virtues the Proper Starting Point for Morality?', p. 100 (145 in this volume). There was a joke in the philosophy department at the University of Auckland that regardless of what you said, you were never going to have a paper on political philosophy well received: if you didn't use a Rawlsian framework, Gillian Brock would stop listening, and if you did, Rosalind Hursthouse would stop listening.

The problem, Hursthouse thought, was that rights get enshrined as the first principles of justice before we ask what we need those rights *for*. Hume was one of the few philosophers who noticed how nonsensical this was, hence going to him as a source of inspiration. Hursthouse describes the problematic view as follows:

> In order to find out what is just, we must first determine what is due to everyone, what we do owe to each other, what are our rights. So we come up with some supposedly incontestable premises about our rights, say that we have rights to life and liberty, and then infer 'and so a just law protects/enshrines these rights'. This way of arguing encapsulates the concept of rights that I referred to at the outset as the one Hume is attacking and, in my view, rightly.[26]

The alternative is to ask first what a good, well-functioning society is, and then think about the general principles and norms that would be conducive to bringing about such a society. Of course, this requires a substantive conception of the good from the beginning, but Hursthouse argues that we have a good and objective conception of human flourishing from Aristotelian ethical naturalism, and could thus formulate a conception of a good society in a framework that doesn't fall prey to the objections of parochialism or cultural relativism.

Moreover, Hursthouse found Rawls's focus on adults particularly objectionable. She mentioned in conversation that she could never shake the idea that what was really going on in the original position was a group of men sitting on the banks of the Potomac listing the ways in which they wanted to be left alone while their wives made their lunch and took care of the children. Of course this isn't totally fair to Rawls, but Hursthouse was always amazed at how little contemporary political philosophers had to say about the development of children, and she writes approvingly that 'Aristotle is one of the few philosophers who remembers that we were once children, and that how life goes then matters a great deal for how life goes later.'[27] Thus Hursthouse isn't just following Susan Moller Okin's influential critique of Rawls, but draws our

---

[26] 'Hume on Justice', 273 (264 in this volume).
[27] See 'Environmental Virtues Ethics', 164–7 (222–5 in this volume) for a wonderful discussion of how we might teach children a new virtue with respect to the environment. Even though she had set out to write something on the Stoics and the sufficiency thesis for Julia Annas's Festschrift, Hursthouse found herself irresistibly drawn to what the Stoics had to say about children, hence 'Excessiveness and Our Natural Development'.

attention to the need for a good society to ask first and foremost what is required to ensure that people have good childhoods. Though Rawlsians will undoubtedly protest, Hursthouse's point is that starting with the liberties and relative wealth levels of adults leads to a very different vision of a just society than one that begins by asking what children need to grow up well.[28] Those interested in virtue politics will surely find many ideas in these chapters worth developing.

Although Hursthouse has been very influential and has played an integral role in establishing virtue ethics as a distinctive approach in ethical theory, many of her earlier writings in more obscure venues contain a wealth of philosophical insights, engaging examples, and further explanations of often-misunderstood points. Similarly, many of her later writings develop important themes from her more famous works, and provide the groundwork for fresh new discussions that deserve further attention. We hope that this volume will allow Hursthouse's writings to be better and more widely appreciated, and that her thought will captivate others as it has captivated us.

The editors have made only those changes necessary to render the typography of the papers consistent, to correct typographical errors, and to complete references.

Bibliography

1980. 'Denoting in the Principles of Mathematics', *Synthese* 45(1): 33–42.

1980–81. 'A False Doctrine of the Mean', *Proceedings of the Aristotelian Society* 81: 57–72.

1984. 'Acting and Feeling in Character: *Nicomachean Ethics* 3.I', *Phronēsis* 29: 252–66.

1984. 'Plato on the Emotions [response to Martha Nussbaum, "Plato on Commensurability and Desire"]', *Proceedings of the Aristotelian Society, Supplementary Volumes* 58: 55–96 [81–96].

1986. 'Aristotle: *Nicomachean Ethics*', *Royal Institute of Philosophy Supplement* 20: 35–53.

---

[28] It is worth noting how mundane Hursthouse takes this project to be in practice: 'Social and political philosophers tend to go for ideals rather than modest aims. It is exciting to discuss the nature of the ideal family and argue for one's favored detailed specification of what is involved in nurturing and socializing the next generation really well, less exciting to garner the sad and sometimes sordid facts about dysfunctional families and think about the nitty-gritty details of how they might be helped in a modest way' ('The Good and Bad Family', 67 (298 in this volume)).

1987. *Beginning Lives*. Oxford: Basil Blackwell.

1988. 'Moral Habituation: A Review of Troels Engberg-Pedersen's *Aristotle's Theory of Moral Insight*', *Oxford Studies in Ancient Philosophy* 6: 201–19.

1990–91. 'After Hume's Justice', *Proceedings of the Aristotelian Society* 91: 229–45.

1991. 'Arational Action', *Journal of Philosophy* 88(2): 57–68.

1991. 'Virtue Theory and Abortion', *Philosophy and Public Affairs* 20(3): 223–46.

1993. 'Slote on Self-Sufficiency', *Journal of Social Philosophy* 24: 57–67.

1995. 'Applying Virtue Ethics'. In Rosalind Hursthouse, Gavin Lawrence, and Warren Quinn (eds), *Virtues and Reasons: Philippa Foot and Moral Theory, Essays in Honor of Philippa Foot*. Oxford: Clarendon Press: 57–75.

1995. 'Fallacies and Moral Dilemmas', *Argumentation* 9(4): 617–32.

1995. 'Hume: Moral and Political Philosophy' In Stuart Brown (ed.), *British Philosophy and the Age of Enlightenment*. Abingdon: Routledge: 179–202.

1995. 'The Virtuous Agent's Reasons: A Reply to Bernard Williams'. In Robert Heinaman (ed.), *Aristotle and Moral Realism*. Boulder, CO: Westview Press: 24–34.

1996. 'Normative Virtue Ethics'. In Roger Crisp (ed.), *How Should One Live? Essays on the Virtues*. New York: Oxford University Press: 19–36.

1997. 'Virtue Ethics and the Emotions'. In Daniel Statman (ed.), *Virtue Ethics*. Washington, DC: Georgetown University Press: 99–117.

1998. 'Reproduction and Ethics'. In Edward Craig (ed.), *Routledge Encyclopedia of Philosophy*. New York: Routledge.

1999. *On Virtue Ethics*. New York: Oxford University Press.

1999. 'Virtue Ethics and Human Nature', *Hume Studies* 25(1–2): 67–82.

2000. *Ethics, Humans, and Other Animals: An Introduction with Readings*. New York: Routledge.

2000. 'Intention'. In Roger Teichmann (ed.), *Logic, Cause and Action (Royal Institute of Philosophy Supplement, 46)*. Cambridge: Cambridge University Press: 83–106.

2000. 'Intention', *Royal Institute of Philosophy Supplement* 46: 83–105.

2000. 'Practical Wisdom: A Mundane Account', *Proceedings of the Aristotelian Society* 106: 283–307.

2000. 'Virtue Ethics vs. Rule Consequentialism: A Reply to Brad Hooker', *Utilitas* 14(1): 41–53.

2002. 'Review of Bennett W. Helm: *Emotional Reason: Deliberation, Motivation and the Nature of Value*', *Mind* 111(442): 418–22.

2004. 'On the Grounding of the Virtues in Human Nature'. In Jan Szaif and Matthias Lutz-Bachmann (eds), *Was ist das für den Menschen Gute?*

Menschliche Natur und Gueterlehre/What is Good for a Human Being? Human Nature and Values. Berlin and New York: De Gruyter: 263–75.

2006. 'Applying Virtue Ethics to Our Treatment of the Other Animals'. In Jennifer Welchman (ed.), *The Practice of Virtue: Classic and Contemporary Readings in Virtue Ethics*. Indianapolis: Hackett: 136–55.

2006. 'Are the Virtues the Proper Starting-Point for Morality?' In James Dreier (ed.), *Contemporary Debates in Moral Theory*. Oxford: Wiley-Blackwell: 99–112.

2006. 'The Central Doctrine of the Mean'. In Richard Kraut (ed.), *The Blackwell Companion to Aristotle's Ethics*. Oxford: Wiley-Blackwell: 96–115.

2007. 'Aristotle for Women Who Love Too Much', *Ethics* 117(2): 327–36.

2007. 'Environmental Virtue Ethics'. In Rebecca L. Walker and Philip J. Ivanhoe (eds), *Working Virtue: Virtue Ethics and Contemporary Moral Problems*. New York: Oxford University Press: 155–71.

2007. 'The Good and Bad Family'. In Laurence Thomas (ed.), *Contemporary Debates in Social Philosophy*. Oxford: Wiley-Blackwell: 57–68.

2007. 'Human Dignity and Charity'. In Jeff Malpas and Norelle Lickiss (eds), *Perspectives on Human Dignity: A Conversation*. Dordrecht: Springer: 59–72.

2007. 'Virtue Theory'. In Hugh Lafollette (ed.), *Ethics in Practice*. Oxford: Wiley-Blackwell: 45–55.

2008. 'Aristotle's Ethics, Old and New'. In Lorna Hardwick and Christopher Stray (eds), *A Companion to Classical Receptions*. Oxford: Wiley-Blackwell: 428–39.

2008. 'Discussing Dilemmas', *Christian Bioethics* 14(2): 141–50.

2008. 'Two Ways of Doing the Right Thing'. In Colin Farrelly and Lawrence B. Solum (eds), *Virtue Jurisprudence*. Basingstoke: Palgrave Macmillan: 236–55.

2009. 'Hume on Justice'. In Charles Pigden (ed.), *Hume on Motivation and Virtue*. Basingstoke: Palgrave Macmillan: 264–76.

2010. 'Doctor-Assisted Suicide: A Commentary on Lesser', *Journal of Evaluation in Clinical Practice* 16(2): 335–6.

2010. 'Virtuous Action'. In Timothy O'Connor and Constantine Sandis (eds), *A Companion to the Philosophy of Action*. Oxford: Wiley-Blackwell: 317–23.

2011. 'Virtue Ethics and the Treatment of Animals'. In Tom L. Beauchamp and R. G. Frey (eds), *The Oxford Handbook of Animal Ethics*. New York: Oxford University Press: 119–43.

2011. 'What Does the Aristotelian *Phronimos* Know?' In Lawrence Jost and Julian Wuerth (eds), *Perfecting Virtue: New Essays on Kantian Ethics and Virtue Ethics*. New York: Cambridge University Press: 38–57.

2012. 'Excessiveness and Our Natural Development'. In Rachana Kamtekar (ed.), *Oxford Studies in Ancient Philosophy: Supplementary Volume in Honour of Julia Annas*. Oxford: Oxford University Press: 171–96.

2012. 'Human Nature and Aristotelian Virtue Ethics'. In Constantine Sandis and Mark J. Cain (eds), *Human Nature*. New York: Cambridge University Press: 169–88.

2012. 'Philippa Ruth Foot, 1920–2010', *British Academy Biographical Memoirs of Fellows* XI: 179–96.

2013. 'Moral Status'. In Hugh LaFollette (ed.), *The International Encyclopedia of Ethics Online*. Hoboken, NJ: Wiley-Blackwell.

2013. 'Neo-Aristotelian Ethical Naturalism'. In Hugh LaFollette (ed.), *The International Encyclopedia of Ethics Online*. Hoboken, NJ: Wiley-Blackwell.

2013. 'Philippa Foot'. In Hugh LaFollette (ed.), *The International Encyclopedia of Ethics Online*. Hoboken, NJ: Wiley-Blackwell.

2015. 'How Do We Reason about What is Right? Virtue Ethics'. In Gideon Rosen, Alex Byrne, Joshua Cohen, and Seana Shiffrin (eds), *The Norton Introduction to Philosophy*. New York: W. W. Norton: 781–7.

2016. 'Virtue Ethics'. In Edward N. Zalta (ed.), *Stanford Online Encyclopedia of Philosophy*, updated with Glen Pettigrove as co-author.

2018. 'The Grammar of Goodness in Foot's Ethical Naturalism'. In John Hacker-Wright (ed.), *Philippa Foot on Goodness and Virtue*. Cham: Palgrave Macmillan: 25–46.

PART I
ARISTOTLE AND ANCIENT VIRTUE ETHICS

1
The Central Doctrine of the Mean

I shall claim that there is no truth in the doctrine of the mean as ordinarily understood, and that we see this quite clearly when we look at it outside the context of Aristotle's ethical works. The latter contain, however, at least two great insights expressed in its terms which I aim to extract from the distorting influence of Aristotle's use of the doctrine. One may even be called 'the central doctrine of the mean' when that is understood in a certain way—hence the title of this chapter.

1. The Doctrine of the Mean outside Aristotle's Ethical Works

Intimations of the doctrine of the mean—in literature, medicine, mathematics, and philosophy—seem to have been around well before Aristotle, but, for the purposes of this chapter, I will go no further back than Plato, beginning with the *Statesman* at 283c–284e. Here 'length and brevity, and excess and deficiency in general' are said to be the things to which the art of measurement relates (283c), and a distinction is drawn between measuring things that are large and small relative to each other, and things that exceed and fall short of 'the due measure' (*metrion*) (283e). Later on, this is filled out as measuring the 'lengths, depths, breadths, and speeds of things in relation to what is opposed to them' and measuring 'in relation to what is in due measure/moderate [*metrion*], what is proper/fitting/appropriate [*prepon*], what is fitting/appropriate/timely/[*kairon*], what is as it ought to be/fitting/necessary [*deon*] and whatever avoids the extremes for the mean [*meson*]' (284e). (Note that, although some translators render the verb not as 'measuring' but as 'assessing', and 'the due measure' in a variety of ways, including 'the mean', it is the same root all the way through.) Plato also claims that exceeding and falling short of due measure is what differentiates bad and good people (283e), and that, quite generally, all skills produce all the good and fine things they do produce by avoiding the more and the less than what is in due measure and by preserving measure (284a–b).

As features of the doctrine of the mean here we might note: (1) the casual alignment of the large and the small, or the more and the less, with excess and deficiency (note that the ambiguity of the Greek comparative, which can mean both 'more' and 'too much', makes the transition much easier than it is in English); (2) the assumption that the mean (what is in due measure) is, or is what produces, what is good or best; (3) the assumption that all the skills, including virtue, aim at the mean; and (4) the plethora of terms—*metrion, prepon, kairon*, which in different contexts are more or less interchangeable—with which it is associated.

In the *Statesman*, where he is discussing the art of statesmanship, Plato does not extend the scope of the doctrine beyond the skills. But in the *Timaeus* (for example, at 31b–32b, 35a, 36a, 43d) it acquires the status of a general explanatory principle, shaping the account of the creation of the cosmic body and the cosmic soul, the human soul, the human body, the physiology of sensation, and the nature of disease. As Tracy (1969) and Hutchinson (1988) note, in the latter area at least, Plato is in close accord with prevailing medical theory, which held (roughly, with many variations) that health depended on the due measure/proportion/balance/moderate blending of opposites, and that illness came about through their excess and deficiency. So, as further features of the doctrine of the mean, we might note: (5) its status as a principle in medical theory; and, more generally; (6) its status as a quite general explanatory or 'scientific' principle.

Aristotle, of course, does not share Plato's passion for the mathematical knowledge that the latter no doubt has in mind when he speaks of the mean in relation to the art of measurement in the *Statesman*; nor will he be so inclined to think of *metrion* and *to mesotēs* as mathematical proportion as Plato is clearly doing in the *Timaeus*. Indeed, translators note that Aristotle uses *to meson* and *to mesotēs* indifferently in the ethical works. But he takes over from Plato all the features of the doctrine identified above.

Here he is, for example, confidently employing it as a general explanatory principle in *De Generatione et Corruptione*:

> [so that] hot and cold, unless they are equally balanced, are transformed into one another [and all other contraries behave in a similar way]. It is thus, then, that in the first place the elements are transformed; and that out of the elements there come to be flesh and bones and the like—the hot becoming cold and the cold becoming hot when they have been brought to the mean ... Similarly, it is in virtue of a mean condition that the dry and the moist and the rest produce flesh and bone and the remaining compounds.
>
> (*Gen. et Corr.* II.7.334b22–30).

And in *De Anima*: 'the sense itself is a mean [*mesotēs*] between any two opposite qualities' (II.11.424a2). And in *De Generatione Animalium*:

> for all things that come into being as products of art or nature exist in virtue of a certain proportion [*logō tini*]. Now if the hot preponderates too much [is excessive?] it dries up the liquid; and if it is very deficient it does not solidify it; whereas for the artistic or natural product it is necessary to have this proportion—the proportion of the mean. (*Gen. An.* IV.2.767a16–20).

And in *De Partibus Animalium*, where the general principle 'now everything has need of an opposite as counterbalance in order that they may achieve moderation/due measure and a mean [*metrion kai ton meson*]; for it is the mean that contains the substance and proper proportion and not either of the extremes apart from it' (II.13.652b17–20), leads him to his unfortunate conclusions about the three cavities or chambers in the heart:

> Of these three cavities it is the right that has the most abundant and the hottest blood... the left cavity has the least blood of all and the coldest; while in the middle [*meson*] cavity the blood, as regards quantity and heat, is intermediate [*mesai*] between the other two, being however of purer quality than either. (*Part. An.* III.4.667a1–4).

In fact, it has a big influence on Aristotle's views on the heart, with respect to the three cavities in *Historia Animalium*: 'the right-hand one the largest of the three, the left-hand one the smallest and the middle one [*mesen*] intermediate in size [*meson*]' (*Hist. An.* I.17.496a20–2), and its being the most important organ of the body, in *Parva Naturalia*: 'this [the common organ] must be situated midway [*meson*] between what is called "before" and "behind"... further, since in all living beings the body is divided into upper and lower... clearly the nutritive principle must be situated midway [*en mesōi*] between these regions' (467b28–468a1), and on his views on blood in *Historia Animalium*: 'In very young animals it resembles ichor and is abundant; in the old it is thick and black and scarce; and in middle-aged animals its qualities are intermediate [*mesos*]' (*Hist. An.* III.19.521a32–b4).

What should our reaction be to Aristotle's use of the doctrine of the mean in his ethical works once we have noted the way it operates in his 'scientific' works? (The passages above are not the only examples.) Urmson (1973) defended what, following Curzer (1996), we may call a 'quantitative' interpretation of the doctrine of the mean. Aristotle says that our target is to act and feel 'on the right occasions, about/with respect to the right people, for the right reasons, in the right way or manner [which] is the mean and best' (*NE* II.6.1106b21–2). According to the quantitative interpretation, we read this as claiming that our target is to act and feel on neither too many nor too few occasions, about or toward neither too many nor too few things, with respect to neither too many nor too few people, for neither too many nor too few reasons (or 'with neither too many nor too few ends'). The quantitative match for 'in the right way or manner' has to be varied from case to case rather than having a general statement. We may have, for example, 'neither a too great (strong/intense) nor a too small (weak) an extent/amount' or 'neither too quickly nor too slowly' or 'for neither too long nor too short a time' and so on.

Urmson also claimed that the doctrine thus interpreted was by and large true and 'at the very least...a substantial doctrine worthy of Aristotle's genius'. I claimed (Hursthouse 1980–81) that, on the contrary, thus interpreted it was not only a false doctrine but a silly one and hence should not be ascribed to Aristotle. And, more recently, Curzer, defending an 'Urmsonian' interpretation, claims that it is a plausible view and hence that (given the textual support) there is no reason not to ascribe it to Aristotle.

Claiming that (under a certain interpretation) the doctrine is true, or at least plausible, is, for Urmson and Curzer, obviously important. Most of us who work on Aristotle's ethics do so in the belief that he is one of the greatest moral philosophers of all time and that (almost) everything he says about ethics is either true or worth taking very seriously indeed. So we are reluctant to attribute implausible views to him, and that was why I was so puzzled, in the earlier article, by the prevalence in the ethical works of the implausible (in my view) talk about excess and deficiency, and Aristotle's commitment to the mysterious mathematical symmetry of there being precisely two, opposed, vices corresponding to each virtue (Hursthouse 1980–81: 59–60). But that was before I became aware of the use of the doctrine of the mean as a general explanatory principle in Aristotle's predecessors and in his other works. This casts it in an entirely different light.

If we regard it as peculiar to the ethical works, we are bound to take it seriously, to work on the assumption that there must be something right about it, just as we assume that there must be something right about the idea that we have a final end, or that *megalopsuchia* is a virtue. (Of course, we may try our hardest and still fail to find anything, but we remain open to the possibility that someone else will do better.) But if it is not peculiar to the ethical works, the principle of charity does not apply to it in the same way. We do not work on the assumption that there must always be something right in what Aristotle says in his 'scientific' works, and we assess the doctrine of the mean as it appears there on its own merits.

When we do, it stands revealed as, to be blunt, simply whacky, emphatically not a principle 'worthy of his genius' (in contrast, say, to his hylomorphism) but a bit of completely misguided science-cum-metaphysics that appears to have been generally accepted in his day. Thereby we lose any reason to try to find something right about it in the ethical works, for its presence there, notwithstanding its implausibility, is no longer puzzling. Suppose we think we have, as a general principle that can be fruitfully employed in physiology, physics, and astronomy, in medicine and other *technai*, the view that what is 'intermediate'—a *meson*, a mean, a midpoint—is appropriate, fitting, in due measure, right, correct, best, a stable mode of being. Suppose further that we have a tradition of seeing some version of this principle as obviously applicable in ethics. Then nothing could be more natural than to apply it there.

However, the fact that the doctrine is simply whacky, that there is no truth in it whatsoever, does not entail that its application in ethics will always have the factitious effect it has when Aristotle so hilariously applies it to the heart. If you lack knowledge in a particular area, the doctrine will be no aid in discovering the truth. But if you already know a lot about an area, as we assume Aristotle does about ethics, its effect may be fairly harmless. What you know may sometimes be expressed in slightly distorting terms but its truth should still be discernible. And it is the true things Aristotle has to tell us about ethics that we should be looking for, not any truth in the doctrine of the mean itself. So let us have a look.

2. The 'Mean' in Action and Feeling

I shall begin by going through the bits of the texts where the doctrine of the mean is first introduced, being sceptical about whether it is contributing anything useful. The introduction of the doctrine of the mean in the *Eudemian Ethics* is abrupt. Although the preceding discussion has covered what virtue is produced and destroyed by, and drawn the analogy between virtue and physical well-being, it has done so with no mention at all of the mean, excess, and deficiency. These all appear for the first time at II.3.1220b21–3 in relation to 'every divisible continuum'. Before this, the emphasis is not on what is between excess and deficiency but on what is best: 'the best disposition is produced by the best things... for example, the best exertions and nourishment are those from which physical wellbeing results' (II.1.1220a22–5).

The parallel passages in the *Nicomachean Ethics* (II.2.1104a12–26) do bring in the doctrine in relation to what virtue is produced and destroyed by and the medical analogy, where it is said that 'the sorts of things we are talking about', viz. excellences of character, are destroyed by deficiency and excess, just as strength and health are. Excessive training and too little training destroy our strength; eating or drinking too much (and presumably too little) destroy our health, whereas drinking and eating 'proportionate' (*symmetra*) amounts creates, increases, and preserves it. Similarly (II.2.1104a25–6), temperance and courage are destroyed by excess and deficiency and preserved by 'what is intermediate' (*mesotētos*).

Is this an improvement on the *Eudemian Ethics*? Does the doctrine of the mean contribute anything true? At first sight, one might suppose so. When we first read these remarks about strength and health, they may seem obviously true and in an obviously quantitative way. We all know middle-aged people who are undermining their strength and health by taking no exercise and eating gross amounts; we have all at least heard of people who damaged their strength and health by becoming fitness or diet freaks. But a moment's thought should remind us of cases where strength and health have been harmed not by large or small quantities of exercise or food but by the wrong quality of either. This person destroyed their knee joints by jogging on hard pavements; that one undermined their health by eating only fast foods. Having the right—the best—sorts of food or exercise is at least as important as avoiding excess and deficiency; that is why we need doctors and trainers to tell us what they are.

How does the analogy work with respect to the individual virtues? The discussions in the *Nicomachean Ethics* that precede the formal introduction of the doctrine of the mean in II.6 nearly all look quantitative. But it also seems that there the examples are being only sketched in, and will be qualified later. (As he emphasizes at II.7.1107b14, 'we are talking in outline, and giving the main points, contenting ourselves with just that.') So he says 'Someone who runs away from everything, out of fear and withstands nothing becomes cowardly' (II.2.1104a21–2), but, as he will say later (VII.5.1149a6ff), 'someone who is naturally of the sort to fear anything—even a mouse rustling—is cowardly with a brutish cowardice.' Similarly, someone 'who is frightened of nothing at all and advances in the face of just anything becomes rash' (II.2.1104a22–3), but he will say later (III.7.1115b25–6) that someone who fears nothing would be 'some sort of madman'. Again, at II.4.1105b2 he says that we are badly disposed in relation to becoming angry if we are violently or sluggishly disposed, but well disposed if we are disposed 'in an intermediate way'. But when he comes to discuss 'mildness' in IV.5, he makes it clear that 'violently' and 'sluggishly' are not the only ways of being badly disposed.

So the quantitative remarks that express the doctrine of the mean are to be qualified later in non-quantitative terms. Finally, from these early passages, we should note that at II.3.1104b21 Aristotle says, in relation to pleasures and pains, that people become bad 'by pursuing them and running away from them', but here he does not say 'too much' or 'to excess' as the doctrine of the mean would suggest. He says, rather, that we become bad 'through pursuing or avoiding the wrong ones, or at the wrong time, or in the wrong manner or in any of the other ways distinguished by reason'. And he will have no reason to qualify that later.

The formal introduction of the doctrine in both texts draws a distinction between one sort of mean and the mean 'relative to us'. This distinction is proper to the Aristotelian ethics, not a variant on the doctrine of the mean to be found in his other works, so it is worth looking carefully at what it is doing and whether the doctrine of the mean is contributing anything in this unique context.

Apart from telling us that 'the mean relative to us is best' and that it also produces the best state (II.3.1220b26–30), the *Eudemian Ethics* says nothing about what either sort of mean is, but this (we assume) is made clearer in the parallel passage which begins at *NE* II.6.1106a26, where the distinction is drawn in terms of the mean 'with reference to the object' and the mean relative to us. The mean 'with reference to the object' is the simplest form of *meson* or *mesotēs* in mathematics, the arithmetical mean. It is what is (a) equidistant from each of its two extremes, which is (b) one and (c) the same for all. The mean 'relative to us' is the sort of thing that (a) neither goes to excess nor is deficient, and this is (b) not one thing, nor (c) is it the same for all.

Does this make it clear what is meant by the mean 'relative to us?' And, if so, is the illumination provided by the contrast between the (a)s or the contrast between the (b)s and (c)s? According to Woods (1982), commenting on both passages, it is provided by the (a)s. 'The contrast seems to be that between the midpoint ["mean", *meson*] on some scale, which is a matter of calculation' (Woods 1982: 111) and '[t]he second mean, which involves an evaluative element, since it refers to what is intermediate between excess and defect, i.e. what avoids too much and too little, and therefore cannot be determined without reference to human needs and purposes—hence the phrase "relative to us"' (Woods 1982: 112). The *EE* apparently confounds the (a)s by saying that 'in every divisible continuum there exists excess, deficiency and a mean', bringing in the 'evaluative element' straightaway, instead of, as the *NE* has it, 'in every divisible continuum one can take more, less or an equal amount.' So, on this reading, the doctrine of the mean makes a significant contribution to our understanding of the mean 'relative to us' by introducing 'the evaluative element'.

But what I noted above as a feature of Plato's discussion of the doctrine of the mean in the *Statesman* (to which Aristotle's distinction between the two sorts of mean is standardly compared), namely the 'casual alignment' of the more and the less with excess and deficiency, is not peculiar to the *EE*. Aristotle does it in the *NE* too, saying of both sorts of mean that the 'equal' is a kind of mean between what exceeds and what falls short (II.6.1106a29) and, with explicit reference to the *arithmetical* mean, that it exceeds and is exceeded by the same amount. So I do not think we can claim that the mean 'relative to us' introduces 'an evaluative element' *because* Aristotle mentions excess and deficiency in its (a), and understand it thereby.

Let us look instead at the other clauses, (b) and (c), with which he draws the distinction in relation to the Milo example. As far as weight of food to be eaten is concerned, there is just one arithmetical mean, namely six minae, and, given that there is just one, it is, inevitably, 'the same for all'. But 'relative to us', this is not so. The trainer, the expert who is 'looking for the mean' will choose, say, eight for Milo and four for someone else who is just beginning their training. So 'the' mean is not the same for all and hence not just one thing.

But if these—(b) (not) one thing and (c) (not) the same for all—are bound to stand or fall together, why does Aristotle explicitly mention them both? This suggests that the Milo example is rather condensed, and needs to be filled out. And the various ways in which 'extremes' are to be balanced (in proportion) for a healthy, 'mean' diet, described in the ancient medical literature, show us how to do so.

They took the weight and age of the patient to be relevant, for example. So, we might say, the mean relative to even one of us is not one thing, because the trainer may have prescribed eight minae for Milo at the beginning of his training to build him up and four later on when he has put on some weight, and it is not the same for all, because he may have prescribed different amounts at corresponding times for older or younger men, for bigger or smaller ones. Unsurprisingly, they also took account of different sorts of food. We may suppose the minae of food to be eaten in a week to be made up of different proportions of, say, meat, fruit, and bread. Let us say 80 per cent meat is a lot, 20 per cent a little. The arithmetic mean is thus 50 per cent. The trainer, seeking the mean relative to us, starts Milo off on 40 per cent and rapidly raises it as his training progresses. He makes corresponding adjustments to his intake of fruit and bread. They also took account of external factors which upset the internal balance. So suppose Milo gets sick, has to stop training and, following doctor's orders, eat only bread and fruit. When he comes back, the trainer starts him off on a slightly different regimen. They took account of the seasons, so the trainer prescribes in one way in winter and another in summer and so on.

This gives real point to the double insistence of 'not one thing and not the same for all'. But why, one might wonder, is this called the mean relative to us? True, it is relative to human beings, Milo, and the other people the trainer is prescribing for, but that seems to be the accidental upshot of the fact that we happen to be talking about prescribing for them. Surely a horse-trainer, responsible for choosing the diet of the horses in his care, will not choose just one diet, nor the same for all, but prescribe differently for old Bucephalus and spirited young Pegasus and pregnant Xanthippe and in summer and winter, and according to how much exercise they have been getting recently and so on. And he will, thereby, be 'choosing the mean, not in the object but relative to us'—to us, not to horses (cf. Brown 1997). For Aristotle, echoing Plato, claims quite generally that every expert 'tries to avoid excess and deficiency' and seeks the mean relative to us (*NE* II.6.1106b5–7), even though not every expert is concerned with what is the mean—and best—for some of us in the way Milo's trainer is.

Why, for example, does Aristotle not follow Plato further, and, having said there are two standards for more and less (and hence for what is equal or intermediate), describe his second mean as 'the due measure', *to metrion*? Well, no doubt, in emphasizing that the mean 'relative to us' is not one thing and not the same for all, Aristotle wants to cancel any Platonic suggestion that in ethics, or medicine, or the various *technai*, there are absolute standards, that could, in theory, determine what was 'the due measure' with mathematical precision (cf. Hutchinson 1988). The arithmetical mean is, as Woods says, 'a matter of calculation and can therefore be ascertained in abstraction from particular circumstances' (1982: 111–12); the mean 'relative to us', according to Aristotle, is not and cannot.

Why, then, does he not describe his second mean as 'relative to the circumstances/the situation', which seems so obviously to be what it amounts to? One reason must surely be that 'relative to the circumstances/the situation' cannot be substituted for 'relative to us' when Aristotle is speaking of virtue itself as a mean disposition. But, more to the point, even in the context of the mean as something that is aimed at on a particular occasion, it cannot be relativized to circumstances without the assumption of a goal or end. I cannot aim at the mean relative to 'the circumstances' or even relative to my circumstances in a vacuum, for in the absence of an end, there is no answer to the question 'Which of the circumstances are relevant?' It is Tuesday, spring, the sun is shining, I cannot swim, I owe Jake $10.00, I am in a foreign country, Bucephalus is old, Milo is a well-trained wrestler, and so on.

But if we allow any end to be assumed, we surely depart too far from Plato's absolute standard. Aristotle agrees with him that it is the experts, and the virtuous, who succeed in hitting the mean, not just anyone; and a mean that is 'relative to the circumstances', where the relevant circumstances are determined simply by the agent's personal end, collapses into something that the incompetent and the vicious could hit upon equally well. I am not interested in making a good pot; I just want to have fun trying. Given my end, I will hit 'the mean relative to the circumstances' if it does not take me too long to make a sort of pot (and I don't accidentally make rather a good one too quickly in which case I shall want to have another go) and I don't get too dirty or tired trying, and don't waste too much expensive clay. And, similarly, bent on deceiving my husband, I aim at 'the mean relative to the circumstances', being careful to avoid appearing too eager that he should go away for a week, without annoying him by appearing too indifferent, arranging to visit some of his relatives but not so many as to leave me without enough time to spend with my lover—and may well hit upon it readily enough if I am clever. So the mean 'relative to the circumstances' is either not the sort of thing that can ever be aimed at, or, if made sufficiently determinate to be a target by the individual agent's end(s), can be hit upon by the incompetent and vicious as well as by the experts and the virtuous.

So we have to find a way of reading 'relative to us' that preserves the second mean as something that the experts and the virtuous hit upon and others miss. And the right place to look is surely at the beginning of Book I. The various experts, and the virtuous, all have certain ends. All of these are the sorts of goods a human being can pursue in action or possess, human goods or 'goods for us'. And it is these human goods, things that are good relative to us humans, that, taken as ends, determine which circumstances are relevant. In the context of the *technai*, the expert's end—about which *qua* expert he does not deliberate—is to bring about a good product, a good pot or a good (strong, healthy) wrestler or horse. Thereby, experts aim at the mean 'relative to us', but the dilettante does not. In the context of ethics, our end just is *the* human good, the supreme good 'relative to us'; this involves excellent activity, acting and feeling well, and it is that, assumed as an end, that determines which circumstances are relevant for the agent in a given situation.

The mean 'relative to us' in the ethical context is, then, the mean relative to such relevant circumstances. (Modern philosophers might say relative to 'the morally relevant circumstances' but, in practice, that phrase tends to have a much narrower extension.) Of course, such circumstances may well include facts about the agent. As Brown (1997: 86) says, 'obviously whether your conduct counts as generous depends on how wealthy you are' and whether or not I am being intemperate in eating a large steak may be determined by how big I am and/or whether or not I am in training. But even if I am huge, and in training, eating the steak will fail to be a temperate act if I turn a blind eye to the fact that it was someone else's meal or that I can't afford it, disregarding the constraints of the other virtues (cf. *NE* III.11.1119a19–20). The mean 'relative to us' in the ethical context can be one thing for you and another for me if (but only if) a difference between us makes for different circumstances relevant to the end of each of us acting or feeling well.

So, yes, the contrast between the arithmetical mean and the mean 'relative to us' is a contrast between what is always the same and what varies according to the particular circumstances; and, yes, the mean 'relative to us' cannot be determined without reference to human goods. But our understanding of this all-important notion of the mean 'relative to us' does not come from the mention of 'excess and deficiency', nor is its 'evaluative element' (if that is what the reference to 'human goods' is) introduced by it. So the doctrine of the mean has contributed nothing to it.

3. The Central Doctrine of the Mean

Whenever Milo's trainer prescribes, he is aiming at the mean 'relative to us'. He is thereby, on each occasion, aiming at something determined by the variety of circumstances which are relevant, given his end *qua* trainer. And, when the example is filled out, we can see that this could be summed up by saying that his target is to prescribe the right food, in the right amounts, on the right occasions, in relation to the right people, for the right reason. This is strictly parallel to the II.6.1106b21–2 passage, according to which our target is to act and feel 'on the right occasions, about/with respect to the right things, with respect to the right people, for the right reasons, in the right way or manner'.

For reasons that will emerge later, I shall label this passage—the above claim about our target, just as it stands with no mention of the mean, excess, or deficiency—'the central doctrine'. My question now is: is anything illuminating added by *calling* this a doctrine of the mean and adding (as Aristotle does) that our target is hitting upon 'what is the mean and best'?

The passage gives us what Curzer (1996) has helpfully described as five 'parameters' with respect to which we can go wrong in a particular sphere. According to the Urmsonian quantitative interpretation, calling our target a mean does add something because it tells us that the '*deon*' in the various parameters (the right Xs or the Xs one should) can be captured in terms of too many/much and too few/little, and so on. In my earlier article (Hursthouse 1980–81) I argued against that view. I began by pointing out that the very idea that the concept of 'for the right aim or reason' could be captured by specifying it as a mean between too many and too few aims or reasons had only to be stated to be seen as absurd. I then went on to argue, with respect to courage, temperance, and 'patience', that the *qualitative* idea that there are objects or people it is right to fear or enjoy or be angry with and others it is wrong to fear or enjoy or be angry with could not be captured in such a way either. Fearing the right objects with respect to courage, for example, is not a matter of fearing, say, three, some figure in a mean between two or less and four or more. I do not count as courageous if, as a 'fearless phobic', the three objects I fear are the dark, enclosed spaces, and mice, but only if they are death, pain, and physical damage—the *right* objects. I now want to pursue this line of thought.

What the quantitative version of the doctrine of the mean latches on to is that almost all the parameters seem to be straightforwardly measurable. Objects, people, and occasions are, surely, all countable, and amount, though not countable, is still measurable. (The exception is 'way or manner'. 'How did she do it? Let me count the ways.' Or should I measure them? How do I set about doing either?) And, it seems, where you can count or measure, you can mark points on a continuum from 0 to whatever, and thereby speak of the more or 'too much' and the less or 'too little' and the mean between them.

But this is where the talk about the mean misleads us, for counting objects is not a straightforward matter; nor, in the present context, is counting people. How both are to be counted is determined by how they are described. At the buffet, there are, let us say, six plates-of-food, but only three plates-of-healthy-food. At the bar, there are six bottles-of-wine but only two bottles-of-wine-within-my means. At the party, there are ten people other than me, but only five men and only one unmarried one. In my city, there are, no doubt, scores of people of bad character, dozens of people I associate with, eight friends of mine, six people to whom I owe money, just one man who is my father. And right and wrong objects and people are identified as such by the way they are described.

The wrong objects enjoyed by the self-indulgent are 'the pleasures of the table, wine and sex' (VII.14.1154a18) that fall under the descriptions 'unhealthy', 'unaffordable', or 'contrary to what is fine'; the right objects fall under the contrary descriptions (III.11.1119a16–20). The wrong people to whom the wasteful give, or on whom they spend, are those who fall under the descriptions 'bad character' or 'acquaintance rather than friend' (or 'friend rather than debtor' or 'someone other than one's father' [cf. IX.2.1164b30–1165a5]). The right people with whom to get angry include those who can be described as making you or people close to you a target of abuse (IV.4.1125b8–9) (though perhaps we may infer from VII.5.1149a9–14 that one's father is usually a wrong object even if he has insulted you or those close to you). Aristotle does not give us an example of wrong people, but we all know at least some of the descriptions they fall under—people who have reminded you of your obligations, people who catch you out in making a mistake, or voice mild criticism of you, people who innocently and/or unintentionally fail to give you what you want or prevent you from getting or doing what you want.

Moreover, although we, and Aristotle, find it natural to talk about fearing things or objects, 'they' are much harder to identify than the things for which most people have an appetite. When we first think of the 'objects' of fear, we may think in terms of things one can name and count, and thereby in terms of someone fearing numerically more, or fewer, things than the one who is courageous. Our background assumptions save us from construing Aristotle's claim that someone who is 'cowardly with a brutish cowardice' fears anything (VII.5.1149a7–8) literally. We don't suppose he is afraid of flowers or books, but imagine him to be easily frightened by large dogs, noises such as the rustling of a mouse, his own shadow, being in a boat, horses, goats—as well as a whole lot of other things which are more common amongst sane adults (poverty, disease, earthquakes, death, and pain). It is not clear whom Aristotle means by the 'brutish'—if he is referring to people who we would say were mentally handicapped (and also perhaps people born deaf, and neglected?) then perhaps we would just accept that they found all these things fearsome and leave it at that. But certainly when we are training ordinarily timorous children, we talk to them as though we were assuming that mostly 'what they fear' is pain or some vaguely conceived sort of harm, assuring them that the large animals will not hurt them, that they are safe in the boat, and that the noises and shadows do not mean that there is 'anything' there, teaching them that the right objects of fear are what can be described truly as dangerous or fearsome things (cf. III.7.1115b15).

The importance of, as we would say, getting objects under a certain description is strikingly obvious in the case of death as a fearsome object. Someone who is the sort not to fear death at all is presumably a sort of madman (III.7.1115b26) and beyond the pale as far as courage, cowardice, or rashness is concerned. But without being any sort of madman, someone may not fear death under a certain description. Death as a way of escaping from poverty, or sexual passion, may not be something the coward fears on the battlefield but something he accepts (III.7.1116a13–14). Similarly, the courageous man does not fear a death on the battlefield that can be described as fine, though he is the sort to fear death. And what 'the central doctrine' latches on to is precisely the importance of describing objects and people.

Now, the interesting thing about 'the central doctrine' (II.6.1106b22–3) as quoted above (p. 105) is that it is not, as it stands, a doctrine of 'the mean', as we understand that phrase in English, i.e. as something lying between excess and deficiency. Taken out of its context, which indeed bristles with references to excess and deficiency, it reads naturally as suggesting, not an image of something intermediate *between* two other things, but the very image Aristotle gives us at II.9.1109a25, namely that of the centre of a circle. When we think of the centre of a circular target as what we are supposed to hit, we see immediately that 'there are many ways of going astray...whereas there is only one way of getting it right (which is exactly why the one is easy and the other difficult—missing the mark is easy, but hitting it is difficult)' (II.6.1106b29–33).

The 1106b22–3 passage gives us five parameters within which we can go wrong but, as Curzer notes, '[M]ost virtues do not involve exactly these five parameters, but instead involve fewer, more, or different parameters' (1996: 130). For example, II.9.1109a27–8 adds 'to the right extent' and drops 'about the right things', with respect to both anger and giving and spending. The target for feeling anger seems, uniquely, to need a further parameter—right length of time. (One might think that this fell under the very general 'in the right way or manner/as one should', but Aristotle is clearly not assuming that this is so, for at IV.5.1125b32–3 we get both. Nor can it fall under 'to the right extent/amount' because we get failures in both at IV.5.1126a10–11.)

So we have something like six to eight parameters within which we can go wrong. Indeed, if we add in the complication of continence in the modern (not Aristotelian) sense, we may have as many as twelve to sixteen. (In the modern sense, 'continence' is not restricted to the same areas as temperance [VII.4.1148b12–13], but covers, quite generally, hitting the target in action but missing it in feeling.) Thereby we arrive at what I regard as one of Aristotle's most illuminating and profound insights—the *detailed* account of why 'there are many ways of going astray...whereas there is only one way of getting it right'.

It is not only a great insight into what is required for acting (and feeling) well, it is also one of his most practically instructive, the best corrective to our tendency to think that if we, for example, tell the truth, or give a man his due, or put ourselves out of pocket, we can congratulate ourselves on having 'hit the mark'. It not only tells us to examine our consciences before reaching this satisfying conclusion, but also gives us, in all the different parameters, the detailed instructions about how to do so. It is not easy to delude oneself if one goes through all of them carefully, and not often that one emerges from the process convinced that one did indeed hit the mark bang on. And it thereby shows us exactly how we can set about improving ourselves.

Having got this great insight clearly in our sights, we can discard as simply distorting effects the surrounding talk of excess and deficiency. Failures to hit the centre obviously cannot be divided up into those that are excessively or deficiently off target. If you are 'excessively' far to the right you are thereby 'deficiently' close to the left, excessively high is deficiently low and so on. No individual miss-hit is excessive rather than deficient or vice versa; *any* miss-hit is 'too far' from the centre. It is part and parcel of the image of hitting the centre that we attach significance to landing more or less far from it, and strongly suggests that the centre itself need not be a single point but, like a bull's-eye, something that we may count as having hit even if we are not precisely in the centre of it (cf. II.9.1109b19–21 and IV.5.1126a31–b4). We are not, after all, in an area where mathematical precision is called for.

However, we need not do such violence to the text as to discard all talk about hitting the mean. For the centre—the middle—of a circle, that brilliant image, is 'a mean', a *meson* (though for reasons best known to themselves, even the most helpfully literal translators conceal this fact). Hence we can retain 'the central doctrine' as, indeed, 'the central doctrine of the mean' if we remember that, *qua* the centre of a circle, 'the mean' does not involve excess and deficiency. (One might wonder how Aristotle could have supposed for a moment that it did. Well, distressing as it is to recognize, he was prepared to assert [*De Incessu Animalium* 4.706a20-2, 5.706b10-14] that the right is superior to the left and higher to lower, so he can attach sense to missing the meson of a circle by going deficiently high and excessively low, deficiently right and excessively left, deficiently NNE and excessively SSW, and so on.)

4. Virtue as a Mean Disposition and the Moral Education of the Passions

So much for a doctrine of the mean in action and feeling. What about virtue as a mean disposition? Aristotle says in both ethical texts that virtue is a kind of mean insofar as it is effective in hitting the mean, but there is clearly more to his thought than that. Virtue as a mean disposition unavoidably has something to do with being neither excessive nor deficient. What is it?

When Aristotle comes to telling us what virtue is (*EE* II.2.1220b6ff and *NE* II.5.1105b19ff), he does not, as a modern reader might expect, say that the virtues are dispositional states (*hexeis*) with respect to actions, but that they are states 'in terms of which we are well...disposed in relation to passions' (II.5.1105b26–7). In both texts, when he goes on to run through the virtues and vices on his chart, he begins by bringing this feature out (though he abandons it in favour of actions such as giving and spending pretty quickly). If we are to look for truths in Aristotle in relation to virtue and vice anywhere, which he expresses in terms of a mean between excess and deficiency, we should follow Curzer in concentrating on the 'passion parameters'. But instead of looking, as Curzer does, for truth in a quantitative doctrine of the mean, we should rather be looking for truths about being well disposed in relation to the passions.

Let us return again to the medical doctrine of the mean. Plato and Aristotle both accept it, and they both see the health of the human body as obviously analogous to the health or goodness of the human soul. Thereby they see goodness—virtue—as a mean state, a *meson* or *mesotēs* between opposite extremes in the soul (or the affective soul). The medical idea is that these opposing extremes must be blended or balanced or brought closer together for health, so that there is neither excess nor deficiency in any one. But instead of being distracted by excess and deficiency, let us be struck by something else. The hot and the cold, the wet and the dry (or whatever elements your fancy lights on when you use the doctrine of the mean in medicine) are all supposed to be *there* in the human body. Disease is not conceived of as an alien something getting in to the human body (as we now know it often is) but as its natural elements getting out of balance (or harmony or due measure or proportion or symmetry).

Now that is a *wonderful* way to think about virtue and being well-disposed in relation to the passions. What it yields is the idea of the human passions as natural elements in the human *psychē*, things that are supposed to be there, which can be brought into a balance or harmony—from which virtue arises. This gives substantial content to Aristotle's view that, although we do not have the virtues by nature, they are not contrary to nature; indeed, we are fitted by nature to receive them (II.1.1103a24–5). Although there are, as he notes (II.6.1107a9–11), some passions which are singled out by name as ones we should never have, for the most part the capacities to have the passions are part of the natural endowment of a psychologically healthy human child.

What is so wonderful about it can be seen if we contrast it with the different way in which Plato regards the passions in his darker moments. In *Republic* 440C–D, 588B–591D and in the *Phaedrus*, we have what Annas nicely dubs 'the suppressed-beast model' (1999, where she argues forcefully that the model is atypical in Plato). The passions, or at least some of them, especially the appetites, appear as animals to be controlled, coerced, dominated, even enslaved, by superior (and unsympathetic) reason. On this picture, the virtues *are* contrary to (our) nature—not, of course, the nature of our best part, just the dirty animal part. On the other picture, our natural passions are not, in themselves, things that virtue, in the form of knowledge, has to subdue or extirpate, but the very material from which virtue is constituted. It is their presence in us, as much as our reason, that makes us 'fitted by nature to receive the virtues'.

If you thought of the physical appetites as something that should not be there, then you should welcome a baby who was not eager to feed, or a toddler who early became very picky about his or her food and always had to be cajoled into eating. But such a baby or child would not have the natural virtue of temperance; it would clearly be defective. Moreover, it would not be defective because it was showing early signs of tending toward the adult human vice or defect of being 'insensate', but simply because it is an unhealthy animal. (What could that adult vice or defect be? Aristotle says three times that people with that disposition hardly occur [II.7.1107b7, III.11.1119a7, 1119a11] and, in the latter two, that such people are not human. Is it the doctrine of the mean [and thereby the necessity to find a vice opposed to self-indulgence] that prevents him from saying that they could not occur because they would have died in infancy? Or has he heard tales of the Indian ascetics such as Alexander later encountered, and assumed that, having initially taken pleasure in eating, they had so perverted it by their 'barbarian' beliefs as to kill it off altogether? Either way, the idea that what we call, advisedly, a 'normal healthy appetite' for food is supposed to be there in the human *psychē* from birth is operative.)

So, on the medical analogy, the passions that, for the most part, small children characteristically display—and their innate capacity to display a number of others later on—are an important part of what fits us to receive the virtues. This seems to be the obvious point to read into Aristotle's claim, speaking of some (it is not quite clear which) 'natural' passions, that 'since they are natural, they tend to the natural virtues; for, as will be said later, each virtue is found both naturally and also otherwise, viz. as including thought' (*EE* III.7.1234a27–30) and his cryptic remark that 'we are just, prone to temperance, courageous and the rest from the moment we are born' (*NE* VI.13.1144b6–7).

So the medical analogy is fruitful. It yields what I believe is the second of Aristotle's great insights in ethics, namely the idea that the capacities for various passions with which we are born are part of what fits us to receive the virtues. But, as we have seen, the relation between the medical case and the insight is fortuitous; the medical doctrine of the mean is pre-scientific nonsense.

It does not follow that we should discard everything Aristotle says in relation to virtue's being 'a mean between two vices' (*NE* II.6.1107a3), for here too we may find many truths. However, rather than pursuing them, I want to concentrate on this second insight, which has nothing to do with virtue being 'in a mean'.

The question arises: *how* do the innate capacities for the passions fit us to receive the virtues? Well, given that all passions are accompanied by pleasure or pain (II.5.1105b22), I think we may assume that, according to Aristotle, we come into the world, for the most part, set up to enjoy and be distressed by, broadly speaking, some of the right things: for example, eating, being liked or loved, and others' enjoyment, on the one hand, and physical damage, being thwarted, and others' distress or anger, on the other. However, it is also clear that this is not enough, for, notwithstanding the VI.13.1144b6–7 passage quoted above, we know we do not have the virtues from birth, by nature. We must be brought up from childhood onward to delight in and be distressed by the right things (II.3.1104b11–13).

As long as we remember that the claim is that our natural passions in childhood set us up to enjoy and be distressed by just *some* of the right things, *broadly speaking*, there is no contradiction here. Certain as it is that a healthy baby enjoys eating, it is equally certain that it will stick anything it can into its mouth, and as we start teaching it language, we simultaneously start teaching it that some things it wants to eat are 'nasty', 'dirty', 'horrid', and bad and others it is not so enthusiastic about are 'yummy' and good, thereby beginning to fine-tune its healthy appetite regarding right things. Certain as it is that toddlers are distressed by pain, it is equally certain that they have no instinct for danger and we have to teach them that some things that they want to approach or touch will hurt them and are bad. But such early 'correct education' (II.3.1104b13) has to have something to fine-tune; it cannot, in small children, conjure enjoyment and distress about the right things out of total indifference.

It is clear that, amongst the many 'right things', it is pre-eminently important that we should come to delight in doing fine/noble actions and be distressed by doing bad/base ones. But how do we get from the early tuning of toddlers' passions to the enjoyment of fine action? Just what educational programme is suggested by the second insight?

'Habituation', Aristotle tells us, but, as everyone notes, he tells us little about what this involves. Moreover, the mention of punishment at II.3.1104b16–17, his consistent coupling of children with the other *logos*-lacking animals, and the suggestion at VI.13.1144b1–11 that habituated virtue can exist without something in the faculty of reason (however we take *nous* here) tends to give the impression that habituation from childhood onward is to be conceived of as analogous to horse-breaking, that is, as a mindless process of aversion therapy. (*Politics* VII.17.1336a23–VIII.5.1340b19 goes some way to correcting this impression, but is still not much help.)

But, on Aristotle's own grounds, this cannot be right. At the very least, we need something more akin to horse-whispering to get us the beginnings of taking delight in fine actions. We also need something that reflects the fact that children are not mindless and that out of this early training, not only habituated virtue but also full virtue and hence *phronēsis* must somehow eventually grow. Training children to do just, temperate, and courageous acts is not like training a horse to do trotting and cantering acts, even by the horse-whispering technique. It is all bound up with thought and talk. But how?

For an answer, we naturally turn to Burnyeat's (1980) unsurpassed account of Aristotle on moral education—but only to find that his account begins after the phase we are interested in, with young men rather than with children, leaving unexplained *how*, from 'being habituated to noble and just conduct', the students in Aristotle's lecture class could have acquired 'the *that*', that is the ability to know 'of specific actions that they are noble or just in specific circumstances' (1980: 72). Beginning at this later stage, he also leaves unexplored why, or how, early habituation brings about 'a taste for... the pleasure of noble and just actions'. It is surely unlikely that any form of habituation will do. Do we not know that children who are forbidden all sweet foods and vilified as 'greedy' and 'disgusting' and 'bad' when caught eating them on the sly not only fail to develop any enthusiasm for temperate actions (in this area) but dislike them increasingly? An instructive place to look is outside academic philosophy in the Virtues Project[TM] books (Popov 1997, 2000). These have been designed for parents and school-teachers to use to 'help children develop the virtues' and have, in a short period, proved strikingly successful. The Virtues Project[TM] has been recognized by the United Nations as a model programme for parents in all (N.B.) cultures, is currently operating in over eighty-five countries, and is being highly praised by a wide variety of schools.

It is a grassroots movement, and no doubt philosophers would cavil at some of its details. For example, it identifies fifty-two different virtues (one for each week of the year) and we might complain that some of them are indistinguishable (trustworthiness, truthfulness, honesty) and that others (cleanliness, orderliness, enthusiasm, peacefulness, humility, modesty) are not really virtues in the full Aristotelian sense. However, unlike anything we philosophers have managed to produce, it is an extremely detailed and practical educational program and well worth our attention. Its admirable pedagogy makes it clear that the actual doing of the virtuous acts is not all there is to 'helping children to develop the virtues', important as this is, and contains two features that any Aristotelian should find striking.

One is the emphasis on the use, from the earliest days, of the fifty-two virtue words, often in the context of praising a child for doing something (including reacting emotionally) which can (perhaps with a little license) be correctly described by one of them, also in the context of specifically naming a virtue which is called for in a given situation. ('Please be considerate—speak quietly'; 'You need perseverance here—keep trying.') However, not all the recommended uses are confined to action-reinforcement or action-guidance. For slightly older children, at school or in the home, activities and practices are outlined which develop understanding of the words. The children are encouraged to recognize and describe their practice of named virtues, and the occasions on which others have practiced them, and to describe, or play-act, what would happen if a particular virtue was not, and then was, practiced in a particular situation. (One of many interesting examples, for courage: 'You see another child being teased or hurt by other children' [Popov 2000: 151]. Another, for honesty: 'You say something cruel to someone and later tell yourself he deserved it' [2000:179].) And they are also encouraged to consider and discuss what a particular virtue, say courage, is, why we practise it, and how we practise it.

So, from very early days, there is the application of the relevant words to a variety of imagined as well as real instances, and the beginning of reflection, a detailed picture of how the training is bound up with thought and talk, where the talk centres around the use of virtue words in *specific circumstances*. All of this is consistent with, but provides a much-needed supplement to, philosophers' reflections; it provides a detailed answer to the question: 'How do we begin to give children the *that*?'

The other striking feature of the project is that it shares the Aristotelian premise that, in some sense, we have the virtues from the moment we are born. It claims that 'all children are born with all the virtues', 'in potential', 'waiting to grow', and that 'authentic self-esteem and real happiness come *naturally* as children experience the emergence of their virtues' (Popov 1997: 2–3, emphasis added). This premise strongly shapes the pedagogy, which stresses, constantly, looking for something to be praised by a virtue word in a child's action (or reaction) rather than for something to be condemned. But it is not, thereby, permissive. In fact, it is markedly strict, by contemporary standards, about 'setting boundaries' (obedience is one of the fifty-two virtues) and offers a number of techniques for doing so by, once again, emphasizing the virtues (and hence 'Dos' rather than 'Don'ts'). Naming a virtue which is called for in a given situation, which I mentioned above, is one: 'Please be considerate—speak quietly' rather than 'Don't shout.' A related one involves offering the child a choice confined by a virtue: 'Which toys are you willing to be generous with and which don't you want to share?' (to a child who keeps grabbing every one off a visiting child). And then, of course, the child is praised for doing the virtuous action. Others, for older children who are behaving badly, involve asking them what virtue is called for in the situation, or what virtue they are forgetting, or what would be the V (kind, respectful, peaceful) thing to do. The idea is that, rather than making children think of themselves as bad and lacking in virtue, the way poor Huck Finn does, they are enabled to think of themselves as potentially good, as able to recognize and practise the virtues, and find pleasure in doing so.

All very homey stuff, you may say. Well, yes. It is more impressive—very impressive I thought myself—when you read the books and see Popov handling questions, but still homey. But how could bringing up children correctly be anything other than a homey business? Moreover, it encapsulates what I have claimed in this chapter are two of the insights shrouded in the doctrine of the mean: it starts by training children, not to follow general rules but to recognize their central target in particular circumstances, and it develops their natural dispositions toward virtue.

Acknowledgements

I would like to thank Karl Steven and Frans Svensson for helpful comments on an earlier draft of this chapter.

References

Annas, J. 1999. *Platonic Ethics, Old and New*. Ithaca, NY: Cornell University Press.
Brown, L. 1997. 'What is "the Mean Relative to Us" in Aristotle's Ethics?', *Phronēsis* 42: 77–93.

Burnyeat, M. F. 1980. 'Aristotle on Learning to be Good'. In A. O. Rorty (ed.), *Essays on Aristotle's Ethics*. Berkeley, CA: University of California Press: 69–92.

Curzer, H. J. 1996. 'A Defense of Aristotle's Doctrine that Virtue is a Mean', *Ancient Philosophy* 16: 129–38.

Hursthouse, R. 1980–81. 'A False Doctrine of the Mean', *Proceedings of the Aristotelian Society* 81: 57–72.

Hutchinson, D. S. 1988. 'Doctrines of the Mean and the Debate concerning Skills in Fourth-Century Medicine, Rhetoric and Ethics'. In R. J. Hankinson (ed.), *Apeiron*, vol. 4: *Method, Medicine and Metaphysics*. Edmonton, Canada: Academic: 17–52.

Popov, L. K. 1997. *The Family Virtues Guide*. New York: Penguin.

Popov, L. K. 2000. *The Virtues Project^{TM} Educator's Guide*. California: Jalmar Press.

Tracy, T. 1969. *Physiological Theory and the Doctrine of the Mean in Plato and Aristotle*. Chicago: Loyola University Press.

Urmson, J. O. 1973. 'Aristotle's Doctrine of the Mean', *American Philosophical Quarterly* 10: 223–30.

Woods, M. 1982. *Aristotle's Eudemian Ethics, I, II and VIII*. Oxford: Clarendon Press.

Further Reading

Bosley, R., Shiner, R. A., and Sisson, J. D. (eds) 1995. *Apeiron*, vol. 4: *Aristotle, Virtue and the Mean*. Edmonton, Canada: Academic.

Broadie, S. 1991. *Ethics with Aristotle*. New York: Oxford University Press.

Hutchinson, D. S. 1986. *The Virtues of Aristotle*. London: Routledge & Kegan Paul.

Müller, A. W. 2004. 'Aristotle's Conception of Ethical and Natural Virtue: How the Unity Thesis Sheds Light on the Doctrine of the Mean'. In J. Szaif and M. Lutz-Bachmann (eds), *What is Good for a Human Being?* New York: Walter de Gruyter: 18–53.

Stocks, J. L. 1969. 'The Golden Mean'. In D. Z. Phillips (ed.), *Morality and Purpose*. London: Routledge & Kegan Paul: 82–98.

2
Practical Wisdom

A Mundane Account

Be wisely worldly, be not worldly wise.
—Francis Quarles

1. Introduction

Aristotle's *phronimos* has *phronēsis*, which we usually translate as 'practical wisdom'. Practical wisdom is, according to Aristotle in Book VI,[1] an excellent dispositional state of the intellectual/rational part of the soul. Thereby it is a state that enables its possessor to attain truth, and also thereby it contrasts with overall virtue of character, which is a dispositional state of the desiderative/appetitive part of the soul. He who has it, unlike those who have not, characteristically attains 'practical truth'; that is, he gets things right in action in what we would call 'the moral sphere', which Aristotle describes as the sphere of what is good or bad for human beings (1140b6). He is, because of his practical wisdom, outstanding in conduct, and his state, instead of resembling virtue, is 'full virtue' or virtue 'in the primary sense' (1144b13). Whether he always gets things right and is thereby an unattainable but necessary standard-setting ideal, or whether Aristotle thinks he is a rare but not unknown phenomenon who gets them right 'for the most part' need not concern us here. Either way, at least most of us are a fair way from having practical wisdom and (if we are decent people) we are interested in acquiring it. And since, according to Aristotle, we are engaged in studying not what virtue is but how to become good (1103b27-8), we might reasonably expect him to help us.

So we might expect Aristotle to answer the question 'What special knowledge does the Aristotelian *phronimos* have that we lack, that enables him to avoid the mistakes in action to which we are all no doubt prone? What does he

---

[1] References are to *Nicomachean Ethics* throughout unless otherwise stated; most translations are from Aristotle (2000).

know that we lesser mortals don't know that enables him to hit the mean in action?' That way of putting it suggests that the answer would be of the form 'He knows *that* such and such',[2] and then, thinking in terms of the aspirations of modern ethical theory, we might well assume that what he knows is a system of what we would call 'moral principles'. Pursuing this line of thought, some commentators arrive at the idea that knowledge of, say, *eudaimonia* the good life or how one should live or *eupraxia* acting well is propositional knowledge that *eudaimonia/eupraxia* is doing..., where, ideally, the dots are filled in with a system of what we would call 'moral principles'. Call this the generalist model.

But when we read Book VI, we do not find Aristotle telling us that the *phronimos* knows *that*... Instead we find him distinguishing practical wisdom from various sorts of theoretical knowledge-that, and then, when he comes to discuss it, exploring a number of states that all look like intellectual capacities or skills rather than knowledge-that. This leads commentators who favour the generalist model to suppose that Aristotle has simply failed to deliver the goods. At the beginning of Book VI he admits that what he has said so far, while discussing the virtues of character as intermediate (mean) states, is only an unilluminating truism, and says that 'we must not only offer this truism but also determine what correct reason[3] is' (1 138b25–34), but does not go on to do so.

According to a more charitable interpretation, Aristotle has not failed to deliver the goods, we have asked the wrong question. Instead of asking for the *phronimos*'s propositional knowledge we should have asked something like 'What intellectual capacities does he have that we lack that enable him to avoid the mistakes in action to which we are prone?' Answering that question in a rather limited way, what we may call 'the perceptual model' takes the special knowledge the *phronimos* has to be (akin to) a perceptual capacity to see correctly what he is to do or what acting well is in a particular situation. This may share with the generalist model the idea that the *phronimos* has an especially superior conception of the universal *eudaimonia* or *eupraxia* which he puts into practice when he makes his choice to do such-and-such here and now, but if so, denies that there is anything more to his superior conception than his capacity to get things right. (Of course these two models are extremes on a spectrum of interpretations.)

---

[2] Cf. McDowell (1979: 57): 'We tend to assume that the knowledge must have a stateable propositional content.'

[3] *orthos logos*, also translated in this context as 'the correct prescription' (Rowe), 'the right principle' (Tredennick), 'the right rule' (Ross).

The perceptual model concentrates on what Aristotle says about practical *nous* in Book VI, and, in stressing the point that practical *nous* is akin to a perceptual capacity rather than the knowledge that some general principles hold, it has proved a needed corrective to the generalist model. But practical *nous* can't be all there is to practical wisdom because of all the other things Aristotle discusses in Book VI—*euboulia* (good deliberation), *sunesis* ([good] comprehension) and *gnōmē* (correct discernment). Aristotle says of the latter two and *nous* (though oddly omitting *euboulia*) that all these capacities tend in the same direction and that we attribute them, and practical wisdom, to the same people, 'saying that they have discernment and thereby nous and that they are practically wise and able to comprehend' (1143a25-9). So we have quite a few capacities to learn about. But the current prevalence of the perceptual model has led to the neglect of the others and a corresponding neglect of the importance of experience (*empeiria*). It is these that I want to discuss in this paper.

One source of the neglect, I think, is that the current generalist versus perceptual/particularist debate seems to be set largely against the background of considering the intellectual dispositional state of the virtuous as contrasted with that of the wicked or the incontinent. Now, it will surely be the case that the intellectual state of the *phronimos* is superior to that of the wicked and the incontinent (and indeed to that of the continent), since none of them has the virtue of temperance, whereas practical wisdom is supposed to carry with it possession of all the virtues (1145a1-2). But Aristotle's final remarks about practical wisdom—the ones that answer the question (raised at the beginning of VI 12) 'Why do we need it if we already have virtue of character?'—force us 'to reconsider the nature of virtue' (1144b2) and distinguish the natural virtue of, for example, temperance from the full virtue of temperance, temperance 'in the primary sense'. The intellectual state of the *phronimos*, we then see, is superior not only to that of the incontinent and the continent but also to that of anyone with only the natural virtue of temperance (or any other natural virtue). And we will not have understood the nature of practical wisdom until we have understood in what way this is so.

This immediately suggests a need to concentrate on the significance of experience. Aristotle tells us several times that practical wisdom requires experience. What sort? I mean, 'What of?' Well, the claim that practical wisdom requires experience might just be an alternative description of the parallel between practical wisdom and *technē* (technical expertise) as regards habituation. Just as *technē* requires experience—of habitual potting or boat-building or healing—so practical wisdom, being ultimately indistinguishable from virtue, requires experience of habitually doing what is virtuous. But at the beginning of Book II Aristotle *contrasts* the way the intellectual virtues are acquired (which he says takes experience) with habituation. We know that those with only natural virtue lack practical wisdom, and common sense suggests that it is unlikely to be found in adolescents, however well they have been brought up and habituated. (Aristotle explicitly links inexperience and lack of practical wisdom with youth [1142a12–16].) So suppose we are to think of 'the experience' that is required for practical wisdom as something that can, in thought at least, be distinguished from the experience that goes into the habitual performance of virtuous actions to preserve natural/innate virtue and generate habituated virtue.[4] And we want to work out what *this* experience contributes to practical wisdom.

It will be helpful to bear in mind the sorts of mistakes that well-habituated but inexperienced adolescents are likely to make as typical of those with only natural virtue. I hope to show that the capacities of correct discernment, good comprehension, and good deliberation are all acquired through experience, and that when we consider them we can see what sort of experience we need and hence what sort the people in Aristotle's lecture class—and probably us—should be trying to acquire. If this is right, then Book VI really does give us the help that Aristotle promised us at its beginning.

2. Mistakes about Moral Dilemmas

It is generally recognized that practical wisdom comes into play in the correct resolving of difficult dilemmas (even if Aristotle himself says very little about them). In the favoured case, the agent is faced with a resolvable dilemma, one in which good reasons conflict, recommending different and incompatible actions, and it is not obvious, to those who lack *phronēsis*, that one of the actions, not the other, is the right thing to do in the situation.[5] Typically, those with only natural virtue will make a mistake, whereas the *phronimos* knows which is the right thing to do and acts accordingly. (We should note that the qualification 'difficult' is important, because people sometimes write as though practical wisdom was needed to reach a decision about what to do in any

---

[4] Broadie (Aristotle 2002) notes that natural virtue 'may be a place-holder for any good character state unfinished by wisdom, in which case it includes tendencies acquired through upbringing. (These are put on a par with natural (i.e. innate) excellence at VII 8, 1151a18–19.)' (383).

[5] Some philosophers reserve the term 'moral dilemma' for irresolvable conflicts of reasons. Anyone who prefers this way of using the term can substitute 'conflict' for 'dilemma' throughout.

situation that presents the agent with conflicting reasons, and that cannot be right. Knowing that you have to stop the toddler from smashing the neighbour's china, even though the toddler will be upset, is the kind of thing that responsible older siblings, however affectionate towards the younger, know very young, hardly the sort that calls for practical wisdom.)

The generalist and perceptual/particularist models of practical wisdom mentioned above give different accounts of what enables the *phronimos* to reach the correct resolution, the latter favouring the view that his practical *nous* just enabled him to see that one, but not the other, action was the one to do. I would support that rather than the generalist account, but only with the caveat that the favoured case is far from exhausting the number of ways in which those with only natural virtue will fail to resolve dilemmas correctly, and only after bringing in the relevance of experience and the other intellectual capacities Aristotle discusses in Book VI.

The trouble with the perceptual model is that it leaves us in the dark about how experience might enable those with natural virtue to develop practical *nous*, and when we do not have any examples of what the *phronimos* sees, it is impossible to tell what we should be on the lookout for. Michael Woods offers a couple of suggestive examples. He supposes 'that the propositions that the person with intuition (*nous*) sees the truth of are ones that ascribe a virtuous or evaluative character to a certain possible action open to the agent', and gives as examples 'The magnanimous thing to do would be to abandon the claim' and 'The courageous thing to do would be to resign.'[6]

I take it that the point of these is that they are examples of judgements whose truth it would be hard for the inexperienced and naive to recognize. The well-brought-up young would tend to suppose that abandoning one's claim was servile or pusillanimous, even though their natural generosity prompted them to do it, and to suppose that it would be cowardly to resign even though 'mildness' (perhaps? or justice?) suggested one should. But although it may be plausible to assign to practical *nous* the capacity to see the truth of such judgements, it is worth raising the question of whether we might not assign it instead to discernment (*gnōmē*).

Aristotle's description of discernment is tantalizingly brief. He says no more than that it is 'correct judgement of what is reasonable/equitable/decent [*epieikēs*]' and leaves us to follow up his other remarks on 'equity' in Book V of the *Nicomachean Ethics* and the *Rhetoric*. The discussions there specifically concern correcting universal laws when they are in error regarding a

---

[6] Woods (1986: 157).

particular exceptional case, but may be taken to apply more generally in the context of his discussion of *phronēsis*; it is discernment that enables the *phronimos* to judge, correctly, such things as that (in this rather unusual case) the magnanimous thing to do would be to abandon the claim, where those with only natural virtue think of the magnanimous man as so concerned with his honour that he would never, universally, do such a pusillanimous thing.

Might we then simply assign the capacity to make such judgements to discernment rather than to practical *nous*? No, for discernment is obviously like comprehension (*sunesis*) insofar as it is not prescriptive but only makes judgements (cf. 1143a9–10). As Woods notes, the experienced and practically wise may come out with such 'remarks' when giving advice or commenting on the actions of others, whereas the assumption is that practical *nous* is exercised only in the context of an agent's own practical reasoning. However, it is clear that you couldn't have practical *nous* without having discernment, and thereby we learn how those with only natural virtue can, through experience, acquire the former capacity.

One can think of other examples of similar naivety about what the virtues do and do not require, and correspondingly about what does or does not fall under a vice term. It is not mean to spend no more on presents than you can afford; on the contrary, it is prodigal, not generous, to do otherwise. It is not always cowardly to run away, and not always intemperate to eat a lot. The non-Aristotelian dilemma with which modern virtue ethicists are standardly confronted is described as one in which the requirements of kindness and honesty conflict, giving the agent reason, on the one hand, to lie (that is how it is always presented), and on the other, to tell the hurtful truth. But, on some occasion, the dilemma may be resolvable when one realizes that the kindest thing to do would be to tell the hurtful truth, and, on another, when one realizes that it would not be dishonest to remain discreetly or politely silent.

It seems plausible to suppose the well-brought-up but inexperienced tend to think about what the virtues require and the vices rule out in terms of rather conventional generalizations or paradigms. It is only with the experience of exceptions—when an admired figure does what you thought only a pusillanimous coward would do and is widely praised, when the action of someone you respect surprises you until she explains why she did it, when you hear accounts of such examples—that you come to the more sophisticated understanding—the discernment-that the *phronimos* has. And, as you develop the discernment, you develop the practical *nous*.

So there is our first bit of help about how to get closer to full virtue—briefly, don't rely unthinkingly on generalizations about, and paradigms of, the virtues and vices, take good note of the exceptions when you come across them, and watch out for others. And, given how often Aristotle stresses that we are in the area where things are true 'for the most part', I think we may assume that he regards this as worth getting across to his lecture class.

Of course, this pertains to no more than a part of practical *nous*.[7] No doubt there are many other aspects covered by the perceptual model's general idea of 'the capacity to read predicaments correctly',[8] and as the 'proper responsiveness to the details of situations'.[9] But rather than pursuing those, I want to move away from failures in moral perception and turn to consider another way in which the naive and inexperienced will tend to go wrong about dilemmas.

What is done is always done in a particular situation, but so far nothing has been said about what might be involved in getting 'the situation' right in the first place. It seems odd that Aristotle should say nothing about this, since clearly if I get it wrong my reasoning about what to do will be flawed in some way, and, for all that the *phronimos* is not infallible, it would be astonishing if he were not better at getting situations right than those with natural virtue. Is it not typical of the inexperienced that they 'get hold of the wrong end of the stick' as we say? (His remarks about culpable negligence [1113b30–1114a11] don't mention practical wisdom, and he doesn't refer back to anything like them in Book VI.) However, if we pay attention to his brief remarks on comprehension (*sunesis*) we find something very suggestive.

If you have *sunesis*, (good) comprehension, you are able to judge, rightly or well, what others say about matters within the scope of practical wisdom (1143a15). Like discernment and practical *nous*, it depends on age (1143b8) and is one of the rational capacities of the *phronimos*. Though usually neglected, it is well worth looking at.

The need for it reminds us of something it is easy to overlook if we focus too determinedly on the image of the *phronimos* being faced with 'the situation' and coming to a decision about what is to be done here and now, namely the following. A 'situation' which calls for my doing something may not be *facing* me at all, waiting for me to read it, but rather something whose details I have to work out from what other people say about it. And until I can make a correct judgement about *their* accounts of the relevant matters, any practical conclusion I reached about what to do in 'this situation' would be made in the dark.

---

[7] Woods does not claim that 'judgements about the virtuous or unvirtuous character of actions of a certain sort in particular circumstances' are the only sort that *nous* enables one to see the truth of, 'only that these should be possible and central examples' (ibid., 158).
[8] McDowell (1998a: 26). [9] Ibid., 22.

Whether we suppose I come to my decision by perceiving what is salient in it, or arriving through reflection at a proper appreciation of it, or applying a general principle to it, I can't do any of these until I know, in some detail, what it *is*. And I often do not. Say I hear a rumour that a friend is in trouble, or that my university has treated a student unjustly or is doing something improper with its finances, or that there is a new political movement afoot in my country to throw people off their land... *If* the rumour has some truth in it, there is probably something I should do, but I can have no idea of what until I know the details.

We should, I think, allow ourselves to be struck by how *often* finding out exactly what 'the situation' is, with a view to acting well, involves judging what other people say, particularly about their own, or someone else's, actions and/ or feelings, past, present, or future. It is an absolutely indispensable part of knowing one's way about in the human world, which is a world of language-using creatures. In this respect practical wisdom, pertaining as it does to action 'in the sphere of human goods', contrasts with most of the various 'crafts' (*technai*). (I take it that the exception is medicine.) Although, no doubt, when I need to know more about 'the situation' before I set about making a pot or building a house or a boat or..., it may be useful to find out what other people have to say about the available clay or site or wood. But I may well be able to find out the relevant details by myself. In contrast, given practical wisdom's sphere of action, what other people are saying and thinking and feeling about things that have been done, and themselves, and each other, rightly or wrongly, may well be the relevant details themselves. And if I get them wrong I may believe, incorrectly, that 'the situation' is a dilemma, where my choice lies between two regrettable alternatives, and go for one, when in fact neither was necessary at all.

Closely related to such cases are those in which I am, roughly speaking, faced with a situation, but someone else reads it to me, incorrectly. We should not assume that it is guaranteed that, if I had practical wisdom myself, I would be able to read it correctly straight off; not every present situation is an open book, even to the *phronimos*. But what the *phronimos*, given his comprehension, will often be able to do is judge, correctly, that the other person's account, though it might be right, should not be relied upon (and so one must withhold final assessment about what's what until one has found out more) or that it just can't be quite right (and so again, final assessment must be withheld).

The others' incorrect account of the situation may be deliberate deception— as, say, in the Milgram experiments, or something more straightforwardly self-serving ('This is a bargain—you won't get anything better', 'You needn't worry about what's going to happen to so-and-so—I'll make that all right'). It might be a sincere but wicked or defective account: for instance, the sincere but false assertion that the situation is such that this bad aspect of it is something that has to be done, that it is necessary for some greater good, or isn't really bad at all. And thereby we come to two of the most common mistakes made about dilemmas:

(i) Accepting someone else's description of a situation as a dilemma (in which, unfortunately, the alternatives both involve acting ill), as in 'You'll have to tell him the brutal truth or lie in your teeth.'
(ii) Accepting someone else's description of a situation as one in which there is only one way out (which, unfortunately involves acting ill), as in 'You/we can't do such-and-such, so you/we must be realistic and face up to doing so-and-so.'

3. More Mistakes, and Wickedness

Although accepting others' accounts when they are not true is a very common source of mistakes specifically about difficult dilemmas, and hence a common source of wrongdoing, it is obvious that defective comprehension leads to many other mistakes. But does it lead to wrongdoing? When I act in response to (what I think is) a resolvable difficult dilemma, I knowingly do something that, if I have virtue, is not the sort of thing I do gladly. I do it perforce, compelled (as I think) by the circumstances. I know it is the sort of thing that is prima facie wrong and calls for justification, and if I am mistaken about the justification I have done what is just plain wrong, no prima facie about it.

But, we might think, when not compelled by circumstances to risk wrongdoing in this way, those with natural virtue will intend only what is good, even if it does not come off. You intended to help me, but you have, unwittingly, made everything much worse. You intended to bear the burden of the insult to yourself 'mildly', but unwittingly you have broken your father's heart. You intended to save the day, but you have lost not only the battle but the kingdom. And each time it is because, lacking comprehension, you got the situation wrong. But did you *do* wrong? Some would say yes, and others no, and others that it depends on whether your misjudgement of people's accounts of the situation was culpable, but in the Aristotelian context we need not engage in this debate. Our concern, after all, is not the mere avoidance of wrongdoing or being blameless. We are aspirants to full virtue, to practical wisdom; we aspire to get things right in action. And however blameless and well-intentioned those with natural virtue may be, that is not what they achieve, because they lack comprehension.

So we may now think of these points—that I may have to find out what the situation is by asking around, and may have it incorrectly read to me—as generating a whole range of examples of how those with natural virtue but lacking practical wisdom go wrong. For the young and inexperienced are typically both gullible about many things from many sources and also (believing themselves very sapient in this) too incredulous regarding some things from some sources. They ascribe mendacity where they shouldn't, do not consider it as a possibility when they should, fail to ask themselves 'But how could she know?', or 'Why should I accept that?', or 'Isn't it quite likely he is just mistaken?', and rush to judgement too readily. Lacking comprehension, they make incorrect judgements about what others say, and thereby frequently get 'the situation' wrong in such a way that they couldn't exercise practical *nous* even if they had it.

Comprehension is an intellectual dispositional state that comes from not only experience but also instruction (1103a16). It is from experience that one learns, for example, in what sorts of circumstances one really should be suspicious or incredulous, what sorts of things most people lie about, whom amongst one's acquaintances can and can't be relied on and about what, the extraordinary range of different descriptions you get of an event from those who witnessed it, and so on. And, post-Hume at least, there is useful instruction to be gained from what he says about testimony regarding the occurrence of miracles.

So there is our next bit of help about how to get closer to full virtue. We have to learn to think critically about other people's accounts, to remember to ask ourselves the right questions about them, and to make a point of noticing who is and who is not reliable and about what. Hume is helpful, especially when one takes his discussion beyond the realm of statistical induction into the 'sphere of human goods' with which we are concerned. Then we see him as directing us to consider the question 'Which do I think is more likely—that what this person has just told me is true or that he is mistaken, self-deceived, lying or simply not to be trusted on this matter?', and our answers are not just determined by statistics. Both loyalty and charity require one to think well of others when one can. It is neither disloyal nor uncharitable to think of a stranger that they must surely have made some mistake if they tell you that a long-known friend, or someone of known probity, has done something disgraceful. But it is disloyal and uncharitable to take the stranger's word for it.

(Anscombe once remarked on the absurd way in which supposedly decent characters in murder mysteries so often accept the detective's claim that one of their nearest and dearest has committed the murder rather than taking it as overwhelmingly likely that he has made a mistake.) Finding oneself in agreement with a recognizable ratbag should give the virtuous pause for thought about whether one had judged another's account correctly, and similarly if one finds oneself disagreeing with someone one had reason to think was wiser than oneself.[10]

At this point, a perhaps surprising thought may occur to us. Anyone clever, not just those interested in acquiring full virtue, might read Hume on testimony and pick up useful ideas about circumstances in which testimony about almost anything should be viewed with scepticism. And, with age and experience, they may become very good at judging when someone's account is likely to be reliable. Surely wickedness is not, in itself, a bar to acquiring comprehension; the successful conmen of this world must be pretty well qualified in it, much better at it, indeed, than those with natural virtue.

Why might that be a surprising thought? Well, it is no accident that *phronēsis* is often translated as 'moral' rather than 'practical' wisdom, despite the fact that there is no corresponding Greek word for 'moral'.[11] That translation reflects a certain picture that people have of *phronēsis* (even though they may not use that translation), namely of its being something rarefied and exalted, *exclusively* 'moral'. Hence the concentration on the *phronimos*'s superior grasp of *eudaimonia* or *eupraxia* in both the generalist and the perceptual models, the concentration on moral rules in the former and moral perception in the latter, and the oft-drawn contrast between the *phronimos* and the wicked or incontinent.

If this picture were correct, it would indeed be surprising if there turned out to be something that some of the wicked as well as the *phronimos* were better at than those with natural virtue. Where the *phronimos* is better than those with natural virtue, he would be morally better, and how could the wicked be morally better than anyone, let alone those with natural virtue?

But it isn't correct according to Aristotle. The literally mundane, worldly, capacity of cleverness (*deinotēs*, which enables its possessor to find the really effective means to her proposed goal, whatever that may be) is essential to

---

[10] This may be the sort of point Aristotle is making when he says that for (good) comprehension, one must judge what the other says 'nobly/finely' (*kalōs*) since this is judging it well (1143a16).

[11] In this use. Of course it has a word for 'ethical' which corresponds in other uses, as when we harmlessly translate '*ēthikē aretē*' as 'moral character'. But no one thinks of calling *phronēsis* 'ethical wisdom'.

practical wisdom, and the unscrupulous may have it too (1144a25–30). Some of the wicked, as well as the *phronimos*, are better at deliberating cleverly than those with natural virtue. So there should be nothing surprising about the fact that, aspiring to full virtue, we should seek to improve a capacity that, under a fairly general description, we would share with the successful conmen. For, with natural virtue, we will not be trying to acquire exactly the same version, and we won't wind up in the same place.

Just as 24-carat *excellence* in deliberation (*euboulia*) calls for more than just cleverness, so real excellence in comprehension (*eusunesia*) will require more than just meeting some threshold in the capacity to judge what other people say about situations. There will be times when those with excellent comprehension get it right, and the conmen, with their shared but nameless capacity, get it wrong. We may note, for instance, that the virtuous and the wicked will not bring the same assessments of likelihood to Hume's question, for the latter will be quick to assume that the supposedly virtuous are probably venal. And we have already noted that the wicked are, typically, the very promulgators of some of the false accounts, not through mendacity but because they view things differently, and, with respect to such cases, it will be inevitable that they sometimes accept each other's as accurate when in fact they are not.

But we must not forget that, as with cleverness, the mundane capacity that the successful conmen have is something that we have to acquire or develop for full virtue. And this suggests that we might return, briefly, to what might be involved in the perceptual capacity of the *phronimos*.

That there is much variation in the literature about just what the *phronimos* perceives is understandable, given how enigmatic Aristotle's remarks about *nous* in Book VI are and how corrupted the text is. I do not want to enter that debate, but to mention (without committing myself to how it relates to practical *nous*) the importance of a perceptual capacity, born of experience, that again the wicked may share (to a fair degree) with the *phronimos* while those of natural virtue lack it.

'Is there', Wittgenstein asks, 'such a thing as "expert judgement" about the genuineness of expressions of feeling?' 'No', he implies, but there is better and worse, and continues, 'Correcter prognoses will generally issue from the judgements of those with better knowledge of mankind.'[12]

People with such knowledge have a better understanding of other people than the inexperienced, and can make better judgements than them about more than the genuineness of expressions of feeling. They have a perceptual

---

[12] Wittgenstein (1963: 227e) (and 193e in the third edition).

capacity, 'perceptiveness' or 'sensitivity', to see or hear that, despite a smiling front, others are hurt, embarrassed, uncertain, angry, frightened, worried, or that their apparent shiftiness or brazen- ness is no more than embarrassment, that their expression of gratitude, though awkward, is genuine, or... This is the perceptual capacity that Nussbaum has discussed and vividly illustrated, and rightly so. Like comprehension, it is a capacity absolutely requisite for finding out what 'the situation' is in many central cases in which action is called for. It is needed when the situation is right in front of us, in all its detail, and if we fail to perceive, or misperceive, one of the details, as the inexperienced do, we will make the insensitive blunders that the inexperienced, with natural virtue, typically make.

However, Nussbaum has not, as far as I know, highlighted the point that successful Iagos are pretty good at perceiving these things too. Though love may sharpen this sort of perception, so may hatred, jealousy, resentment, and misanthropy. If only the wickedness of would-be manipulative people guaranteed that they were imperceptive of such things, how much easier life would be! And once we recognize the fact that the *phronimos* and some of the wicked may share this perceptual capacity, we should find it unproblematic that there are other sorts of 'non-moral' details that experience will enable the *phronimos* to perceive which the inexperienced fail to perceive, and thereby blunder. I am thinking of such things as that someone is out of his mind, or in need of immediate medical attention.[13]

As before, there may be nothing culpable about the failure, but as before, given our aim, that is beside the point. As before, it shows us what we should be trying to get better at, what sort of experience we should be on the lookout for. We can learn from our own and other people's failures in perception, and also by taking note of the successes, even when these take a repellent form. When the cruel and cynical mock and sneer, this is not always mere misanthropy, but because they have perceived a weakness we missed; while we are still missing things, we should not turn up our noses at the superiority of their capacity though we may deplore the use to which it is put.

---

[13] There are several accounts of commanding officers going clean off their heads under the stress of war and issuing orders which those with the natural virtue of courage unquestioningly, albeit unhappily, obeyed when they should not have, because they simply could not see how far gone the officer was. I know of a case wherein a young lecturer failed to realize that a student's ravings about his first encounter with *Philosophical Investigations* were not merely understandable excitement and lack of sleep but the onset of acute schizophrenia, and so failed to report it. In another case, someone with acute brain damage was seen by some as 'behaving rather oddly', but they didn't see that he was in need of immediate medical attention and they should have called an ambulance straight away.

So there are at least two areas, getting other people's accounts right, and perceiving the details of situations correctly, where the *phronimos*, because of his experience, shares with some of the wicked a nameless intellectual capacity that those with natural virtue lack. Of course, since he has virtue as well as experience, he has a superior version, but nevertheless he must reach the mundane threshold of 'worldly wisdom' which is involved in both. Recognition of this should pave the way for accepting the relevance of the supposedly 'merely technical' aspects of the *phronimos*'s capacity for good deliberation, where the shared capacity does have a name.

4. Experience and Good Deliberation (*euboulia*)

One thing that seems uncontroversial about the text is that most of what it tells us regarding what practical wisdom involves is about *deliberation*, but neither the generalist nor the perceptual model seems to fit well with what Aristotle has to say about it. Most of what Aristotle tells us about deliberation explicitly says, or strongly suggests (i) that it is a time-consuming process (1142b4) with a beginning and an end, (ii) that its beginning is a clockable moment when agents establish an end, and (iii) '*then* go onto think about how and by what means it is to be achieved' (1112b15–16; my italics). This involves (iv) selecting the easiest and 'most fine' (*kallistos*) means from those available, if there is more than one, or (v) if there is only one, 'how this will bring it about and *by what further means* this means is itself to be brought about' (1112b18–19; my italics).

Nearly all these remarks come from Book III, and the discussion there used to be dismissed as concerned merely with 'technical', 'means-end', deliberation. The idea was that Book VI introduced a new sort of 'rule-case' deliberation uniquely suited to the (moral) sphere of practical wisdom. Those who incline towards the perceptual model now regard this sharp distinction between the Book III and the Book VI discussions as a mistake,[14] but this has not led them to a renewed interest in the 'technical' aspects of good deliberation. What is emphasized, in varied ways, is either the *phronimos*'s reassessment of his proposed end in the light of his discovery that it can only be brought about by some less than honourable means, or, once again, his immediate response to the perceived details of the situation.[15] But this too is a mistake.

---

[14] See, especially, Wiggins (1975–6).
[15] Even Broadie (1991), though she acknowledges that the *phronimos* must be 'factually canny about means' (247), puts this whole capacity under the umbrella of 'practical intelligence' (*nous*) and does not give it any individual attention. (This is not to say she subscribes to the 'perceptual' model.)

Practical wisdom is, after all, the excellence of the *calculative* part of the intellectual part of the soul, and deliberation and calculation are the same thing (1139a1–12). The excellence of each of the parts of the intellectual soul must relate to the part's characteristic activity (*ergon*), and so practical wisdom must be excellence in deliberation, excellence in the very activity that skill (*technē*), which is also in the calculative part of the soul, engages in (in its own inferior way). Moreover, in the sphere of practical wisdom, as with the skills, experience is needed for good technical deliberation, and inexperience leads to mistakes. If we pay no attention to the 'merely technical' deliberation, we will, once again, not see what sort of experience we need and hence what we should be looking out for.

It is true that both common sense and 1117a17–22 compel us to regard Aristotle's discussion of deliberation as sometimes 'aimed at the reconstruction of reasons for action not necessarily thought out in advance'.[16] It is easy to think of examples of situations which not only prompt, but *call for*, an immediate action from the virtuous; anyone who fails to respond by acting will count as failing in virtue. But unless we are careful to think of the right examples, and then think about those in the right way, we will overlook how the reconstruction of reasons might be supposed to go, and thereby miss out on the significance of experience in deliberation.

When the small child slips under the bathwater, we hope the older observer will leap forward and yank them up again, seeing (perceptual model) or realizing in an instant (generalist model) what she must do without having to search for it. But that is not a good example to think about as an exercise of practical wisdom, because failing to respond in that way is not characteristic of those with natural virtue as opposed to practical wisdom. Rather it would be characteristic of the very wicked. The unambiguous exercise of practical wisdom (in an immediate case) should be an action that someone with natural virtue would typically fail to do. And there are at least two different sorts of cases.

One is the sort already discussed, namely that in which the agent is faced with a resolvable moral dilemma that calls for immediate action. Here are two examples of the other sort. The small child on water wings drifts out of his depth into the river current, which bears him, with increasing speed, towards the weir. The onlooker with natural virtue immediately flings herself into the water and starts swimming after him. The onlooker with practical wisdom immediately starts running along the bank to get well ahead of the child *before*

---

[16] McDowell (1979: 66, n. 22).

flinging herself into the water. Or, to adapt Aristotle's own example of immediate action, as the two soldiers are woken by the unmistakable sounds of the enemy invading the camp, the one with natural virtue grabs his sword and rushes straight out of the tent towards the fray and the one with practical wisdom pauses just long enough to strap on his helmet and find his shield as well.

The immediate action dilemma cases, as I noted above, generate a debate about whether the generalist can provide some kind of ranking of reasons (moral concerns, morally relevant properties, principles, whatever) which could plausibly figure in the reconstruction of the *phronimos*'s reasons, or whether we just have to accept that he saw one but not the other feature of the situation as salient, and that this is an appreciation that may not be articulable or comprehensible to those who lack his practical wisdom (and thereby his virtue). But that debate does not get a grip on the second sort of case. *Post hoc*, everyone, even the wicked, can immediately reconstruct the *phronimos*'s reasons and see that (relative to his aim) he did the right thing. Given the aim of saving the child or repelling the enemy, he found what everyone can see were by far the better means to achieving it; if the actions of the agents with natural virtue succeed, they will have been very lucky.

The second sort of case should make it clear that immediacy does not render correctness in the technical deliberative steps 'how and by what means' irrelevant. Overlooking their relevance is, perhaps, made easier by being too struck by certain descriptions of actions called for in a presented situation— saving the child, helping a friend in trouble, the noble facing of danger, abstaining from an available but illicit bodily pleasure[17]—as unproblematically identifying *the* thing to be done (the right thing to do/what virtue requires) in that situation. But, in most situations, all such descriptions leave room for 'how and by what means'. They are descriptions of action-types[18] which may be realized by a variety of actual action-tokens, and we don't get right (rather than well-intentioned) conduct unless we get them realized in the right ways. Sometimes, though rarely, there will be just one, obvious, right way—but then anyone with natural virtue will find it without the need for practical wisdom. More usually, there are more and less effective ways, in a particular situation, of helping a friend in trouble or nobly facing danger, and more and less effective (as well as inoffensive and discreet) ways of abstaining from the available but illicit bodily pleasure offered by someone else's partner. And it

---

[17] These last three examples are all from McDowell (1988).
[18] Less anachronistically, 'possible actions' as in Woods (1986).

is the *phronimos* who finds the more effective ways, and the one with natural virtue who characteristically does not.

Book II has emphasized time and time again how difficult it is to hit the mean, because there are so many ways of missing it, and everything Aristotle says about deliberation in Books III and Book VI suggests that good deliberation is also difficult, because there are so many bits that have to be got right. And as soon as we think about real examples, it surely becomes obvious that it is often very difficult indeed. Just getting going on the deliberation may be very difficult. My son is in trouble, increasingly doing drugs. Of course I must do something to help him. But 'how and by what means?' I don't know where to start. It may well be that for this kind of thing, even the *phronimos* must call in others because he distrusts, rightly, his own ability to reach a good decision about the effective means (1112b17).

Being able to find the effective means, in the way that the runner on the riverbank and the soldier above are, is at least in part a matter of knowing what does and doesn't work. But 'finding the effective means' covers more than finding what will work as opposed to that which will almost certainly fail. There is, as Aristotle notes, the question of finding the means that will achieve the end most easily (1112b17). Life is short and time is precious, after all, and there is no virtue in making a meal of something that could have been done much more easily (though people who have gone to unnecessary trouble often expect gratitude as though there were, and even resent it when someone pulls off a morally grand result [for example, saving someone's life] with a brilliantly simple stroke). He also notes that, in the course of any drawn-out deliberation (about the means by which the means by which...the end will be achieved), one may 'encounter an impossibility' and give up (1112b25). (I assume he means 'give up that line of enquiry' rather than 'immediately give up entirely and abandon the end one set'.) This is usually discussed in terms of encountering a moral impossibility, but it may be a failure in technical deliberation. I think that something is 'technically' impossible because I lack the experience that enables the *phronimos* to find an ingenious way around it, and so I give up when I shouldn't, missing out on what is in fact by far the more effective means.

In the above cases, it is clear that the runner on the riverbank and the experienced soldier are not necessarily *phronimoi*, because either might be quite wicked. Nevertheless, this entirely mundane, non-moral, sort of 'technical' expertise is essential to practical wisdom. Finding the effective means to one's proposed end is an essential, indeed major, part of deliberating well, and hence one of the things the *phronimos* must be excellent at, and Aristotle makes this explicit when he insists that practical wisdom implies cleverness (*deinotēs*), a faculty that the unscrupulous can exercise pretty well too.

Once Aristotle has introduced cleverness, and distinguished it from practical wisdom, it may look as though the latter is just a hybrid, that is, expertise in 'technical' deliberation gained from experience, which in the virtuous happens to be directed to the right end.[19] But this hybrid picture underestimates the ways in which maturing virtue will shape the experience gained, and thereby the expertise.

The experience might be of one's own failures or of learning about others'. Or it might be of learning about others' successful methods. Whichever it is, 'the experience' will not be of much use to one unless one recognizes it for what it is (incompetence or effectiveness rather than bad or good luck) and takes it to heart. And whether we are keen to be effective in certain sorts of action and take our failures to heart or do not care much, are on the watch for ways in which to improve our performance or fairly satisfied with the way we are managing, will be part of our characters and reflected in the ways in which we do, or don't, continue to develop our virtue and our effectiveness in action.

Suppose the youthful swimmer isn't lucky, and the child goes over the weir. Someone points out, or she realizes later, thinking about it, that she probably would have managed to save him if she had run along the bank first. That fact will strike someone with natural virtue in a way it wouldn't strike someone who had dived in merely for a lark, thinking it would be great to get one's picture in the papers as a heroine. The latter will shrug it off with faint damns; the former will probably never forget it. One way we can acquire experience nowadays is through newspapers—we read accounts of other people's successes and failures in achieving their proposed end. Will the naturally virtuous and those who lack natural virtue be struck by the same accounts? I assume not. The former will hardly be interested in the precise details of the ways in which the fraudster proceeded, but will, or should, be very interested in how someone achieved a great deed, or what made them fail and whether, thinking about it, they can see a way in which they could have succeeded.

Consider the area of 'people management'. (I use this horrid term advisedly, to remind us that the Iagos of this world are good at finding effective means to their proposed ends in the area of our dealings with other people.) Like the Iagos, the *phronimos* must have enough understanding of people, born of

---

[19] Cf. Broadie (Aristotle 2002: 50): 'Wisdom, then, turns out to be impossible without excellence of character, just as excellence of character is impossible without wisdom. When Aristotle "puts them together" in his exposition, what in fact he puts together is an unfinished infrastructure of character-excellence with an abstract or ethically footloose capacity called "cleverness".'

experience, to know what sorts of things would make things worse for them, not in order to do it of course, but to avoid it, and to avert it if he sees it coming from elsewhere. But does he know more than the Iagos about what would make things better for them? Of course he does! Practically, it is quite implausible that they would acquire the needed experience because they have so little reason to be on the watch for it all the time and put it into practice, as someone with natural virtue should be. The wicked do not know what love and trust, for example, can do for people, and couldn't set about using the knowledge if they had it. Their cleverness can only take them so far.[20]

I claimed above that in order to get situations right in the first place the *phronimos* must reach a threshold of worldly wisdom concerning two areas. He must be good at judging the reliability of other people's accounts, and he has the sort of 'knowledge of mankind' that enables him to perceive the details of (broadly speaking) 'how it is' with other people—whether they are embarrassed, or frightened, or mad. But I also claimed that he had a superior version of the capacities in question, because those with natural virtue do not garner exactly the same experience as those who lack it, and the capacities they wind up with are not exactly the same.

We may now note that 'getting situations right' is essential *throughout* technical deliberation, not merely at the point where it begins in response to a presented one. Wherever one's means involve dealing with other people, there is another situation, and if one gets it wrong, one's means-end reasoning will not (except fortuitously) be effective. So here too the cleverness of the unscrupulous can only take them so far. The *phronimos* is cleverer than they are—wisely worldly rather than worldly wise, in Quarles's perspicuous terms.

5. Conclusion

This momentary return to the area of the moral should not distract us from the upshot of the preceding discussion, namely that a lot of what the *phronimos* must gain from experience to ensure his expertise in 'technical' deliberation is just plain worldly knowledge. I do not, of course, want to

---

[20] Stephen Watt pointed out to me that an Iago will know, in detail, how to do some things—drive someone to suicide perhaps, or torture them effectively, which the *phronimos* (for the most part) wouldn't know how to do, because he would lack knowledge (unless it had been forced upon him) of certain horrible facts. This, I take it, is no reflection on *his* cleverness, because they are not means to any end he would set himself. But although the virtuous cannot have wicked ends, the wicked may, occasionally, have good ones.

underestimate the importance of the ethical aspects of practical wisdom. To acquire it we must indeed gain an understanding of what the individual virtues require, and reflect on our life as a whole and how our competing and perhaps incommensurable concerns can be encompassed within the realization of the ideal life of virtuous activity at which we are aiming. But this has all been ably discussed by others, and my concern has been to point out that it is not *enough*. We must also, more prosaically, but just as essentially, seek to acquire the experience that will give us comprehension, the required sort of perceptiveness, and the capacity for effective deliberation.

A final objection to my emphasizing this point is the following. If practical wisdom does have to involve such empirical knowledge, shouldn't the knowledge be, as Irwin puts it, 'encyclopaedic'.[21] This seems not only absurd but elitist, guaranteeing that practical wisdom, and thereby full virtue, is open only to the academically intelligent, those who are capable of absorbing such a vast amount of varied information.

Philippa Foot has the right answer to this, derived from Aquinas. Discussing the point that it is 'quite wrong to suggest that [practical] wisdom cannot be a virtue because virtue must be within the reach of anyone who really wants it', she says, '[Practical] wisdom, in so far as it consists of knowledge which anyone can gain in the course of an ordinary life, is available to anyone who really wants it. As Aquinas put it, it belongs 'to a power under the direction of the will'.[22]

Real effectiveness in deliberation, of the sort that can be acquired from experience in 'an ordinary life', is something any aspirant to full virtue should want. Its acquisition is not supposed to disrupt an ordinary human life, but to form part of it, as the regular looking out for, and taking note of, successes and failures, and reflection on them, can do. But it still requires more effort than most of us have noticed. Acquiring the medical knowledge of a doctor would require years of one's life, but, nowadays, for nearly everyone likely to be reading this paper, learning elementary first aid is just a matter of enrolling in a class that lasts a few hours, so Foot is right to say that 'it is contrary to charity to fail to find out about elementary first aid'.[23] How many of us have done so?[24]

---

[21] Irwin (1988): 'If wisdom is to meet the demand for success, apparently it has to include a large body of empirical techniques. [A completely virtuous person would have to be] a doctor or a plumber or to acquire all sorts of other empirical knowledge that might come in handy on some occasion. Aristotle seems to have no escape from an encyclopaedic conception of virtue and wisdom' (75).
[22] Foot (1978: 6), my italics.   [23] Ibid., p. 4.
[24] I am grateful to Julia Annas, William Charlton, and Stephen Watt for helpful comments on an earlier version of this paper.

References

Aristotle. 2000. *Nicomachean Ethics*. Edited and translated by Roger Crisp. Cambridge: Cambridge University Press.

Aristotle. 2002. *Nicomachean Ethics*. Translated by Christopher Rowe, introduction and commentary by Sarah Broadie. Oxford: Oxford University Press.

Broadie, S. 1991. *Ethics With Aristotle*. Oxford: Oxford University Press.

Foot, P. 1978. 'Virtues and Vices'. In *Virtues and Vices and Other Essays in Moral Philosophy*. Oxford: Blackwell.

Irwin, T. 1988. 'Disunity in the Aristotelian Virtues'. In Julia Annas and Robert Grimm (eds), *Oxford Studies in Ancient Philosophy, Supplementary Volume*. Oxford: Clarendon Press: 61–78.

McDowell, J. 1979. 'Virtue and Reason', *Monist* 62: 331–50. Reprinted in McDowell 1998b.

McDowell, J. 1988. 'Comments on T. H. Irwin's "Some Rational Aspects of Incontinence"', *Southern Journal of Philosophy* 27, Supplement: 89–102.

McDowell, J. 1998a. 'Some Issues in Aristotle's Moral Psychology'. In McDowell 1998b: 23–49.

McDowell, J. 1998b. *Mind, Value, and Reality*. Cambridge, MA: Harvard University Press.

Wiggins, D. 1975–6. 'Deliberation and Practical Reason', *Proceedings of the Aristotelian Society* 76: 29–51.

Wittgenstein, L. 1963. *Philosophical Investigations*, 2nd edn. Translated by G. E. M. Anscombe. Oxford: Blackwell.

Woods, M. 1986. 'Intuition and Perception in Aristotle's Ethics', *Oxford Studies in Ancient Philosophy* 4: 145–66.

3
What Does the Aristotelian *Phronimos* Know?

The question above is a way of asking, 'What is moral knowledge, according to Aristotle?' For the Aristotelian *phronimos*—the practically wise man[1]—has *phronēsis*, which is a form of knowledge, and it is this that enables him (characteristically) to make correct decisions about what he should do. What the *phronimos* is excellent at, *because* of his *phronēsis*, is practical reasoning.

What normative ethical theory aspires to do is enable those agents who apply it to reach correct decisions about what they should do, to provide a model of excellent practical reasoning. Hence modern moral philosophers who believe that we have much to learn from Aristotle have turned to his account of *phronēsis* for insights about, among other things, the possibility of normative ethical theory. This generated a debate between particularists and generalists about codifiability and the role of moral principles, which overlapped with that between virtue ethicists and their critics over whether virtue ethics failed to be action-guiding because it failed to provide them.

Now I take it that, with respect to a normative ethical theory's providing action-guidance, the virtue ethicists have prompted new insights among the generalists. Some of the latter, at least, used to say that they were seeking not just a guide but 'hopefully a determinate decision procedure' (Louden 1984: 228–9) for resolving dilemmas, and now they don't. Indeed, the author of that quotation now says that of course no one ever thought that there could be such a decision procedure, and that everyone has always recognized that 'informed judgment' and 'practical wisdom' are needed to apply rules and principles correctly (Louden 1998: 494). But, in my view, the most significant aspect of Aristotelian *phronēsis*, namely that it is impossible without virtue, has been rather obscured by the generalist vs. particularist debate, and hence its impact

---

[1] It is, unfortunately, impossible to translate 'phronimos' as 'the practically wise person', so this chapter has to be couched in Aristotle's sexist terms. [Editors' note: *phronimos* is a two-termination adjective, such that the masculine form is the same as the feminine form; so both 'person' and 'woman' are in fact grammatical.]

on the pretensions of philosophers' normative ethical theorizing is still not appreciated by non-virtue ethicists. This is what this chapter is about.

Too new (as a technical term in moral philosophy) to have made it into the second edition of *The Cambridge Dictionary of Philosophy* (Broadie 1999), 'particularism' is already old enough to have become unclear, and so, as far as possible, I shall avoid it, and use the less contested terms 'anti-generalism' and 'anti-codifiability' instead.

1. Anti-Codifiability: Two Red Herrings

McDowell and Nussbaum began with an interest in what the Aristotelian *phronimos* knows, with what he possesses that enables him, unlike the rest of us, to be excellent at knowing what to do. And they were both concerned to deny a certain generalist picture of his knowledge; one according to which the *phronimos* has knowledge of a code by following which he is able to live and act well.

Hence the first statement of anti-generalism in relation to Aristotle, in McDowell's 'Virtue and Reason', where it is stated as an anti-codifiability claim about a certain sort of ethical generalization or principle. What McDowell originally denied was that 'the virtuous person's views about how, in general, one should behave are susceptible of codification, in principles apt for serving as major premisses in [practical] syllogisms' (McDowell 1979: 148).

That amounts to denying the existence of a set of (correctly) *action-guiding* ethical principles, viz., principles or generalizations that could figure as the starting points of practical reasoning, a set sufficiently large to constitute a code for acting well in general. Taking this denial as the basic anti-codifiability claim, I want to note a few points about it to get a couple of red herrings out of the way.

The first red herring is the (possible) existence of a few absolute prohibitions. At *NE* 1107a10–14, Aristotle does indeed tell us that 'adultery', theft, and murder are themselves bad and that one must always be wrong in doing them. But this is quite consistent with the denial of codifiability. What is denied is that the *phronimos* has, and employs, a *general* procedure, subsuming new cases under the rules in his code in order to reach a correct decision about what to do, day to day, and this need not involve the blanket rejection of all absolute prohibitions. All it requires is the plausible claim that they are few and far between and that, whatever they may be, they provide very little in the way of action-guidance in day-to-day life. If I want to know what the *phronimos* knows, so that I shall know how to act well, day to day, knowing that, say, theft, murder, and adultery cannot form part of a well-spent day still leaves me pretty much in the dark. So I put the issue of whether there are any absolute ethical generalizations or moral principles aside as a red herring.

At this point, we should remind ourselves of two features of the *phronimos*. One is that, *qua* virtuous, the *phronimos* knows what anyone minimally decent knows. We may not agree with Aristotle that murder, theft, and adultery are always wrong, but whether we do or not, I assume that we all think that they *are*, roughly speaking, wrong, and moreover that everyone, short of the shameless and wicked, knows that this is so. It is ordinary, common or garden moral knowledge. And of course the *phronimos*, being neither shameless nor wicked, knows it too.

However (I want to add, pointedly), this hardly marks out what the *phronimos* knows as special, and the second feature of the *phronimos* is that he has special knowledge. This point must be stressed, because, when we consider the question 'What does the *phronimos* know?' it is only his special (or 'peculiar') knowledge that we are after, that is, the knowledge he has *qua phronimos* that distinguishes him from everyone who lacks *phronēsis*, not the knowledge he has *qua* ordinary intellectually competent adult, nor the knowledge he has *qua* neither shameless nor wicked. And it is to the *phronimos*'s special knowledge that the anti-codifiability claim pertains.

These two features give us a further reason to put the few exceptionless action-guiding rules or generalizations we can untendentiously ascribe to Aristotle and to his *phronimos* to one side as red herrings. They also come into play with respect to the second red herring, namely the existence of a fair number of other action-guiding ethical generalizations which are not exceptionless but hold 'for the most part' (*hōs epi to polu*). Aristotle does not mention many, but several occur in the following passage, and it is instructive to consider what we should make of it.

> [S]hould someone help a friend rather than a good person, and show gratitude to a benefactor rather than offer a service to a companion if he cannot do both? It is, of course, no easy matter to make precise decisions in cases like this, because they allow all sorts of variations in respect of importance and unimportance, of what is noble, and of what is necessary. But it is quite clear that we should not give everything to the same person. In general, we should return a benefit instead of doing a favor for our companions, just as we should repay a debt instead of giving the money to a companion. But perhaps even this is not always so. For example, if you have been ransomed

from kidnappers, should you ransom in return the person who freed you, whoever he is? Or if he has not been kidnapped, but asks for his money back, should you repay him, or ransom your own father instead? It seems that you should ransom your father even in preference to yourself. As we have said, then, in general debts should be paid, but if a gift is overriding in its nobility or necessity, we should incline in favor of these considerations.

(*NE* 1164b30–1165a5).

The action-guiding ethical generalizations we can find here are (i) for the most part, we should sooner return a benefit than give to a companion; (ii) for the most part, we should sooner repay a debt than give favours to companions; (iii) you should ransom your father rather than repay a debt, indeed, even in preference to ransoming yourself; and (iv) for the most part one should repay what is owed, but if giving is overridingly fine or necessary we should incline in favour of it. We may infer, given these and his earlier discussion, that Aristotle will also accept (v) for the most part we should repay debts; (vi) for the most part we should return benefits; and (vii) for the most part we should give (favours) to companions.

Here, as with a few absolute rules, the anti-codifier should have no objection to ascribing knowledge of (v)–(vii) to the *phronimos*. But, as before, we may deny that such ascription goes any distance towards ascribing any *special* knowledge to him.

However, there are some places in *Love's Knowledge*, taken up by Irwin (2000),[2] in which it looks as though Nussbaum (1990) denies that there is any sense in which the *phronimos* is guided by rules such as (v)–(vii), or brings them to bear on his decision. For there she seems to be committed to regarding such rules 'not as normative... the ultimate authorities against which the correctness of particular choices is assessed, but more as summaries or rules of thumb, highly useful for a variety of purposes, but valid only to the extent to which they correctly describe good concrete judgments, and to be assessed, ultimately, against these' (68). She mentions three of their uses later—as part of moral education, as worth sticking to when you think you might be subject to emotional bias, and as things to use when 'there is not time to formulate a fully concrete decision in the case at hand' (73). We should note that the first two do not pertain to the choices of the *phronimos* but that the third might.

---

[2] It should be noted that Irwin targets Nussbaum's 'An Aristotelian Conception of Rationality' and does not take account of her view in 'Finely Aware and Richly Responsible' that 'perceptions "perch on the heads of"' standing obligations and 'do not displace them' (Nussbaum 1990: 155).

These remarks strike me as sounding disquietingly similar to what act utilitarians used to say about moral rules. Moral rules don't have any sort of normative authority—only the greatest happiness principle has that; individual acts are not to be assessed as right or wrong in terms of *them*, but only in terms of it. The so-called true or correct ones are correct only insofar as they summarize a large number of true judgements about the rightness or wrongness of individual acts. And, as such, they are useful in the three ways that Nussbaum mentions, even though sometimes a particular true judgement will show that the rule is, in this instance, incorrect.

Now *if* this is what rules such as 'debts should be repaid' and 'benefits should be returned' are like, it is surely the case that the *phronimos* will hardly ever rely on them. His moral education is complete, and he is not subject to bias since his emotions are in harmony with his reason. Such rules may be useful to others, but why should he employ them when there is a correct concrete decision he can come to that the rule might have disallowed? His sole employment of them would be in those rare cases where he does not have time to find out much about the situation at hand and has to jump to a practical conclusion instead of reasoning to it, and hope for the best. But in these cases we might well say he isn't really employing his practical reason anyhow, or at least only in a non-standard way. So *qua phronimos* (rather than *qua* human being who, inevitably, sometimes finds himself having to act on inadequate information) he is never guided by such rules in his decision making. Irwin finds this implausible, and so—though for rather different reasons—do I.

Insofar as learning such rules as 'debts should be repaid', 'benefits should be returned', and 'favours should be done for companions' is an important part of moral education, we should not think of the successful inculcation of such rules only in terms of being habituated to act in accordance with them (for the most part). Is it not plausible to say that the *phronimos* thinks of debts as the sorts of thing that are to be repaid, of benefits as the sorts of thing that are to be returned, and of friends as the sorts of people you put yourself out for? This is part of his virtue and one of the many ways in which he contrasts with the shameless and wicked, who think of debts as money for jam, of benefits as the harvest to be reaped from suckers, and of friends merely as people you know it is fun to be with. It is part of what he came to know, not by induction, but when he was receiving his good moral education in childhood. And there is no reason for him to discard that knowledge as merely statistical, because that is not what it is.

So if this is what Nussbaum was committed to, I agree with Irwin that it should not be ascribed to Aristotle. Someone who has been so badly brought up that he does not realize that, for the most part, benefits should be returned, debts repaid, and favours done for one's companions, will hit on correct decisions about what to do only by accident; the *phronimos*'s knowledge of these mother's-knee rules surely, as Irwin (2000) puts it, 'contributes essentially to (his) correct decision about what to do' in many cases in the relevant areas, in at least the same sense as a minimally decent upbringing does (122).

But these *are* mother's-knee rules, and the *phronimos* has moved well beyond what he—and we—learnt at our mothers' knees in such an upbringing. So it is innocuous to allow that the *phronimos* is often, in relevant situations, guided by such rules, since, as that is all they are, this point does not get us any closer to understanding what his special knowledge consists in. They, and the *phronimos*'s possible employment of them, are another red herring.

2. Anti-Codifiability: The *Phronimos*'s Special Knowledge

Let us now return to the passage and consider Aristotle's two 'ranking rules' (i) and (ii). Here I am much less certain that these are ethical generalizations that Aristotle might assume everyone with a minimally decent upbringing knows. If they are, the above remarks apply, so let us assume more interestingly that they are not, but examples of the sort of thing that the *phronimos*, especially, knows. And let us assume, with the codifiers, that his knowledge of them essentially informs some of his characteristically (or 'peculiarly') correct decisions. That is, it is *because* he knows them that, unlike the nicest sort of prodigal person (who is not base but foolish [*NE* 1121a26]) he does not give to a companion when he shouldn't—for instance when unreturned benefits or debts are outstanding.

Is there any objection those committed to the anti-codifiability claim might make to ascribing knowledge of these two ranking rules to the Aristotelian *phronimos* as examples of his special knowledge? If so, it should not, I think, be that the ascription is false. Rather, the objection should be that it is either misleading or not *perspicuous*.

Let us suppose that part of what is special about the *phronimos*'s knowledge is that he knows these two ranking rules. How do we go on from there in our consideration of the question 'What does the *phronimos* know?' Are we to infer, as an interpretation geared towards codifiability would suggest, that he knows lots and lots of such ranking rules, that what often—even usually, perhaps?—enables him to reach the correct decision in cases where those lacking *phronēsis*, albeit fairly well brought up, reach the wrong one, is his knowledge of a large set of such ranking rules? Well, we certainly don't find *them* in Aristotle's text, nor any suggestion that we will find them if we think a bit harder, nor that Aristotle is seeking them. So if we take the ascription of these two ranking rules to the *phronimos* as *indicative* of a whole lot of them somewhere in the offing, the ascription is misleading; nothing in the text supports their being thus indicative.

So should we say, 'There is nothing to infer from the *phronimos*'s knowledge of these two rules, nothing in general to learn about his special knowledge from this bit of the text, just this rather odd fact that he knows a couple of ranking rules (and perhaps a very specialized rule about ransoming one's father)'? Well, that might be true, but it is hardly a *perspicuous* answer to 'What does the *phronimos* know?'

For the anti-codifier, there is something more perspicuous in the offing. What we have in (i) and (ii), she may say, are examples of the *phronimos*'s especially good grasp of the important, the fine (or 'noble'), and the necessary (at least). (Note the opening sentence of the discussion: 'It is, of course, no easy matter to make precise decisions in cases like this, because they allow all sorts of variations in respect of importance and unimportance, of what is noble, and of what is necessary.') The examples here happen to be of a rather rare sort, insofar as his understanding of these concepts in this area can be roughly expressed in a couple of what nowadays we call ranking rules. For the most part, it is not disgraceful (contrary to what is fine) to refuse a favour to a companion *when* this is incompatible with repaying a debt or, more generally, what one owes; for the most part, repaying the debt or returning the benefit is necessary/what has to be done in such a case, and it would be disgraceful not to do it. On the occasions on which the rule holds, the *phronimos* can say truly to a friend or benefactor, 'I *can't* give you this $20, much as I would like to, because I *have* to/must repay it to so and so', where the 'can't' and the 'have to' or 'must' deploy the concept of the necessary. 'Of course returning benefits and doing favours to companions are important, but first things first; for the most part, repaying debts is more important—and this is one of the cases in which that is so.'

But remember (iv)—'for the most part one should repay what is owed, but if giving is overridingly fine or necessary we should incline in favour of these considerations.' There can be cases in which it would be more fine or necessary (and no doubt important) to do the favour rather than pay the debt or return the benefit. And the *phronimos*, with his special, true understanding or conception of the important, the fine, and the necessary (which enables him to make the correct decision in all sorts of cases where none of us can come up with remotely plausible ranking rules) can recognize such a case when he encounters it.

So the *phronimos* has a grasp of the important, the fine, and the necessary superior to that of most of us. And this suggests a way to go on in our consideration of the question, 'What does the *phronimos* know?' which immediately proves fruitful. From other bits of the text, we see that he has a superior grasp of other concepts too, such as those of the fine (again), the expedient or useful, the (truly) pleasant and their opposites (*NE* 1104b30–33). He has a superior grasp of the right or correct as it occurs 'to the right extent, towards the right people, for the right reason, etc.'. He also has a superior grasp of *eupraxia*—acting well—and *eudaimonia*. And he has a superior grasp of the virtues and vices.

Given the content of the second half of Book III and all of Book IV, namely the extended discussion of various virtues and what they may be confounded with (which includes their corresponding vices), at the very least what we ascribe to the Aristotelian *phronimos* in this area is knowledge of what courage (or temperance or generosity or 'mildness', etc.) really is; we ascribe to him, in our modern terminology, a full mastery of the concept. This mastery is what enables him always to apply it correctly—something that the wicked and the well-brought-up-but-still-lacking-full-virtue people are not able to do. We know that the vicious do not have such mastery of the concepts because we know from the text that 'the coward calls the brave man rash and the reckless call him a coward and so for all the other cases' (*NE* 1108b25–6). That the well brought up but not yet fully virtuous lack it is interpretation, but not of a tendentious sort. When Aristotle goes to the trouble of distinguishing the character of the (truly) courageous from five other types who are thought to be courageous, we may plausibly suppose that quite a few ordinary people, not just the shameless and wicked, tend to confound the genuine article with one or some of these other five. Similarly, they confound the buffoon with the ready-witted and tend to commend certain irascible men as 'manly' and 'natural leaders' (*NE* 1128a15, 1126b1–2). Perhaps, too, they sometimes take the open-handed prodigal to be generous.

Any such mistake is liable to lead to error in action, as one praises and imitates where one should condemn and eschew. But the *phronimos*'s special knowledge enables him not to make these mistakes.

So what we have so far are the beginnings of an account—far from complete,[3] but quite substantial—of the *phronimos*'s special knowledge, which

---

[3] 'Far from complete' because nothing has been said about the close relation between political knowledge and *phronēsis* ('same state, but their being is different' [*NE* 1141b24–5]), nor what is involved in deliberative excellence. I still don't know what to say about the former, but address the latter, and its relation to experience, in Hursthouse (2006).

emphasizes not his knowledge of a code of action-guiding rules, but his mastery of a large number of concepts, a mastery he displays in applying them correctly, case by case.

However, at this point, a codifier might say, triumphantly, 'Suppose the *phronimos* knows what courage, temperance, generosity, mildness, etc. really are (which most people don't) and that it is this special knowledge that enables him, uniquely, to live and act well. Surely then his correct views about how in general one should behave *are* susceptible to codification in principles apt for serving as major premises in practical syllogisms, contrary to the basic claim of anti-codifiability. The principles or rules in question (the v-rules) are something like "one ought to do what is courageous, one ought not to do what is cowardly or reckless", "one ought to do what is temperate, one ought not to do what is licentious", "one ought to do what is generous", etc. The relevant minor premise in each case would be "Doing such and such would be courageous or doing so and so would be cowardly", and thereby he reaches his correct practical decision.'

Now as an objection to the basic anti-codifiability claim that looks pretty strong. So what are we to say about it?

3. Beyond Anti-Codifiability

The debate about anti-codifiability began as one between the particularists and the generalists. The generalist said the *phronimos* knows a code; the particularist denied it. But that debate began well before explicit talk about the v-rules appeared in our philosophical literature, and it is plausible to suppose that they are not quite the sort of rules or principles the generalists, or the particularists, initially had in mind.[4] For they have the following two features.

Firstly, they do not consist of anything recondite that philosophers have painstakingly formulated or discovered, but only common moral knowledge.

---

[4] Space does not permit defending this in detail, but we may briefly note the following. As Roger Crisp has argued (2000), the examples that form the main support for Dancy's particularism about reasons in *Moral Reasons* (1993) all involve 'non-ultimate' reasons such as my having borrowed a book from you, or a claim's being a lie, rather than 'ultimate' such as an action's being just or dishonest, which he does not discuss. It is only in the recent *Ethics without Principles* (2004) that he has a go at them. Nussbaum, as we have seen, was thinking of the sort of moral rules that might plausibly be thought of as 'rules of thumb'. The target of McDowell's 'Virtue and Reason' (1979) is perhaps a very general conception of moral philosophy that he thinks most of his contemporaries mistakenly hold and is hence difficult to pin down, but it is hard to believe that he has the v-rules in mind when he says, 'As Aristotle consistently says, the best generalizations about how one should behave hold only for the most part.' (I return to this claim below, n. 9.)

But the generalist picture surely was, and still is, as Irwin (2000) describes it—that it is the moral philosophers' task to '*seek* general principles that will guide agents in deciding that one course of action is morally right and another is wrong' (100), to find 'in ethics *as in natural science*, theoretically significant generalizations', which, in ethics, 'are significant for the primarily practical purpose of ethical inquiry' (129, my italics). What they sought, and are still seeking, is something superior to the folk wisdom of the v-rules, as 'natural' philosophers sought, and scientists now seek, something superior to folk wisdom about the natural world.

Secondly, insofar as the v-rules are only common moral knowledge they do not, of course, capture the *phronimos*'s special knowledge. Once again, any minimally well-brought-up Aristotelian child knows that one ought to do what is courageous, not what is cowardly, what is temperate, not what is licentious, etc., and can understand and apply such rules to some extent. What is special about the *phronimos*'s knowledge is the special understanding he brings to these rules, his unique mastery of the concepts involved. All the difficult practical work, one might say, is done by this superior understanding, not by the rules themselves. To lack *phronēsis* is to lack such mastery; so these rules, the v-rules, cannot be fully understood by those lacking *phronēsis*. But thereby they fail to be the sort the generalists initially had in mind, which (I assume) were rules or principles that could be understood, albeit to differing effect, by the virtuous and non-virtuous alike. The generalists' drive was, and is, to formulate the principles they seek in 'non-moral' or 'descriptive' terms, articulating, in detail, the *phronimos*'s special knowledge.

If the generalist vs. particularist debate was about *any* sort of code, it was a pretty trivial debate. But I do not believe that it was. As a debate about what the *phronimos* knows, there was always more to it than that. The crucial feature of *phronēsis* which the anti-codifiability claim on its own quite fails to capture is that its acquisition is inseparable from the acquisition of (full) virtue. And virtue, according to Aristotle, can be acquired only by habitually engaging in virtuous action, not, for example, from 'discourses'.[5] So *phronēsis*—excellence in practical reasoning—can be acquired only by habitually engaging in virtuous action, not, for example, just by learning a code of action-guiding principles comprehensible to the virtuous and non-virtuous alike. And I take this, rather than anti-codifiability per se, to be the basic insight of anti-generalism in relation to Aristotle.

---

[5] *NE* 1103a25–b25, 1105b10–19, 1179b1–7; cf. 1142a12–20.

So we might take the central claim of an anti-generalist interpretation of Aristotle as, not just anti-codifiability tout court, but the following: the *phronimos*'s special knowledge—that which enables him to get practical decisions right—is not susceptible of codification in rules that are both action-guiding and fully comprehensible to those lacking virtue (and thereby *phronēsis*).[6]

And I think we have good reason to suppose that Aristotle accepts that. Note that if we express the claim in this way, the issue of whether the *phronimos* follows a code of v-rules becomes, strictly speaking, as much of a red herring as the issue of whether he brings 'Debts should be repaid' to bear on a particular case in reaching his correct decision about what to do.[7] There is no significant generalist point to be made by insisting on it, but neither is there any significant anti-generalist point to be made by denying it and insisting that we talk instead of his mastery of a wide range of concepts.

There might indeed be a point in the denial (with regard to truth rather than interpretation of Aristotle), but it could not be made alongside insistence on the *phronimos*'s mastery of a wide range of concepts. It is this. The virtues and vices, and hence concepts of them and the corresponding v-rules, are fairly culturally specific. It may be that Aristotle thought that his lists were not only correct but complete and that *phronēsis*, and hence virtue, was impossible for anyone unfortunate enough to know only a culture with somewhat different lists. We are not so sanguine. Nor, surely, should any sensible philosopher commit herself to the claim that a proper moral education would be impossible in a culture that lacked virtue and vice terms. So, for the sake of avoiding committal to cultural relativism, an anti-generalist might well avoid committal to either the v-rules or to the *phronimos*'s mastery of a wide range of specified concepts. And this may be why McDowell tends to keep his discussion at the highly abstract level of the *phronimos*'s conception of 'doing well' or of 'what virtue requires'.

It is, of course (returning to the *phronimos*'s special mastery of the virtue terms in the v-rules), open to a generalist to claim that what such mastery involves is knowledge of the necessary and sufficient conditions of their correct application expressed in 'non-evaluative' or 'purely descriptive' terms. So what the Aristotelian *phronimos* knows is, at the very least, something roughly of the form 'An act is courageous if and only if it is such and such, and/or so and so and/or if thus and so then this and that, etc.' *That* debate cannot be closed here. But in an Aristotelian context, the claim is distinctly problematic.

---

[6] I owe this formulation to Eric Brown. [7] Cf. Broadie (1991: 248–49 and 264n. 67).

Given Aristotle's committal to some version of the unity of the virtues, what the *phronimos* knows about, say, courage, cannot be isolable from what he knows about temperance, generosity, 'mildness', justice, etc. So those rules that articulate in detail his special understanding of 'Do what is courageous' would have to have written into them something that connected them (some of them?) essentially with the other sets that articulate his understanding of the other virtue and vice terms. That does not certainly show them to be impossible, but it certainly presents anyone who is seeking them with a formidable task.

And it suggests a further problem. If the rules are to be couched in 'descriptive' terms understood alike by the virtuous and non-virtuous, then there are surely a number of terms that must not figure in them—such as 'the fine', 'the necessary', 'the important', 'the advantageous', 'the beneficial', 'the pleasant'. (Not all of these may be terms that philosophers will confidently classify as 'moral', but nor are they terms whose application the virtuous and the non-virtuous agree on.) But how could we possibly give the necessary and sufficient conditions for the application of 'courage' without reference to the relevance of facing danger for a fine and thereby important but not a trivial end? Well, it might be said, these terms too are to be provided with necessary and sufficient conditions for their application in 'descriptive' terms which, in their turn, can be understood by someone who lacks *phronēsis*. But that only the *fully* virtuous, and thereby the *phronimos*, has the really correct conception of these, and that this conception *cannot* be acquired theoretically, just by attending lectures or reading books but only through virtuous activity itself, is another unquestionably Aristotelian thesis.

Quite generally, if there were indeed some way to articulate the *phronimos*'s code that could be understood by someone who lacked virtue, then this is just what Aristotle should be seeking or offering in his lecture courses, for, contrary to what he says, it should be possible to acquire *phronēsis* and thereby full virtue by attending lectures—given a minimally decent upbringing, it could replace the experience he says is needed. But it could not. *Phronēsis*—excellence in practical reasoning, moral knowledge—can be acquired only by habitually engaging in virtuous action, not, for example, just by learning a written code of conduct.

4. *Phronēsis* and Perception

So far, I have left untouched two other themes in Aristotle that figure prominently in the generalist vs. particularist debate.

One is found in his claims that the subject matter of ethics does not allow for a high degree of exactness, that we must be content to draw conclusions that are true only for the most part and that it is not easy to define by rule, or give an account of, this area or that. The other is found in the claims that, in at least some of these cases, 'the judgment rests with perception' and in the passages that relate action and *phronēsis* to perception.[8]

Are these two themes connected? And if so, how? Aristotle's claim that 'the judgment rests with perception' is usually quoted in the context in which Ross quoted it (1988: 42), namely that in which two prima facie duties or rules conflict. This suggests an obvious connection. Ethical generalizations hold only for the most part, as we see most clearly when two of them conflict and one is overridden and thereby shown to have an exception. Which one is overridden in a particular case is not determined by some exceptionless ranking rules, for they too hold only for the most part. So reaching the correct judgement about what to do in cases of conflict between rules rests with perception.

That sounds very plausible, but it is worth noting that nothing in Aristotle's text supports it directly. The two occasions on which he says that 'the judgment rests with perception' both relate to the same example, and it is not an example of a conflict, but of hitting the mean or of judging how far one can deviate from it without incurring blame (*NE* 1109b12ff and 1126a31ff). And that we should be angry on the right occasions in the right way with the right people with the right end for the right amount of time and so on is not one of the generalizations that seems to call for qualification by 'for the most part'. What could possibly count as an exception to it?

Moreover, there is not much in the text that looks like a discussion of conflicts between Rossian prima facie duties. All we have is the short passage discussed above concerning repaying debts and returning benefits, and the discussion of 'mixed actions' in Book III, which Aristotle thinks ought to be chosen in return for what, since there are many differences in particulars (*NE* 1110b7) with nary a mention of perception. Furthermore, what is notably—from a modern perspective—lacking in him is any suggestion that the v-rules can conflict. He is seemingly unworried by the thought that, say, courage and *philia*, or generosity and justice, might make competing demands in a particular situation.[9] Instead, there is the serene claim of the unity of the virtues: that if one possesses *phronēsis*, all the virtues of character will be present as well.

---

[8] *NE* 1112b34–1113a2, 1142a25–31, 1143a25–b14.
[9] This is why I said above (n. 4) that McDowell cannot have had the v-rules in mind when he said, 'As Aristotle consistently says, the best generalizations about how one should behave hold only for the most part.' There is nothing in Aristotle one could quote to support the idea that a case would ever turn up in which doing what was courageous or generous or temperate would strike us as wrong.

So it may be that rather than moving to the importance of perception in Aristotle via the anachronistic concern with the resolution of dilemmas when rules conflict, we should look elsewhere.

The capacity for a certain sort of intellectual (rather than sensory) perception (*NE* 1142a30), now often called, following Wiggins (1987), 'situational appreciation' (237), is standardly taken to be something the *phronimos* is especially good at, one of the things that enables him to avoid the mistakes that lesser mortals make. Few generalists now dispute the necessity for this capacity for discerning the relevant features of particular situations. Many generalists accept, that is, that the correct application of their rules in a particular context requires recognizing its relevant and/or salient features.

However, accepting the latter does not quite amount to assigning the importance to the intellectual perceptual capacity that is assigned to the practical *nous* uniquely possessed by the *phronimos*. The generalist thought might be that although, granted, the *phronimos* is especially good at seeing everything that is relevant immediately, the non-virtuous, although they tend to overlook it initially, can recognize it when it is pointed out. (After all, ex hypothesi, it is *there*.) And perhaps the thought is that this recognition is best brought about by appeal to ethical generalizations.

In some cases that is a plausible thought (as long as we do not take the non-virtuous to include the shameless and wicked), since it is obvious enough that we often allow ourselves to drift into wrongdoing by turning a blind eye to what is relevant. (I heard of Elizabeth Anscombe's bringing a debate about whether the imminent danger of a scandal should be averted by telling the newspapers *this* or *that* to an embarrassed halt by saying, 'But both of those involve telling lies.' Everyone present was virtuous enough to accept that this was so relevant that a third course of action should be sought, but they had overlooked it before she pointed it out. The generalist gloss on this would be that everyone accepted 'Lying is wrong' [or 'Lying is a wrong-making feature'] and that all that was missing was the recognition of the relevant feature.)

But things are not so straightforward if we suppose that what the *phronimos* often recognizes as a relevant and indeed decisive feature is that, for example, a proposed course of action is not 'unspirited' but 'mild', or not generous but prodigal, or that it will not bring true pleasure or advantage to its proposed recipient, or that, in this case, giving to the friend is more important than paying the debt.[10] For in these sorts of cases, it is not plausible to suppose that

---

[10] I take it these would all count as examples of perceiving what was relevant or salient. Woods (1986) suggests that the *phronimos* sees that a certain possible action is courageous (rather than cowardly), magnanimous (rather than pusillanimous) (see esp. 157).

those lacking *phronēsis* will recognize the feature as soon as it is pointed out. On the contrary, one rather imagines them saying, 'I don't see that.'

Is there anything the *phronimos*—or the ideally articulate *phronimos*—can say to make the feature recognizable to them? A stress on (intellectual) perception need not be taken to the point of denying that no doubt there are often things he could say that might often work: 'This is not generous but prodigal' and 'This is more important than that' are not just like 'This is not green but blue' or 'This is greener than that.' They are more like 'This is a *babiana* plant not a *sparaxis*—can you see that the foliage is just a little less shiny and branches in a slightly different way?' which the trained botanist can sometimes say.[11] But they have an important similarity to both, viz., that mastery of the terms they employ can be acquired only through a training in which they are applied to particular instances. There is nothing the *phronimos* could say that would fully articulate his (intellectual) perceptual capacity, because there is nothing that could be written down that could replace the training through which he has acquired it, just as no amount of written information will enable the unpractised eye of the amateur botanist to spot, reliably, the *babiana* plants.

Here we see how a general Wittgensteinian move could be brought in but also that anti-Wittgensteinian Aristotelians should accept the point anyhow. A Wittgensteinian will say, 'We acquire a large number of our concepts in practice. What I bring to a new example of, say, a game, is my mastery of "game" which is part of the mastery of English I acquired through my childhood training, engaging in the practice of the application of the term to particular instances. (I do not bring a definition.) Similarly, what the *phronimos* brings to a new situation is his virtue (with all that that entails) acquired through his childhood training in doing what is just or temperate or courageous, and fully developed by habituation (not a set of definitions).'[12]

Anti-Wittgensteinians think that there must be a definition that someone brought up in a culture where games were unknown could use to work out, reliably, whether the activity going on before her was a game, absent any ostensive training. But be that as it may, *no* Aristotelian should believe that there is something, say a set of definitions, that someone who lacked virtue could, in theory, use to work out, reliably, whether something was important, fine, truly pleasant, or advantageous, prodigal rather than generous... or, quite

---

[11] I owe the analogy to the identification of different species of plant to Anthony Price.
[12] Cf. McDowell (1988: 94).

generally, an instance of *eupraxia* or acting well, absent appropriate ostensive training in childhood and subsequent habituation in virtuous actions.

The anti-generalist dispute about the 'priority of perception' is indeed, as Irwin (2000) says, not just about the 'temporal priority of learning' (103). Everyone agrees that, as a matter of fact, our moral education begins with our being taught to see that particular situations have certain features and trained to act accordingly. It is about whether, in theory, there could be a substitute for this early training, something else, such as a set of definitions, that would enable someone untrained in virtuous action to see, reliably, that something was generous rather than prodigal, or not disgraceful, or more important than something else, or not truly pleasant, or necessary... or an instance of acting well. And the Aristotelian claim is that there could not be.

5. Conclusion

So we return again to what I called the 'basic insight', namely that *phronēsis*— excellence in practical reasoning, moral knowledge—can be acquired only by habitual engagement in virtuous action. There is no short cut to what the *phronimos* knows. Nothing but the acquisition of personal virtue will yield it.

When we bring this feature of *phronēsis* right to the surface, it clearly suppresses (on the assumption that Aristotle is right) a significant amount of the pretensions of contemporary normative ethical theory. Most startlingly, it entails that we moral philosophers, notwithstanding our claims to a grasp of what is reasonable or consistent or universalizable or objectively the case which is superior to that of the non-philosophical adults who taught us in our youth are, *qua* philosophers, no better equipped than they to give guidance on what we should do. And, most embarrassingly, it entails that we can claim to be better equipped only by claiming virtue.

Who teaches us, or professes to teach us, how we should conduct ourselves? Well, parents and other adults who contribute to the upbringing and moral education of children, by training them to act in accordance with virtue (or not). And moral philosophers, who write and give 'discourses'. (I take it that legislators impose codes of conduct rather than teach them.) But, according to Aristotle's view of *phronēsis*, the discourses of philosophers are useless to those who have not been well trained in childhood, because they will not listen to argument and would not understand it if they did (*NE* 1179b16–17). Moreover, since it is only the *phronimos*, complete with his virtue, who has knowledge of how we should conduct ourselves, it is only the discourses of (fully) virtuous moral philosophers that could justifiably be claimed to teach those who are prepared to listen.

If the generalists agree that there is no way to become excellent at knowing what to do without acquiring virtue, why should they continue to seek to formulate action-guiding principles? (Of course that is a big 'if', but I know of no generalist who has explicitly claimed that it is false. And no doubt there are some who do indeed think of themselves as wiser and more virtuous than most of the rest of us.)

One possible generalist reply is that, although there is no short cut to *phronēsis*, there may nevertheless be some ways that are shorter than others. The philosopher's search for principles that are not just part of common moral knowledge leads, it may be said, to the invention or discovery of terms or concepts that make virtue easier to teach, and hence easier to acquire, providing action-guidance in that sense.

An example might be the term 'informed consent'. Prior to its coinage, the few (at least fairly) virtuous doctors who were making the correct decisions about how to engage with their patients before treatment—about the circumstances in which to discuss the treatment with their patients, and in which not to, and on what occasion, and in what way, and with how much giving of information and with what aim, and so on—no doubt found it very difficult to pass this aspect of their *phronēsis* on to medical students. Even a medical student who spent a year or so with such a doctor and aspired to act as she did might well not catch on to imitating what was at issue, since neither he, nor the doctor, would have the term to group the relevant instances together, distinguishing them from all the other things that the doctor was doing day by day. He might, for example, catch on to the gentle vagueness as to gruesome details present *here*, without noticing that here the gentleness related to soothing fears regarding a treatment already fully discussed—and go on to become untruthful. Or he might catch on to being genuinely informative but, missing the gentleness, go on to become a brutally honest bully. But the philosophers, abstracting from the instances in which the virtuous doctors made the correct decisions, worked out that what such doctors were doing was, where possible, seeking informed consent. The principle 'Health practitioners should seek the informed consent of their patients to treatment' does not give medical students instant virtue, but it makes it much easier for them than hitherto to begin to habituate themselves in this area of virtuous activity. They can learn quite quickly—and moreover from lectures—a substantial part of what they have to see as salient in their engagement with a patient before treatment.

Irwin (2000), I think, regards Aristotle's doctrine of the mean in a somewhat similar light (115–18). Of course 'We should hit the mean' is hardly an illuminating piece of action-guidance as it stands, but, by the time Aristotle has unpacked it into 'the mean in actions and feelings', given the general account of this as 'to feel or act towards the right person to the right extent at the right time for the right reason in the right way', placed it between excess and deficiency, and then run through its specific versions by discussing the individual virtues, he winds up by offering something quite substantial. As before, it does not give instant virtue to those who lack it. But, it might be said, it makes it much easier for the proto-virtuous to habituate themselves along the path of improvement rather than falling away from it. We can learn quite quickly—and moreover from a 'discourse'—a substantial part of what we have to see as salient in our conduct and thereby learn to start looking out for it.

'We should aim at hitting the mean', we might say, once elaborated, gives the aspirant to virtuous action an instructively and formatively demanding checklist. (Action towards right person? Yes. Feeling towards right person [not necessarily the same one]? Not all of them—I do take an improper pleasure in outdoing so and so, and should work on that. To the right extent? Action—rather over the top. Feeling—covered already. Occasion? I did rush it a bit—must curb my impulsiveness. Grounds? Motives, alas, mixed. Etc.) Philosophers with no interest in virtue ethics may well regard the consideration of such a checklist as beneath their contempt, but I would be surprised to hear from any of its adherents that they had not found illuminating Aristotle's list of the many ways in which one can go wrong, and that they did not regard the list as one of their most powerful tools in making virtue ethics plausible to their students.

These are two very specialized examples, and thereby hard to generalize from. Do they suggest that normative ethical theorists should still be seeking as yet unrecognized action-guiding ethical principles? Well, they certainly suggest that ethics is not an area in which we should say that our ordinary language and current knowledge is all right as it is. There may well be rules as yet unformulated that would enable us to train our children and indeed ourselves in virtue more easily than we do now. So it might well be worth seeking new terms that could be enshrined in new rules, or indeed new rules in our already available vocabulary. Of course, the purpose would be educative, rather than intended to find rules to resolve difficult cases, but none the worse for that.

But would what we think of as normative ethical theorizing then be the obvious way to proceed? One might say that a more obvious method would be to look for currently untranslatable terms or unfamiliar rules in other cultures that were embedded in what seemed to us to be ethically good practice. If part of the drive to generalism is, as it is in O'Neill (1996), the fear that our ordinary virtue and vice terms are too culturally specific and thereby parochial (67–8), then surely we should look for what other cultures could, specifically, teach us, not seek abstractions within the confines of our own.

Another method might be to try to coin catchy new terms for bad practice—the grass-roots creation of 'sexist' and 'racist' made it much easier (for those of us who were willing) to recognize, and thereby try to avoid, the actions and reactions that fall under them.[13] Another might be to look for easy-to-teach rules whose normative authority would be obvious to all but the shameless and wicked and which would make a substantial difference in a limited area. Would that a moral philosopher had come up with 'Don't drink and drive', which quite transformed my generation. (Those who grew up with the rule find it hard to believe how recklessly self-indulgent, irresponsible, imprudent, and light-minded we were.)

So there may indeed be important and as yet unrecognized—if somewhat unexpected—rules for normative ethical theorists to seek. But Aristotelian anti-generalism, as characterized here, still carries a nasty sting, for it entails that, unless the theorists have *phronēsis* and hence virtue themselves, their 'shorter ways' may well make it harder, rather than easier, to acquire virtue. I believe myself that 'informed consent' was a winner, but I also believe that the contemporary elevation of 'person' (as a philosopher's term that contrasts with 'human being') has already proved to be a short cut to vice rather than a shorter way to virtue.

References

Broadie, S. 1991. *Ethics With Aristotle*. Oxford: Oxford University Press.

Broadie, S. 1999. *Cambridge Dictionary of Philosophy*, 2nd edn. Cambridge: Cambridge University Press.

Crisp, R. 2000. 'Particularizing Particularism'. In Hooker and Little 2000: 23–47.

Dancy, J. 1993. *Moral Reasons*. Oxford: Blackwell.

Dancy, J. 2004. *Ethics without Principles*. Oxford: Clarendon Press.

---

[13] I owe these two excellent examples to Chris Cuomo.

Hooker, B. and M. Little (eds). 2000. *Moral Particularism*. Oxford: Clarendon Press.

Hursthouse, R. 2006. 'Practical Wisdom: A Mundane Account', *Proceedings of the Aristotelian Society* 106: 283–307.

Irwin, T. H. 2000. 'Ethics as an Inexact Science: Aristotle's Ambitions for Moral Theory'. In Hooker and Little 2000: 100–29.

Louden, R. 1984. 'On Some Vices of Virtue Ethics', *American Philosophical Quarterly* 21: 228–94.

Louden, R. 1998. 'Virtue Ethics'. In Ruth Chadwick (ed.), *Encyclopedia of Applied Ethics*, vol. IV. New York: Academic Press: 491–8.

McDowell, J. 1979. 'Virtue and Reason', *Monist* 62: 331–50.

McDowell, J. 1988. 'Comments on T. H. Irwin's "Some Rational Aspects of Incontinence"', *Southern Journal of Philosophy* 27, Supplement: 89–102.

Nussbaum, M. 1990. *Love's Knowledge*. New York: Oxford University Press.

O'Neill, O. 1996. *Towards Justice and Virtue*. Cambridge: Cambridge University Press.

Ross, W. D. 1988. *The Right and the Good*. Oxford: Clarendon Press.

Wiggins, D. 1987. *Needs, Values and Truth*. Oxford: Blackwell.

Woods, M. 1986. 'Intuition and Perception in Aristotle's Ethics', *Oxford Studies in Ancient Philosophy* 4: 489–532.

4
Aristotle for Women Who Love Too Much

Having goodwill (*eunoia*) toward someone is, according to Aristotle, wishing him well, or wishing good things to him for his own sake (1155b31). As Talbot Brewer notes, Aristotle 'seems to contradict himself' on the issue of whether mutual goodwill is present in friendship based on utility or pleasure as well as in those based on virtue ('character friendships'), and the different claims in the texts have sustained considerable scholarly debate.[1] On good textual grounds, Cooper and Broadie favour the interpretation according to which goodwill is present in all three,[2] and, on good textual grounds, Brewer rejects Cooper's interpretation, taking Aristotle to claim that people in pleasure and utility friendships 'do not in fact have *eunoia* toward each other, since they seek to benefit each other only because, and insofar as, they expect a reciprocal benefit for themselves', a claim that he endorses as seeming like 'exactly the right thing to say'.[3]

Brewer thus sets up a rather stark opposition, between pleasure and utility friends, on the one hand, who do not wish the other well 'for his own sake' at all, but only with a view to their own benefit, and character friends, on the other, who do wish each other well for the other's own sake and hence have mutual goodwill. But he does not consider the interesting interpretation favoured by Price, which offers 'the parties wish one another well in the way in which they love one another, this being either for the other's own sake, or in a way that bears enough resemblance to wishing another well for his sake.'[4] His idea is that 'the notion of well-wishing is Protean'; it takes different forms in the different forms of friendship and its primary form in character

---

[1] Talbot Brewer, 'Virtues We Can Share: Friendship and Aristotelian Ethical Theory', *Ethics* 115: 721–58, 730.

[2] John Cooper, 'Aristotle on the Forms of Friendship', in his *Reason and Emotion: Essays on Ancient Moral Psychology and Ethical Theory* (Princeton, NJ: Princeton University Press, 1998), 312–35; Sarah Broadie, 'Philosophical Introduction and Commentary', in *Aristotle: Nicomachean Ethics*, ed. Sarah Broadie and Christopher Rowe (Oxford: Oxford University Press, 2002), esp. 58, and the commentary on 1155b28–9 (409), 1156b7–11 (410), and 1167a12–14 (420).

[3] Brewer, 'Virtues We Can Share', 730–31. Brewer's reference is to 1167a13–18; see Broadie (*Aristotle: Nicomachean Ethics*, 420) for a different interpretation.

[4] A. W. Price, *Love and Friendship in Plato and Aristotle* (Oxford: Clarendon Press, 1989), 144.

friendship where each friend wishes to forward the other's *eudaimonia*.[5] Like Brewer, he denies that goodwill is part of pleasure and utility friendships, but, significantly, he emphasizes the point that the divergence between himself and Cooper is one 'of nuance'.[6] 'Aristotle's general characterization of friendship was itself abstract, and to be enriched by reference to one kind, that of perfect friendship. Cooper supposes that it is the notion of goodwill that has to adapt itself to the shape of the facts; I suppose it is well-wishing.'[7]

Now on this (surely correct) reading of Cooper, Brewer has no need to set up such a stark opposition. What is essential to Brewer's uplifting account of character friendship is that the goodwill in it takes a special form not to be found in the other kinds of friendship. The goodwill involves a strongly focused interest in the other's virtuous character, or 'evaluative outlook', for the 'good thing' above all one wishes for one's character friend is the objective human good, *eudaimonia*, or the life of virtue.[8] So all Brewer needs to deny is that this form of goodwill (or indeed, well-wishing in Price's version) is present in the other kinds of friendship, with which Cooper and Broadie could readily agree. He need not go to the lengths of rejecting the Cooper-Broadie interpretation without qualification and claiming that in the other kinds, the friends wish good things for the other only 'for instrumental reasons, in hopes of securing egoistic benefits'.[9]

I would like to urge acceptance of the Cooper-Broadie interpretation, not by rehearsing, again, the textual grounds but for a different reason. On the Cooper-Broadie interpretation, we find Aristotle passing on to his youthful audience a truly splendid piece of worldly wisdom (hinted at in my eye-catching title), which we lose if we deny it outright in the way Brewer does. And since, as I say, Brewer does not need to deny it, we might as well have both the worldly wisdom and the edification.

The piece of worldly wisdom turns on noting how readily, in some cases, we can draw the distinction between 'benefiting someone "for his own sake"' and 'loving/liking him for (or "as" or "in") himself'.

We should begin by noting that pleasure and utility friendships are friendships, not merely associations. People can be associates without being friends, because friends (*philoi*), tautologically, have to like/love (*philein*) each other, and we don't like everyone with whom we associate.

As a familiar example of a utility friendship, I want us to consider our relationships with our academic colleagues. True, given the ancient Greeks'

---

[5] Ibid., 145. [6] Ibid., 161. [7] Ibid., 154. [8] Brewer, 'Virtues We Can Share', 724.
[9] Ibid., 731 n. 23.

lofty disdain for anything as vulgar as a job, not all of Aristotle's remarks about utility friendships apply to them, but I doubt that many of us have business friendships or mutual practical enterprise friendships (as some neighbouring landowners do), and I need an example that will be familiar to us all.[10] So, consider your colleagues. Unless you are very lucky, it will be with you as it is with me; there will be some you do not like as well as some you like. (If we are unlucky, there will be some we actively dislike, but not liking is not as strong as disliking.) Among the ones we like, at least some will like us; we are friends. What does this mutual liking/friendship consist in?

Well, to a limited extent, we enjoy each other's company. We enjoy lunches and after-work drinks and chats with each other, as we don't with the ones that we don't like, though collegiality and politeness will sometimes require that we engage in them. And, unless you are a monster of self-centredness (in which case it seems unlikely that any of your colleagues will like you) you have, as I do, goodwill toward the ones you like who like you, your friends. It is not only that you wish good things to them, you actually put yourself out for their sake. You listen sympathetically to their troubles, readily offer to take one of their classes when they want to be away, offer to drive them to the airport to meet their mother when their car has broken down, offer to babysit, buy a book for them you know they would like when it catches your eye, and so on. And you expect the same sort of goodwill from them because, ex hypothesi, they like you; you are friends.

With respect to the colleagues that we don't like and/or who don't like us, things are different; we won't usually offer to do such things. Naturally, we might sometimes offer for special reasons. I might offer to do an extra lecture on a course I was team teaching to enable a colleague I didn't like to speak at a conference for the sake of the unity of the course. I might offer to babysit as part of a deal—'I'll babysit on Thursday if you will give me a lift into work on Friday.' Then, when I do these things, I don't do them out of goodwill, for the sake of the colleague in question, but for those special reasons. But, with the ones I like, such modest acts of altruism come quite naturally. I do them for David or Julia because I like them, because they are my friends, and I do them for their sake, not for the special reasons I need when it comes to Vivian and Peter. (Obviously, I would, if minimally decent, do things for Vivian's or Peter's sakes when they really need it and no one else has offered. But I'm not going to be the first to offer, as I do with those of my colleagues who are my friends.)

---

[10] For similar modern examples, see Broadie, *Aristotle: Nicomachean Ethics*, 58.

Nevertheless, in many of the cases of such friendly relationships with our colleagues, we do not like the other 'for himself'—we are not friends with the other 'as himself' but as a colleague.[11] This is shown by the fact that when we cease to be colleagues the liking, the friendship, dissolves. One of us changes departments, or retires, and it is 'out of sight, out of mind'. We don't miss each other, never think of each other unless especially reminded; meeting each other by accident we may well find we have little or nothing to talk about. It usually wouldn't occur to me to ring them up out of the blue and ask them to put themselves out for me in some way, and if they rang me up, expecting me to do that, I would be very surprised and slightly irritated. (Again, given minimal decency, it would be different if one of us were in desperate straits.)

We all, I assume, are familiar with this phenomenon. We don't expect these friendships to survive the breakup of the work relationship; that we work together is the basis of the friendship. But this does not lead us to ascribe ulterior motives to their, or our, modest beneficence to each other when we were colleagues. That such friendships, such mutual likings and goodwill, just come and go according to circumstances is unsurprising, simply how things happen.

Aristotle implies (1156b1–3) that there are pleasure friendships that are not erotic, without giving us any hint as to what they may be. Let us guess that they are, for example, the friendships that spring up in groups of (typically young) people who, in Aristotle's day, hunt, drank, or trained for the Olympics together, and in our day, drink, go clubbing, or engage in some sporting activity together. And, again in our day, groups of, typically, the old, who go on luxury cruises together.

In such groups, as with colleagues, there will nearly always be some who like each other and some who don't. Insofar as there is any room for modest beneficence, it will, as with colleagues, occur between the ones who like each other, who are friends, spontaneously, and without calculation, for the sake of the friend. As with colleagues, this standing goodwill between those who like each other, who are friends, contrasts with the occasional beneficent acts those who are not friends might do either for special reasons or out of minimal decency.

And, as with colleagues, the parties to the friendship do not like the other 'in himself'. They are not friends with the other 'as himself' but as a sharer in a

---

[11] Not in all cases, of course. I would be the last to deny that a shared and mutually recognized dedication to one's subject is a promising ground for a character friendship.

pleasurable activity. And this is shown by the fact that such friendships, the mutual liking and goodwill, simply evaporate when one or both parties to the friendship leave the group, or the group dissolves, and they are no longer enjoying themselves together. Once again, this is a familiar and unsurprising fact. (People who have been friends on cruises always exchange addresses when they part, sincerely, and often tearfully, promising to keep in touch. And they very rarely do. And no one is surprised.)

Aristotle's perspicuous piece of worldly wisdom is that of course the same is true of pleasure friendships when they are erotic. There is mutual liking and goodwill, based on mutual pleasure; the other is loved/liked not as himself but as a pleasure-giving companion. And when the sexual attraction, and hence the pleasure in the company of the other goes, the liking/love and the goodwill just evaporate, as they do in all the other friendships in which the others are not liked/loved 'for themselves'. Why is this worth his pointing out?

It is worth Aristotle's pointing it out to his youthful audience because they are particularly prone to sexual passion and going wrong about pleasure. Passion combined with mutual liking/loving gives erotic pleasure friendships a number of features that the non-erotic pleasure friendships and utility friendships do not share, and this makes it difficult to discern their fundamental similarity and hence the transitoriness of the goodwill involved.

Consider how the erotic friendships, with their extra features, will appear to the young on the Brewer interpretation. Suppose that I am a young Athenian man, passionately involved with an older one. I see him manifesting goodwill to me. It is quite unmistakable—he goes to endless trouble, is so patient and thoughtful. And of course I would do anything for him. That is, after all, how passion so often takes one—the enjoyment of each other's company and the willingness to do things for the other are so unlimited, so, in those respects, different from the other pleasure and utility friendships. As Aristotle says, the lover 'promises everything' (1164a6), and this is very different from the way things are among friendly colleagues and shipmates. So now let us suppose that Aristotle, instead of (seemingly) saying contradictory things, says, unambiguously, what Brewer would have him say. 'If there is real mutual goodwill, rather than merely instrumentally motivated beneficence, this cannot be a pleasure (or utility) friendship, but must be a character one, in which each friend loves the other as himself.' How readily I will believe that! Exalted by passion, I have invested him with all the virtues (passion does that too), and I am more than happy to think that I have them, albeit imperfectly, as well. (How nice of Aristotle to allow that, when he elsewhere seems to have been telling me that I have a long way to go.)

But I am probably in for a bad shock. The circumstances that form the bases of the other transitory friendships are external relations, such that a change in one party to the friendship necessarily brings about a corresponding change in the other. (If you leave, we are no longer colleagues.) But the circumstance that forms the basis of the erotic friendships is passion, and if my erstwhile lover ceases to find me sexually attractive this will not, alas, bring about a corresponding change in me; I may still love him as much as ever. Of course, given the convention of the *erastēs/erōmenos* relationship in ancient Greece, it is highly unlikely that I shall have been expecting that our relationship would be permanent. I may well not have thought, even vaguely, that we would wind up as friends at all after we were both married. But I certainly was not expecting that the goodwill was going to evaporate, completely, in only a day, as it may well do.

When it does, I would then find myself in the bewildered state that, nowadays, I think is more common among women. I must have spent hours (perhaps weeks?) of my life listening to my women friends bewailing the breakup of an affair and saying they 'didn't understand'. What they didn't understand was how it could be that he was (apparently) so sweet and loving if he didn't really care for them. If he just cared about them as a sexual object instead of 'for themselves', why had he gone to so much trouble about their birthday, looked after them so tenderly when they had flu (and looked revolting), and been so delightful with their cranky child, so patient with their tiresome mother, so interested in their work,...and 'promised everything'? It only made sense if all of these beneficent acts were done for ulterior reasons, not for their sake, but that didn't make sense. He could have acted in those ways only for their sake. *So* he must have loved them for themselves alone and not their yellow hair.[12] But then, how could he have stopped doing so so suddenly? They hadn't necessarily been thinking in terms of settling down for ever—but nor had they been expecting that he would just turn the sweetness off, like a tap. How could he have—it was incomprehensible.

That '*So* he must have loved them for themselves...' relies on the same stark dichotomy that the Brewer interpretation draws. If goodwill in friendship exists only in character friendships, then my poor friends' bewilderment is

---

[12] Never shall a young man,
Thrown into despair
By those great honey-coloured
Ramparts at your ear,
Love you for yourself alone
And not your yellow hair.
—W. B. Yeats, 'For Anne Gregory'

inescapable. Either they had, and have inexplicably lost ('I haven't changed!' 'I didn't do anything!'), a character friendship wherein they were loved for themselves, or they cannot make sense of other people's beneficent actions at all.

But on the Cooper-Broadie interpretation, with the examples of the other pleasure friendships and the utility friendships in place, the 'So...' is the obvious mistake in the reasoning. I know that my colleague friends do the nice things they do do for me for my sake, as I do mine for theirs. It would be absurd to try to understand their actions in terms of their calculating that somehow they must do these things in order to preserve me as a useful colleague or guarantee that I will reciprocate; such an 'explanation' would make nonsense, not sense, of their actions. But I don't infer, 'So they must really like me for myself and will miss me dreadfully when they go off to their exciting new job in another department.'

In the context of these examples, we have no difficulty in separating 'does things for me for my sake' and 'likes me for myself, not just as a colleague'. To escape from the bewilderment over the breakup of an erotic friendship, one has only to separate 'did (lots and lots of) things for my sake' and 'loved me for myself alone'. We know, from the other examples, that these two things just don't automatically go together, and they do not go together in erotic friendships either.

Hence it should not be surprising, when the basis of an erotic pleasure friendship dissolves—which requires only one party to the friendship to cease to feel sexual attraction—that the liking and the goodwill go too. And we do not find it at all surprising when we are the one who first ceases to feel the sexual attraction. Looking back on our slavish goodwill, we laugh and say, 'I must have been mad.'

We probably were. *Erōs* is a dangerous god, tempting us to believe that in our transitory erotic pleasure friendships we are loved for ourselves. But we are not; that happens only in character friendships, and on the Cooper-Broadie interpretation, the extravagant goodwill involved in erotic friendship is not grounds for supposing that the form of the friendship is anything other than what it is. This form of goodwill is peculiar to erotic relationships and in its pure form (which is perhaps rare) a far cry from the form celebrated in Brewer's account.

However, as Brewer notes, few actual friendships are likely to be pure cases of the three forms that Aristotle distinguishes. This may be particularly true of erotic pleasure friendships between decent people, who, one might think, may well have at least some interest in each other's good characters. Such pleasure friendships are the starting point of many good marriages for us, at least, and possibly in a few cases in Aristotle's day too.[13]

References

Brewer, T. 2005. 'Virtues We Can Share: Friendship and Aristotelian Ethical Theory', *Ethics* 115: 721–58.

Broadie, S. 2002. 'Philosophical Introduction and Commentary'. In *Aristotle: Nicomachean Ethics*. Edited by S. Broadie and C. Rowe. Oxford: Oxford University Press.

Cooper, J. 1998. 'Aristotle on the Forms of Friendship'. In *Reason and Emotion: Essays on Ancient Moral Psychology and Ethical Theory*. Princeton, NJ: Princeton University Press: 312–35.

Price, A. W. 1989. *Love and Friendship in Plato and Aristotle*. Oxford: Clarendon Press.

---

[13] Price notes that Aristotle acknowledges that pleasure friendships may develop into character friendships when the friends 'are alike in character and have come to be fond of each other's characters through familiarity' (1157a3–12) and speculates, on the basis of a passage in *Prior Analytics*, that, in his lost *Eroticus*, Aristotle may have done more to develop his idea that eros 'may generate a different kind of loving, less erotic and more faithful... linking individuals not merely as satisfiers of one another's incidental needs, but as partners in a life of personal self-realization' (*Love and Friendship*, 249).

5
Excessiveness and Our Natural Development

According to Stoic doctrine, the Sage, although he feels good passions (*eupatheiai*), is never subject to bad ones (*pathē*). At first, given the sufficiency thesis, it seems obvious enough why. The *pathē* involve, firstly, a false evaluative judgement about present or impending good or evil, false because whatever is judged to be good or evil is, at best, a preferable or dispreferable indifferent. This clearly guarantees that there is something irrational about the second judgement involved in a passion (the judgement that I should act or react in a certain way to this good or evil), namely that it is based on a false assumption. But the second judgement constitutes an impulse which is not only irrational but *excessive*, and it is unclear why these irrational impulses are guaranteed to be so violent.

More than twenty-five years ago, Brad Inwood said that the question of what the excessiveness of the 'pathetic impulse' (as I shall call it) consisted in was 'perhaps the most difficult aspect of the [Stoic] theory of the passions',[1] and I think that is still true. I shall argue that we need to distinguish the violent, 'literal', form of excessiveness from an 'ethically loaded' form, but that Chrysippus' account of excessiveness as being 'out of control' applies to both. Moreover, if, as he does not, we push the story of our natural development as rational animals back to where it truly starts, namely with speech in toddlers, his view that excessive impulses come from a defective rational soul, one that has not developed in accordance with nature, also applies to both.

1. The Stoics' Monistic Psychology

Why should a modern Aristotelian consider abandoning his distinction between the desiderative and the rational parts of the soul in favour of the

---

[1] B. Inwood, *Ethics and Human Action in Early Stoicism* (New York: Oxford University Press, 1985), 154.

Stoics' monistic psychology? Let us begin with an idea the Stoics shared with Aristotle—that thought, by itself, moves nothing. Now the things that, in Aristotle, can move us to action—'desire' (*orexis*) in its most general sense—seem to be a rather mixed bunch which, atypically, he hasn't sorted out. They range, after all, from the appetites (*epithumiai*) we share with the other animals through the *pathē* such as anger, fear, confidence, envy, joy, love (*philia*), hatred, longing, emulation, pity (*NE* 1105b21), spite (1107a10), love of honour (1125b5–25), and shame (1128b10–35), some of which we share with them and others of which are peculiar to us as rational animals, to the special case of rational choice (*prohairesis*). This is indeed a desire (thought-related desire, *orexis dianoētikē*) but of such a strange sort that it can also be described as not being one at all but only desire-related (desire-related intellect, *orektikos nous*).

Why does Aristotle want *prohairesis*? Because, taking it as a premise that, for us, a good life, or living well, has to involve a special sort of acting which only we rational animals can do, he wants to identify how it is that we are moved to acting well, *eupraxia*. From a modern, post-Hume-and-Kant perspective, this looks to be one of his most brilliant moves. We think that Kant was right to say that, when we act morally, we act from reason—only rational animals are moral agents—but we also think, with Hume, that reason alone cannot move us to act. And so we hail Aristotle with relief, as showing us how to reconcile these two apparently contradictory beliefs.

But from an earlier perspective, it would surely have looked arbitrary rather than impressive. One objection that springs to mind is that our capacity to *act* in a special way is not the only thing that distinguishes us from the non-rational animals. As just noted, we also, in virtue of our rationality, are capable of feeling *some* passions that the other animals could not conceivably feel, for example spite, shame, envy, love of honour. Moreover, there does not seem to be a hard and fast line to be drawn between the two classes. What should we say about 'spirit' (*thumos*), given its own part of the soul in Plato's tripartite division, but apparently collapsed into anger (*orgē*) and placed in the desiderative part along with the appetites by Aristotle? On the face of it, children and the other animals are capable of *thumos* (*Rep.* 441a–b) and surely of *orgē*, but, on the other hand, whatever they are (or it is), it seems clear that, as we become old enough to grasp the concept of honour and thereby of being slighted (*Rhet.* 1378a32), they develop into a passion peculiar to us as rational animals.

Hence, without having previously adopted a monistic psychology, we might be led, quite naturally, to the very plausible thought that in *us*, not just some of the passions, but all of them, and, moreover, the appetites, are not quite the same as they are in the other animals, thereby coming to the Stoic view. In us, the passions are different, involving our reason.

We might say that Aristotle had already made that move. After all, according to the end of Book I of the *Nicomachean Ethics*, his desiderative element of the soul is not non-rational as it is in the other animals but 'partakes in reason', for this element listens to reason and can be brought into harmony with it. However, that claim of Aristotle's does not go all the way to the Stoics' claim. In Aristotle, it is clear that the desiderative element partakes of reason in the souls of the self-controlled and the virtuous, but far from clear that it does so in the souls of the incontinent and the masses who live *kata pathos*, by their feelings. The implication in Book I is that reason can only be right reason, whereas the Stoics' claim clearly invites a distinction between right reason and wrong reason.

It is true that Aristotle quite often uses the phrase 'right reason', and if there is any point in saying *orthos logos* it must surely be possible for reason itself to go wrong, even if the phrase 'wrong reason' sounds as odd in the Greek as it does in English. What about the wicked? Is it not clear in Aristotle that, in at least some of them, the desiderative element in their souls partakes of their wrong reason? Presumably this cannot be true of the wicked as described in *NE* 9, whose souls, like those of the incontinent, are in a state of faction (1166b20). However, as is often noted, Aristotle also seems to envisage the possibility of their souls being in harmony (1148a6–20, and 9.8 passim), and it is hard to imagine that the villainous would be called clever (1144a28) if they inevitably made themselves as subject to regret and self-hatred as the bad people in Book IX. But although it seems that, in the villainous, wrong reason is commanding, generating rational choices from a false first principle, this disturbing state of affairs is laid at the door not of reason or the intellect but of the defective state of the desiderative part of the soul, vice, which 'thoroughly deceives us about the first principles of actions' (1144a35).

This takes us back to the nature of vice, as being badly disposed in relation to the passions (*NE* 1105b25–6). And here we find what seems to be the obvious way in which Aristotle invokes the distinction between right and wrong reason. For a virtue is a state 'in respect of which we are well... disposed in relation to feelings', and he emphasizes again and again the importance for virtue of feeling the passions about the right things, towards the right people, at the right time, etc., contrasting this with feeling them regarding the wrong things, people, time, etc. And what can this be but the contrast between the operation of right reason in the virtuous and wrong reason in those who lack it? But he tells his audience very little about what the wrong things, in particular, are in each case, and, in the grip of the doctrine of the mean, he has an unfortunate tendency to imply, and even explicitly say, that what is wrong about the wrong things is that they are too many or too few. This, apart from being clearly false in many cases, leaves us quite in the dark about why spite and envy are passions that are bad in themselves (1107a10–14).

The result of his being so non-committal is that he gives us little or no guidance about how to improve ourselves. If I suspect that I am rather badly disposed in relation to some passions, what should I do? The little piece of advice he gives us about 'dragging ourselves in the opposite direction' (*NE* 1109b5) from that to which we find ourselves particularly prone is hard enough to apply to actions, but really no help at all with passions. Moreover, it seems overwhelmingly certain that the way that I would set about trying to change my tendency to be subject to certain passions is by concentrating on the judgements involved. If I tended to greed and foolish fear and wanted to change, I would try to convince myself that there was something bad about fast food and chocolate and nothing bad about mice and spiders.

Hence we are led further into the Stoics' view: the *pathē*, occurrent passions, in us, involve our reason, and the way our reason is involved is that our *pathē* involve true or false judgements about good and bad (or benefit and harm).

So we can say that all of them, even the appetites, are not the same in us as they are in the other animals and maintain, plausibly, that this is because the other animals, lacking reason, cannot make judgements about what is good or bad.[2] But is it equally plausible to say that of children—that they are not subject to the passions the way we are? According to Galen, Posidonius objected that this was obviously false (*PHP* 5.1.10–11; 5.5.8–26),[3] and I agree. But Posidonius is objecting to the view that the passions involve judgements while leaving unquestioned the view that children lack rationality, and my objection is different. Obviously, children have passions—he is right about that. But equally obviously, as they learn to talk, they make judgements, among them, we may say, those that, on the Stoic view, constitute the *pathē*. So that part of the Stoic view remains intact. What I want to reject here is the view

---

[2] We might want to qualify this with 'by and large'. R. Sorabji, *Emotion and Peace of Mind: From Stoic Agitation to Christian Temptation* (New York: Oxford University Press, 2000) goes so far as to say that he 'would not object to saying that in some sense certain animals are capable of judging things good or bad' (129), though the pages he cites in *Animal Minds and Human Morals: The Origins of the Western Debate* [*Morals*] (London: Duckworth, 1993), namely 43 and 83, are not obviously about evaluative judgements.

[3] References and translations are from the CMG edition: Galen, *On the Doctrines of Hippocrates and Plato*, ed., trans., comm. P. De Lacy, 3 vols. (Berlin: Akademie-Verlag, 1978–84).

of rationality, and thereby the capacity to make judgements, as something that children entirely lack. To this day, we speak of children as 'not having reached the age of reason' but we do not think for a moment that they acquire reason on some particular birthday, not having had it before. That this just is how things are seems to be a view that the Stoics never thought to question, and it is true that it gets Chrysippus into trouble. But it is his account of the passions as judgements, not the Galen/Posidonius one, that will extend easily and plausibly as far back as toddlers.

2. Including Children

Elizabeth Anscombe has a nice story. 'A child saw a bit of red stuff on a turn in the stairway and asked what it was. He thought his nurse told him it was a bit of Satan and felt dreadful fear of it. (No doubt she said it was a bit of satin.)'[4] It is quite possible that, in a Catholic household, the child was no more than two and a half, and yet its 'impression' of the bit of stuff was surely a rational impression, involving thought, produced by 'inference and combination'.[5] It is perhaps only in a post-Freudian age which highlights the significance of early childhood, and further, in a post-Wittgensteinian one, that we could have become so conscious of the fact that, from the very beginning, the bringing up of children is all bound up with 'thought and talk'. Of course, we talk to our pets, but we do not, by and large, utter the same words and we do not expect them to learn to talk in response. But with our children, one might say, we address their rational soul right from the word go, beginning by teaching them how to name us. (I believe this is thought to be universal.)

Although this is a distinctively modern view, it chimes well with the Stoics' picture of speech as essentially rational, and with what Long describes as their 'central insight', namely that 'the human soul is a capacity for living as a language animal.'[6] All it does not chime with is the absurd assumption that the 'utterances' of children, like those of crows and parrots, do not issue from thought until they have reached seven or fourteen.[7]

---

[4] G. E. M. Anscombe, *Intention*, 2nd edn. (Oxford: Basil Blackwell, 1963), 16.

[5] A. A. Long and D. N. Sedley, *The Hellenistic Philosophers*, 2 vols. (Cambridge: Cambridge University Press, 1987), 318T.

[6] A. A. Long, 'Soul and Body in Stoicism', in *Stoic Studies* (Cambridge: Cambridge University Press, 1996), 224–49 at 246.

[7] Commenting on the Ciceronian passage I shall discuss shortly, A. A. Long says 'A young child is "not yet rational", but the development of rationality is a continuous process which must be assumed to be well under way, though not perfected, at Cicero's third stage' (A. A. Long, *Hellenistic Philosophy*, 2nd edn. (London: Duckworth, 1986), 190). He takes the Stoic doctrine to be that there is a gradual development of rationality from birth to maturity and hence that the Stoics do not subscribe to the

It seems that actually Posidonius allowed that humans have the rational 'element' from birth, albeit only as something 'small and weak' (*PHP* 5.5.34), but (in common with most other philosophers until recent times) overlooked the fact that adults start affecting that 'element' as soon as they start teaching the child such words as 'nice' and 'nasty', 'good' and 'bad', and correcting its own use of such words.

We are now very conscious of the ways in which that teaching shapes some of the ways the child will turn out; that is in part why we now condemn overtly racist and sexist discourse. But the rationality that enables children to learn to talk also enables them to do much more than apply their vocabulary in just the way that they hear others apply it. From early on, they use it to express views of their own, and as for how they come by those views, we have, in many cases, no idea. Following Posidonius, Galen sneers at Chrysippus for being 'puzzled about the origin of vice... [and] unable to discover how it is that children err' (*PHP* 5.5.9–10) but, two millennia later, we are just as puzzled, unable to attribute it (in most cases at least) to inborn nature—for have we not evolved to be social animals?—nor simply to their upbringing, since it seems that even well-brought-up children sometimes turn out badly. In fact, Chrysippus' explanations—that they are corrupted by 'the conversation of the majority of men' and 'the very nature of the things (around them)' (*PHP* 5.5.14)— sound like the ancient Greek version of our vague thought that it must have a lot to do with the deplorable influence of our materialistic society and the media. All that needs to be added is that the effects of 'the conversation' begin as soon as the child is learning to talk, rather than kicking in suddenly at fourteen. The conversation a child grows up with really matters even if it is not the whole story, as we know from the fact that our efforts to eliminate sexist and racist language *have* made us a bit better, whereas we can be confident that 'a regimen of rhythms and scales' (*PHP* 5.6.20) applied to the desiderative element of our souls would have been no help at all.

3. Our Natural Development

The insistence that children are *alogoi*, irrational, not only chimes ill with the Stoic recognition of the significance of our being 'a language animal'. It also chimes ill with the Stoic account of human development given to us by Cicero

---

absurd view that young humans are not rational at all until they reach 'the age of rationality', be that seven or fourteen. I argue that this is indeed what their doctrine should have been, but whether the Ciceronian passage, and other texts, can be read in this way is controversial.

(*De finibus* 3.20–1), creating such a hiccup in it that, contrary to what is usually said, I do not think it can be rightly called an account of our natural *development* at all.[8] The familiar starting-point looks strikingly plausible from our post-Darwinian perspective—that every animal, and hence the human animal, is born endowed by Nature with impulses to self-preservation and acts (or perhaps one should say 'carries on') appropriately. The two oft-cited illustrations of this universal phenomenon in the case of human infants are apt. A baby 'does' very little, but it does, at least, seek nourishment, having a natural tendency to suck at its mother's breast, thereby maintaining itself in its natural condition, and it struggles to master walking and thereby train itself to 'do what nature demands' (Sen. *Ep.* 121.8).

There are also many nice illustrations of the *other* animals acting in accordance with nature as they 'seek for what conduces to their safety and reject the opposite' (Cic. *Fin.* 3.16). But we do not find any illustrations of children's activities exhibiting the same providential general pattern, and I think we can be sure that this is not because they are in lost texts. It is because there *aren't* any.

Aristotle, to his credit, noticed that, with respect to the way they act, children are not at all like the other animals. In his biological works he takes many of the activities of the other animals as showing that they have *phronēsis*, since they clearly calculate means to ends in a way that leads them to their good,[9] but rightly, he never suggests that children have the same capacity. The Stoics however, when they consider children in the context of human development, lump them together with the other animals as if they naturally seek their good—the good appropriate to their nature—the way the other animals seek the good appropriate to theirs.

The Stoics seem, quite generally, to have overlooked the fact that young humans are singularly ill-equipped by providential Nature with innate impulses to self-preservation. Whoever it was did well to cite the newborn baby's natural tendency to suckle, universal among mammals, but must have failed to notice that the recklessly general prescription 'Suck it and see' is one they naturally go on to follow; the other animals are naturally more cautious.

---

[8] Although Annas quotes the Cicero passage without criticism (J. Annas, *The Morality of Happiness* (Oxford: Oxford University Press, 1993), 264), I hope that she would be happy to accept what I am about to say. Her interest in 'our' natural development towards virtue has consistently been, I think, focused on the conscious self-development that begins only when we start to reflect on our life as a whole, which, as she rightly remarks, we do not usually do 'when we are young' (ibid., 29), and this is indeed well captured in Cicero's third to fifth stages.

[9] J. G. Lennox, 'Aristotle on the Biological Roots of Virtue', in J. Maienschein and M. Ruse (eds), *Biology and the Foundation of Ethics* (Cambridge: Cambridge University Press, 1999), 10–31.

Seneca overlooks the fact that, while the very young struggle to master walking, thereafter they are into everything, with no instinct to avoid what is harmful. Nothing could be further from the truth than that young humans 'seek for what conduces to their safety and reject the opposite'. It is the burnt child that fears the fire; the unburnt one has to be taught to.

All of this, as I shall argue below, should be grist to the Stoics' mill, and yield something in the way of a proper account of our natural development. But if they lump the children in with the other animals, they cut themselves off from it.

It is clear that there is development from the third to the fifth of Cicero's stages, and *if* he had been right that children were just like the other animals and sought to preserve themselves, there would have been development from the first to the second. But, even on that assumption, there is no development at all between the second and third stages. At the second stage we would have a population of mostly strong, healthy, non-defective young human beings doing what they should be doing, consistently pursuing what benefits them and avoiding what is harmful or dangerous to them, in accordance with nature; at the third stage we have an *entire* population of psychologically weak or diseased, defective older ones who are doing very little in accordance with nature. That is not *development*.

Nor can it be made out to be development by saying that, at the third stage, 'reason supervenes as the craftsman of impulse' (D.L. 7.85–6). All that yields is 'We start like this and naturally develop thus. And *then* we undergo a great metamorphosis and we become like so and have to develop in a different way', as though one were describing the life cycle of a species of insect from whose chrysalis emerges, not a fully fledged butterfly, but something that, in its turn, has a lot of developing to do before it reaches its *telos* (end). Conceivably, somewhere in the universe, there are rational animals with just such a life cycle, but ours does not involve metamorphosis.

Finally, it will not do to say that 'the analogical continuity provided by the concept of living according to nature'[10] will bridge the break between the second and third stages because, in Cicero's story, the human children are not, and *could not be*, living 'in accordance with nature' the way the other animals are.

Each of the other animals, if not defective, is preserving *itself*, maintaining itself in *its* natural condition, acting in relation to *its* good or *telos*. What *its* natural condition and *its* good are are determined by what *it* is, its nature—

---

[10] Inwood, *Ethics*, 195.

that is, by what sort of animal it is. But the only possible answer to 'What sort of animal is a human child?' is 'A human'. 'A child' is not a sort of animal, except metaphorically, and we have to be careful, in this context, with Seneca's claim that 'Each period of life has its own constitution, different in the case of ⟨the baby⟩ [*inserted because he adds it later on*], the child, the youth, and the old man...' (Sen. *Ep*. 121.15). It must not be taken to mean that the baby, *that* sort of animal, if not defective, is maintaining 'its' natural constitution and 'its' good, and the child, a different sort of animal, if not defective, is maintaining 'its' different constitution and different good, and the youth 'its'. Rather, it should mean that, at each period of human development—as with many of the other animals—the non-defective human will be acting (or 'carrying on') in ways that, at that period, are appropriate to its eventual attainment of the human *telos*, and thereby in accordance with nature.

The children in Cicero's story, even if they were successfully pursuing the (biologically) beneficial and eschewing the harmful as the other animals do, would not thereby be acting in accordance with nature because they would not, merely thereby, be carrying on in the way appropriate in early childhood to attaining the *human* good, namely the full development of their rational soul. If that were all they were doing, they would be sadly defective human children (as wolf children would have been), for it is essential to the development of the rational soul that one acquire language. Although it is no defect in a baby that it cannot talk, something is probably amiss with a child who has not learnt to do so a bit by eighteen months. If young humans are acting in accordance with nature, they should have started to focus on their parents' speech in their first few months (as indeed they do), not just their mother's breast—as if, we might imaginatively say, their rational soul sought the further nourishment it needs to grow, namely language—and begun to imitate what they hear.

So, having given children their proper place in the Stoic picture of our natural development, I now turn to exploring whether this will enable us to give an account of the excessiveness found, on the Stoic account, in pathetic impulses.

4. Literal Excessiveness as Being Irrational/Out of Control

Saying that the *pathē* are excessive seems, at first, basically and literally right. Our *pathē* shake or stir us, they are turbulent, unruly vehement. To non-philosophers 'the calm passions' is an oxymoron. This striking feature of them is a proper object of philosophical analysis and it is what Chrysippus is apparently discussing when he connects the excessiveness of the *pathē* with their irrationality.

Galen (*PHP* 4.4.9–18) says that the word *alogon* (irrational or without reason) is used in two senses, which, following Aristotle on privation (*Met.* 1022b22), he compares to the two uses of 'voiceless' and 'neckless'. In one use, the word is used to describe the sorts of creature that do not have voices or necks at all, say, fish. In the other they describe an individual creature which has a voice or neck, say, one of us, but an impaired one—they can't sing in tune or they have a very short neck. Similarly, 'irrational' is used to describe those creatures that do not have reason at all, namely non-humans, and is also used to describe as impaired an operation of reason in an individual which does have it.

He then goes on to say that Chrysippus recognizes these two uses of *alogon* but, in his use of them, contradicts his claim that the human soul is all rational and does not contain an irrational (in the first sense) part. For Chrysippus says (a) that the passions, or excessive impulses, are irrational, but (b) explicitly denies that he means they are irrational in the second sense, namely that in which reason's operation is impaired and it makes a mistake. So he has to mean that they are irrational in the first sense—the sort of thing that does not have reason at all.

But Galen has been misled by his analogies. He sums up their ambiguity by saying 'they refer either to the absence of voice or neck, or to their impairment', and that is indeed what his examples are of. However, in concentrating on examples of impairment in the case of voices, and in choosing 'neckless' rather than one of his other 'similar' expressions (footless, legless, handless), he overlooks a corresponding ambiguity in 'absence of voice or neck'. A creature which is such as to have a voice (a human, not a fish) can be voiceless not only in having an impaired voice but in not having one at all, either momentarily because she has a cold and has lost it, or permanently, because her throat has been permanently damaged. Galen can say plausibly that 'no man would be neckless in the sense that he lacked a neck completely', but this is false for footless, legless, and handless, which, applied to us, cover everything from impairment of one or both to complete absence of one or both. So he is right to identify an ambiguity in *alogon* (irrational, reasonless) and he has rightly specified the first use—it is used to describe a sort of living thing that does not have reason at all—but he has not succeeded in specifying the second.

This cannot be done without recognizing that it is an attributive adjective. We might say that 'irrational' is used to describe us, and things such as our actions, impressions, passions, and desires, and our statements, beliefs, inferences, and arguments, but not our bodies or bodily parts. That gets us halfway there, in line with saying that, in its first use, it is used to describe a *sort of living thing*, but it doesn't say much about what we are ascribing, apart from, very vaguely, something's being amiss somewhere. Thereby, it is an attributive adjective, like 'bad' and 'strong'. This constitutes its second sense, and Galen is right that there is not a third. However, like 'bad' and 'strong', just what it ascribes in application to a particular sort of thing will vary from case to case, and so it will amount to, or 'mean', something different in different cases, despite being used in the same, second, sense.

In the passages in which Galen finds the contradiction, Chrysippus is talking about our *pathē* as excessive impulses and thereby irrational, disobedient to reason, without reason or judgement, and so on. Of course, as a Stoic who holds the sufficiency thesis, he would say that, insofar as these impulses are false judgements about the appropriateness of reacting to a false value judgement, they are irrational, disobedient to reason, etc. in the way that *all* false judgements are. But he is not talking about them as irrational judgements but as *impulses*, and uncovering the point that impulses are irrational in their own way, a way appropriate to impulses rather than judgements. That is what he is making clear when he says that what he means is *not* that the person with the excessive impulse 'is carried away by error and from a misapprehension of something that is in accord with reason' (*PHP* 4.2.12)—though that too is true—but something else. And he goes on to make his meaning clearer by giving the example of running (4.2.14–18).

When I set about running as fast as I can it would be foolish not to look first towards where I am going to run, because once I am running full tilt I shall not be able to stop quickly. I should be mindful of the fact that when I set out to run full tilt, I relinquish myself, to some extent, to the forces of nature and it may be that, willy-nilly, I shall 'do' something (run smack into someone who appears unexpectedly from around a corner) which, in a way, will be no doing of mine, no operation of my rational soul. In the same way, when I make the second judgement, taking the first evaluative judgement to be true, and thereby let loose the excessive impulse, I relinquish myself to the forces of nature, and some of my subsequent actions or movements will be no operation of my rational soul. 'For they [runners and angered people] could not be said, like those who are in control of their movement, to be moving in conformity with themselves, but instead to be moving in conformity with some force external to themselves' (*PHP* 4.6.35–6). The runner is carried forward, the person with the passion is carried away, willy-nilly. And there we have a way in which certain impulses are irrational, namely that they are not obeying reason, and are such as to disobey it, which is quite different from being false, which an impulse, *qua* impulse, cannot be.

One mark of the fact that we are out of the control of our reason when acting from a pathetic impulse is that, as Chrysippus rightly observes, 'we behave towards these persons suffering from affection as we do towards persons out of their minds, and we talk to them as to persons who have taken leave of their senses and are not in their right minds or in possession of their faculties' (*PHP* 4.6.24–5). I take it that what he is pointing to here is that we do not (if we have any sense) attempt to remind people in a passion of the excellent reason(s) they have for not doing whatever it is they are doing because we know they are deaf to reason. After all, we hear angry people and 'lovers and persons with other violent desires' saying 'that they want to gratify their anger and to let them be, whether it is better or not, and to say nothing to them, and that this is to be done by all means, even if they are wrong and it is not to their advantage' (*PHP* 4.6.27). There is clearly no point in trying to bring reason to people in that sort of state, as there is no point in shouting 'Look out, be careful!' to someone running full tilt. An excessive impulse is irrational, beyond the reach of reason.

Another, albeit closely related, mark is that, in the grip of a passion, we do such completely idiotic things, as Chrysippus so wonderfully illustrates. 'For in disappointment we are "outside of " or "beside" ourselves, and, in a word, blinded so that sometimes if we have a sponge or a bit [ball?] of wool in our hands, we pick it up and throw it, as if that would achieve something... And often, through the same blindness, we bite keys, and beat at doors when they do not open quickly, and if we stumble over a stone, we take revenge on it by breaking it or throwing it somewhere' (*PHP* 4.6.44–5).

Thus we come to an interesting way in which the second judgement will almost inevitably be false, which is independent of any presumed falsity in the first. Presented with a malfunctioning key or a sticking door, there must be *some* true judgement to be made about how I should react. After all, if I don't make some judgement which will constitute an impulse that gets me moving, I shall stand immobile before a door that I cannot open until I drop. What is wrong with the second judgements in Chrysippus' examples above is obviously, given the pointless, idiotic actions they produce, that they are foolish. They have to be judgements to the effect that I should act *this* way, where *this* way is really foolish.

So we might think of the essential characteristic of the second judgements, the feature that guarantees that they constitute the excessive impulses, as their being judgements to the effect that one should react in a certain vehement, 'this-is-going-to-be-uncontrollable' *way*. Where that way of acting is foolish, which is invariably (or almost invariably?) so, then the judgement that I should react in that way is guaranteed to be false.

This makes the falsity of the second judgement strictly independent of the truth value of the first, which, at this stage, I think is important. This is not because I am seeking to undermine the view that the first judgements in the *pathē* are nearly always false because they misapply 'good' and 'bad' to things that are indifferent. Rather, I am aiming to make sense of the excessiveness explored so far, Chrysippus' examples and his remark 'For we do not speak of these infirmities as being in the judgement that each of these things is good, but in *also* being drawn to them in excess of what is natural' (*PHP* 4.5.21–2, emphasis added). When we think of the excessiveness and the foolishness, it seems plain that true first judgements, even when limited to those that the Stoics count as true, might be followed by false second ones. If I am cast into such raptures by the manifest virtue of Socrates that I have an excessive impulse to, say, throw my arms about him, or weep when reproached by him, or, when drunk at a symposium, make fervent speeches in his praise which include far too many 'I drink to him!'s', I have undoubtedly made a false judgement about the way in which I should react to his virtue.

Might Galen complain that we are back with the first sense of 'irrational'? Isn't Chrysippus indeed claiming that 'excessive impulses are *the sort of thing* that does not have reason at all'? But, given how bizarre it would be to say 'excessive impulses are irrational, like fish', we can see the significance of stipulating, as I did above, that the first sense of 'irrational' is limited—or strongly tends to be limited—in its application to the sort of *living* thing that does not have reason at all. If, but *only* if, you think there is, in us, an independent desiderative soul with a life of its own, as Galen and Posidonius do, then that would count as a living thing and you would naturally interpret 'excessive impulses are like fish' as a shorthand for 'the desiderative soul is like a fish—it doesn't have reason at all'. But if you do not hold that view, it just sounds like a category mistake.

What Chrysippus has done is make clear just what it is we ascribe to our pathetic impulses—as opposed to, say, our judgements or impressions or arguments—when we say they are irrational but not in the sense of being based on a false first judgement. They are, in their very nature, out of control (*akrateis*) and make us out of control. Furthermore, it seems to me that he is right that this is exactly what we often mean when we say they are excessive (another attributive adjective), and, one might add on his behalf, usually what we mean when we say they are bad and when we say they are strong.

The *pathē*, by definition, involve an excessive impulse. The literally excessive impulses, as we now see, are irrational in the way described. So the *pathē* should be eradicated—and we reach this conclusion without any mention of the falsity of the first judgements. But if the literally excessive impulses are irrational in their own right, independently of the falsity of the first judgement, how come we have them? Posidonius is entitled to press the question 'What causes the excess?' (*PHP* 4.3.4–9).

5. Literal Excessiveness as Childishness

Chrysippus' answer is that in 'inferior men' the cause is their disease or weak or defective souls; they are constituted in such a way as to be subject to the *pathē*, those excessive impulses, in a way similar to that in which someone with an unhealthy body is subject to 'fevers and chills', in a random way, at 'the incidence of small causes' (*PHP* 5.2.14–15). Galen pooh-poohs him for not being able to give a further account of the nature of the 'disease', which he thinks he has readily to hand in the Platonic account. But if one thinks that the appeal to imbalance and lack of harmony between the three elements of the soul is no better than an appeal to the dormitive powers of something that puts one to sleep, one would do better to stick to saying that the inferior men's souls just *are* constituted this way (though we do not know the details of the mechanics—or psycho-thermodynamics—of such a constitution) and explain why their souls' being like that counts as their being diseased.

This Chrysippus is not in a strong position to do, but if we give a proper account of our natural development by bringing the children in, we have rather a nice explanation.

Very small children do indeed live *kata pathos*, in accordance with their *pathē*, as Aristotle claimed more broadly—they are constantly subject to the excessive impulses. This is so universally the case that we must assume that it is in accordance with the inscrutable workings of nature, and it would be absurd to think that all children, excepting any apathetic ones, are defective, just as (as Chrysippus might say) it would be absurd to think there was something wrong with their bodies because they are so much smaller and weaker than that of a grown-up. That they are so subject to the *pathē* is appropriate to this stage of human life, just as their small bodies are. But it becomes increasingly inappropriate as they get older. Children begin by trying to grab the chocolate cake as soon as they see it and being distressed or angry when they can't have it right now. But they quickly learn to say "Please" and only *then* grab, and later not to grab at all. They begin by resisting and screaming with anger when we try to get them to do something they don't want to do, but they quickly learn something in the way of good-tempered compliance.

Training children out of these immediate excessive impulses is in some ways not unlike training dogs to beg and then hold back from the proffered treat until the command 'Take it', or to stay at one's side growling until the command 'Attack'. But in other ways it is completely different, since it takes place in the context of the development of the language-mediated concept acquisition sketched above. Unlike dogs, children can be taught to reconceptualize things and activities which initially appeared to be good as no good at all, and to conceptualize other children who still grab and scream as bad or silly *because* they do such things. We think there is something wrong with them if they do not learn such things, just as, pursuing Chrysippus' analogy, one would come to suspect bodily disease in a small child who did not start to grow and develop rapidly, for again, that is the universal pattern in nature that we see. What counts as the rational soul's 'growing and developing' on this analogy, would be, increasingly, its becoming less subject to the literally excessive impulses. We recognize the inferior men who are subject to them as diseased because we recognize them, grown men, as not having developed 'in accordance with nature', but as having remained, in this respect, like small children.

I cannot remember when women first started describing angry men in terms of their throwing their toys out of their pram, but I do remember that it came as an excellent corrective to a prevailing tendency to see male anger as, though no doubt regrettable in a way, a rather noble adult phenomenon related to a sort of pride that only men were entitled to have. But usually it is no such thing. When, scarlet in the face with rage, grown men beat the sticking doors and act in other violent this-is-uncontrollable ways, their actions are not those of a rational *adult*; they are obviously nothing but (rational) toddlers' temper tantrums.

Of course, in adults, the actions the second judgements give rise to are rarely as harmless as they are in small children. Just after he has described what we do in anger with harmless objects, Chrysippus says 'and if we happen to be holding a dagger or some other weapon, we do the same with that'. We might add that, in a passion, adults not only beat at doors and throw stones that frustrate them, but do the same to their infants. They have judged that they should react in *that* way to the child's incessant crying. (I live in a country with a shockingly high incidence of infant mortality caused by rage.)

Hence, in an adult rather than a child, a literally excessive impulse really matters. It may well be that, on a particular occasion, the gratification of the anger, or the love, or some other violent desire is harmless, and that, in the circumstances, there is not much to be said against it beyond 'You are behaving like a child/an idiot.' However, in adults, serious folly is nevertheless guaranteed to be present, lying in the truth of the counterfactual that, had the circumstances been otherwise, or changed after the excessive impulse had been let loose, in such a way that virtue would have required desisting immediately, the agent, *ex hypothesi*, would not have desisted. There are not many cases in which it would be anything other than reckless and irresponsible for an adult to make the judgement 'I should now act in a vehement, this-will-be-out-of-control way' and thereby relinquish rational control. That is why it is *within* the class of actions arising from literally excessive pathetic impulses that we find what we call the cases of weakness of will—those in which the agent subsequently regrets what he has done, recognizing that it was wrong.

Without suffering any such regrets, the wicked may also act from such impulses. However, that is not to say that it is in *this* class of pathetic impulses—the literally excessive ones—that we find all the impulses that impel us to wrongdoing. The Stoic view that being subject to the *pathē* is the source of all evil should not be taken to be the implausible thesis that the wicked can readily be identified as those who are characteristically in a frenzy shouting 'I don't care! I *will* have my way', and cheerfully say the same afterwards. Life would be much easier if that were so but it is not so: the wicked are not, as such, prone to acting in a vehement out-of-control way. So there is more to be said about the way being subject to the *pathē* is the source of evil.

6. Responsiveness to Reasons

It is clear that the Sage never has literally excessive impulses; he is, after all, to the highest conceivable degree, always ready and able to act in accordance with reason.

Does this mean that the Sage's impulses differ from the literally excessive ones in virtue of his corresponding hormetic (second) judgement having 'an added clause' in it, which registers a mental reservation, as Inwood influentially claimed?[11] I agree with Brennan that this is not

---

[11] Ibid., 121.

right,¹² though for an intuitive reason rather than his scholarly ones. Surely the Sage's impulses as hormetic judgements are not perfectly in accordance with reason and true because they have an extra bit, any more than his other judgements are perfectly in accordance with reason and true because they have an extra bit. They are perfectly in accordance with reason because they are *his*—that is, because they are produced by a soul whose rationality has been perfected.

The Sage, undoubtedly, 'adapts smoothly' to circumstances.¹³ As Brennan says, more explicitly, he 'changes his desires and impulses *in response to* what happens',¹⁴ unlike the agent who is out of control and beyond reason. But it is essential to make it explicit that, being a Sage, he always does so in accordance with right reason in every respect, for here we encounter the difficulties of the different uses of 'rational/irrational' again.

Although it is 'in accordance with reason', i.e. rational, to be responsive, not blind, to features of the circumstances in which one is acting, such responsiveness is not necessarily in accordance with right reason and rational in *that* way. The Sage's responsiveness will, *ex hypothesi*, always be thus, but not anyone else's. As Iago works his evil way to Othello's undoing, he encounters many unforeseen obstacles, but they do not throw him; he adapts smoothly, responding cleverly to them as they arise. What is wrong with him is that, from the very outset, and throughout, he is undeterred from his course of action by any considerations pertaining to virtue and he continues to be unresponsive to them as they come up. All along he fails to adapt to things he should always be responsive to, but his irrationality does not consist in lack of responsiveness per se.

So if we are to say that the Sage's reservation enables him to adapt responsively, as opposed to rushing blindly headlong, we had better distinguish his reservation from Iago's, and the only satisfactory way of doing this is to say that his perfected rationality (or knowledge or virtue) always *informs* his hormetic judgements. Iago, and a number of other fools of various sorts, can be credited with being responsive to reasons, in particular to reasons pertaining to their stopping whatever course of action they have embarked on, but the ways in which their reasons would differ from the Sage's reasons cannot be spelt out in advance. All we can say is that his are always right, and give obvious illustrations of what would count as wrong ones, such as Iago's, or

---

¹² T. Brennan, 'Reservation in Stoic Ethics' ['Reservation'], *Archiv für Geschichte der Philosophie* 82 (2000): 149–77.
¹³ Inwood, *Ethics*, 121 and 123.   ¹⁴ Brennan, 'Reservation', 163 (emphasis added).

those of a miserly and licentious fool who is deterred from continuing his pursuit of another man's wife by her turning out to expect expensive presents, or of a cowardly fool who takes it that he 'can't' after all eliminate a political rival as he intended because his proposed victim has turned out to have a very powerful family, and so on.

Such examples bring us to a new problem about impulses and actions that are irrational. The impulses and the actions of the fools above are obviously irrational in being contrary to virtue, and thereby reason, but are we to say that the fools are acting from *pathē*, implying that their actions come from the literally excessive impulses, notwithstanding the fact that they have all been described as *not* like the person running full tilt, but responsive to reasons? On the face of it, this seems absurd. What was the point of the oft-reiterated analogy with the runner if it turns out not to be an analogy after all? And why are Chrysippus' examples so predominantly examples of people in a frenzy, quite unresponsive to reasons, if in fact these are not even typical? However, on the other hand, if these actions do not come from literally excessive impulses, what sort of impulse do they come from?

Chrysippus, typically, has yet another brilliant example, or rather a pair, which, unlike his others, present us with exactly this problem: the two people who were so money-loving that, at the end of their lives, 'one of them swallowed a great deal of gold before he died, and the other had gold sewn into a sort of cloak and then put it on, enjoining his intimates to bury him just so, without cremation or other preparation.'[15] It is, I suppose, conceivable that we are to imagine the first man falling on his gold in a frenzy as soon as he heard he was about to die, and gulping it down as if he were starving, but since the second man has obviously had to make some arrangements about getting the cloak made and the two are mentioned in the same breath, it is more plausible to think of both of them as going in for unfrenzied, deliberated actions as Iago does.

To imagine them thus is to imagine them as responsive to a *certain range* of reasons, namely considerations that pertain to better means to their respective ends. The first man would perhaps consider the suggestion that he increase the value of what he was capable of swallowing by using a lot of it to buy a single very valuable though quite small piece, the second that he might consider a gold coffin as well. So there is a way in which we can talk to them as men who

---

[15] *SVF* iii.195, quoted in T. Brennan, 'The Old Stoic Theory of Emotions' ['Old Stoic'], in J. Sihvola and T. Engberg-Pedersen (eds), *The Emotions in Hellenistic Philosophy* (Dordrecht: Kluwer, 1998), 21–70 at 42.

are in possession of their faculties, unlike the ones who are waving the bits of wool and the daggers around and shouting. However, in another way, presumably, we cannot—there is no point in trying to get them to recognize that their end is contrary to reason, though it certainly is. And the same is true of the preceding examples.

Hence we have a family of cases—those in which the agent is engaged in doing such things as bringing about the undoing of someone he hates, seeking to seduce his neighbour's wife, eliminating a political rival, arranging to die with gold in his gut—which are not the same as the frenzied ones in which the agents act from the literally excessive pathetic impulses. Nevertheless, the actions are irrational, so they must come from impulses that are in some way irrational, and surely, given the premise that the *pathē* are the root of all evil, in a way that is related to the *pathē*.

7. Ethically Loaded Excessiveness

Thus we come to a different conception of 'the pathetic impulse', for which I shall use the term 'rational pathetic impulse'. Although the *pathē* are themselves what we would call occurrent passions—instances of feeling *pathē* such as love or hatred are clockable events—we know that Chrysippus also recognized what we call dispositional passions and he called diseases (*nosēmata*), such as love of wine or women or money, and hatred of mankind. We can safely assume, I think, that he would also recognize dispositional love or hatred of a particular person. Whence occurrent delight or grief at one person's death if not from dispositional hatred or love of them, after all? All the cases above are of people with a dispositional passion, and now, at last, the significance of the falsity of the first judgement involved in any *pathē* and the *consequent*, not independent, falsity of the second, which constitutes the 'rational pathetic impulse', emerges fully.

All the agents above have a dispositional false evaluative belief about the goodness of achieving what is, in fact, a bad end. It disposes them to, among other things, series of certain occurrent evaluative beliefs as first judgements, namely those of the form 'Doing such and such would be good (as a means to that good end)'—which they may endorse in their second judgements, and thereby impel themselves to a series of actions directed towards what they falsely believe is a good end. However, their occurrent first judgements, since they concern only instrumental goodness, are not unlike occurrent judgements that doing such and such is indifferent but to be preferred, in that the agents are responsive to reason to the extent that they may withhold or change their second judgement when circumstances change in certain ways, or when onlookers offer them better means. So their second judgements do not constitute the violent impulses.

Nevertheless, whatever judgements about means to be taken the agents make, they are out of control, beyond the reach of right reason, insofar as no considerations pertaining to virtue could deter them, *given* the dispositional false evaluative belief which generates the occurrent false beliefs about the value of the means. And so their impulses are excessive, though now in an ethically loaded way. As we have seen, 'out of control' meant 'out of the control of reason' in the cases of literal excessiveness, and it means the same here, even though the excessiveness is no longer violent, since considerations pertaining to virtue are, pre-eminently, *the* reasons for action that properly developed reason recognizes. That the excessiveness does not, here, carry the further implication of being given over to the forces of nature is insignificant; we can now see that the point of the examples of frenzy is to illustrate vividly what momentary false evaluative beliefs do to those of us who are far from being wicked—they make us temporarily utterly foolish or mad—and thereby make vivid that when such beliefs are not momentary but settled opinions, they make us fools or lunatics.[16]

Claiming that '*no* considerations pertaining to virtue' would deter *any* of the agents in the above examples is obviously too strong. The agent setting out to do down his political rival might, after all, be deterred from his course of action by the reappearance of his long-lost noble father, which reanimates his appreciation of the value of virtue. It seems clear that being beyond the reach of right reason is a matter of degree, as is being beyond reason more broadly in the case of literal excessiveness. We do not, I think, have enough material to be clear about what the significant differences between diseases (*nosēmata*), ailments (*arrhōstēmata*), proclivities (*euemptōsiai*), and weaknesses of the soul are, nor, relatedly, whether Chrysippus actually wanted to distinguish being women- or money-loving from being women- or money-mad. However, we certainly have enough to suggest that some significant distinctions were being drawn to reflect degrees of being out of control, and, if we think in terms

---

[16] Brennan has some interesting speculations about the original Stoic emphasis on examples of *pathē* involving the literally excessive impulses (which he identifies as those with 'feeling-tone') in 'Old Stoic', 38.

of our natural development, it is not difficult to think of what some of them would have been.

In the development of the rational soul from its early stages to anything even approaching the perfection of the Sage's we can discern two (just) distinguishable strands.

One involves learning to act 'from reason' or rationally, in a sense that does not assume that 'reason' here means 'right reason'. Among the many rational capacities that go into acquiring that general capacity we could note, for a start, the one mentioned above: that, in response to impressions of what they take to be good or bad, children learn to make fewer of the second judgements that constitute the literally excessive impulses (they say 'Please' and then take rather than grab). We could add that they acquire the concept of 'better' and learn to prioritize. Furthermore, their reason stocked, by their acquisition of language, with many more concepts than that of merely wanting one thing more than another, they come to prioritize goods by giving enriched descriptions of them which provide *reasons* for one being better than the other. They learn to engage in courses of action, to work out how to do things towards securing a distant good, and come to understand our suggestions that they could do it more effectively another way.

All of this is natural, distinctively human, development; when a young child does not develop in these ways, we know that they are psychologically impaired in some way—that is, that their rational soul is not developing as it should, given their age.

It is the second strand which introduces right reason. As noted at the outset, children quickly acquire evaluative concepts and apply them to things and activities not only as they are taught to, but also on their own account. It seems that children do not have to be taught explicitly that it is good to be with and play with other children. Unless they are somehow put off doing so, they come to seek it of their own accord around the age of three. And, by the time they are four, they are playing cooperatively, like to share, and are beginning to have 'best friends'. Again, this is natural, and again, when a child does not develop in this way, we assess it as psychologically impaired.

So, in Stoic-speak, it is part of children's natural development that, for example, the rational impression they have of the friendly overtures of other children will naturally come to be, quite early, an impression of something good (not threatening or bad) in prospect. This will be but one among many such rational impressions that are, with our teaching, increasingly assented to—that it is good to share one's toys, to take one's turn, to tell the truth, good that this other child be happy, bad that this one is upset, good to give and bad to take. Moreover, we expect them to catch on to the idea that there is something special about the goodness and badness at issue here.[17] All this is very important. If a child does not readily pick up this sort of ethical conceptualization, which we know as the necessary beginnings of virtue and right reason, we see that something is very seriously amiss indeed, quite different from a failure to pick up on 'acting from reason'.

(Note that I speak here as someone who, with the Stoics, is presupposing that it is good and natural for human beings to live cooperatively together, to help each other, to have fellow feeling, and as someone who believes that the possession of perfect virtue is the human *telos*. If I actually believed that we live together only *faute de mieux* and that we are all naturally selfish, I would not believe what I said above, and would, I suppose, notice children's egocentric tendencies (which are certainly there) and think that *they* were natural. As indeed they are, to their age, but I see them as ways they will grow out of if their rational soul develops properly, whereas if I had the other standpoint, I would see them only as tendencies that needed to be modified by more accurate opinions about how it is best to get one's own way—a development of only the first strand.)

Although I have been insisting from the outset that even small children make evaluative judgements, I would not deny that many of these are unlike the evaluative judgements of the fully adult. The child's judgement that it is good to offer this other child her doll now is no more a reflexion of 'her values' than her judgement that it is good to build a sandcastle now. It is only as children get older that they begin to have values at all, and quite some time before we can say that those values are their own, rather than the possibly temporary influence of their good parents or the deplorable media.

As they come to have them, in early adolescence, we are more concerned about some manifestations of the values than others. The false judgement about the importance of one's appearance may show up in the sobs and tantrums that follow the discovery of a new spot, and the near hysterical delight and constant prinking at the mirror that follow the fashionable new haircut. However, if such literal excesses are by and large the only manifestation of the opinion, if the adolescent freely admits in calm moments that she was being a bit silly, and shows herself to be sensibly indifferent to how she looks on other occasions, we take it that she simply has a temporary tendency,

---

[17] As Annas has noted, there is a well-established body of empirical research in social psychology which shows that, by the age of three to four, children can come to understand the difference between what falls under conventional rules and what falls under ethical ones and recognize the latter as more serious (*Intelligent Virtue* [Oxford: Oxford University Press, 2011], 175).

not unusual at her age, to form the belief, just on some clockable occasions, that her appearance is important but will—quite naturally—grow out it. We worry more about the adolescent who, largely free of such excesses, spends all his pocket money on his appearance despite reminders that he should keep some by for presents for others at Christmas. Rather than going through a regrettable but normal phase, it seems he might be acquiring a dispositional belief that his appearance is really important, inculcating a defect in his rational soul. But then again, given his age, he is still far from having the strongly entrenched, global, trait of vanity. Not only may the dispositional belief turn out to be as temporary as the other adolescent's tendency, but also, given his limited experience of different situations, it is manifesting as a relatively local trait, largely confined to reasoning about how to attract young women, and can coexist in him with other local traits to act in accordance with virtue. If these develop well, he may grow up to have nothing more than a tendency to feel slight pain when he is reminded of his thinning hair and otherwise be as near to being a Sage as anyone gets to be.

So we shall certainly, mindful of our natural development through adolescence to adulthood, want the distinctions between a possibly temporary, a more settled, and a very well-entrenched emotional disposition, and between more and less local and global ones. And, in keeping with the two distinguishable strands of the natural development of children's practical reason, we shall count those that involve getting one's ends wrong and thereby, to a greater or lesser extent, failing to recognize that virtue is the only good, as more serious impairments of the rational soul than others.

Acknowledgements

Only once, I think, has Julia [Annas] said to me that I ought to pay attention to the Stoics, and she did so then quite casually. But over the years I have felt the weight of the magisterial authority which lay behind the casual remark pressing me towards heeding it, and it seemed *kathēkon* that I do so for her Festschrift. I had intended to engage with her on the sufficiency thesis, having been drawn much closer to her position on it, but I became so fascinated by excessiveness that I wound up writing this paper instead. So I have Julia to thank for leading me to Chrysippus, as for so many other things she has taught me over the years.

I am grateful to Tad Brennan and Carol Voeller for very helpful comments on earlier drafts of this paper.

References

Annas, J. 1993. *The Morality of Happiness*. Oxford: Oxford University Press.

Annas, J. 2011. *Intelligent Virtue*. Oxford: Oxford University Press.

Anscombe, G. E. M. 1963. *Intention*, 2nd edn. Oxford: Basil Blackwell.

Brennan, T. 1998. 'The Old Stoic Theory of the Emotions'. In J. Sihvola and T. Engberg-Pedersen (eds), *The Emotions in Hellenistic Philosophy*. Dordrecht: Kluwer: 21–70.

Brennan, T. 2000. 'Reservation in Stoic Ethics', *Archiv für Geschichte der Philosophie* 82 (2000): 149–77.

De Lacy, P. 1978–84 (trans., comm.). Galen, *On the Doctrines of Hippocrates and Plato*. 3 vols. Berlin: Akademie-Verlag.

Inwood, B. 1985. *Ethics and Human Action in Early Stoicism*. New York: Oxford University Press.

Lennox, J. G. 1999. 'Aristotle on the Biological Roots of Virtue'. In J. Maienschein and M. Ruse (eds), *Biology and the Foundations of Ethics*. Cambridge: Cambridge University Press: 10–31.

Long, A. A. 1986. *Hellenistic Philosophy*, 2nd edn. London: Duckworth.

Long, A. A. 1996. 'Soul and Body in Stoicism'. In *Stoic Studies*. Cambridge: Cambridge University Press: 224–49.

Long, A. A. and D. Sedley (eds). 1987. *The Hellenistic Philosophers*, 2 vols. Cambridge: Cambridge University Press.

Sorabji, R. 1993. *Animal Minds and Human Morals: The Origin of the Western Debate*. London: Duckworth.

Sorabji, R. 2000. *Emotion and Peace of Mind: From Stoic Agitation to Christian Temptation*. New York: Oxford University Press.

PART II
NORMATIVE VIRTUE ETHICS

6
Virtue Theory and Abortion

The sort of ethical theory derived from Aristotle, variously described a virtue ethics, virtue-based ethics, or neo-Aristotelianism, is becoming better known, and is now quite widely recognized as at least a possible rival to deontological and utilitarian theories. With recognition has come criticism, of varying quality. In this article I shall discuss nine separate criticisms that I have frequently encountered, most of which seem to me to betray an inadequate grasp either of the structure of virtue theory or of what would be involved in thinking about a real moral issue in its terms. In the first half I aim particularly to secure an understanding that will reveal that many of these criticisms are simply misplaced, and to articulate what I take to be the major criticism of virtue theory. I reject this criticism, but do not claim that it is necessarily misplaced. In the second half I aim to deepen that understanding and highlight the issues raised by the criticisms by illustrating what the theory looks like when it is applied to a particular issue, in this case, abortion.

1. Virtue Theory

Virtue theory can be laid out in a framework that reveals clearly some of the essential similarities and differences between it and some versions of deontological and utilitarian theories. I begin with a rough sketch of familiar versions of the latter two sorts of theory, not, of course, with the intention of suggesting that they exhaust the field, but on the assumption that their very familiarity will provide a helpful contrast with virtue theory. Suppose a deontological theory has basically the following framework. We begin with a premise providing a specification of right action:

P.1. An action is right iff it is in accordance with a moral rule or principle.

This is a purely formal specification, forging a link between the concepts of *right action* and *moral rule*, and gives one no guidance until one knows what a moral rule is. So the next thing the theory needs is a premise about that:

P.2. A moral rule is one that...

Historically, an acceptable completion of P.2 would have been

(i)   is laid on us by God
or
(ii) is required by natural law.

In secular versions (not, of course, unconnected to God's being pure reason, and the universality of natural law) we get such completions as

(iii) is laid on us by reason
or
(iv) is required by rationality
or
(v)   would command universal rational acceptance
or
(vi) would be the object of choice of all rational beings

and so on. Such a specification forges a second conceptual link, between the concepts of *moral rule* and *rationality*.

We have here the skeleton of a familiar version of a deontological theory, a skeleton that reveals that what is essential to any such version is the links between *right action, moral rule,* and *rationality*. That these form the basic structure can be seen particularly vividly if we lay out the familiar act-utilitarianism in such a way as to bring out the contrasts.

Act-utilitarianism begins with a premise that provides a specification of right action:

P.1. An action is right iff it promotes the best consequences.

It thereby forges the link between the concepts of *right action* and *consequences*. It goes on to specify what the best consequences are in its second premise:

P.2. The best consequences are those in which happiness is maximized.

It thereby forges the link between *consequences* and *happiness*.

Now let us consider what a skeletal virtue theory looks like. It begins with a specification of right action:

P.1. An action is right iff it is what a virtuous agent would do in the circumstances.[1]

This, like the first premises of the other two sorts of theory, is a purely formal principle, giving one no guidance as to what to do, that forges the conceptual link between *right action* and *virtuous agent*. Like the other theories, it must, of course, go on to specify what the latter is. The first step toward this may appear quite trivial, but is needed to correct a prevailing tendency among many critics to define the virtuous agent as one who is disposed to act in accordance with a deontologist's moral rules.

P.1a. A virtuous agent is one who acts virtuously, that is, one who has and exercises the virtues.

This subsidiary premise lays bare the fact that virtue theory aims to provide a nontrivial specification of the virtuous agent *via* a nontrivial specification of the virtues, which is given in its second premise:

P.2. A virtue is a character trait a human being needs to flourish or live well.

This premise forges a conceptual link between *virtue* and *flourishing* (or *living well* or *eudaimonia*). And, just as deontology, in theory, then goes on to argue that each favoured rule meets its specification, so virtue ethics, in theory, goes on to argue that each favoured character trait meets its.

These are the bare bones of virtue theory. Following are five brief comments directed to some misconceived criticisms that should be cleared out of the way.

First, the theory does not have a peculiar weakness or problem in virtue of the fact that it involves the concept of *eudaimonia* (a standard criticism being

---

[1] It should be noted that this premise intentionally allows for the possibility that two virtuous agents, faced with the same choice in the same circumstances, may act differently. For example, one might opt for taking her father off the life-support machine and the other for leaving her father on it. The theory requires that neither agent thinks that what the other does is wrong (see note 4), but it explicitly allows that no action is uniquely right in such a case—both are right. It also intentionally allows for the possibility that in some circumstances—those into which no virtuous agent could have got herself—no action is right. I explore this premise at greater length in 'Applying Virtue Ethics', in R. Hursthouse, G. Lawrence, and W. Quinn (eds), *Virtues and Reasons: Philippa Foot and Moral Theory, Essays in Honor of Philippa Foot* (Oxford: Clarendon Press, 1995), 57–75.

that this concept is hopelessly obscure). Now no virtue theorist will pretend that the concept of human flourishing is an easy one to grasp. I will not even claim here (though I would elsewhere) that it is no more obscure than the concepts of *rationality* and *happiness*, since, if our vocabulary were more limited, we might, *faute de mieux*, call it (human) *rational happiness*, and thereby reveal that it has at least some of the difficulties of both. But virtue theory has never, so far as I know, been dismissed on the grounds of the *comparative* obscurity of this central concept; rather, the popular view is that it has a problem with this which deontology and utilitarianism in no way share. This, I think, is clearly false. Both *rationality* and *happiness*, as they figure in their respective theories, are rich and difficult concepts—hence all the disputes about the various tests for a rule's being an object of rational choice, and the disputes, dating back to Mill's introduction of the higher and lower pleasures, about what constitutes happiness.

Second, the theory is not trivially circular; it does not specify right action in terms of the virtuous agent and then immediately specify the virtuous agent in terms of right action. Rather, it specifies her in terms of the virtues, and then specifies these, not merely as dispositions to right action, but as the character traits (which are dispositions to feel and react as well as act in certain ways) required for *eudaimonia*.[2]

Third, it does answer the question 'What should I do?' as well as the question 'What sort of person should I be?' (That is, it is not, as one of the catchphrases has it, concerned only with Being and not with Doing.)

Fourth, the theory does, to a certain extent, answer this question by coming up with rules or principles (contrary to the common claim that it does not come up with any rules or principles). Every virtue generates a positive instruction (act justly, kindly, courageously, honestly, etc.) and every vice a prohibition (do not act unjustly, cruelly, like a coward, dishonestly, etc.). So trying to decide what to do within the framework of virtue theory is not, as some people seem to imagine, necessarily a matter of taking one's favoured

---

[2] There is, of course, the further question of whether the theory eventually describes a larger circle and winds up relying on the concept of right action in its interpretation of *eudaimonia*. In denying that the theory is trivially circular, I do not pretend to answer this intricate question. It is certainly true that virtue theory does not claim that the correct conception of *eudaimonia* can be got from 'an independent "value-free" investigation of human nature' (John McDowell, 'The Role of Eudaimonia in Aristotle's Ethics', in A. Rorty (ed.), *Essays on Aristotle's Ethics* (Berkeley and Los Angeles: University of California Press, 1980), 359–76). The sort of training that is required for acquiring the correct conception no doubt involves being taught from early on such things as 'Decent people do this sort of thing, not that' and 'To do such and such is the mark of a depraved character' (cf. *Nicomachean Ethics* 1110a22). But whether this counts as relying on the concept of right (or wrong) action seems to me very unclear and requiring much discussion.

candidate for a virtuous person and asking oneself, 'What would they do in these circumstances?' (as if the raped fifteen-year-old girl might be supposed to say to herself, 'Now would Socrates have an abortion if he were in my circumstances?' and as if someone who had never known or heard of anyone very virtuous were going to be left, according to the theory, with no way to decide what to do at all). The agent may instead ask herself, 'If I were to do such and such now, would I be acting justly or unjustly (or neither), kindly or unkindly [and so on]?' I shall consider below the problem created by cases in which such a question apparently does not yield an answer to 'What should I do?' (because, say, the alternatives are being unkind or being unjust); here my claim is only that it sometimes does—the agent may employ her concepts of the virtues and vices directly, rather than imagining what some hypothetical exemplar would do.

Fifth (a point that is implicit but should be made explicit), virtue theory is not committed to any sort of reductionism involving defining all of our moral concepts in terms of the virtuous agent. On the contrary, it relies on a lot of very significant moral concepts. Charity or benevolence, for instance, is the virtue whose concern is the *good* of others; that concept of good is related to the concept of *evil* or *harm*, and they are both related to the concepts of the *worthwhile*, the *advantageous*, and the *pleasant*. If I have the wrong conception of what is worthwhile and advantageous and pleasant, then I shall have the wrong conception of what is good for, and harmful to, myself and others, and, even with the best will in the world, will lack the virtue of charity, which involves getting all this right. (This point will be illustrated at some length in the second half of this article; I mention it here only in support of the fact that no virtue theorist who takes her inspiration from Aristotle would even contemplate aiming at reductionism.)[3]

Let me now, with equal brevity, run through two more standard criticisms of virtue theory (the sixth and seventh of my nine) to show that, though not entirely misplaced, they do not highlight problems peculiar to that theory but, rather, problems that are shared by familiar versions of deontology.

One common criticism is that we do not know which character traits are the virtues, or that this is open to much dispute, or particularly subject to the threat of moral scepticism or 'pluralism'[4] or cultural relativism. But the parallel roles played by the second premises of both deontological and virtue theories

---

[3] Cf. Bernard Williams' point in *Ethics and the Limits of Philosophy* (London: Collins, 1985) that we need an enriched ethical vocabulary, not a cut-down one.
[4] I put *pluralism* in scare quotes to serve as a warning that virtue theory is not incompatible with all forms of it. It allows for 'competing conceptions' of *eudaimonia* and the worthwhile, for instance, in the

reveal the way in which both sorts of theory share this problem. It is at the stage at which one tries to get the right conclusions to drop out of the bottom of one's theory that, *theoretically*, all the work has to be done. Rule deontologists know that they want to get 'don't kill', 'keep promises', 'cherish your children', and so on as the rules that meet their specification, whatever it may be. They also know that any of these can be disputed, that some philosopher may claim, of any one of them, that it is reasonable to reject it, and that at least some people claim that there has been, for each rule, some culture that rejected it. Similarly, the virtue theorists know that they want to get justice, charity, fidelity, courage, and so on as the character traits needed for *eudaimonia*; and they also know that any of these can be disputed, that some philosopher will say of any one of them that it is reasonable to reject it as a virtue, and that there is said to be, for each character trait, some culture that has thus rejected it.

This is a problem for both theories, and the virtue theorist certainly does not find it any harder to argue against moral scepticism, 'pluralism', or cultural relativism than the deontologist. Each theory has to stick out its neck and say, in some cases, 'This person/these people/other cultures are (or would be) in error', and find some grounds for saying this.

Another criticism (the seventh) often made is that virtue ethics has unresolvable conflict built into it. 'It is common knowledge', it is said, 'that the requirements of the virtues can conflict; charity may prompt me to end the frightful suffering of the person in my care by killing him, but justice bids me to stay my hand. To tell my brother that his wife is being unfaithful to him would be honest and loyal, but it would be kinder to keep quiet about it. So which should I do? In such cases, virtue ethics has nothing helpful to say.' (This is one version of the problem, mentioned above, that considering whether a proposed action falls under a virtue or vice term does not always yield an answer to 'What should I do?')

The obvious reply to this criticism is that rule deontology notoriously suffers from the same problem, arising not only from the fact that its rules

---

sense that it allows for a plurality of flourishing lives—the theory need not follow Aristotle in specifying the life of contemplation as the only one that truly constitutes *eudaimonia* (if he does). But the conceptions 'compete' only in the sense that, within a single flourishing life, not everything worthwhile can be fitted in; the theory does not allow that two people with a correct conception of *eudaimonia* can disagree over whether the way the other is living constitutes flourishing. Moreover, the theory is committed to the strong thesis that the same set of character traits is needed for any flourishing life; it will not allow that, for instance, soldiers need courage but wives and mothers do not, or that judges need justice but can live well despite lacking kindness. (This obviously is related to the point made in note 1.) For an interesting discussion of pluralism (different interpretations thereof) and virtue theory, see Douglas B. Rasmussen, 'Liberalism and Natural End Ethics', *American Philosophical Quarterly* 27 (1990): 153–161.

can apparently conflict, but also from the fact that, at first blush, it appears that one and the same rule (e.g., preserve life) can yield contrary instructions in a particular case.[5] As before, I agree that this is a problem for virtue theory, but deny that it is a problem peculiar to it.

Finally, I want to articulate, and reject, what I take to be the major criticism of virtue theory. Perhaps because it is *the* major criticism, the reflection of a very general sort of disquiet about the theory, it is hard to state clearly—especially for someone who does not accept it—but it goes something like this.[6] My interlocutor says:

> Virtue theory can't *get* us anywhere in real moral issues because it's bound to be all assertion and no argument. You admit that the best it can come up with in the way of action-guiding rules are the ones that rely on the virtue and vice concepts, such as 'act charitably', 'don't act cruelly', and so on; and, as if that weren't bad enough, you admit that these virtue concepts, such as charity, presuppose concepts such as the *good*, and the *worthwhile*, and so on. But that means that any virtue theorist who writes about real moral issues must rely on her audience's agreeing with her application of all these concepts, and hence accepting all the premises in which those applications are enshrined. But some other virtue theorist might take different premises about these matters, and come up with very different conclusions, and, within the terms of the theory, there is no way to distinguish between the two. While there is agreement, virtue theory can repeat conventional wisdom, preserve the status quo, but it can't get us anywhere in the way that a normative ethical theory is supposed to, namely, by providing rational grounds for acceptance of its practical conclusions.

My strategy will be to split this criticism into two: one (the eighth) addressed to the virtue theorist's employment of the virtue and vice concepts enshrined in her rules—act charitably, honestly, and so on—and the other (the ninth) addressed to her employment of concepts such as that of the *worthwhile*. Each objection, I shall maintain, implicitly appeals to a certain *condition of*

---

[5] E.g., in Williams' Jim and Pedro case in J. J. C. Smart and Bernard Williams, *Utilitarianism: For and Against* (Cambridge: Cambridge University Press, 1973).

[6] Intimations of this criticism constantly come up in discussion; the clearest statement of it I have found is by Onora O'Neill, in her review of Stephen Clark's *The Moral Status of Animals*, in *Journal of Philosophy* 77 (1980): 440–46. For a response I am much in sympathy with, see Cora Diamond, 'Anything But Argument?' *Philosophical Investigations* 5 (1982): 23–41.

adequacy on a normative moral theory, and, in each case, I shall claim, the condition of adequacy, once made explicit, is utterly implausible.

It is true that when she discusses real moral issues, the virtue theorist has to assert that certain actions are honest, dishonest, or neither; charitable, uncharitable, or neither. And it is true that this is often a very difficult matter to decide; her rules are not always easy to apply. But this counts as a criticism of the theory only if we assume, as a condition of adequacy, that any adequate action-guiding theory must make the difficult business of knowing what to do if one is to act well easy, that it must provide clear guidance about what ought and ought not to be done which any reasonably clever adolescent could follow if she chose. But such a condition of adequacy is implausible. Acting rightly *is* difficult, and *does* call for much moral wisdom, and the relevant condition of adequacy, which virtue theory meets, is that it should have built into it an explanation of a truth expressed by Aristotle,[7] namely, that moral knowledge—unlike mathematical knowledge—cannot be acquired merely by attending lectures and is not characteristically to be found in people too young to have had much experience of life. There are youthful mathematical geniuses, but rarely, if ever, youthful moral geniuses, and this tells us something significant about the sort of knowledge that moral knowledge is. Virtue ethics builds this in straight off precisely by couching its rules in terms whose application may indeed call for the most delicate and sensitive judgement.

Here we may discern a slightly different version of the problem that there are cases in which applying the virtue and vice terms does not yield an answer to 'What should I do?' Suppose someone 'youthful in character', as Aristotle puts it, having applied the relevant terms, finds herself landed with what is, unbeknownst to her, a case not of real but of apparent conflict, arising from a misapplication of those terms. Then she will not be able to decide what to do unless she knows of a virtuous agent to look to for guidance. But her quandary is (*ex hypothesi*) the result of her lack of wisdom, and just what virtue theory expects. Someone hesitating over whether to reveal a hurtful truth, for example, thinking it would be kind but dishonest or unjust to lie, may need to realize, with respect to these particular circumstances, not that kindness is more (or less) important than honesty or justice, and not that honesty or justice sometimes requires one to act unkindly or cruelly, but that one does people no kindness by concealing this sort of truth from them, hurtful as it may be. This is the *type* of thing (I use it only as an example) that people with

---

[7] Aristotle, *Nicomachean Ethics* 1142a12–16.

moral wisdom know about, involving the correct application of *kind*, and that people without such wisdom find difficult.

What about the virtue theorist's reliance on concepts such as that of the *worthwhile*? If such reliance is to count as a fault in the theory, what condition of adequacy is implicitly in play? It must be that any good normative theory should provide answers to questions about real moral issues whose truth is in no way determined by truths about what is worthwhile, or what really matters in human life. Now although people are initially inclined to reject out of hand the claim that the practical conclusions of a normative moral theory have to be based on premises about what is truly worthwhile, the alternative, once it is made explicit, may look even more unacceptable. Consider what the condition of adequacy entails. If truths about what is worthwhile (or truly good, or serious, or about what matters in human life) do *not* have to be appealed to in order to answer questions about real moral issues, then I might sensibly seek guidance about what I ought to do from someone who had declared in advance that she knew nothing about such matters, or from someone who said that, although she had opinions about them, these were quite likely to be wrong but that this did not matter, because they would play no determining role in the advice she gave me.

I should emphasize that we are talking about real moral issues and real guidance; I want to know whether I should have an abortion, take my mother off the life-support machine, leave academic life and become a doctor in the Third World, give up my job with the firm that is using animals in its experiments, tell my father he has cancer. Would I go to someone who says she has *no* views about what is worthwhile in life? Or to someone who says that, as a matter of fact, she tends to think that the only thing that matters is having a good time, but has a normative theory that is consistent both with this view and with my own rather more puritanical one, which will yield the guidance I need?

I take it as a premise that this is absurd. The relevant condition of adequacy should be that the practical conclusions of a good normative theory *must* be in part determined by premises about what is worthwhile, important, and so on. Thus I reject this 'major criticism' of virtue theory, that it cannot get us anywhere in the way that a normative moral theory is supposed to. According to my response, a normative theory that any clever adolescent can apply, or that reaches practical conclusions that are in no way determined by premises about what is truly worthwhile, serious, and so on, is guaranteed to be an inadequate theory.

Although I reject this criticism, I have not argued that it is misplaced and that it necessarily manifests a failure to understand what virtue theory is. My rejection is based on premises about what an adequate normative theory must be like—what sorts of concepts it must contain, and what sort of account it must give of moral knowledge—and thereby claims, implicitly, that the 'major criticism' manifests a failure to understand what an *adequate normative theory* is. But, as a matter of fact, I think the criticism is often made by people who have no idea of what virtue theory looks like when applied to a real moral issue; they drastically underestimate the variety of ways in which the virtue and vice concepts, and the others, such as that of the *worthwhile*, figure in such discussion.

As promised, I now turn to an illustration of such discussion, applying virtue theory to abortion. Before I embark on this tendentious business, I should remind the reader of the aim of this discussion. I am not, in this article, trying to solve the problem of abortion; I am illustrating how virtue theory directs one to think about it. It might indeed be said that thinking about the problem in this way 'solves' it by *dis*solving it, insofar as it leads one to the conclusion that there is no single right answer, but a variety of particular answers, and in what follows I am certainly trying to make that conclusion seem plausible. But, that granted, it should still be said that I am not trying to 'solve the problems' in the practical sense of telling people that they should, or should not, do this or that if they are pregnant and contemplating abortion in these or those particular circumstances.

I do not assume, or expect, that all of my readers will agree with everything I am about to say. On the contrary, given the plausible assumption that some are morally wiser than I am, and some less so, the theory has built into it that we are bound to disagree on some points. For instance, we may well disagree about the particular application of some of the virtue and vice terms; and we may disagree about what is worthwhile or serious, worthless or trivial. But my aim is to make clear how these concepts figure in a discussion conducted in terms of virtue theory. What is at issue is whether these concepts are indeed the ones that should come in, that is, whether virtue theory should be criticized for employing them. The problem of abortion highlights this issue dramatically since virtue theory quite transforms the discussion of it.

2. Abortion

As everyone knows, the morality of abortion is commonly discussed in relation to just two considerations: first, and predominantly, the status of the foetus and whether or not it is the sort of thing that may or may not be innocuously or justifiably killed; and second, and less predominantly (when, that is, the discussion concerns the *morality* of abortion rather than the question of permissible legislation in a just society), women's rights. If one thinks within this familiar framework, one may well be puzzled about what virtue theory, as such, could contribute. Some people assume the discussion will be conducted solely in terms of what the virtuous agent would or would not do (cf. the third, fourth, and fifth criticisms above). Others assume that only justice, or at most justice and charity,[8] will be applied to the issue, generating a discussion very similar to Judith Jarvis Thomson's.[9]

Now if this is the way the virtue theorist's discussion of abortion is imagined to be, no wonder people think little of it. It seems obvious in advance that in any such discussion there must be either a great deal of extremely tendentious application of the virtue terms *just, charitable*, and so on or a lot of rhetorical appeal to 'this is what only the virtuous agent knows.' But these are caricatures; they fail to appreciate the way in which virtue theory quite transforms the discussion of abortion by dismissing the two familiar dominating considerations as, in a way, fundamentally irrelevant. In what way or ways, I hope to make both clear and plausible.

Let us first consider women's rights. Let me emphasize again that we are discussing the *morality* of abortion, not the rights and wrongs of laws prohibiting or permitting it. If we suppose that women do have a moral right to do as they choose with their own bodies, or, more particularly, to terminate their pregnancies, then it may well follow that a *law* forbidding abortion would be unjust. Indeed, even if they have no such right, such a law might be, as things stand at the moment, unjust, or impractical, or inhumane: on this issue I have nothing to say in this article. But, putting all questions about the justice or injustice of laws to one side, and supposing only that women have such a moral right, *nothing* follows from this supposition about the morality of abortion, according to virtue theory, once it is noted (quite generally, not with particular reference to abortion) that in exercising a moral right I can do

---

[8] It seems likely that some people have been misled by Foot's discussion of euthanasia (through no fault of hers) into thinking that a virtue theorist's discussion of terminating human life will be conducted exclusively in terms of justice and charity (and the corresponding vice terms) (Philippa Foot, 'Euthanasia', *Philosophy & Public Affairs* 6(2) (1977): 85–112). But the act-category *euthanasia* is a very special one, at least as defined in her article, since such an act must be done 'for the sake of the one who is to die'. Building a virtuous motivation into the specification of the act in this way immediately rules out the application of many other vice terms.

[9] Judith Jarvis Thomson, 'A Defense of Abortion', *Philosophy & Public Affairs* 1(1): 47–66. One could indeed regard this article as proto-virtue theory (no doubt to the surprise of the author) if the concepts of callousness and kindness were allowed more weight.

something cruel, or callous, or selfish, light-minded, self-righteous, stupid, inconsiderate, disloyal, dishonest—that is, act viciously.[10] Love and friendship do not survive their parties' constantly insisting on their rights, nor do people live well when they think that getting what they have a right to is of pre-eminent importance; they harm others, and they harm themselves. So whether women have a moral right to terminate their pregnancies is irrelevant within virtue theory, for it is irrelevant to the question 'In having an abortion in these circumstances, would the agent be acting virtuously or viciously or neither?'

What about the consideration of the status of the foetus—what can virtue theory say about that? One might say that this issue is not in the province of *any* moral theory; it is a metaphysical question, and an extremely difficult one at that. Must virtue theory then wait upon metaphysics to come up with the answer?

At first sight it might seem so. For virtue is said to involve knowledge, and part of this knowledge consists in having the *right* attitude to things. 'Right' here does not just mean 'morally right' or 'proper' or 'nice' in the modem sense; it means 'accurate, true'. One cannot have the right or correct attitude to something if the attitude is based on or involves false beliefs. And this suggests that if the status of the foetus is relevant to the rightness or wrongness of abortion, its status must be known, as a truth, to the fully wise and virtuous person.

But the sort of wisdom that the fully virtuous person has is not supposed to be recondite; it does not call for fancy philosophical sophistication, and it does not depend upon, let alone wait upon, the discoveries of academic philosophers.[11] And this entails the following, rather startling, conclusion: that the status of the foetus—that issue over which so much ink has been spilt—is, according to virtue theory, simply not relevant to the rightness or wrongness of abortion (within, that is, a secular morality).

Or rather, since that is clearly too radical a conclusion, it is in a sense relevant, but only in the sense that the familiar biological facts are relevant. By 'the familiar biological facts' I mean the facts that most human societies are

---

[10] One possible qualification: if one ties the concept of justice very closely to rights, then if women do have a moral right to terminate their pregnancies it *may* follow that in doing so they do not act unjustly. (Cf. Thomson, 'A Defense of Abortion'.) But it is debatable whether even that much follows.

[11] This is an assumption of virtue theory, and I do not attempt to defend it here. An adequate discussion of it would require a separate article, since, although most moral philosophers would be chary of claiming that intellectual sophistication is a necessary condition of moral wisdom or virtue, most of us, from Plato onward, tend to write as if this were so. Sorting out which claims about moral knowledge are committed to this kind of elitism and which can, albeit with difficulty, be reconciled with the idea that moral knowledge can be acquired by anyone who really wants it would be a major task.

and have been familiar with—that, standardly (but not invariably), pregnancy occurs as the result of sexual intercourse, that lasts about nine months, during which time the foetus grows and develops, that standardly it terminates in the birth of a living baby, and this is how we all come to be.

It might be thought that this distinction—between the familiar biological facts and the status of the foetus—is a distinction without a difference. But this is not so. To attach relevance to the status of the foetus, in the sense in which virtue theory claims it is not relevant, is to be gripped by the conviction that we must go beyond the familiar biological facts, deriving some sort of conclusion from them, such as that the foetus has rights, or is not a person, or something similar. It is also to believe that this exhausts the relevance of the familiar biological facts, that all they are relevant to is the status of the foetus and whether or not it is the sort of thing that may or may not be killed.

These convictions, I suspect, are rooted in the desire to solve the problem of abortion by getting it to fall under some general rule such as 'You ought not to kill anything with the right to life but may kill anything else.' But they have resulted in what should surely strike any non-philosopher as a most bizarre aspect of nearly all the current philosophical literature on abortion, namely, that, far from treating abortion as a unique moral problem, markedly unlike any other, nearly everything written on the status of the foetus and its bearing on the abortion issue would be consistent with the human reproductive facts' (to say nothing of family life) being totally different from what they are. Imagine that you are an alien extraterrestrial anthropologist who does not know that the human race is roughly 50 per cent female and 50 per cent male, or that our only (natural) form of reproduction involves heterosexual intercourse, viviparous birth, and the female's (and only the female's) being pregnant for nine months, or that females are capable of childbearing from late childhood to late middle age, or that childbearing is painful, dangerous, and emotionally charged—do you think you would pick up these facts from the hundreds of articles written on the status of the foetus? I am quite sure you would not. And that, I think, shows that the current philosophical literature on abortion has got badly out of touch with reality.

Now if we are using virtue theory, our first question is not 'What do the familiar biological facts show—what can be derived from them about the status of the foetus?' but 'How do these facts figure in the practical reasoning, actions and passions, thoughts and reactions, of the virtuous and the non-virtuous? What is the mark of having the right attitude to these facts and what manifests having the wrong attitude to them?' This immediately makes essentially relevant not only all the facts about human reproduction I mentioned above, but a whole range of facts about our emotions in relation to them as well. I mean such facts as that human parents, both male and female, tend to care passionately about their offspring, and that family relationships are among the deepest and strongest in our lives—and, significantly, among the longest-lasting.

These facts make it obvious that pregnancy is not just one among many other physical conditions; and hence that anyone who genuinely believes that an abortion is comparable to a haircut or an appendectomy is mistaken.[12] The fact that the premature termination of a pregnancy is, in some sense, the cutting off of a new human life, and thereby, like the procreation of a new human life, connects with all our thoughts about human life and death, parenthood, and family relationships, must make it a serious matter. To disregard this fact about it, to think of abortion as nothing but the killing of something that does not matter, or as nothing but the exercise of some right or rights one has, or as the incidental means to some desirable state of affairs, is to do something callous and light-minded, the sort of thing that no virtuous and wise person would do. It is to have the wrong attitude not only to foetuses, but more generally to human life and death, parenthood, and family relationships.

Although I say that the facts make this obvious, I know that this is one of my tendentious points. In partial support of it I note that even the most dedicated proponents of the view that deliberate abortion is just like an appendectomy or haircut rarely hold the same view of spontaneous abortion, that is, miscarriage. It is not so tendentious of me to claim that to react to people's grief over miscarriage by saying, or even thinking, 'What a fuss about nothing!' would be callous and light-minded, whereas to try to laugh someone out of grief over an appendectomy scar or a botched haircut would not be. It is hard to give this point due prominence within act-centred theories, for the inconsistency is an inconsistency in attitude about the seriousness of loss of life, not in beliefs about which acts are right or wrong. Moreover, an act-centred theorist may say, 'Well, there is nothing wrong with *thinking* "What a fuss about nothing!"

---

[12] Mary Anne Warren, in 'On the Moral and Legal Status of Abortion', *Monist* 57 (1973): 43–61, sec. 1, says of the opponents of restrictive laws governing abortion that 'their conviction (for the most part) is that abortion is not a *morally* serious and extremely unfortunate, even though sometimes justified, act, comparable to killing in self-defense or to letting the violinist die, but rather is closer to being a *morally neutral* act, like cutting one's hair' (italics mine). I would like to think that no one *genuinely* believes this. But certainly in discussion, particularly when arguing against restrictive laws or the suggestion that remorse over abortion might be appropriate, I have found that some people *say* they believe it (and often cite Warren's article, albeit inaccurately, despite its age). Those who allow that it is morally serious, and far from morally neutral, have to argue against restrictive laws, or the appropriateness of remorse, on a very different ground from that laid down by the premise 'The foetus is just part of the woman's body (and she has a right to determine what happens to her body and should not feel guilt about anything she does to it).'

as long as you do not say it and hurt the person who is grieving. And besides, we cannot be held responsible for our thoughts, only for the intentional actions they give rise to.' But the character traits that virtue theory emphasizes are not simply dispositions to intentional actions, but a seamless disposition to certain actions and passions, thoughts and reactions.

To say that the cutting off of a human life is always a matter of some seriousness, at any stage, is not to deny the relevance of gradual foetal development. Notwithstanding the well-worn point that clear boundary lines cannot be drawn, our emotions and attitudes regarding the foetus do change as it develops, and again when it is born, and indeed further as the baby grows. Abortion for shallow reasons in the later stages is much more shocking than abortion for the same reasons in the early stages in a way that matches the fact that deep grief over miscarriage in the later stages is more appropriate than it is over miscarriage in the earlier stages (when, that is, the grief is solely about the loss of *this* child, not about as might be the case, the loss of one's only hope of having a child or of having one's husband's child). Imagine (or recall) a woman who already has children; she had not intended to have more, but finds herself unexpectedly pregnant. Though contrary to her plans, the pregnancy, once established as a fact, is welcomed—and then she loses the embryo almost immediately. If this were bemoaned as a tragedy, it would, I think, be a misapplication of the concept of what is tragic. But it may still properly be mourned as a loss. The grief is expressed in such terms as 'I shall always wonder how she or he would have turned out' or 'When I look at the others, I shall think, "How different their lives would have been if this other one had been part of them."' It would, I take it, be callous and light-minded to say, or think, 'Well, she has already *got* four children; what's the problem?'; it would be neither, nor arrogantly intrusive in the case of a close friend, to try to correct prolonged mourning by saying, 'I know it's sad, but it's not a tragedy; rejoice in the ones you have.' The application of *tragic* becomes more appropriate as the foetus grows, for the mere fact that one has lived with it for longer, conscious of its existence, makes a difference. To shrug off an early abortion is understandable just because it is very hard to be fully conscious of the foetus's existence in the early stages and hence hard to appreciate that an early abortion is the destruction of life. It is particularly hard for the young and inexperienced to appreciate this, because appreciation of it usually comes only with experience.

I do not mean 'with the experience of having an abortion' (though that may be part of it) but, quite generally, 'with the experience of life'. Many women who have borne children contrast their later pregnancies with their first successful one, saying that in the later ones they were conscious of a new life growing in them from very early on. And, more generally, as one reaches the age at which the next generation is coming up close behind one, the counterfactuals 'If I, or she, had had an abortion, Alice, or Bob, would not have been born' acquire a significant application, which casts a new light on the conditionals 'If I or Alice have an abortion then some Caroline or Bill will not be born.'

The fact that pregnancy is not just one among many physical conditions does not mean that one can never regard it in that light without manifesting a vice. When women are in very poor physical health, or worn out from childbearing, or forced to do very physically demanding jobs, then they cannot be described as self-indulgent, callous, irresponsible, or light-minded if they seek abortions mainly with a view to avoiding pregnancy as the physical condition that it is. To go through with a pregnancy when one is utterly exhausted, or when one's job consists of crawling along tunnels hauling coal, as many women in the nineteenth century were obliged to do, is perhaps heroic, but people who do not achieve heroism are not necessarily vicious. That they can view the pregnancy only as eight months of misery, followed by hours if not days of agony and exhaustion, and abortion only as the blessed escape from this prospect, is entirely understandable and does not manifest any lack of serious respect for human life or a shallow attitude to motherhood. What it does show is that something is terribly amiss in the conditions of their lives, which make it so hard to recognize pregnancy and childbearing as the good that they can be.

In relation to this last point I should draw attention to the way in which virtue theory has a sort of built-in indexicality. Philosophers arguing against anything remotely resembling a belief in the sanctity of life (which the above claims clearly embody) frequently appeal to the existence of other communities in which abortion and infanticide are practised. We should not automatically assume that it is impossible that some other communities could be morally inferior to our own; maybe some are, or have been, precisely insofar as their members are, typically, callous or light-minded or unjust. But in communities in which life is a great deal tougher for everyone than it is in ours, having the right attitude to human life and death, parenthood, and family relationships might well manifest itself in ways that are unlike ours. When it is essential to survival that most members of the community fend for themselves at a very young age or work during most of their waking hours, selective abortion or infanticide might be practised either as a form of genuine euthanasia or for the sake of the community and not, I think, be thought callous or light-minded. But this does not make everything all right; as before, it shows that there is something amiss with the conditions of their lives, which are making it impossible for them to live really well.[13]

The foregoing discussion, insofar as it emphasizes the right attitude to human life and death, parallels to a certain extent those standard discussions of abortion that concentrate on it solely as an issue of killing. But it does not, as those discussions do, gloss over the fact, emphasized by those who discuss the morality of abortion in terms of women's rights, that abortion, wildly unlike any other form of killing, is the termination of a pregnancy, which is a condition of a woman's body and results in *her* having a child if it is not aborted. This fact is given due recognition not by appeal to women's rights but by emphasizing the relevance of the familiar biological and psychological facts and their connection with having the right attitude to parenthood and family relationships. But it may well be thought that failing to bring in women's rights still leaves some important aspects of the problem of abortion untouched.

Speaking in terms of women's rights, people sometimes say things like, 'Well, it's her life you're talking about too, you know; she's got a right to her own life, her own happiness.' And the discussion stops there. But in the context of virtue theory, given that we are particularly concerned with what constitutes a good human life, with what true happiness or *eudaimonia* is, this is no place to stop. We go on to ask, 'And is this life of hers a good one? Is she living well?'

If we are to go on to talk about good human lives, in the context of abortion, we have to bring in our thoughts about the value of love and family life, and our proper emotional development through a natural life cycle. The familiar facts support the view that parenthood in general, and motherhood and childbearing in particular, are intrinsically worthwhile, are among the things that can be correctly thought to be partially constitutive of a flourishing human life.[14] If this is right, then a woman who opts for not being a mother (at all, or again, or now) by opting for abortion may thereby be manifesting a flawed grasp of what her life should be, and be about—a grasp that is childish, or grossly materialistic, or shortsighted, or shallow.

---

[13] For another example of the way in which 'tough conditions' can make a difference to what is involved in having the right attitude to human life and death and family relationships, see the concluding sentences of Foot's 'Euthanasia'.

[14] I take this as a premise here, but argue for it in some detail in my *Beginning Lives* (Oxford: Blackwell, 1987). In this connection I also discuss adoption and the sense in which it may be regarded as 'second best', and the difficult question of whether the good of parenthood may properly be sought, or indeed bought, by surrogacy.

I said '*may* thereby': this *need* not be so. Consider, for instance, a woman who has already had several children and fears that to have another will seriously affect her capacity to be a good mother to the ones she has—she does not show a lack of appreciation of the intrinsic value of being a parent by opting for abortion. Nor does a woman who has been a good mother and is approaching the age at which she may be looking forward to being a good grandmother. Nor does a woman who discovers that her pregnancy may well kill her, and opts for abortion and adoption. Nor, necessarily, does a woman who has decided to lead a life centred around some other worthwhile activity or activities with which motherhood would compete.

People who are childless by choice are sometimes described as 'irresponsible', or 'selfish', or 'refusing to grow up', or 'not knowing what life is about'. But one can hold that having children is intrinsically worthwhile without endorsing this, for we are, after all, in the happy position of there being more worthwhile things to do than can be fitted into one lifetime. Parenthood, and motherhood in particular, even if granted to be intrinsically worthwhile, undoubtedly take up a lot of one's adult life, leaving no room for some other worthwhile pursuits. But some women who choose abortion rather than have their first child, and some men who encourage their partners to choose abortion, are not avoiding parenthood for the sake of other worthwhile pursuits, but for the worthless one of 'having a good time', or for the pursuit of some false vision of the ideals of freedom or self-realization. And some others who say 'I am not ready for parenthood yet' are making some sort of mistake about the extent to which one can manipulate the circumstances of one's life so as to make it fulfil some dream that one has. Perhaps one's dream is to have two perfect children, a girl and a boy, within a perfect marriage, in financially secure circumstances, with an interesting job of one's own. But to care too much about that dream, to demand of life that it give it to one and act accordingly, may be both greedy and foolish, and is to run the risk of missing out on happiness entirely. Not only may fate make the dream impossible, or destroy it, but one's own attachment to it may make it impossible. Good marriages, and the most promising children, can be destroyed by just one adult's excessive demand for perfection.

Once again, this is not to deny that girls may quite properly say 'I am not ready for motherhood yet', especially in our society, and, far from manifesting irresponsibility or light-mindedness, show an appropriate modesty or humility, or a fearfulness that does not amount to cowardice. However, even when the decision to have an abortion is the right decision—one that does not itself fall under a vice-related term and thereby one that the perfectly virtuous could recommend—it does not follow that there is no sense in which having the abortion is wrong, or guilt inappropriate. For, by virtue of the fact that a human life has been cut short, some evil has probably been brought about,[15] and that circumstances make the decision to bring about some evil the right decision will be a ground for guilt if getting into those circumstances in the first place itself manifested a flaw in character.

What 'gets one into those circumstances' in the case of abortion is, except in the case of rape, one's sexual activity and one's choices, or the lack of them, about one's sexual partner and about contraception. The virtuous woman (which here of course does not mean simply 'chaste woman' but 'woman with the virtues') has such character traits as strength, independence, resoluteness, decisiveness, self-confidence, responsibility, serious-mindedness, and self-determination—and no one, I think, could deny that many women become pregnant in circumstances in which they cannot welcome or cannot face the thought of having *this* child precisely because they lack one or some of these character traits. So even in the cases where the decision to have an abortion is the right one, it can still be the reflection of a moral failing—not because the decision itself is weak or cowardly or irresolute or irresponsible or lightminded, but because lack of the requisite opposite of these failings landed one in the circumstances in the first place. Hence the common universalized claim that guilt and remorse are never appropriate emotions about an abortion is denied. They may be appropriate, and appropriately inculcated, even when the decision was the right one.

Another motivation for bringing women's rights into the discussion may be to attempt to correct the implication, carried by the killing-centred approach, that insofar as abortion is wrong, it is a wrong that only women do, or at least (given the preponderance of male doctors) that only women instigate. I do not myself believe that we can thus escape the fact that nature bears harder on women than it does on men,[16] but virtue theory can certainly correct many of the injustices that the emphasis on women's rights is rightly concerned about. With very little amendment, everything that has been said above applies to boys and men too. Although the abortion decision is, in a natural sense, the woman's decision, proper to her, boys and men are often party to it, for well or

---

[15] I say 'some evil has probably been brought about' on the ground that (human) life is (usually) a good and hence (human) death usually an evil. The exceptions would be (a) where death is actually a good or a benefit, because the baby that would come to be if the life were not cut short would be better off dead than alive, and (b) where death, though not a good, is not an evil either, because the life that would be led (e.g., in a state of permanent coma) would not be a good. (See Foot, 'Euthanasia'.)

[16] I discuss this point at greater length in *Beginning Lives*.

ill, and even when they are not, they are bound to have been party to the circumstances that brought it up. No less than girls and women, boys and men can, in their actions, manifest self-centredness, callousness, and light-mindedness about life and parenthood in relation to abortion. They can be self-centred or courageous about the possibility of disability in their offspring; they need to reflect on their sexual activity and their choices, or the lack of them, about their sexual partner and contraception; they need to grow up and take responsibility for their own actions and life in relation to fatherhood. If it is true, as I maintain, that insofar as motherhood is intrinsically worthwhile, being a mother is an important purpose in women's lives, being a father (rather than a mere generator) is an important purpose in men's lives as well, and it is adolescent of men to turn a blind eye to this and pretend that they have many more important things to do.

3. Conclusion

Much more might be said, but I shall end the actual discussion of the problem of abortion here, and conclude by highlighting what I take to be its significant features. These hark back to many of the criticisms of virtue theory discussed earlier.

The discussion does not proceed simply by our trying to answer the question 'Would a perfectly virtuous agent ever have an abortion and, if so, when?'; virtue theory is not limited to considering 'Would Socrates have had an abortion if he were a raped, pregnant fifteen-year-old?' or automatically stumped when we are considering circumstances into which no virtuous agent would have got herself. Instead, much of the discussion proceeds in the virtue- and vice-related terms whose application, in several cases, yields practical conclusions (cf. the third and fourth criticisms above). These terms are difficult to apply correctly, and anyone might challenge my application of any one of them. So, for example, I have claimed that some abortions, done for certain reasons, would be callous or light-minded; that others might indicate an appropriate modesty or humility; that others would reflect a greedy and foolish attitude to what one could expect out of life. Any of these examples may be disputed, but what is at issue is, should these difficult terms be there, or should the discussion be couched in terms that all clever adolescents can apply correctly? (Cf. the first half of the 'major objection' above.)

Proceeding as it does in the virtue- and vice-related terms, the discussion thereby, inevitably, also contains claims about what is worthwhile, serious and important, good and evil, in our lives. So, for example, I claimed that parenthood is intrinsically worthwhile, and that having a good time was a worthless end (in life, not on individual occasions); that losing a foetus is always a serious matter (albeit not a tragedy in itself in the first trimester) whereas acquiring an appendectomy scar is a trivial one; that (human) death is an evil. Once again, these are difficult matters, and anyone might challenge any one of my claims. But what is at issue is, as before, should those difficult claims be there or can one reach practical conclusions about real moral issues that are in no way determined by premises about such matters? (Cf. the fifth criticism, and the second half of the 'major criticism'.)

The discussion also thereby, inevitably, contains claims about what life is like (e.g., my claim that love and friendship do not survive their parties' constantly insisting on their rights; or the claim that to demand perfection of life is to run the risk of missing out on happiness entirely). What is at issue is, should those disputable claims be there, or is our knowledge (or are our false opinions) about what life is like irrelevant to our understanding of real moral issues? (Cf. both halves of the 'major criticism'.)

Naturally, my own view is that all these concepts should be there in any discussion of real moral issues and that virtue theory, which uses all of them, is the right theory to apply to them. I do not pretend to have shown this. I realize that proponents of rival theories may say that, now that they have understood how virtue theory uses the range of concepts it draws on, they are more convinced than ever that such concepts should not figure in an adequate normative theory, because they are sectarian, or vague, or too particular, or improperly anthropocentric, and reinstate what I called the 'major criticism'. Or, finding many of the details of the discussion appropriate, they may agree that many, perhaps even all, of the concepts should figure, but argue that virtue theory gives an inaccurate account of the way the concepts fit together (and indeed of the concepts themselves) and that another theory provides a better account; that would be interesting to see. Moreover, I admitted that there were at least two problems for virtue theory: that it has to argue against moral scepticism, 'pluralism', and cultural relativism, and that it has to find something to say about conflicting requirements of different virtues. Proponents of rival theories might argue that their favoured theory provides better solutions to these problems than virtue theory can. Indeed, they might criticize virtue theory for finding problems here at all. Anyone who argued for at least one of moral scepticism, 'pluralism', or cultural relativism could presumably do so (provided their favoured theory does not find a similar problem); and a utilitarian might say that benevolence is the only virtue and hence that virtue theory errs when it discusses even apparent conflicts between the requirements of benevolence and some other character trait such as honesty.

Defending virtue theory against all possible, or even likely, criticisms of it would be a lifelong task. As I said at the outset, in this article I aimed to defend the theory against some criticisms which I thought arose from an inadequate understanding of it, and to improve that understanding. If I have succeeded, we may hope for more comprehending criticisms of virtue theory than have appeared hitherto.

Acknowledgements

Versions of this article have been read to philosophy societies at University College, London, Rutgers University, and the Universities of Dundee, Edinburgh, Oxford, Swansea, and California-San Diego; at a conference of the Polish and British Academies in Cracow in 1988 on 'Life, Death and the Law', and as a symposium paper at the Pacific Division of the American Philosophical Association in 1989. I am grateful to the many people who contributed to the discussions of it on these occasions, and particularly to Philippa Foot and Anne Jaap Jacobson for private discussion.

References

Diamond, C. 1982. 'Anything But Argument?', *Philosophical Investigations* 5: 23–41.

Foot, P. 1977. 'Euthanasia', *Philosophy & Public Affairs* 6(2): 85–112.

Hursthouse, R. 1987. *Beginning Lives*. Oxford: Blackwell.

Hursthouse, R. 1995. 'Applying Virtue Ethics'. In R. Hursthouse, G. Lawrence, and W. Quinn (eds), *Virtues and Reasons: Philippa Foot and Moral Theory, Essays in Honor of Philippa Foot*. Oxford: Clarendon Press: 57–75.

McDowell, J. 1980. 'The Role of Eudaimonia in Aristotle's Ethics'. In A. Rorty (ed.), *Essays on Aristotle's Ethics*. Berkeley and Los Angeles: University of California Press: 359–76.

O'Neill, O. 1980. 'Review of Stephen Clark's *The Moral Status of Animals*', *Journal of Philosophy* 77: 440–46.

Rasmussen, D. 1990. 'Liberalism and Natural End Ethics', *American Philosophical Quarterly* 27: 153–61.

Smart, J. J. C. and B. Williams. 1973. *Utilitarianism: For and Against*. Cambridge: Cambridge University Press.

Thomson, J. J. 1971. 'A Defense of Abortion', *Philosophy & Public Affairs* 1(1): 47–66.

Warren, M. A. 1973. 'On the Moral and Legal Status of Abortion', *Monist* 57: 43–61.

Williams, B. 1985. *Ethics and the Limits of Philosophy*. London: Collins.

7
Are the Virtues the Proper Starting Point for Morality?

An instructive way to trace the rise of modern virtue ethics is through the successive editions of Beauchamp and Childress's *Principles of Biomedical Ethics*. The first edition (1979) perfectly reflects the contemporary state of play—biomedical issues have been under discussion for some time and although many of the utilitarians and deontologists who have been writing about them remain implacably opposed, some have benefited from reading each other and begun to think that they have enough common ground regarding rules and principles to make progress together. The book is mostly about these rules and principles and how they are to be applied to issues in biomedical ethics. Virtue ethics is not mentioned and 'virtues' (not 'virtue') has just four entries in the index, all of which refer to a very brief section in Chapter 8 on 'Virtues and Character'.

The second edition (1983) is not very different but the third (1989) is strikingly so. Now 'virtue' is in the index, and only a couple of its fifteen entries refer to the greatly expanded section on 'Virtues and Character'. In the fourth (1994), the real sea change occurs. Much of that expanded section now appears, not in the 'Here are some other important bits and pieces', Chapter 8, but in the major early chapter on 'Types of Ethical Theory'.

The fourth (and fifth) editions might well be said to reflect the state of play as it still is now—viewed that is, from the perspective of many consequentialists and deontologists. As moderately anti-virtue ethicists, they claim that 'what we need' (for a complete ethical theory) is an ethics of virtue *and* an ethics of rules, since (a) the concept of virtue is 'irreducible' (hence the need for an ethics of virtue), but (b) an ethics of virtue cannot provide action-guidance and hence must be supplemented by an ethics of rules such as consequentialists and deontologists provide. Less moderate opponents of virtue ethics, agreeing with (b), deny (a) and aim to give an account of the virtues in terms of their favoured normative approach. This is now called 'virtue *theory*' as distinct from 'virtue *ethics*'.

Virtue ethicists, naturally, support (a) and deny (b). Their positions on the two are related, for many of the criticisms of virtue ethics as a normative approach are, virtue ethicists maintain, based on an inadequate account of what a virtue is. Most contemporary virtue ethicists acquire their concept of virtue from Aristotle and hang on to it. Many contemporary consequentialists and deontologists do not, and hence the virtue theories they produce are, from the virtue ethical point of view, quite inadequate. I think myself that this is, at least in part, because they are working within a reductivist framework which I want to dismantle before continuing.

1. Against the Rawlsian Framework

One explanation of why the first supporters of virtue ethics had such a hard time getting their audience to hear their claim that virtue ethics really did offer a third type of normative approach is the exceptionally pervasive—and deleterious—influence of Rawls's *A Theory of Justice* (1971).

According to Rawls, as is well known, there are just two types of ethical theory: deontology is an example of one, utilitarianism of the other. The reason why there are just two types is that there are just two 'main concepts' or 'basic notions' in ethics, the 'right' and the 'good', and the differentiating structures of the two types are (largely) determined by how they define and connect these two. Might one not have expected to read that *virtue* was a third (albeit recently neglected) main concept in ethics? Well, the word 'virtue' does not even appear in Rawls's index, but a sentence sweeps the thought away— the concept of a 'morally worthy person', Rawls believes, is derived from the other two.

If only Rawls had said nothing about Aristotle, the first supporters of virtue ethics might have had an easier time. After all, a lot of people in their audience had not read Aristotle and might have been receptive to the unsurprising idea that three great moral philosophers of the Western tradition, namely Aristotle, Kant, and Mill could each inspire a distinctive type of normative ethical approach that was worth considering, giving us three rather than two. But alas, Rawls did say a bit about Aristotle, suggesting that he is, not a utilitarian, but in the same camp—a 'teleologist' (or, as we would now say, a 'consequentialist') committed to a maximizing principle. This was simply an unfortunate howler, but to this day one hears consequentialists saying to virtue ethicists: 'Surely the virtuous agent must aim at maximizing virtue (or virtuous action or *eudaimonia*) because that is what your theory maintains is the good.'

Rawls himself asserts the attractively simple slogan that 'teleological' theories define the right in terms of the good but did not commit himself to a parallel one for deontological theories. However, his many followers quickly supplied one, and several other pairs as well. And so we get such claims as: 'Utilitarianism defines the right in terms of the good and deontology defines the good in terms of the right'; 'Utilitarianism begins with the good and derives the right, whereas deontology begins with the right and derives the good'; 'The basic/most important concept in utilitarianism is that of the good, whereas in deontology it is that of the right.' Belief in the truth of such slogans made it well nigh impossible to recognize that virtue ethics could be a third, distinctive approach. For surely it would have to opt for the good or the right and hence align itself with one of the two established approaches? After all, its only alternative is to derive both the good and the right from the concept of virtue, and that is obviously an impossible task.

But the slogans should be dismissed as nonsense, not merely because they block getting virtue ethics off the ground, but because, as I have argued elsewhere (Hursthouse 1999), they seriously distort deontology and utilitarianism too. It would, for instance, be a travesty of Kant to describe him as 'taking the good as his basic concept' on the grounds that he attaches such importance to the good will. But any such crudity would be a travesty of any great moral philosopher. The important thing to do with them is not to look for their 'basic' concept (especially not if it is settled in advance that this must be one of the good, the right, or virtue), but to understand what they say about a whole host of concepts relevant to moral philosophy, including what they say about how those concepts connect and knit together.

It is noteworthy that the new wave of Kantian interpretation places much more emphasis on *connecting* what Kant has to say about virtue with what he has to say about the good will and the kingdom of ends than on trying to define virtue in 'more basic' terms. Unfortunately, other deontologists, and most consequentialists, are still working within the confines of the Rawlsian reductivist slogans, aiming for derivations rather than connections—and demanding that virtue ethics do the same. But no virtue ethicist remotely inspired by Aristotle aims for the reduction of significant moral concepts to others. On the contrary, we seek acknowledgement of a much larger number than is common—not only *good* in contexts other than those pertaining to consequences, but also *evil* and *harm*, the *worthwhile*, the *advantageous*, the *pleasant*, the *important*, the *necessary*. We are not even, as I shall argue later, out to reduce or derive the concept of the right.

2. The Aristotelian Concept of Virtue

What of those who are still seeking to derive the concept of virtue? Well, there are, I suppose, stricter and looser derivations, but the concept of virtue we acquire from Aristotle is rich, far too rich one suspects, to emerge in all its required complexity from anything that could be described as a derivation from one or two abstract concepts. As Julia Annas has argued (2006), what we tend to get in the non-virtue ethical virtue theories are 'reduced' accounts of virtue which simply leave out important features of the classical account.

The full Aristotelian concept of virtue is the concept of a complex character trait, that is, a disposition that is well entrenched in its possessor and, as we say, 'goes all the way down'. The disposition, far from being a single-track disposition to do, say, honest actions, or even honest actions for certain reasons, is multi-track, involving many other actions as well: desires, emotions and emotional reactions, perceptions, attitudes, interests, and expectations. This is because your virtues (and your vices) are a matter of what sort of adult you are, and involve, most particularly, your values—what you regard as worth pursuing or preserving or doing and what you regard as not so. Christine Swanton encapsulates this complexity by describing a virtue as a disposition 'to respond to, or acknowledge, items within its field' (2003: 19) and emphasizing the plurality of 'kinds of responsiveness'.

Anti-virtue ethicists typically pay lip service to the idea that virtues (and vices) are complex character traits, but it is often the case that, when they are arguing against virtue ethics, they forget this fact. Brad Hooker (2002) thinks my 'naturalism' will have the distasteful consequence that homosexuality is a vice; my response, in brief, is that homosexuality, like heterosexuality, is *not* a character trait, and hence not the sort of thing that even gets into the running for being assessed as a virtue or a vice. I appeal to the following fact: that if all I know about a man is that he is heterosexual, I know *nothing* about his character—about what he typically does, for what reasons, about whether he loves women or hates them, is disgusted by heterosexual intercourse or revels in it, about his values or what he counts as worth pursuing or preserving—at all. He might be licentious or temperate, violent or gentle, cruel or compassionate, wise or foolish, and so on. And, to the unprejudiced, the same (*mutatis mutandis*) is obviously true if all I know about him is that he is homosexual.

By the same token, I take it as obvious that water phobia is not a character flaw, whereas Julia Driver takes it as obvious that it is. As before, it seems to me that, if all I know about a man is that he has a water phobia, I know nothing about his character, for well or ill, at all. He might be kind or cruel, just or unjust, honest or dishonest, courageous or cowardly, wise or foolish. All I know about him, *ex hypothesi*, is that if he gets into water, he freezes and is likely to drown, which isn't even a disposition to action.

Given that the virtuous disposition is multi-track, no virtue ethicist would dream of making 'the fundamental attribution error' and ascribing honesty or charity to someone on the basis of a single honest or charitable action or even a series of them. Quite aside from anything else, well-brought-up adolescents will behave thus, and in some sense, for the right sorts of reasons, but we do not attribute the Aristotelian concept of virtue until we have some grounds for supposing that the agent has made the reasons she has been taught her own.

When we bear in mind that an agent with a particular virtue (or vice), V, reasons to action in a characteristic way, we recognize that the result may well not be what we would call a V action. For example, recognizing a proposed end as worthless, the courageous agent may well avoid danger as carefully as the coward, while the reckless plunge ahead. Another common mistake is to think only in terms of a thin disposition to V acts.

Driver (2001) has made much of the 'virtues of ignorance', but it seems to me that she has slipped into regarding the 'virtues' in question as no more than such thin dispositions. If we think seriously about the way her V agents reason, her virtues of ignorance turn out not be virtues even by her own lights (i.e. more conducive than not to the good).

According to Driver, the 'modest' agent underestimates her own worth and is thereby disposed to 'modest' actions such as not bragging and giving up her share of scarce goods to those she believes are more deserving than her, both of which are conducive to the good. But is that all that someone who underestimates herself typically does? Aristotle's diagnostic of the 'small-souled' man, who 'thinks himself worthy of lesser things than he is worthy of' is no less accurate than Driver's—'these people abstain from noble actions and projects' as well as from external goods, 'because they feel unworthy of them'. In praising modesty as both charming and conducive to the good, Driver must surely have overlooked the fact that her modest person is the one who will never volunteer to do the difficult and responsible jobs and who resists taking them on even when her turn is well overdue, saying: 'I can't, I'm no good at that sort of thing, I'll only make a mess of it.' She speaks with perfect sincerity, but, *ex hypothesi*, what she says is not true and everyone resents her resistance, especially if it is successful and the job has to fall on the shoulders of someone who doesn't do it as well as she could have, none of which conduces to the good at all.

This is not to deny the common-sense view that modesty is a virtue. It is, rather, to insist on the Aristotelian view (supported incidentally by the *Oxford*

English Dictionary) that modesty involves correctly estimating oneself as moderately worthy.

Driver similarly overlooks, in my view, the obvious ways in which the 'blind charity' possessed by Jane Bennett in *Pride and Prejudice* will fail to conduce to the good. Jane is indeed an exceptionally sweet-natured young woman, and her sister Elizabeth needs to emulate her 'wish not be hasty in censuring anyone', which the sharp-eyed, sharp-tongued Elizabeth still actually enjoys. But it is significant that she is *young*, with older people to care for her and no one yet in her care. If she is not to become a disastrously irresponsible parent, she had better acquire some of Elizabeth's eye for what is bad in people.

Driver wants to reject a feature of the Aristotelian concept of virtue that I have not yet made explicit, namely the point that the virtuous (excellent) person's practical reasoning is itself excellent; she gets things right. What makes someone excellent in practical reasoning is the excellence (virtue) of *phronēsis* or practical wisdom, which is inseparable from the full version of any of the other virtues. The introduction of *phronēsis* is sometimes thought to bring with it not only the idea that virtue is rare, but further that it is guaranteed to be limited to the intellectually sophisticated. It is true that, when talking about moral knowledge (and *phronēsis* is a form of moral knowledge), most philosophers find it hard to avoid talking as though they believed that it could only be acquired by studying academic philosophy; it's an occupational hazard we tend to share whatever our favoured theory. But practical wisdom is certainly not supposed to be something that only the intellectually sophisticated can acquire. You cannot possess the virtue of courage without a correct grasp of which goals or ends are worth pursuing or preserving and in what circumstances, and accordingly reasoning with a view to such ends. (Risking your life for a worthless and trivial end is not courageous, but reckless.) But recognizing that risking your life by donating a kidney may well be worthwhile, whereas risking it to have your body sculpted into a sexier shape is not, seems to be the sort of thing that any ordinary grown up is capable of.

As I said above, an agent with a particular virtue, V, reasons to action in a characteristic way. The requirement of *phronēsis* as part of virtue embodies the idea that an agent who does not do such reasoning tolerably well cannot be said to have the virtue in question.

We appeal to the norm of practical wisdom when we say such things as 'She should have known, realized, recognized, appreciated that...', and we don't say that about the recondite. It comes up, for instance, in relation to the cases where we recognize good intentions but deplore their outcome. We don't usually criticize small children when, trying to help without being asked for the first time, they smash some of the best china. They don't know some china is better than others and they don't know they are clumsy, and we don't expect them to. But we do expect clumsy adults to have noticed that they are clumsy and that this is something that they must take into account in their practical reasoning if they are to avoid distressing other people. When, without asking or telling you, they do the washing up 'because you looked so tired', and, inevitably, smash the irreplaceable teapot lid and thereby ruin the whole teaset, you can reasonably complain that they should have recognized they were quite likely to break something you cherished and should have appreciated that it would be considerate to ask you so that you had a chance to say, 'Oh yes, the dirty saucepans please, but not the teapot because it's part of the set I had from my mother.'

So to give up on *phronēsis* as requisite for virtue is to give up the notion of culpable ignorance, leaving us with nothing to say in criticism of the mature Jane when, unwilling to censure, she leaves her daughter in the hands of her uncle despite her knowledge that he is a twice-convicted child molester, or entrusts her health to a notoriously incompetent doctor. And we lose more than the notion of culpable ignorance.

We noted above that the Aristotelian concept of virtue is the concept of a character trait that involves actions *and* feelings, and any account of virtue that does not depart too far from Aristotle preserves his distinction between *enkrateia*, continence or strength of will, and virtue. 'Virtuous conduct gives pleasure to the lover of virtue' (*Nicomachean Ethics* 1099a12) because reason and inclination/desire are in harmony in such a person; they characteristically do what is virtuous desiring to do it. (Characteristically, but not invariably; see Hursthouse 1999: 92–8.)

We should be clear about why, within the Aristotelian tradition, the distinction is important. It is not just that the enkratic might be less reliable in action, or that the world would be a cheerier place if it contained agents' good feelings about their right actions as well as the actions, but that the enkratic are still imperfect in practical rationality. The Aristotelian view of human nature is that, *qua* rational, it can be perfected by getting our inclinations into harmony with our reason. If my inclinations are not in harmony with my reason, and if getting them into harmony is something that human rationality can achieve, then the people whose inclinations are in harmony are, *ceteris paribus*, better human beings, closer to excellence (virtue), than I am.

Given that we are, by nature, rational animals, I do not see how one can maintain that someone who has a failing in human rationality that pertains to their character may still possess full virtue, without abandoning the idea that virtue is *excellence*. As I understand her, this is something that Driver is not only willing but eager to do. But abandoning this idea is very serious indeed, because it is to abandon the idea of virtue as an ideal—something for us to strive to attain in our own lives, and hope to see more closely attained by our children and in better societies than our own. That full justice and charity—justice and charity that bring the emotions into complete harmony with reason—are probably well nigh impossible to achieve if one has been brought up in a racist society is a reason (amongst others) for lamenting the state of society at the time, not a reason for allowing or encouraging those who have done their best within it to congratulate themselves with the thought that no one could be better than they are.

We need not deny that 'virtue', in modern parlance, is a threshold concept (Swanton 2003: 24). (Perhaps even 'excellence' is. After all, we say A- [or perhaps A] to A+ on our students' essays means 'Excellent'.) If someone gets over the threshold then they certainly are not vicious. But grammatically, 'virtue', and the terms for the individual virtues, accept a whole range of qualifications—'quite V, admirably V, for his age/for her time/in his society/given her disadvantages'—where the qualifications enable us both to give credit where credit is due but also to register the point that the ideal standard has not yet been met. Giving due credit to people such as Huck Finn or the supportive husbands of the Victorian suffragettes (who, like their wives, remained blindly indifferent to their exploitation of working-class women) is one thing; giving up on the idea that human beings can be better is another thing entirely.

The mention of excellence in practical reasoning brings us not to the full doctrine of the unity of the virtues (according to which you cannot possess one virtue without possessing them all), but to some limited version of it. This is the idea that at least the major or 'core' virtues are not isolable dispositions, but are interconnected by the characteristic reasoning each involves. One's own life is usually worth preserving, the good of others is usually worth pursuing and preserving, and the latter is, sometimes, truly worth risking or even sacrificing the former for. So someone who is courageous cannot be callous but must be at least well on the way to being benevolent or charitable—how can she not be, if she is prepared to lay down her life for others? Charity or benevolence requires a correct conception of what is beneficial (and harmful) to human beings. What is truly beneficial to them is, quite often, hearing the truth, or the truth's being told. So if someone is benevolent or charitable he must be at least on the way to being honest—at the very least, he cannot be someone who just tells lies or conceals the truth to suit himself. How could he be if he is prepared to go out of his way in truthfulness for the sake of others? And if someone is honest, they cannot lack courage in every way. They may be honest and a physical coward, but they cannot be honest without having 'the courage of their convictions', as we say, and someone quite incapable of defending others in physical ways may still boldly tell the truth in their defence in full knowledge of the fact that doing so is a death warrant.

This limited unity, governed by the norm of *phronēsis* as necessary for full virtue, makes it much harder than Driver supposes to say, without careful qualification, that virtuous people may act wrongly precisely because of their virtue. If I can't bring myself to kill the bird my cat has mauled and am thereby forced to leave it to perish miserably, I should be berating myself for my squeamishness, not congratulating myself on my compassion. It may well be that the perfect harmony Aristotle envisages is not in fact possible for human nature, that those who are capable of 'tough love' are inevitably thereby less capable of tender sympathy and vice versa. That is still not a reason for lowering the standard and giving up on the idea that if I could—as perhaps I can—make myself just a bit tougher or a bit more tender I would be better, and so should try.

3. Right Action

How then is this Aristotelian concept of virtue related to the concept of right action?

During the 1980s, virtue ethics seemed vulnerable to 'the application problem', the objection that it can't provide action guidance or be applied and is hence unable to do what a normative ethical theory is pre-eminently supposed to do. The objection was based on the premise that the only guidance virtue ethics could come up with was that you should do what the virtuous agent would do in the circumstances and it is true that the earlier virtue ethics literature offered little more. The stress on 'in the circumstances' went hand in hand with the same literature's professed scorn for the very idea of ethical choices or conduct as rule-guided or rule-governed. And this made it not at all implausible to believe that virtue ethics simply could not get off the ground as a normative theory. When, anxious to make the right moral decision, I turn to it, what does it tell me to do? Apparently, to find a virtuous person and ask them what they would do in my circumstances. But suppose I can't, or not soon enough? Then it seems I am left with nothing. Or suppose I think I can, and they say 'I would do so and so.' It would surely be reasonable for me to ask 'Why?' and, unfortunately, much of the available virtue ethics literature suggested that the only answer I would receive would be, 'My *phronēsis* (practical wisdom) enables me to perceive that so and so would be the virtuous thing to do in the circumstances.' At which point it might occur to me that anyone sufficiently confident, whether virtuous or corrupt but self-righteous, could give me that answer, and hence that if virtue ethics could not tell me how to identify a virtuous person, its telling me to find and ask one was no guidance at all. ('How do I get to Amarillo?' 'Find the right road and follow it.')

I realized that there was an obvious way to elaborate on 'The right action is what a virtuous person would do (in the circumstances)' which completely blocked this form of the application problem. By and large, we do not need to find a virtuous agent, because in one way, we know what she does and would do. She does, and would do, what is virtuous, not vicious; that is, she does what is courageous, just, honest, charitable, loyal, kind, generous—and does not do what is cowardly or reckless, unjust, dishonest, uncharitable, malevolent, disloyal, unkind, stingy. So each virtue generates a prescription—'Do what is courageous, just, etc.'—and every vice a prohibition—'Do not do what is cowardly or reckless, unjust, etc.'—and in order to do what the virtuous agent would do in the circumstances, one acts in accordance with these, which I have called 'v-rules'. And so I committed myself to the view that 'An action is right iff it is what a virtuous agent would, characteristically (i.e. acting in character), do in the circumstances', and triumphantly pointed out that, contrary to the premise that virtue ethics did not offer any action-guiding rules or principles, it thereby came up with an impressively long and helpful list: the v-rules.

It seems to me that, in the specific context of the application problem, the most interesting aspect of this view is not the biconditional itself but the discovery of the v-rules. The existence of these, expressed in the vocabulary of the virtues and vices, refutes (literally) the premise on which the objection was based.

Naturally, the v-rules have been criticized, but the standard criticisms fall foul of obvious *tu quoque* responses. Of course, the requirements of the different virtues may, at least apparently, conflict. Honesty points to telling the hurtful truth, kindness or compassion to remaining silent or even lying. But so too do the related deontologists' and rule-consequentialists' rules, rightly reflecting the fact (ignored by the old act utilitarians) that life does present us with dilemmas whose resolution, even if correct, should leave us with a remainder of regret. Like the other two approaches, virtue ethics seeks resolutions of such conflicts in a more refined or nuanced understanding or application of the rules involved; and as with the other approaches, its proponents may disagree about the correct resolution.

Perhaps over-impressed by MacIntyre's early work (1981; but see his 1999 for a very different account), critics of virtue ethics have commonly asserted that the v-rules are inherently culturally specific and conservative because they are developed within existing traditions and societies. Virtue ethicists may take heart from the empirical fact of the Virtues Project (go to www.virtuesproject.com), an international educational programme based on 52(!) virtues found to be common to seven of the world's cultural traditions, which has been translated into numerous languages and successfully used in schools all over the world. At a more theoretical level, virtue ethicists are amused by the implicit assumption that what their opponents find 'reasonable' or 'rationally acceptable' is not shaped by modern Western culture and (predominantly) American society, and ask their rivals to join them in admitting that none of us has reason to suppose that our lists of rules are complete or beyond revision. And we all share 'the justification problem', that is, the problem of finding ways to validate whatever list we have come up with so far.

However, virtue ethicists do point out that their list of rules is remarkably long in comparison with any that their rivals have produced, and grows naturally (albeit within our own culture) as people's experience of modern life contributes new terms. This is perhaps particularly noticeable with respect to rules couched in terms that connote, if not strictly, vices, at least ways of falling seriously short of virtue. And they appeal to their list to rebut the charge that the guidance they offer is less specific than that provided by others. 'Tell the truth', even if filled out to provide plausible answers to 'All of it? Always? To anyone?' is still much less specific than what is yielded by 'Do what is honest', 'Do not do what is disingenuous, rude, insensitive, spiteful, hypocritical, untrustworthy, treacherous, phony, sneaky, manipulative...'.

The claim is that these provide better action-guidance than the sorts of rules that deontologists and rule-consequentialists come up with (because there are so many more and they are so much more specific and subtly nuanced), and better action-guidance than straight act utilitarianism, which notoriously prescribes far too many hair-raisingly wrong actions. It is this claim, rather than the biconditional itself, which is the denial of (b) above, namely that we need an 'ethics of rules' (by which is meant rules that are not expressed in virtue and vice terms). To establish (b), you have to argue against the claimed adequacy of the v-rules in general, which, as far as I know, no one has attempted to do, not just find fault with the biconditional itself. (Merely pointing to the inadequacy (which I admit) of 'Do what is just/do not do what is unjust' will not suffice, for it too is open to the *tu quoque* response.)

But what of the biconditional? Well, what is the point of any simple biconditional with 'An action is right iff...' on the left-hand side? It is only within the reductive Rawlsian framework that it is taken to offer a definition or derivation of 'the right' in relation to just one other concept which appears on the right-hand side. As I noted above, though this may, perhaps, be a plausible way of taking the biconditional that captures the crudest form of act utilitarianism, it will not do justice to one that captures deontology. I originally described all of them as 'forging a link' between the concept of right action and the concept that appeared on the right-hand side and that still seems to me much better. For what we should all recognize, regardless of our allegiance to one normative approach or another, is that we employ the concept of right action in a variety of ways; it is essentially linked to a number of concepts and those to others. What will distinguish our approaches most clearly is which concept—if indeed any one—we take as our entry point and focus, and how, starting where we do, we treat the others. Virtue ethics starts with the concept of the virtuous agent; let us look at some of the other concepts right action is (somehow) linked to.

One is the concept of right decision. (Morally) right decisions are what normative ethical theories are supposed to help or enable us to come up with; that is what action-guidance is all about. They do so by giving some account or specification of right action, for, platitudinously, right action is that at which good decision-making is aimed. When the decision is correct, and moreover comes off—when the agent succeeds in doing what she intended to do—we get right action.

Or rather, that is what we characteristically get. Resolvable dilemmas which present us with a forced choice between morally unpalatable alternatives show that the concept of right action has another link which may pull against right decision in such cases. *Right* as opposed to *wrong* action is the proper object of approval, the kind that merits praise rather than blame, and 'the satisfactory review of one's own conduct' rather than shame or regret on the part of the agent. But the right decision that correctly resolves an unpalatable dilemma results, if it comes off, in an action that apparently calls for justification and regret rather than meriting praise or pride.

What are we to say about this? My biconditional, rather felicitously I thought, directed us to say that, in some cases, the action, though the outcome of a right decision, was not right, not what a virtuous agent would have done in the circumstances. All the cases have the feature that a virtuous agent would never have landed herself in those circumstances in the first place. If it is your own wrongdoing that has brought you to this pass, then resolving the dilemma correctly does not free you from blame and shame; the link between right action and right decision does not hold here.

However, I did not want to deny that agents, including the virtuous, could be faced with unpalatable dilemmas through no fault of their own, and thinking about how it would be when the virtuous resolved them correctly made me realize that there are two ways to read my biconditional which correspond to two ways in which we talk about right action. (If this makes the biconditional 'indeterminate', as Driver claims, the indeterminacy is a point in its favour, for it captures the corresponding indeterminacy of 'right action'.)

We often confidently say that an action was right regardless of the reasons why it was done (say Kant's shopkeeper). We have, after all, a strong interest in people doing what is honest, just, generous, charitable, or benevolent, etc.; to a large extent that's what keeps society ticking over and enables us to live together fairly pleasantly, and that—or those—purposes are served tolerably well even when a lot of people are doing what is right for the wrong reasons—out of fear of disapproval or the law, or because it suits them better than doing otherwise, or to curry favour or whatever. So a lot of the time we don't raise questions about the reasons for the action, just approve it as right and accept it as a truism that you do not have to be virtuous to do what is right.

But we may also think of what is right and merits approval in contexts relating to moral improvement—of ourselves, of our children, of the way too many doctors behave—and then we up the standard. In these contexts, assessing the actions by the standard of the virtuous agent—with her full panoply of not only right reasons but also right emotions—we frequently assess them not as wrong, but certainly not as deserving unqualified approval. Thinking of the virtuous agent as the one who sets the standard to which we should all aspire, we get a richer notion of 'what is done'. What you *do* does not count as right unless it is what the virtuous agent would *do*, say, 'tell the truth, after much painful thought, for the right reasons, feeling deep regret, having put in place all that can be done to support the person on the receiving end afterwards.' Only if you get all of that right are you entitled to the satisfactory review of your own conduct, and we want the children, and the insensitive arrogant doctors, and ourselves to grant that simply making the right decision, and telling the truth just wasn't good enough to merit approval.

In fact, in these and other contexts in which we are looking for, or hoping for, manifestations of virtue, we sometimes do reassess the actions as just plain wrong when the wrong reasons and/or the accompanying emotions turn out to be strikingly contrary to virtue. There I was, confident in assessing the plain-speaking of a colleague in a meeting as right, because honest—just the kind of straightforwardness we need in order to come to mutual decisions effectively and enable the department to run. And then I discover that the truth-teller is in fact usually evasive, manipulative, and plain mendacious in such meetings, and that his truth-telling on this occasion was motivated purely by spite, and I reassess it. 'The ratbag!' I say. 'What a rotten thing to do, to say that just to upset so and so.' And if you press me on whether his action wasn't, all the same, right in *some* way, because honest, I shall say (a) that it would have been right, because honest, coming from, for example, John, but (b) that it wasn't honest coming from him and he would have done better to hold his tongue.

So my biconditional works so far. But right action, insofar as it is the proper object of approval, cannot be terrible and horrible, and tragic dilemmas, which present the agent with a forced choice between terrible actions, sever the link between right action and the virtuous agent.

Driver (2002) suggested that one might insist that such actions *are* right, in this unusual context, and explain that 'there are good instrumental reasons to balk at calling the action "right" since that seems an honorific.' I am not sure whether her idea was that a virtue ethicist might do this, or that it would be the obvious consequentialist strategy, but either way, I think the suggestion is incoherent. The semantic fact is that 'right' *is* an honorific; I can't even *think* that such actions are right because they are so terrible. Some people thought I should have preserved my biconditional (for what purpose?) by claiming that, in the context of a tragic dilemma, the virtuous agent acts uncharacteristically. But that seemed to me manifestly false. It may be utterly characteristic of a virtuous agent that she resolves a tragic dilemma the way she does (if resolvable) or recognizes it as irresolvable if that's what it is, for such resolving, or recognition, may call on all her virtue and moral wisdom. It would also be utterly characteristic of her to recognize that what she has done is terrible and that her life can never be the same again now she has been forced to do this terrible thing.

The fact that the link is severed by tragic dilemmas, far from inclining me to give up the focus on the virtuous agent, seemed to me to harmonize perfectly with certain aspects of the classical Aristotelian account of virtue and its relation to *eudaimonia* (true happiness, or flourishing). What the virtuous agent is forced to do in a tragic dilemma is not an instance of that *acting well* or *good action* which makes up the *eudaimōn* life, the sort of thing that allows the agent to look back at the end of her life and say truly 'that was a *good* human life.' On the contrary, it is precisely the sort of action that, looking back, the virtuous agent rightly describes as having marred her life.

The action category of the terrible or 'intolerable' is, as Louden (1984) rightly noted, an important one. He thinks such actions (i) can be identified in deontological rules that mark off 'clear boundaries' and (ii) are limited to those which 'produce harm of such magnitude that they destroy the bonds of community and render...the achievement of moral goods impossible', but in my view this is a mistake on both counts (insofar as I understand the second). British, though not US, legal history, testifies to the fact that our attempts to capture in law precisely which cases of homicide—the really *wicked* ones—deserved capital punishment always foundered because they could not provide 'clear boundaries'; that is part of the reason we gave them up. They always had to resort to attempts to lay down what the gratuitously *callous* or *cruel* taking of human life was, attempting to specify the killing as something that, in the particular circumstances, only someone markedly callous or cruel would have done, never, ever, the even minimally virtuous. But that is not a deontological 'clear boundary'. It is a v-rule, and although these can be, as I have stressed, very specific and readily applicable, in difficult cases they could serve the purposes of law only if we were able to select our jurors on the basis of their *phronēsis*.

Moreover, even if a deontological rule could lay out precisely those conditions in which the taking of a human life was, in the circumstances, something that only a wicked person would do, all it would have captured is a type/kind of action that the virtuous would never, ever, do. I agree that the characteristic actions of the really wicked do in some sense strike at the foundations of our moral community. Perhaps, often, they produce striking amounts of unnecessary suffering too. But neither feature, I think, exhausts our concept of 'the terrible' in action. The intentional bringing about of the death of the adult nearest and dearest to you, the companion with whom you have shared much of your life, whose good has been your good, even if it is the right, unavoidable, decision, is terrible, horrible, notwithstanding the fact no one wicked would ever be in a position to do such a thing. Only the (at least fairly) virtuous think that such relationships are worth pursuing and preserving; only they thus give hostages to fortune and run the risk of having their lives marred by, tragically, having to destroy the one they hold most dear.

This is a way to map the terrain of 'the terrible' and 'the tragic'—which any adequate account of act appraisals should do—when you start with the concept of the virtuous agent. Let me turn, finally to the virtue ethics account of the distinction between 'the obligatory' and 'the supererogatory'.

Driver claims to find a deplorable indeterminacy in the phrase 'what the virtuous agent would do *in the circumstances*'. Have I not left it fatally unclear whether 'real character flaws' are included in the circumstances? Well I haven't—as Driver herself works out, if you include *real* character flaws such as cowardice in the circumstances, the account becomes incoherent. In fact it is this very distinction—between the circumstances (which of course do not include character flaws) and the character flaws themselves—that Foot— and following her, I—rely on in giving an account of the supererogatory.

Foot (1978) discusses two apparently clashing intuitions we have: on the one hand, 'the harder it is for a man to act virtuously the more virtue he shows if he acts well' (usually identified with Kant) and, on the other, 'the harder it is for a man to act virtuously, the less virtue he shows if he acts well' (usually associated with Aristotle). Foot brilliantly extracts this clash from the mire in which the Kantian/Aristotelian debate has obscured it and argues that the intuitions do not clash but simply pertain to different cases.

If what makes it hard (on a particular occasion) for an agent to act virtuously is the *circumstances*, then the more virtue he shows if he acts well—as the first intuition had it. But: if what makes it hard (on a particular occasion) for an agent to act virtuously is (not the circumstances but) a flaw or imperfection of his character, then the less virtue he shows if he acts well—as the second intuition had it. So if what makes it 'hard for me' to restore the full purse I saw someone drop is that I am strongly tempted to pocket it and have to conquer the temptation, then what makes it hard for me is an imperfection in my honesty; I am less than thoroughly honest in character and morally inferior to someone who hastens to restore it with no thought of keeping what is not theirs. But there are at least two different sorts of *circumstances* in which the thoroughly honest agent hastens to return the purse with no thought of keeping it. One is that in which she is comfortably off, the other is that in which she is poor. In the former case, it is easy for her to return it; her honesty is not, as Foot puts it, 'severely tested', and what she does, though good and right, is not, given the circumstances, strikingly admirable. However, in the latter case, it is hard for the agent to restore the purse—hard insofar as she is hardily circumstanced—and her honesty is severely tested. If it comes through, and she still restores it with no thought of doing otherwise, what she does is strikingly admirable.

And this distinction, between right action where virtue is not severely tested and right action where virtue *is* severely tested and comes through, is the virtue ethics account of the distinction between 'the obligatory' and 'the supererogatory', a distinction that no adequate account of 'the right' can ignore.

No doubt someone will protest, 'But this isn't what your biconditional says. You are just adding things on.' But no approach's simple biconditional can say anything about the distinction between the obligatory and the supererogatory while the left-hand side is simply 'An action is right', since both the obligatory and the supererogatory are right. That is why it would be stupid to regard any such biconditional as giving a complete definition when 'right action' has these two different uses. My biconditional is consistent with both and, taking the virtuous agent as the starting point as Foot does, leads us easily into an extremely plausible account of each as qualified versions of the original. And this isn't 'just adding things on'. It's a test of the original that it passes with flying colours.

There are other significant uses of 'right action' that my simple biconditional does capture, which space does not permit me to discuss. Swanton's (2003) account, for instance, captures that use of 'right action' which disconnects it from praiseworthiness and Johnson (2003) identifies a very interesting use in the context of moral self-improvement. But none I have seen so far inclines me to give up the idea that, when we want to understand the concept of right action, the concept of the virtuous agent and thereby the virtues, should be our entry point and focus.

References

Annas, J. 2006. 'Virtue Ethics'. In D. Copp (ed.), *The Oxford Handbook of Ethical Theory*. Oxford: Oxford University Press: 515–36.

Beauchamp, T. L. and J. F. Childress. 1979, 1983, 1989, 1994, 2001. *Principles of Biomedical Ethics*. New York: Oxford University Press.

Driver, J. 2001. *Uneasy Virtue*. Cambridge: Cambridge University Press.

Driver, J. 2002. 'On Virtue Ethics (Book review)', *Philosophical Review* 111: 122–6.

Foot, P. 1978. 'Virtues and Vices'. In *Virtues and Vices and Other Essays in Moral Philosophy*. Oxford: Blackwell.

Hooker, B. 2002. 'The Collapse of Virtue Ethics', *Utilitas* 14: 22–40.

Hursthouse, R. 1999. *On Virtue Ethics*. Oxford: Oxford University Press.

Johnson, R. 2003. 'Virtue and Right', *Ethics* 113: 810–34.

Louden, R. B. 1984. 'On Some Vices of Virtue Ethics', *American Philosophical Quarterly* 21: 227–36.

MacIntyre, A. 1981. *After Virtue*. Notre Dame, IN: University of Notre Dame Press.

MacIntyre, A. 1999. *Dependent Rational Animals*. Chicago: Open Court.

Rawls, J. 1971. *A Theory of Justice*. Oxford: Clarendon Press.

Swanton, C. 2003. *Virtue Ethics: A Pluralistic View*. Oxford: Oxford University Press.

8
Discussing Dilemmas

Everyone interested in virtue ethics should reread 'Modern Moral Philosophy' at least once every five years. I made the mistake of not doing so about twenty years ago and thereby did Anscombe an injustice that I am happy to have the opportunity to rectify here. I am usually credited with the idea of the 'v-rules'—rules, such as 'Do what is honest', 'Do not do what is cruel', which provide action-guidance by employing the virtue and vice terms—and indeed, at the time I first wrote about them, I thought it was my idea. But of course it was not. All I had done was recall Anscombe's saying 'It would be a great improvement if, instead of "morally wrong", one always named a genus such as "untruthful", "unchaste", "unjust"',[1] and I had not reread 'Modern Moral Philosophy' sufficiently recently to recognize from whence my thought had come.

It is just as well that, instead of heeding her recommendation to *'banish... ethics totally* from our minds',[2] abandon moral philosophy as unprofitable, and concentrate instead on philosophy of psychology, some philosophers, most notably Foot, MacIntyre, and McDowell, went ahead with talking '(the way) Plato and Aristotle talk'[3] and brought modern virtue ethics into being. The emergence of virtue ethics, though it has not wiped the sort of moral philosophy Anscombe deplored right off the board, has certainly brought about a sea change in it. And contrary to her expectations, consideration of the concept of a virtue, rather than being something we progressed to only after getting a lot of philosophy of psychology sorted out, arrived with virtue ethics and generated a new interest in moral psychology. If we have not explored exactly the psychological concepts she mentioned, certainly work on those of character, emotion, desire, perception, and practical reasoning is widespread and exciting. In fact, looking back, one wonders why, instead of telling us to give up doing secular moral philosophy, she did not just tell us to go back to its roots and see what we could learn from Plato and Aristotle. It is

---

[1] G. E. M. Anscombe, 'Modern Moral Philosophy', in *Ethics, Religion and Politics: The Collected Papers of G. E. M. Anscombe: Volume III* (Minneapolis, MN: University of Minnesota Press, 1981), 33.
[2] Ibid., 38. [3] Ibid., 41.

particularly the modern concentration on the latter that has brought ethics and philosophy of psychology so close together, generated character and motive utilitarianism out of the act utilitarianism she condemned, turned Kantians toward Kant's *Doctrine of Virtue*, and informed Korsgaard's work on practical reason; things do not look anything like as bad in moral philosophy as they did fifty years ago.

Well, perhaps that is an overoptimistic remark. At the level of ethical theory, I think things look better. At the level of bioethics, it is more of a curate's egg; some bits are better but in some areas—particularly those addressing the new biotechnology—things look hair-raisingly worse. But I hope that this is in part because modern virtue ethics is still so new. It has taken the last twenty-five years to get it recognized as a viable normative ethical theory, and the business of actually applying it is only just beginning.[4] Moreover, applying it to real moral issues is very difficult.

Applying it involves, in part, considering *what a virtuous agent would do* in the circumstances at issue. And understanding 'a virtuous agent' to be one who has the virtues—such character traits as justice, compassion, temperance, and generosity—this often amounts to doing exactly what Anscombe recommended. Instead of talking about morally right and morally wrong actions, we talk about actions as just and unjust, compassionate and cruel, temperate and greedy, generous and grasping, employing the vocabulary of adjectives derived from the terms for the virtues and vices. And here, I want to reflect on some of the improvements that do indeed result from doing this when, in moral philosophy, we consider the problem of moral dilemmas.

'Modern Moral Philosophy' is particularly concerned with the consequentialist resolution of dilemmas, in which the agent's forced choice lies between doing something disgraceful or not doing it despite foreseeing that some very bad consequences will result. On the consequentialist approach, forestalling the bad consequences always wins out, and hence doing the disgraceful thing is described as the 'morally right' thing to do, no matter how unjust or dishonest or callous or disloyal... it may be. Anscombe attacks this approach on a variety of fronts but here I want to highlight just one.

It appears only in a footnote, but hearing her elaborate on it when I was young was very instructive and had a profound effect on me. She had come as a guest speaker to an Open University philosophy summer school, and in the

---

[4] Foot's paper on euthanasia and my own on abortion were, as far as I know, the only two 'virtue ethics' articles in bioethics for many years. The first collection of articles explicitly devoted to applying virtue ethics was published this year. Rebecca L. Walker and Philip J. Ivanhoe (eds), *Working Virtue* (Oxford: Clarendon Press, 2007).

discussion with the students afterwards she described a real life case. An old woman in Austria under Nazi rule had given shelter to some Jews in her attic, and one evening, there was the dreaded knock on the door and a young SS officer saying 'We believe you have some Jews here?' 'Clearly', said Anscombe, 'she must not lie.' And there was a long embarrassed silence because we all thought that obviously she must—that this was the 'morally right' thing to do—but did not dare to say so. And she let the pause continue, and then said 'Of course, she mustn't tell the truth either', and we were all greatly relieved, but also puzzled.

She went on to describe what the woman had in fact done; she had turned on a brilliant performance of pretending to believe that the young officer was her sister's son, whom she had not seen since he was a boy. 'Gustav!' she cried, 'how wonderful, come in, come in. How is dear Lotte, I haven't heard from her for so long, I never knew you had become an officer, how tall you have grown...!' And she kissed him and babbled on (never once telling a lie) and insisted he have coffee and cakes and, being young and well-mannered, he was too embarrassed to tell her she had made a mistake and press his official question. So he partook of the coffee and cakes and escaped as soon as he could.

Our initial reaction to Anscombe's saying 'She must not lie' and our puzzlement when she said 'Of course she mustn't tell the truth either' shows how right she is, in the footnote, to pinpoint 'the assumption that only two courses (of action) are open'[5] in a presented forced choice between evils as corrupt. One need not share her belief that lying is always a sin, nor her belief that God's Providence ensures that an agent will be confronted with a forced choice between forbidden acts only through previous wrongdoing of his own, to accept her point. I do not believe either, but I was shocked to realize that, even after she had said 'Of course, she mustn't tell the truth', it still did not occur to me to question the assumption. As I said, this had a profound effect on me. Ever since, I have borne the possibility in mind and never accept 'Well, there's nothing else for it, you/we will just have to do A or B dreadful as they are', however buttressed with exhortations to be 'practical' or 'realistic', without looking for a third possibility.

It is, I think significant, that one can prompt people to do the same if one presents dilemmas in a certain way. If one describes *what appears to be* a conflict situation, a forced choice between evils, as Anscombe did, and asks people 'What is the morally right thing to do here?' nearly everyone will quickly plump for one side or the other, and usually the side that

---

[5] Anscombe, 'Modern Moral Philosophy', 40n.

consequentialists would go for. But I have found that, against a certain background, one can prompt a different response by asking a different question.

One begins by talking a little about virtuous agents, the obvious truth that people who are just, honest, and compassionate characteristically *do* what is just, honest, and compassionate and not what is unjust, dishonest, or callous; one mentions the need for the practical wisdom that enables an agent 'to stretch a point on the circumference'[6] and apply such terms correctly in borderline cases. Then we describe what appears to be a conflict situation. And then instead of asking 'What is the morally right thing to do?' the question presented is 'What do you think a *virtuous agent* would do faced with such a situation?'

Instead of a prompt and usually consequentialist response, there is a puzzled silence, during which one can see people thinking 'Well she wouldn't do that because it's dishonest (and she has the virtue of honesty); but then she wouldn't do *that* because it's unjust, or callous or...' and finding themselves stymied. After a time, someone will assay an answer, but, again, it is different. It is, often, 'Well, she would look for a way to slip between the horns of the dilemma wouldn't she? I can't see what it would be, but with her practical wisdom, she could find something.'

And, as a response, that is surely a marked improvement on the quick plumping for one evil or the other, let alone the describing of it as 'the morally right thing to do'.

Of course, it is not always true that there is a way of slipping between the horns. Even God's Providence does not guarantee that the innocent will not be faced with agonizing forced choices, only that the choice will not lie between sin and sin. And a forced choice that is the result of one's own previous wrongdoing may well be one between sin and sin, with no third way available. And this brings me to the explicit consideration of the resolution of such dilemmas.

I shall claim that modern deontologists and consequentialists tend to present their resolutions in a corrupting way and that we can see how this comes about by reflecting on Anscombe's remarks about the use of 'morally ought' and, by implication 'morally right' in secular moral philosophy.

She claims, as I understand her, that, in secular moral philosophy, 'morally ought' is expected to play two roles at once. On the one hand, it is like 'the ordinary "ought"':[7] used in connection with a *moral* subject-matter: namely

[6] Ibid., 36.   [7] Ibid., 41.

that of human passions and (nontechnical) actions.[8] That is to say, it is used in sentences such as 'X ought (ought not) to f', or 'Such and such ought to be' which, on the analogy of 'owes', and 'needs' can truly be asserted on the basis of facts and, further, have no necessary connection with action. On the other hand, it is used in sentences such as 'X ought (ought not) to f' as if it had some necessary connection with action. It is supposed 'to have an influence on your actions',[9] a 'certain compelling force'.[10] And she claims that the latter use, deprived of a backing from divine law, is 'purely psychological',[11] having been stripped of all 'discernible content'.[12]

Her thought seems to be that, with a divine law backing, the two uses of 'morally ought' are intertwined. I say 'X ought to be done.' My grounds are that, the facts being thus and so, doing X is repaying a debt, or helping someone in need, or that not doing X in these circumstances would be, say, unjust or uncharitable, so I am saying that things are thus and so. But I am also saying that things being thus and so provides a compelling reason for doing X. How can I do the second? After all, it is a significant extra step, this move from 'Things are thus and so' to 'That they are thus and so is a compelling reason to . . .'. I can do it by appeal to divine law; injustice or failures in charity, I say, or failing to pay one's debts or help those in need, is forbidden, things you are required not to do, regardless of what you want. But secular modern moral philosophy cannot take that extra step—there is nowhere for it to go. So its use of 'morally ought' to give reasons and influence our actions has no discernible content; it is just hot air.

I can see why she should say that about Hare's use of 'morally ought', but it is not clear to me why she should say it of the consequentialists. I say 'X ought to be done.' My grounds are that, the facts being thus and so, doing X will have the best consequences; so I am saying that X will have the best consequences. And I am also saying that the fact that X will have the best consequences provides a compelling reason for doing X. How can I take that further step? By appealing to utilitarianism—consequences, I say, are the only things that matter morally.

We might want to say that that's not compelling in the way appeal to divine law is. But in what special way is divine law compelling? We cannot insist it is necessarily so, because Satan flouted it, and in what other way could it be special? One might say that the consequentialist claim is not compelling at all, but I do not think it can be denied that it is *intended* to be. As a consequentialist, I shall naturally claim that the truth that consequences are the only

---

[8] Ibid., 29.   [9] Ibid., 31.   [10] Ibid., 41.   [11] Ibid.   [12] Ibid.

thing that matter morally is one that anyone 'rational' enough to throw off the metaphysical superstructure of religion will recognize, and is not truth (or perhaps rationality?) compelling in the required way?

So I remain puzzled by Anscombe's claim that the act consequentialist's use of 'morally ought' has no discernible content. It seems to me that its content, though lamentable and entirely misguided, is discernible, and it amounts to the claim that only consequences matter.

Be that as it may, her distinction between the two uses of 'morally ought' is extremely valuable in the context of dilemmas because it can also be made with respect to 'morally right'. And this shows us that there is another reason to favour substituting the virtue and vice adjectives for 'morally right' and 'morally wrong' and talking, as Plato and Aristotle talk, about what the virtuous person would do.

Many modern moral philosophers aim to give an 'account' of right (wrong) action in terms of an action's 'right (wrong)-making properties'. (From now on, given we are in the context of moral philosophy, we can drop the 'morally' when it is clumsy.) An action's right-making properties would be, according to a deontological or rule utilitarian theory, such things as its being an instance of paying what one owed, saving someone's life, or telling the truth. Correspondingly, its wrong-making properties would be its being an instance of reneging on a debt, killing someone or letting them die, or telling a lie. In act utilitarianism, there is just one right-making property, namely the action's having better consequences than any available alternative, and correspondingly, just one wrong-making property. In the use that is not necessarily connected to our actions, 'X is morally right' is used to say 'X has at least such and such a property', that is, things are thus and so.

But morally right actions are, obviously, the sorts of actions that people serious about moral matters want to do, and in normative ethical theory, the account of right action is also intended to be action-guiding—to influence the actions of those who consult the theory. When the theory is applied, when it responds to the question 'What shall I do?' we have addressed to it (rather than to our bank manager or doctor or co-conspirator), the answer 'X is morally right' is used to say, not only that X has certain properties but also that the fact that X has, for example, the property of being an instance of telling the truth, or of producing the best consequences is a compelling reason to do it. Absent any countervailing reasons, applying the theory guides us to making right/correct moral decisions and, if we enact them successfully, to 'doing the right thing'.

Since the theories are supposed to be action-guiding, they are expected to resolve serious dilemmas. And their proponents usually go about producing such resolutions in the following way. They present the conflict situation—the forced choice between A and B, where A and B are both pretty bad. Then they ask the question 'What is the morally right thing to do in such a case, A or B?' Then they apply their theory, utilitarian or deontological, resolve the dilemma, and draw the conclusion that A, say, is *the morally right thing to do*. Full stop.

So are they telling me that if I follow the guidance and do A I can rest assured I have done the right thing? I can enjoy, as Hume puts it, that 'inward peace of mind' that arises from 'a satisfactory review of my own conduct'? Congratulate myself even? It seems they must be telling me this, but surely they should not be—what a corrupting idea. After all, what I do after I have correctly resolved a really serious dilemma is bound to be something pretty dreadful—left someone to die when it was within my power to save them, for example, or deceived an honest person who trusted me—and this is not the sort of thing we usually think of when told that someone (good for them) 'did the right thing'. Surely there was *something* bad or wrong about my doing A, even if the dilemma has been resolved correctly and A was indeed the only thing to do in the circumstances, because doing B would have been so much worse. But how so, if doing A was 'doing the morally right thing' without qualification?

When act utilitarians blithely assert that doing something dreadful is the right thing to do, we are not particularly surprised; that they are so often committed to such claims is the standard objection to the theory. But deontology and rule utilitarianism (whose proponents, in practice, frequently produce the same resolutions of serious dilemmas) are not supposed to be open to the same objection. So how does it come about that, when they resolve serious moral dilemmas, they too promote the corrupting idea that doing something which you know falls under at least one truly dreadful description is 'the morally right thing to do', without qualification?

It seems to me it has come about because they have failed to notice that, like 'morally ought', 'morally right' has two uses, and that, in the context of serious dilemmas, the two uses come apart.

When used to pick out a 'right-making feature' of an action, 'A is morally right' can often be used interchangeably with 'A is a good deed.' A is a good deed, in these circumstances, because, in these circumstances it has such and such a 'right-making feature' and no wrong-making ones. Such acts merit praise rather than blame; they are the sort of acts that we encourage each other to do, that virtuous agents typically do, that agents can be happy about doing and review with satisfaction. When used to give action-guidance 'A is morally right' can always be used interchangeably with 'I (you, we) have a compelling reason to do A' or 'Deciding to do A would be the correct moral decision.' And when A is a good deed, deciding to do A would be the correct moral decision because A has its right-making feature and no bad ones; in the circumstances, its right-making feature is a compelling reason to do A.

When we are talking about actions that are good deeds, the intertwined uses of 'morally right action' cause no problems. It does not matter whether I ask 'Which is the good deed, A or B?' or 'Which is the correct decision, to do A or to do B?' The action-guiding normative theory will tell me that owning up to a mistake rather than lying about it, or stopping to help the person who has dropped their shopping rather than pass him by is 'the morally right thing to do' and thereby say both that the first action, not the second has a right-making property which makes it a good deed, and also that deciding to do the first rather than the second is the correct moral decision. The two different uses go hand in hand.

But there are other cases in which this is not true and the two come apart. Consider a famous example of Peter Geach's. A feckless man seduces two women, A and B, promising each of them marriage, and makes both of them pregnant. Ashamed of what he has done, he now wants to 'do the right thing' and clear his conscience. But, in a way he cannot. Suppose his dilemma is resolvable, the evil of abandoning A being less than the evil of abandoning B (perhaps A is stronger and more independent and does not want him). Then there is a right, that is, a correct, moral decision to be made about which way to go. So let us suppose that he makes that right decision and carries it through. But a good deed will not result. It is still the case that, in marrying B, he has abandoned A and her child, and merits not praise but blame for having landed himself in the circumstances that forced him to do so. He has done the sort of thing that no virtuous man would do and he is in no position to view his own conduct with satisfaction.

Serious moral dilemmas—the sort of dilemmas regarding which normative ethical theory is supposed to provide action-guidance—are not dilemmas about which is the good deed to do. They *are* serious and we find them troubling precisely because they seem to present us with a forced choice between actions that are *not* good deeds but bad ones. But this all-important difference—on the one hand a choice between a good deed and a bad or indifferent one and, on the other, a forced choice between bad ones—is glossed over if one approaches the serious dilemmas by asking the question 'Which is the morally right thing to do here, A or B?' because the two uses of 'morally right' no longer coincide. We no longer have a trivially ambiguous question with one answer, but an importantly ambiguous one that calls for different answers according to how it is taken.

If we take the question as 'Which is the correct moral decision, to do A or to do B?' then, if the dilemmas is resolvable, the answer is, say, 'Deciding to do A is the correct moral decision.' But if we take the question as 'Which is the good deed, A or B', the answer is simply 'Neither.' And failing to make *that* clear is what is bad and corrupting in much of the contemporary discussion of moral dilemmas.

If we approach such dilemmas by asking 'What would a virtuous agent do?' we not only avoid coming up with the seriously misleading conclusion 'Such and such is the right thing to do', we also reap further advantages: a number of points naturally arise that are often overlooked.

As I have already noted, the question tends to prompt the thought that we should always begin by looking for a way of slipping between the horns of the dilemma, given that both sides of it are so unpalatable, and that is the first point. But, let us suppose that we have a dilemma where this is not so, and that, having thought about it, we have reached the conclusion that the virtuous agent would, regretfully, decide that she had to do A rather than B.

Does the philosophical discussion naturally end there, having resolved the dilemma? No, because as soon as we imagine a virtuous agent reaching this decision, we know we are imagining her doing something that goes against the grain. She has decided to do something that either falls straightforwardly under a vice description such as 'callous', cruel', 'dishonest', or, even if it does not, is simply not the sort of thing she would normally dream of doing. It is the sort of thing that the vicious characteristically do, not her. So, having reached the painful decision that it has to be done, she will not, typically, just barge ahead and do it. A may well be an action under a rather general description and there may be a number of actions A**, A***, A****, ... under different descriptions which will all count as doing A, some of which are worse than others. So, where appropriate, we are naturally led to reflect on whether there are ways of doing A that are not as bad as some other ways.

Now let us suppose further that we have found one, and think the virtuous agent would do A***. Again, the discussion does not stop there because it must be noted that the virtuous agent, whose emotions are in harmony with his reason, feels regret at having to do A***. As before, we cannot escape the fact that A*** even if not, say, callous is still not kind, if not plain dishonest at least disingenuous, and this obvious fact leads to a further application of our question. What does a virtuous agent do in those circumstances in which he has to do something he regrets? He does not feel remorse of course because, *ex hypothesi*, he was faced with the forced choice through no fault of his own and has made the correct decision—but does this mean that he shrugs off the regret as quickly as he can, saying to himself 'Oh well, I'm blameless, I couldn't do anything else'? No that is not, typically, what virtuous agents do in such circumstances. Landed with a bad job, they do not take the fact that it is not of their making and that they are blameless as a reason let alone an excuse for leaving it as it is. They look around for a way or ways to make the best of it. So, where appropriate, the consideration of what a virtuous agent would do in response to a particular forced choice is naturally lead to looking for a way, say C, to ameliorate the situation after A*** has been done. This generates the possibility of resolving the dilemma not simply by the blanket 'Deciding to do A is the correct decision' nor even 'A*** is the correct decision' but 'A*** *and* C are what should be done in these circumstances' (being what the virtuous agent would do).

And finally, thinking in terms of a virtuous agent, one who leads a life of virtuous activity, we are naturally led to thinking about what such an agent's attitude would be to serious dilemmas. Obviously, she will wish they did not come up, not merely because she does not want to be forced to do regrettable things herself but because she does not want anyone to be forced to do them nor anyone unscrupulous to have an excuse for doing them. Unpredictable misfortune may give rise to some serious dilemmas, predictable human frailty gives rise to others and we still do not know how to prevent them. But some are both predictable and could be averted and no virtuous agent would emerge from one of the latter without going on to give some thought to how it might be prevented from arising again. So, where appropriate, the philosophical discussion of a serious dilemma guided by a consideration of what a virtuous agent would do devotes attention to how we could prevent it from arising again, either so often, or at all, rather than resting content with resolving it. As I learnt from Anscombe all those years ago, it is a failure in virtue to accept, blindly, 'It has to be either A or B' instead of looking for a way of slipping between the horns of the dilemma. And it is equally a failure in virtue to accept, blindly 'It has to go on being either A or B' instead of looking for ways in which that dilemma might be, at least eventually, prevented from arising.

I want to conclude by mentioning another way in which the use of the virtue and vice terms helps us to combat corruption of thought, which would, I think, have delighted her. It arises not in the writings of moral philosophers, but in the context of teaching moral philosophy. She can hardly have anticipated fifty years ago that later generations of English speakers would have become all but incapable of using 'morally right' and 'morally wrong' without scare quotes. But, in my experience, this is now quite a widespread phenomenon, certainly in my home country. Gripped by some vague notion of 'respecting a plurality of values', haunted by the spectre of the question 'Who's to say it's wrong?', New Zealand politicians, journalists, and many of my undergraduates, cannot even bring themselves to say that the sexual abuse of children is wrong. Wanting, sincerely and seriously, to condemn it in the strongest possible terms, they describe it as 'inappropriate behaviour' as if the perpetrator was, not wicked, but merely socially maladroit.

But they are English speakers and they know how to use a large number of vice terms even if they rarely do so. Having said we should 'nam(e) a genus such as "untruthful", "unchaste", "unjust"', Anscombe continues, 'We should no longer ask whether doing something was "wrong", passing directly from some description of an action to this notion; we should ask whether, e.g. it was unjust; *and the answer would sometimes be clear at once*'[13] (my italics). When I ask my students whether the sexual abuse of children is—not wrong of course, or even 'wrong' but—cruel, they agree without hesitation. How could they not? They are English speakers, they know what 'cruel' means and the answer is clear at once. Exceptionally irresponsible? I suggest. Callous? Unbelievably selfish? Everyone nods vigorously. And after a couple of weeks of this sort of exercise, they find themselves able to talk about actions as right and wrong quite unselfconsciously, without the scare quotes.

References

Anscombe, G. E. M. 1981. 'Modern Moral Philosophy'. In *Ethics, Religion and Politics: The Collected Papers of G. E. M. Anscombe: Volume III*. Minneapolis, MN: University of Minnesota Press.

Walker, R. L. and P. J. Ivanhoe (eds). 2007. *Working Virtue*. Oxford: Clarendon Press.

---

[13] Ibid., 33.

9
Two Ways of Doing the Right Thing

1. Introduction

This chapter is about a standard problem in legal ethics which can be roughly stated as follows. Lawyers' professional role often permits—indeed requires—them to do things that would be wrong if they were acting outside their professional role. The usual general examples of the immoral sorts of things their role might permit or require them to do are: enable a client to defeat a just claim on a technicality if they can (*Zabella v. Pakel*), make opposing truthful witnesses look as though they are lying if they can (*Triangle Shirt Waist*), maintain client confidentiality even when this causes serious harm [including being sent to Death Row (Henry Drake)] to an innocent third party (*Lake Pleasant Bodies*) and, arguably, even when this involves remaining silent about a crime in progress or forthcoming.

These permissions and obligations are usually said to arise from the more general role-obligations of a lawyer in the adversarial (as opposed to the inquisitorial) system. These are, roughly, the obligation to pursue, zealously, your client's interests (not just, for instance, the interests of the clients you morally approve of) and the obligation to respect your client's confidentiality.

Now one might say, well we all know this is true—true that lawyers, as lawyers, do such things—but why is it a *philosophical* problem that people who work in legal ethics get tied up in? The answer is that we do not want to say that being a lawyer *necessarily* involves being immoral, the way, say, being a concentration camp commander under the Nazi regime did. We are happy to say that no decent society has any need for concentration camps and hence no need for people to run them, but surely a decent society of some size and complexity does need a legal system and hence does need lawyers. Moreover, surely it needs the adversarial system, so it needs lawyers playing the advocate's role.

Of course, it might be true that a decent society needs advocacy lawyers and it still be true that advocacy lawyers are necessarily immoral. That would be to say that the existence of such lawyers, though an evil, was a necessary evil. That sounds to me like a possible position, but it is not one I have found discussed anywhere, so I will accept here the prevailing assumption. The prevailing assumption in the literature is that, assuming we need advocacy lawyers, it must be possible for a good person to be a good lawyer—that the profession is not necessarily any more inimical to virtue than being a teacher or a business person.

And when we make that assumption explicit, we do indeed have something that looks like a philosophical problem. A lawyer's role sometimes *requires* or *obliges* (we can forget about 'permits' at this point) her to do some really immoral things. If she is a good lawyer she will do them when required or obliged. But of course there is no reason why a good person should not be a good lawyer.

Excuse me? How can it be maintained that there is no reason why a good person could not be someone who did those immoral sorts of things? There is surely a compelling reason why this cannot be so, namely that, on the face of it, someone's doing those sorts of things, voluntarily and intentionally, simply entails that they are immoral and lack virtue. So there is our problem; either we give up the claim that the lawyers' role sometimes obliges them to do immoral things or we have to find some way of explaining how it might be that a good, virtuous person—someone who is, for example, just, compassionate and honest—could, if a lawyer, do what, at least prima facie, is unjust, callous, or dishonest.

Well, that is what *I* think the problem is, but the prevailing literature in legal ethics does not, as far as I can see, actually tackle that problem, though it pursues debates very close to it.

Some of the debate seems to be about whether acceptance of the adversarial system does indeed entail acceptance of the fact that the lawyer's role within that system obliges him to do quite a startling range of immoral sorts of things. This seems to be a debate with no practical interest in it. Let us suppose, with Freedman, that the adversarial system *does* entail this, that is, that *whenever* the advocate zealously pursues his client's interests, and *whenever* he respects their confidentiality (within the limits of the law) he does what his role obliges him to do, no matter how dreadful, in the particular circumstances it is, or how dreadful the ways in which he does it are.

Well then, the obvious commonsense solution is 'so much the worse for the adversarial system *as specified*'; we do not need or want it. This does not mean that we want the inquisitorial one instead; we want an adversarial system with some amendments on the general role-obligations—for example amendments that require the breaking of confidentiality to prevent crime or reveal perjury on the part of one's client. (Freedman may insist, as I believe he has, that the obvious amendments are wrong because they are inconsistent with the values intrinsic to the adversarial system, but at that point the debate does seem to have become entirely academic. Objections to this commonsense solution seem to consist of claiming that the whole adversarial system will break down if such amendments are allowed, but thereby ignore the fact that some countries have introduced such amendments and their adversarial systems have survived intact.)

For practical purposes, concentrating on suitable amendments seems an obvious way to go. Why not look for amendments that would significantly reduce the immoral actions (arguably) required by the general role-obligations and then look to see what might still be required and what we could say about them? But I have not found much discussion on such a programme in the legal ethics literature. It seems that the authors either accept the general role-obligations (with all the immorality that the ABA's Model Rules allow) and say that is fine or they aim to reconceive the lawyer's role as somehow not committed to the role-obligations.

So, on the one hand we have, for example, Hazard,[1] who accepts that the role-obligations may require immoral action but insists that, in thus fulfilling their role-obligations, lawyers are doing the right thing. He implies that, as regular doers of the right thing they are not only blameless, but to be admired for voluntarily taking on their unpalatable task. Now that seems to be simply refusing to face the philosophical problem I have outlined. There is still this question—how *can* doing these immoral things count as doing the right thing? How *can* people who do such things count as admirable?

But the legal ethicists who oppose the sort of position Hazard maintains do not seem to do any better. Luban and Kronman,[2] for example, agree that *if* you take the lawyer's role in the adversarial system to be specified by those two general obligations, then the lawyer would indeed be obliged to do immoral things. But, they say, what this shows is that we have misconceived the lawyer's role. It is not a matter of deferring to those obligations but of taking on a more ethical, personally responsible, virtuous stance and reaching your decisions about what (as a lawyer) you should do, in some other, more 'ethical' way, employing (in Kronman's case) practical wisdom.

---

[1] Geoffrey C. Hazard, Jr., 'Doing the Right Thing', in G. C. Hazard, Jr., and D. L. Rhode (eds), *Legal Profession: Responsibility and Regulation* (Westbury, NY: The Foundation Press, 1994), 161–8.
[2] Anthony Kronman, *The Lost Lawyer: Failing Ideals of the Legal Profession* (Cambridge, MA: Belknap Press, 1993); David Luban, *Lawyers and Justice* (Princeton, NJ: Princeton University Press, 1988).

Precisely what this 'other way' involves is complicated in Luban, and far from clear in Kronman, but in neither of them can I find any clear statement about what the upshot of the (very idealized) lawyer's role would be if instantiated. Is the claim supposed to be that, *if* they reach their decisions about what to do in the recommended way, they will never find themselves deciding to do the immoral things? But this does make it sound as though the original role-obligations just are not going to have any bite at all. Now the problem is not—'How can these people count as doing the right thing or being admirable or good people?' but 'How can they count as *lawyers*?'

It seems to me we must bite on the bullet of saying that lawyers, *as* lawyers, *will* sometimes have to do immoral things and look for a way to make that a less awkward fact. We must try to find, as I said above, some way of explaining how it might be that a virtuous person—someone who is, for example, just, compassionate, and honest—could, if a lawyer, do what is, at least prima facie, unjust, callous, or dishonest.

2. Dilemmas

A good place to start—as some writers in the area do start[3]—is by looking at the fact that it is not only in the case of lawyers that agents' role-obligations may conflict with common morality. Let us, following Hazard, consider whether a good parent can be a good person.

In the days before virtue ethics emerged as a rival to utilitarianism and deontology, expositions of the latter two theories implied (though the issue was not actually raised) that the answer to this had to be 'No', because both theories stressed the view that morality must be impartial. But when the issue was raised, and it became clear that they were committed to denying that a good parent can be a good person, naturally they amended their position, and it is now accepted that of course there are many occasions when the right thing for parents to do is *not* to treat their own children in the way they would treat any other child similarly circumstanced, but to give them special, 'partial', treatment.

This generates the possibility of conflict or moral dilemmas. Sometimes it is quite obvious that I should benefit my own child rather than another—I help my own rather than another with their homework for example. Sometimes it is

---

[3] Hazard, to good effect, *vide supra*, and Richard Wasserstrom 'Roles and Morality', in Luban (ed.), *The Good Lawyer*, 25–37.

equally obvious that I must not benefit my child in circumstances where I would not benefit another in the same way. I must not mark his essay more leniently than I mark others' if I am his teacher for example. But sometimes making the right decision is difficult. Yes, common morality, or the virtue of honesty, generally requires that one not tell barefaced lies, especially to innocent and well-intentioned parties. But one's role-obligations as a parent certainly include protecting one's child from serious harm when one can. So what is the right thing to do when the only way to protect one's child from such a harm is to tell such a lie? It seems that, whichever way you go, you are bound to fail morally in some respect. Either you tell the lie, and then you have done something shamefully dishonest and so cannot be a good or virtuous person, or you do not and thereby fail—through your own intentional omission—to act as a good parent, which is surely a moral failure or a failure in virtue too.

And clearly, other role-obligations also generate dilemmas. Psychiatrists have problems very similar to lawyers' about confidentiality; doctors have rather different ones (do I tell my adolescent patient's parents that she is seeking an abortion). Heads of academic departments have theirs, and also face conflicts between the obligations of that role and those of the common morality of kindness and friendship, and so on.

So good lawyers don't fail to be good people simply in virtue of the fact that their role sometimes compels them to do things which, if virtuous, they would not do if they did not occupy that role. This may happen to all sorts of people who occupy quite different roles. Nor is it simply the fact that they voluntarily took on the role that thus compels them. People voluntarily become psychiatrists, doctors, heads of departments, and, usually, parents. The taking on of *any* such role is giving hostages to fortune, upping the likelihood that bad luck will present one with a moral dilemma, but we do not worry about the question 'Can a good occupier of any of those roles be a virtuous person?'

Perhaps we should? Luban, discussing not just the lawyer's role-obligations, but 'professional role-morality' in general, claims that 'the problem of role-morality stands as a permanent challenge to the coherence of moral thought.'[4] He thinks this is so because role-morality, or role-obligation, is 'particularistic', whereas (real?) moral obligations are 'universal'.[5] But this is a mistake. What is fundamentally at issue is not just the conflict between particular, role-specific,

---

[4] David Luban, 'Professional Ethics', in R. G. Frey and C. Heath (eds), *A Companion to Applied Ethics* (Oxford: Blackwell, 2003), 595.
[5] Ibid., 588.

moral obligations and the 'universal' obligations of common morality, but, quite generally, moral conflicts or dilemmas per se.

These arise in many cases where role-obligations are not at issue. Even if, *per impossibile*, one could avoid taking on any role, one might still be presented with a moral dilemma. Ethical theory literature has long been full of them, since both rule-utilitarians and deontologists constantly come up with cases in which their moral rules give conflicting guidance. Some act-utilitarians were willing to provide brisk resolutions of all such dilemmas, but the rule-utilitarians and deontologists found their resolutions in some cases too unpalatable to accept and continue to disagree amongst themselves about the dilemmas to this day.

So the deep question is not 'How can a good occupier of a role be a good person, given that their specific role-obligations may conflict with more universal moral obligations?' but, more generally, 'How can anyone be a good person given that their moral obligations may conflict?'

To get clear about this, we must get clearer about dilemmas.

Before virtue ethics appeared on the stage, the standard way to set up discussion of serious (or indeed tragic) dilemmas in normative ethics was as follows. One presented an example in which there were, prima facie, good moral reasons against doing A and against doing B and the agent had to do one of them. (Usually, it was one in which the choice lay between killing, or violating another serious right and causing great suffering, or between killing and letting die, or between killing one person or several.) Then one asked the question 'What is the right thing to do in such a case, A or B?' Then one applied one's theory, utilitarian or deontological, resolved the dilemma, and drew the conclusion that A, say, was *the right thing to do*. Full stop.

No one noticed that there was something problematic about such a conclusion but there is, namely that what you do after you have correctly resolved a serious dilemma is bound to be something pretty dreadful—killed someone, for example—and this is not the sort of thing we usually think of when told that someone (good for them) 'did the right thing'. Choosing to 'do the right thing' is after all usually a matter of choosing to do the thing there are good moral reasons for doing, rather than anything there are good moral reasons against. I choose to own up to a mistake rather than lie about it; I choose to stop to help the person who has dropped his shopping rather than pass him by. In such cases, what I do is *the right thing to do*.

But that is not how things are in a serious dilemma—a forced choice between A and B where there are good, even compelling, moral reasons *against* each. If B is even worse than A, then, in deciding to do A, I will have made the right moral decision but my doing A will not thereby be right without qualification. On the contrary, given that there were, *ex hypothesi*, good, even compelling moral reasons against it which still stand, there must, in some sense, have been something bad or wrong about my doing A.

How can we sort this out? Let us begin by noting how the term 'right moral decision' relates to the term 'morally right act'. Suppose we have a morally right act—a good deed. Such acts merit praise rather than blame; they are the sort of acts that we encourage each other to do, that virtuous agents typically do, that agents can be happy about doing with, as Hume so nicely puts it, that 'inward peace of mind' that arises from 'a satisfactory review of their own conduct'. And the same is true of right moral decisions. Such decisions are the sort of decisions that virtuous agents typically make, that we encourage each other to make. We praise those who make such decisions even when they are ineffective and the act does not come off. When someone makes a right moral decision but, through no fault of their own, fails to do what they intended to do, we say well, that's a shame but still, they made the right moral decision, good for them.

This is because, in many cases, effective right moral decisions result in morally right actions; the two go hand in hand. But there are other cases in which this is not true. Consider an example of Peter Geach's.[6] A feckless man seduces two women, A and B, promising each of them marriage, and makes both of them pregnant. Ashamed of what he has done, he now wants to 'do the right thing' and clear his conscience. But, in a way he cannot. Suppose his dilemma is resolvable, the evil of abandoning A being less than the evil of abandoning B (perhaps A is stronger and more independent). Then there is a right, that is, a correct, moral decision to be made about which way to go. So let us suppose that he makes that right decision and carries it through. But a good deed will not result. It is still the case that, in marrying B, he has abandoned A and merits not praise but blame for having landed himself in the circumstances that forced him to do so. He has done the sort of thing that no virtuous man would do, and he is in no position to view his own conduct with satisfaction.

How much of this changes if an agent is faced with a resolvable serious dilemma *through no fault of his own* and resolves it correctly? Anyone, through no fault of their own, may be forced to leave one person to die in order to save five. And not much changes. We will not blame him for having landed himself in the circumstances that created the forced choice, but the fact

---

[6] Peter Geach, *The Virtues* (Cambridge: Cambridge University Press, 1977).

remains that he has wound up doing something that the immoral rather than the virtuous typically do. He left someone to die when he could have saved them, and that is not a good deed. And hence the inadequacy of the way in which the rule-utilitarians and deontologists used to resolve dilemmas and conclude that, say A, was 'the right thing to do' without qualification, thereby implying that A was a good deed, morally indistinguishable from an honest or kind act such as owning up or stopping to help.

When they were engaged in resolving serious dilemmas the utilitarian and deontological theorists were not, I think, entirely clear about what they were doing. On the one hand, they were committed, in those days, to providing action-guidance; their theories were supposed to enable their users to reach correct moral decisions. But they also claimed to have identified, in their respective theory's 'account of right action', which provided the action-guidance, the 'right-making properties' of actions—what it was about them that made them the sorts of actions that the virtuous do and that we all may review with satisfaction. Outside the context of serious dilemmas, the tensions between these two aims were not apparent, since in ordinary cases, an effective right moral decision results in a good deed. But the very reason why we worry about serious dilemmas is that they face us, not with the choice between a good deed and a bad one, but with the unhappy choice between two evils. In such cases there may well be a correct moral decision to be made, the one that latches on to the lesser of the two evils, but no chance that this will result in a good deed.

3. Getting through Dilemmas Virtuously

As is well known, virtue ethics, rather than focusing on the 'right-making properties' of actions, focuses on the virtuous agent. It thereby stands us in good stead when we consider serious dilemmas because it forces on our attention how very different they are from other 'Should I do A or B?' questions. Instead of asking us to think 'Will A or B have the best consequences?' or 'Is it A or B that is in accordance with a correct rule or the highest ranking principle?' and hence think about the actions and their properties, virtue ethics tells us to think about a virtuous agent. Faced with a forced choice between two evils, what would she *do*?

And that is a really *puzzling* question, creating a tension in our thought that the 'A or B?' questions do not. When we try to imagine, concretely, a virtuous agent doing one of these dreadful things, each with the weight of such good moral reasons against them, one's mind tends to boggle.

Asking students to imagine it, I have found they are often unable to do so. They start by saying that an *ideally* virtuous agent would never get herself into the circumstances that presented her with a serious dilemma—it is always through some fault of one's own, albeit perhaps, a very minor one, that one is faced with them. But then I give them examples in which this is clearly not so. Or they say, well, she would reject the forced choice and kill herself. With respect to some examples of dilemmas, that is a good answer—after all, as Aristotle rightly remarks 'There are some things a man must die rather than do'—but as an answer to all of them, it is dodging the issue. So I produce other examples in which killing oneself would clearly be cowardly or irresponsible so the virtuous agent will not do *that*, and they get stuck again. Eventually, one of them, remembering that I am always telling them that virtue involves feelings as well as actions, will say 'Well, I suppose she would have to do A (if that is the way they think the dilemma has to be resolved) but she would feel terrible about it.' Right. And now we can start thinking through what she would do in proper detail.

We start thinking about it this way. Anyone, even the immoral, through the normally fallible or venal, to the virtuous agent with practical wisdom, might be faced with a serious resolvable dilemma through no fault of their own. What we are interested in is, what differentiates them? What would we expect the *virtuous* agent would do in such a situation?

We have already noted that when he does A he will feel badly about it. But why?[7] Because, *ex hypothesi*, A, like B, is the sort of action—unjust, callous, dishonest—that the vicious typically do, not the sort he goes in for. So, when first faced with the dilemma, he is going to be extremely reluctant to do either A or B, and, given that, what would one expect him to do which one would not expect the immoral and the normally fallible to do? Obviously, the first thing *he* is going to do is look for a way to 'slip between the horns of the dilemma', in contrast to the immoral, who will not bother to look, and the normally fallible who, lacking practical wisdom, will not think to question whether they really are faced with a dilemma.

---

[7] The idea that serious moral dilemmas could only be resolved 'with moral remainder' in the form of regret was introduced into the literature by Bernard Williams and has entered the legal ethics literature to some extent. But, as far as I know, no one does more with it than note that 'the agent ought to feel regret.' Cast that in virtue ethics' terms and we get 'the virtuous agent (unlike the immoral) would feel regret' and can start thinking about why and what *follows* from this fact.

Although this too may seem to be dodging the issue, it is, in practice, often indistinguishable from cases that are definitely relevant to it which I will come to in the next paragraph, and it is also an important point to make in the context of teaching legal ethics. It is surely not a good idea to foster in law students the belief that their job is going to face them with a constant stream of forced choices between evils and that, to be good lawyers, they must learn to face the unpalatable choice immediately, identify the lesser of the two evils, grit their teeth and get on with it. The training should consist in directing the students to look *first* for ways of avoiding the presented dilemmas, so they do not have to choose an evil (or such a great one) before moving on to a further step.

Moving on ourselves, let us consider a response to the *Lake Pleasant Bodies* case. Suppose we think that what a virtuous lawyer would have done in that case was send the authorities an anonymous tip-off about the whereabouts of the bodies.[8] Are we to describe this as slipping between the horns of the dilemma between breaking confidentiality and failing to prevent the grief of the relatives, or simply as resolving the dilemma in favour of breaking confidentiality? It seems to me one could say either. If we opt for the former, then it is an example of the first sort of thing a *virtuous* agent does when presented with an apparent serious dilemma. If we opt for the latter, we find the second instance in which the virtuous agent, faced with a serious dilemma, does not do just the same thing as the immoral or the normally fallible.

Suppose a serious moral dilemma between doing A and doing B is correctly resolvable in favour of A. So the virtuous agent decides that A is 'the' way to go. What then? She will not just barge straight ahead but, whenever possible, consider different *sorts of means* of doing A in search of the least bad one and do that (e.g. send the anonymous tip-off). And again, the immoral will not care and so will not bother to search, and the normally fallible will not think to consider anything but the obvious bad means of doing A. So, even when they all decide to 'do A', they will not 'do the same thing' because the virtuous will look for different means to implement that decision and the others will not. Moreover, sometimes she will find it, and wind up doing A* while the others do A** where A*, though bad, is not as bad as A**.

Now let us confront the cases where doing A is the correct moral decision, and all three really do A, the virtuous agent for the right reasons, the normally fallible or venal perhaps for them, perhaps by luck, and the immoral for

---

[8] David Wasserman, 'Should a Good Lawyer do the Right Thing? David Luban on the Morality of Adversary Representation', *Maryland Law Review* 49 (1990): 392–423, 399.

whatever. So we are to imagine that our virtuous agent knowingly does something which is the sort of thing that no virtuous agent would typically do—harms his child, hurts a friend, deceives some good and trusting people, breaks a just law, prompts his wife's suicide...[9] If the immoral, the normally fallible or venal and even the ideally virtuous agent all do the same thing, what now can differentiate them?

At this point, we should bring back the student's point and consider its further implications. Given that virtue is concerned with feeling rightly as much as acting rightly, and assuming that our agent is virtuous, we must assume that he will feel about what he has done as he should, with some pain and regret, perhaps great distress. He certainly will not feel pleased about it. So given that is how he feels, what would we expect him *not* to do? Would he congratulate himself on having done the right thing, feeling pleased about what he has done? Obviously not. Will he boast about it? Obviously not. Will he welcome opportunities to discuss his decision and being congratulated on his perspicacity? Obviously not, even if it was very difficult to arrive at the correct decision and did call on all his practical wisdom. It was *painful*, and who wants to dwell on their pain? But the immoral may well do all of these things (in suitable company) and the normally venal be at least tempted to do so.

Will a virtuous agent, conscious of the fact that pure bad luck landed her with the dilemma, and that she did make the correct decision, shrug off the regret as quickly as she can, saying to herself 'No use crying over spilt milk'? After all, she is, *ex hypothesi*, blameless. If she was faced with the dilemma through no fault of her own, and she resolved it correctly, identifying the lesser of the two evils, she can say, truly, 'It wasn't my fault—I *had* to do A' and that is a watertight excuse and justification.

Now the normally venal may be content with thus excusing themselves (and the immoral will feel no regrets anyhow), but the virtuous are not content with being blameless and able to justify themselves. As virtuous, they are interested not so much in being blameless as in acting well, in the life of virtuous activity. So, landed with a bad job, they do not take the fact that it is not of their making as a reason or excuse for leaving it as it is. They look around for a way or ways to make the best of it.

---

[9] I heard of a tragic case in which a woman was married to a deeply unhappy and neurotic man who abused their children. When she threatened to leave him, taking them with her, he would cry and say he would commit suicide if she did and promise to reform. And lapse again. Having tried everything else without success, she did leave him. And he did commit suicide.

True, there are undoubtedly situations in which nothing further could be done to ameliorate the upshot of a resolved serious dilemma. And in those cases, having tried, and found nothing, the agent can, without showing himself to be irresponsible or considerably less than committed to acting well, move on past the spilt milk. But there usually is something which makes the doing of A, though still regrettable, a little less bad than it would otherwise have been. And the virtuous agent looks for that, and finds it and does it, whereas the immoral and the normally fallible or venal do not look or (if less venal but still fallible) look but fail to find it.

So we find a number of differences between the way in which the virtuous get through serious dilemmas and how the others do.

What makes it, initially, hard to imagine what the virtuous agent would do when faced with such a dilemma is that it is the general version of the problem of explaining the 'awkward fact' I mentioned at the outset. How *could* it be that a virtuous person—someone who is, for example, just, compassionate and honest—does what is unjust, callous, or dishonest? When we hear of someone that they killed an innocent person intentionally, or intentionally allowed one of their children to die when they could have done otherwise, our natural reaction is to assume that they *cannot* be virtuous. These are the sorts of things, we think, that only the immoral do, and one thing we can be sure of is that the immoral and the virtuous do not do the same things.

But once we have worked through what a virtuous agent would do when faced with a serious moral dilemma we see what is wrong about that thought. When—but *only* when—faced with a forced choice between evils—the virtuous, even the ideally virtuous may indeed 'do the same thing' as someone immoral would do. We see that our initial intuition—that the truly, ideally honest never do what is dishonest, the compassionate never what is callous or unkind, the just never what is unjust—was simplistic. Yes, sometimes they do, because they were forced, by the circumstances, to do so.

But it is not enough to say that, resolving a serious dilemma correctly, an agent 'did the right thing' with only the qualification 'given that they were forced to'. There is no virtue in 'doing the right thing' in a dilemma unless it is done in a virtuous way. For we also see what is right about the thought that the immoral and the virtuous do not do the same things. When faced with a (apparent) serious dilemma, the immoral and the virtuous do not 'do the same thing' in the broad sense of 'do'. The virtuous get through the dilemma *virtuously*, doing different things before they reach a decision, sometimes reaching a different decision from the immoral, and when they decide on and do the very same specific action as the immoral, they do different things later on. They feel about it all differently too of course, but it is the differences in action that are of practical interest.

So, quite generally, when faced with serious dilemmas, good people can do bad things, and this may be no reflection on their goodness or virtue. When we discover not only that they have done this bad thing but why (it was a forced choice, and they made the right decision) and how (in the virtuous way outlined above) and how they felt about it all, we are sympathetic about the toll it has taken, not shocked and condemnatory.

4. Lawyers' Dilemmas

Now let us apply the preceding discussion to lawyers' dilemmas. These are serious moral dilemmas in which there is a forced choice between failing to fulfil one's role-obligation, which (*ex hypothesi*) is wrong and doing something else that is (*ex hypothesi*) wrong. And in legal ethics, the question that is standardly addressed is the utilitarians' and deontologists' question—'What is the right thing for the lawyer to do?'—inviting the answer 'A (or B) is the right thing to do, full stop.'

But if we recast that question in virtue ethics' terms we get 'What would the virtuous lawyer do faced with such a dilemma?' and many answers emerge that parallel those in the preceding discussion.

Sometimes the answer is going to be 'Reject the forced choice by giving up on being a lawyer and resigning from her job.' Like the students' even more drastic response ('reject the forced choice and kill herself') this will sometimes, given some examples, be a good answer and it is a possibility that should not be overlooked. However, as before, thinking of it as the answer to all of them is dodging the issue, and we may assume that such examples will be rare. There are doubtless others in which what a particular virtuous lawyer would do, in the circumstances, is arrange for their client to be transferred to another lawyer, and that should not be overlooked either. But in many cases the answer will be that, since she is a virtuous *lawyer*, she fulfils her role-obligations, resolving the dilemma in favour of them and does what common morality would forbid.

But, as a *virtuous* lawyer, he will get through the dilemma, thus resolved, in the way I have detailed above. He will already have looked to see if he can find a way of slipping between its horns. If he cannot, he will look for the least unjust or dishonest or harmful or grief-causing means of fulfilling his role-obligation, not just barge ahead. In particular, he will not ignore the ABA's

Model Rules' grudging permissions to fulfil his role-obligation in a less than hyper-zealous way[10] but take advantage of every single one of them. That would make a substantial difference to what is done in many cases.

A virtuous lawyer will not, while or having fulfilled her role-obligation in such a situation, feel pleased about doing so, nor proud of having done what she has done, nor boast about it, nor write articles or appear on television extolling her perspicacity and legal expertise. She will not congratulate herself smugly on having done the right thing, thinking of what she has done as a good deed. She will, in the course of fulfilling it, and afterwards, be on the lookout for ways in which to mitigate the evils of the situation, rather than rest content with having the perfect excuse ('I had to') and she will find any that are going and do them. And every lawyer who fails to do any of these things fails to do what the virtuous lawyer would do and thereby fails to do what they should.

It will now be obvious that what I think is wrong with Hazard's position is the unqualified claim that the lawyers 'do the right thing' when (whenever? he leaves it unclear) they fulfil their role-obligations, and thereby his unwarranted inference that, as regular doers of such right things, they are virtuous people and merit our esteem.

When in accordance with their role-obligations, they are forced to do something contrary to common morality or virtue, something that is not right 'without qualification', through no fault of their own, lawyers count as 'doing the right thing' *only* if they recognize their choice as one side of a serious dilemma and subsequently act (and react) in the way a virtuous agent would. When, and only when, they regularly 'do the right thing' in this broad sense of 'do' are they candidates for being virtuous people who merit our esteem.

Correspondingly, they are up for moral censure if they fail to find the least immoral means of fulfilling their role-obligations (if there are alternatives), if they congratulate themselves on having done the right thing or make a point of claiming they were blameless, giving the 'adversary system excuse'[11] instead of looking around afterwards for ways to ameliorate the situation. All of which seems a far cry from what Hazard has in mind.

So far, so good. Pointing out that virtuous lawyers must 'do the right thing' *in the way* a virtuous person would takes us away from Hazard and more

---

[10] Tim Dare, 'Mere-Zeal, Hyper-Zeal and the Ethical Obligations of Lawyers', *Legal Ethics* 7 (2004): 24–38.
[11] David Luban, 'The Adversary System Excuse', in Luban (ed.), *The Good Lawyer*, 83–122.

towards Luban's and Kronman's call for more 'ethical lawyering'. A virtuous lawyer has to do a lot more than simply fulfil his role-obligations, and a lot more than fulfil them with an appropriate feeling of regret.

However, we might still wonder whether we have got far enough. In theory, we have found an explanation of the 'awkward fact' with which we began, namely that a virtuous person will, if a lawyer, sometimes do immoral things. The explanation is that virtuous people sometimes *do* do immoral things; they do them when presented with a forced choice between two immoral things through no fault of their own (and then do one of them in a special way which involves doing other things). But there are significant differences between the lawyer's situation and the general case of a virtuous person being faced with a forced choice.

In the general case, it is sheer unpredictable bad luck that brings the forced choice. Ordinarily virtuous people leading ordinary lives have no reason to expect that, lying in wait for them, is some horribly serious dilemma. Minor ones (having to break a promise, let someone down or trick them into doing something, tell a serious lie, cause someone distress, keep a confidence with one and bring serious results for someone else) no doubt crop up quite often. But the 'bad job' can often be not only ameliorated but sometimes entirely dissipated (especially with people one knows, as is often the case) by a subsequent sincere apology ('I *am* sorry; I had to do it because...and I couldn't confess before because...'). So, even in the virtuous, the regret does not have to be deep and does not last long. With a very serious or tragic one, the regret and pain may be long-lasting, even lifelong, but, in ordinary life, these are rare.

This is not true of lawyers. Their being faced with serious dilemmas is not unpredictable bad luck, but all too predictable. Although each particular dilemma may be one they are in through no fault of their own, it is by their own choice that they are in a profession in which they know such dilemmas will face them. Though many involve only relatively minor acts of dishonesty, deception, manipulation, injustice or unkindness, there is no chance of the lawyers' ameliorating the bad job by subsequently apologizing to the strangers they have thus injured. And very serious ones are quite on the cards, not a random blow of cruel fortune which prompts our sympathy when it strikes the virtuous in ordinary life and causes them such distress.

No wonder people claim that lawyers must lack moral integrity! If they were as distressed by acting on their very serious forced choices as the virtuous are in ordinary life, surely they would have broken down and resigned from their profession years ago. How can they have any pretensions to virtue and survive unless they have somehow split themselves in two, leaving their virtuous persona and its emotional reactions at home when they go into the office, and their immoral one (including its consciousness of what it has done) in the office when they go home. And that is not enough for virtue.

So the necessary condition for being a virtuous lawyer, outlined above—that she regularly 'does the right thing' in the virtuous way—is not sufficient. If we are going to hang on to the idea that there can be virtuous lawyers, despite their being forced to do the immoral things they do, something more needs to be said.

Let us again go back to Hazard's reminder that lawyers are not the only role-occupiers who can predict, with confidence, that they are going to be faced with very serious dilemmas. Although I doubt this is true of parents, it certainly seems to be true of some doctors, psychiatrists, and soldiers. Do we suppose of *all* such role-occupiers that they have either split themselves in two, or are on the verge of breaking down under the stress and distress of having to do the things they do, or are immoral and in it just for the money or because it is a more exciting job than any others available to them? I assume we may think that of many—and sometimes see evidence to support it—but not think it of all. I assume we find, if we know some of them, or can imagine, if we do not, that the virtuous ones see themselves as, overall, dedicated to promoting a truly good end—other people's good, or the relief of their suffering. They are thereby enabled to see their forced choices as inseparable from their job-long service to this worthwhile end, not merely as strokes of misfortune, and hence they are less distressed than virtuous people getting through dilemmas in ordinary life. Moreover, they can take heart from their dedication to such an end, and preserve Hume's 'inward peace of mind' and pride in their job.

May we find, or imagine, the same regarding lawyers? Some of them, we may suppose, see themselves as, overall, dedicated to promoting justice. They are thereby enabled to see their forced choices as inseparable, in the inevitable imperfections of any legal system, from their service to that end, and can preserve peace of mind and pride in their job. Well, perhaps—but only if we can find, or imagine, that the dedication is genuine.

An avowal of the dedication, even if manifestly sincere, will not be enough, since self-deception powered by the financial rewards of the profession and the desire for self-esteem is quite enough to guarantee the sincerity. Just as we will doubt the dedication of a psychiatrist with the avowed end of helping others who specializes in wealthy patients suffering from self-indulgence, so, in my view, we may surely doubt the dedication to justice of anyone who has chosen to specialize in corporate law. Even if it were possible for a lawyer to regularly 'do the right thing' in the virtuous way in a US corporate law firm rather than getting sacked the first time he tried it (which I gather from the literature is very unlikely), can they reasonably believe that many of their cases would have just outcomes? There can be no just or fair outcome of two Mafia bosses' battle over the territory in which their gangs operate and, analogously, no just outcome of two corporations' legal battle over profits in the adversarial system when both sides are greedy and unscrupulous. Or so I believe, but I realize this may be a very tendentious view.

Is it as tendentious to claim that we could expect a lawyer dedicated to promoting justice to do pro bono work for 'persons of limited means'? It appears that not many do pro bono work at all unless required by their state, and that some who say they do, do it not by working for the poor but 'by doing free legal work for in-laws and attorneys' country clubs'.[12] They thereby compare unfavourably with those who do do more, particularly those who choose to join law firms that specialize in pro bono work and charge lower fees to the needy, even though this means the lawyers wind up with less money. It is this sort of willingness to 'go the extra mile' that one would expect of the virtuous lawyer, the one who is truly dedicated to promoting justice.

Indeed, we might think that promoting justice was itself a role-obligation of lawyers and that any lawyer who did not manifest the dedication but only fulfilled their other two general role-obligations was not even a good lawyer. After all, the Preamble to the ABA's Model Rules states [in (1)] that a lawyer, as a member of the legal profession, is a public citizen having *special* responsibility for the quality of justice (my italics). To an outsider, this seems to assert that lawyers have a double obligation to promote justice—the one all citizens share, and the one they have in virtue of their role, highlighted here. Still, it might be said, they can discharge the second entirely by discharging the two standard ones effectively; the 'special responsibility' does not require anything further of them as lawyers, and hence is not, as such, a role-obligation. You can be a good lawyer without going the extra mile for justice.

All right, let us accept that. We may still point out that the lawyers' role gives them special opportunities to promote justice. A *virtuous* lawyer will, of course, not pass up such opportunities, and these are not exhausted by the possibility of extra pro bono work.

The specific actions which constitute fulfilling the two general role-obligations are in part determined by the content of specific laws. So if a law

---

[12] See Deborah L. Rhode and David Luban (eds), *Legal Ethics* (Westbury, NY: The Foundation Press, 1995), 794 and preceding.

changes, so do some of the specific actions required. And laws can be changed, sometimes for the better. Lawyers' expertise, experience and authority as lawyers, give them the opportunity to do good and to promote justice in ways that are not open to many others, because they are better positioned than most of the rest of us to be instrumental in changes within the legal system.

A point too obvious to be worth making in the general discussion of getting through serious moral dilemmas virtuously should be made now, namely that only the immoral are indifferent to the prospect of people being faced with a forced choice between two evils and hence doing one of them. The virtuous, and even the minimally decent, just do not want bad things to be done. It is not only that they do not want to do them themselves, they do not want them to *happen*. Given human frailty of course they do happen, and given serious dilemmas they happen, but anything consistent with morality we can do to ensure they happen less often is worth doing. We still do not know what to do about human frailty, and many serious dilemmas arise in ways over which we have no control, but some of the lawyers' dilemmas arise only because of imperfections in the legal system, and something can be done about them.

Tim Dare[13] argues that lawyers are the most appropriate people to take on, occasionally at least, the distinct role of 'reformer'—one who critically evaluates the constitutive rules of a practice. Defending 'the standard conception' of the lawyer's role, he wants to emphasize the necessity of their sticking to their role-obligations. But, as he nicely points out, who would be better positioned than Pakel's lawyer, *after* he had seen the case through, to initiate a change in the relevant statute which would prevent the particular dilemma he resolved in favour of fulfilling his role-obligation from arising again?

Rephrased in virtue ethics' terms we may say that this is exactly the sort of thing one would expect a virtuous lawyer to do. As a lawyer, he pursues his client's interests, venal as they are; as a *virtuous* lawyer, he goes the extra mile for justice and, say, writes to his local law reform commissioner, conforming to the Preamble's (6)—'a lawyer should seek improvement of the law' and 'should employ...knowledge [of the law] in reform of the law'.

One would expect too that virtuous lawyers in the US would be campaigning to get the ABA Model Rules more strictly enforced or tightened up. To the naive reader, they seem to forbid many of the practices deplored by legal ethicists (for example, responding 'to an interrogatory by delivering to the

---

[13] Tim Dare, unpublished manuscript of *The Counsel of Rogues*. He tells me that William Simon makes the same point.

discoverer tons of miscellaneous documents to run up their legal bills'[14]) but apparently they do not, or not unambiguously enough. Young lawyers with aspirations to being virtuous do not need exhortations to 'exercise [...] sensitive professional and moral judgment guided by the basic principles underlying the Rules' [as (9) in the Preamble has it] to find their proper interpretation. They need clearer Rules to which they can appeal, invoking an 'ABA Model Rules Excuse', when under pressure from immoral clients.

I have read much in the legal ethics literature about low morale amongst lawyers and law students. The aim of this chapter has been to show that there are quite a lot of things to be done that would entitle lawyers to think of themselves as virtuous people. Their two, further, general obligations as *virtuous* lawyers are firstly, to do the right thing in a virtuous way, with all the extra doings that entails, and secondly, to go the extra mile for justice. It will not be easy, but virtue never is.

Acknowledgements

Readers interested in a virtue ethics approach to role-generated dilemmas should also read Christine Swanton's rather different version, 'Virtue Ethics, Role Ethics, and Business Ethics' in *Working Virtue* (Rebecca L. Walker and Philip J. Ivanhoe, eds, Oxford: Clarendon Press, 2007), 208–224.

I am grateful to my colleague Tim Dare for generously allowing me to read chapters of his book manuscript *The Counsel of Rogues* (Ashgate, 2008) to which I am greatly indebted in this chapter and for commenting on an earlier version.

References

Dare, T. 2004. 'Mere-Zeal, Hyper-Zeal and the Ethical Obligations of Lawyers', *Legal Ethics* 7: 24–38.

Geach, P. 1977. *The Virtues*. Cambridge: Cambridge University Press.

Hazard, Jr., G. C. 1994. 'Doing the Right Thing'. In G. C. Hazard, Jr., and D. L. Rhode (eds), *The Legal Profession: Responsibility and Regulation*. Westbury, NY: The Foundation Press: 161–8.

Kronman, A. 1988. *The Lost Lawyer: Failing Ideals of the Legal Profession*. Cambridge, MA: Belknap Press.

---

[14] David Luban, *Lawyers and Justice*, p. 51.

Luban, D. 1983. 'The Adversary System Excuse'. In D. Luban (ed.), *The Good Lawyer: Lawyers' Roles and Lawyers' Ethics*. Totowa, NJ: Rowman & Allanheld: 83–122.

Luban, D. 1988. *Lawyers and Justice*. Princeton, NJ: Princeton University Press.

Luban, D. 2003. 'Professional Ethics'. In R. G. Frey and C. Heath (eds), *A Companion to Applied Ethics*. Oxford: Blackwell: 583–96.

Rhode, D. L. and D. Luban (eds). 1995. *Legal Ethics*. Westbury, NY: The Foundation Press.

Wasserman, D. 1990. 'Should a Good Lawyer do the Right Thing? David Luban on the Morality of Adversary Representation', *Maryland Law Review* 49: 392–423.

Wasserstrom, R. 1983. 'Roles and Morality'. In D. Luban (ed.), *The Good Lawyer: Lawyers' Roles and Lawyers' Ethics*. Totowa, NJ: Rowman & Allanheld: 25–37.

10
Applying Virtue Ethics to Our Treatment of the Other Animals

Applying virtue ethics to moral issues should be straightforward. After all, it basically just amounts to thinking about what to do using the virtue and vice terms. 'I mustn't pull the cat's tail because it's cruel', I might say to myself, and surely that is simple enough. But somehow, when one turns, as a virtue ethicist, to engaging in current moral debates, applying virtue ethics becomes very difficult. Of course, applying the virtue and vice terms correctly may be difficult; one may need much practical wisdom to determine whether, in a particular case, telling a hurtful truth is cruel or not, for example, but that does not seem to be the main problem. In my experience, the main problem is just getting started. Why is this? Well, the thing I found most difficult when I was first trying to work out the virtue ethics approach to abortion was shedding the structure of thought about the issue imposed by the other two approaches, and I had the same difficulty trying to think about applying virtue ethics to our treatment of the other animals. We can't get started until we have cleared enough space to think in our own way and have found the right questions to ask.

1. Against Moral Status

In the abortion debate, the question that almost everyone began with was 'What is the moral status of the foetus?' and I wasted a lot of time asking myself 'What is the virtue ethicist's answer to that question?' (and, indeed, 'What does virtue ethics say about that question?' and 'What would the virtuous agent's answer to that question be?' and even 'What would the virtuous answer to that question be?'). Eventually it occurred to me to wonder why we were all trying to determine the moral status of the foetus and, once I saw why everyone else was, it became clear that virtue ethicists needn't bother. For everyone else was assuming the correctness of some moral rule or principle about respecting the rights of, or giving equal consideration to the interests of, or the wrongness of killing, Xs, and so they really needed to know, Are foetuses Xs or not? But we virtue ethicists had roundly declared that normative ethics did not have to consist of a system of such moral principles and that practical ethical thought was better conducted in terms of the v-rules.

The consequentialist and deontological approaches to the rights and wrongs of the ways we treat the other animals (and also the environment) are structured in exactly the same way. Here too, the question that must be answered first is 'What is the moral status of the other animals (or other living things, such as trees, or indeed other natural things such as rocks and mountains)?' Here too, it is supposed that to establish that the other animals (or some subset of them) are Xs would be to establish that they have rights, or that their interests should be given the same moral weight as those of other Xs, or that prohibitions that apply to other Xs apply to them. And here too, virtue ethicists have no need to answer the question.

Moreover, we have reason to reject it. Kant's infelicitous distinction between *persons* and *things* highlights a problem inherent in this structure which virtue ethics, with its case-by-case approach, should be well fitted to avoid. Suppose that the distinction has been drawn in such a way that Xs are, in practice, mostly very similar. Xs are, let's say, rational, or self-consciousness, or human. Then the problem is that the non-Xs are bound to be a very heterogeneous class. Let us grant, for the sake of the argument, that if I am faced with an X then there are certain things I must or must not do to it. But what if I am faced with a non-X? Where is my action-guidance? May I do anything to it I please, however wicked my desires? Well, if it is indeed a thing such as a bit of wastepaper or mud it is hard to imagine any wicked desires engaging with it, and perhaps the answer is, indeed, 'Yes, do as you please.' However, precisely because the class of non-Xs is so heterogeneous, that clearly can't be the right answer every time. Not every non-X is 'just a thing' in a colloquial sense, and much of what I may or may not or ought to do to a particular non-X is going to depend in part on what features it has, other than failing to be an X.

While debates about the status of the foetus were so exclusively concerned with the issue of abortion, this problem was not glaringly obvious. What, after all, did anyone want to do with a human foetus, or embryo, but preserve it or kill it? If it was a non-X, it was something you could kill, and that was all anyone wanted to know. But then it turned out that there were other things people wanted to do with the foetuses or embryos, such as use them for experimental purposes, and the question 'What may I do to this rather special sort of non-X, beyond killing it?' became pressing.

What happens when we turn to debates about the status of the other animals? Most philosophers writing on this come down on the animals' side, classifying them as Xs and thereby generate the complementary version of the problem. Now it is the Xs that form a heterogeneous class, not, it is true, as heterogeneous as Kant's 'things', but still encompassing, arguably, fish and birds, mice, rats, and cockroaches, as well as the familiar domestic animals and mammals quite generally, including us. This heterogeneity makes it extremely difficult to maintain the 'All Xs are equal' stance which, in the name of antispeciesism, had motivated awarding the other animals moral status in the first place.

As is well known, the chick's interest in a few years of simple henny pleasures, or its right to life as something of inherent value, turn out, in Singer and Regan,[1] to guarantee very little when they come up against my consciously contemplated future sophisticated pleasures or my right to life. The quasi-Kantian person/nonperson distinction is now drawn within the class of items accorded moral status and, although Singer and Regan can both plausibly claim that they still avoid speciesism (because of their stances on mentally incompetent humans), they do not avoid (what we might call) animal elitism. In their systems, some animals are more equal—have a higher moral status—than others. Some moral philosophers, working within the same structure, have made this explicit.[2]

Well, one might say, what's wrong with saying that differing animals—and even human beings at differing stages of their development—have differing moral status? Isn't this just to recognize a whole variety of morally relevant features that should be taken into account when deciding what to do, instead of lumping everything together under a single principle, and isn't this what virtue ethics recommends?

I would say there are two things wrong with it.

One is that the 'variety' of features recognized is so paltry, a few psychological capacities selected ad hoc to capture a few crude intuitions about which animal should win in cases where interests conflict. In this context we should note in passing the standard objection environmentalists make to the animal liberationists. It is that the latter draw no distinction between domestic and

---

[1] See Peter Singer (ed.), *In Defense of Animals* (Oxford: Blackwell, 1985) or for full statements of Regan's and Singer's positions, see Tom Regan, *The Case for Animal Rights* (Berkeley: University of California Press, 1985) and Peter Singer, *Animal Liberation*, rev. ed. (New York: Avon, 1990).

[2] For example, Donald VanDeVeer, 'Interspecific Justice', *Inquiry* 22 (1979): 55–70; and Mary Anne Warren, 'Difficulties with the Strong Animal Rights Position', *Between the Species* 2 (1987): 163–73.

wild animals, and that what their positions on 'animals' entail might be all right with respect to the former but are absurd with respect to the latter.[3]

The second is that the assigning of differing moral status is not merely recognizing a few features often relevant to good practical decision-making. It is recognizing them *and ranking* the possessors of those features accordingly. That, after all, is what the concept of status does. In welcoming recognition of (some of) the obvious differences between cats and men as an improvement on always lumping them together as sentient, or experiencing subjects of a life, virtue ethicists are not going to commit themselves in advance to saying that the cited differences will always guarantee that, in cases of conflict, it is the cats that will go to the wall because of their inferior status. After all, we can recognize differences between women and men as features that should often be taken into account when deciding what to do, without for a moment thinking that we thereby commit ourselves to any kind of ranking.

To illustrate the wrongness of both, we might briefly consider me and my cat. On any prevailing assignment of differing moral status, my psychological capacities easily outrank my cat's. If you can only rescue one of us from the burning building without danger to yourself, you should rescue me, preserving the animal that has the higher status. What if I have escaped by myself, should you then rescue the cat? Most people say no, unless you really can do it with no danger to yourself at all, because you outrank the cat too and should preserve the animal with the higher status. Is the same obviously true of me?

I would say that this is, at least, not obvious. For a further feature of the cat relevant to my decision-making is that he is *my* cat, a cat for whom I have assumed responsibility. Although it would, I take it, be sentimental idiocy of me to run a high risk of dying to rescue him, and highly irresponsible if I have family and friends, I am inclined to say that, if the risk, though real, is fairly low, and no one will be devastated by my death, going to rescue him might well be a good decision. After all, despite my superior moral status, my life mightn't be worth much, and although I can't risk your life on the grounds that it isn't worth much, I can surely risk my own.

Moreover, it is not obviously the case that, just because you outrank my cat, you are not in any way called upon to rescue him. I am reliably informed that people with the further feature of being firemen regard rescuing animals from burning buildings (when the risk is not extreme) as part of their normal duties.

---

[3] See J. Baird Callicott, 'Animal Liberation: A Triangular Affair', *Environmental Ethics* 2 (1980): 311–38.

Given these problems, virtue ethics can dismiss the question of the moral status of animals without a qualm. As a tool in the abortion debate, the concept of moral status had its uses. In my view, assigning the embryo or foetus a certain moral status was a clumsy (and often wildly inaccurate) attempt to capture what I called 'the right attitude to the familiar biological facts' of how we come to be, and that's worth doing. However, in the context of the ethics of our treatment of the other animals it is simply useless. There isn't one familiar set of facts concerning *the* other animals, but a whole host of sets of (largely unfamiliar) facts about different species, and another host of sets about individual animals, and another host about groups—pets, zoo animals, the animals we eat, the animals we experiment on... Questions about right and wrong actions in relation to animals arise in a wide variety of contexts, far too many to be settled by a blanket assignment of status.

Since there are so many different questions about right and wrong, I'll just jump into one of the most familiar areas, *viz.*—

2. Vegetarianism

The first thing for a virtue ethicist to say about vegetarianism, to correct a surprisingly common mistake, is that it cannot be a virtue. This is a grammatical, not an ethical, claim. Vegetarianism can't be a virtue because it is not a character trait but a practice, and virtues have to be character traits. Well, is it a virtuous practice? If we take that as asking 'Is it a practice which, as such, manifests or expresses virtue?' the answer is 'Obviously not' because people can become vegetarians for such a range of different reasons. If I become vegetarian on health grounds it might well manifest temperance, but if I go in for it simply because it is fashionable it would be a mark of folly.

However, if we take 'Is it a virtuous practice?' as asking 'Is it a practice that the virtuous, as such, go in for (or ideally, would go in for); i.e., a practice it is right to go in for?' we get to the question that someone employing a normative virtue ethics is supposed to address.

One way I begin to approach it is by taking several leaves out of Singer's first book, *Animal Liberation*. As some reviewers on the Amazon.com website note, you can skip over Singer's philosophy in this book without missing anything important. What is doing the work are the detailed descriptions of factory farming (and animal experimentation). Thirty years ago,[4] they

---

[4] The first edition of Singer's *Animal Liberation* appeared in 1975.

showed his readers that what we are being party to in eating meat is a huge amount of animal suffering that could be substantially reduced if we changed our habits. So I take the leaves on which he does that and think about them in terms of, for example, compassion, temperance, callousness, cruelty, greed, self-indulgence—and honesty.

Can I, in all honesty, deny the ongoing existence of this suffering? No, I can't. I know perfectly well that although there have been some improvements in the regulation of factory farming, what is going on is still terrible. Can I think it is anything but callous to shrug this off and say it doesn't matter? No, I can't. Can I deny that the practices are cruel? No, I can't. Then what am I doing being party to them? It won't do for me to say that I am not actually engaging in the cruelty myself. There is a large gap between not being cruel and being truly compassionate, and the virtue of compassion is what I am supposed to be acquiring and exercising. I can no more think of myself as compassionate while I am party to such cruelty than I could think of myself as just if, scrupulously avoiding owning slaves, I still enjoyed the fruits of slave labour.

What if I needed to eat meat to survive? That would, of course, be a very different situation. No one would think of many Africans, situated as they are, as being short of compassion solely on the grounds that they ate whatever the aid agencies provided. But that is not how it is with me, nor with anyone in a sufficiently privileged position to be reading this book. Once again, honesty compels me to admit that I do not *need* meat, I just *like* it. A lot. It gives me an enormous amount of pleasure. However, precisely what temperance requires is that I do not pursue such pleasure while ignoring the claims of the other virtues. Pursuing the pleasures of consuming meat, in the teeth of the claims of compassion, is just plain greedy and self-indulgent.

Suppose that, on occasion, I eat meat not in the pursuit of pleasure, but for some other reason? I have many hospitable meat-eating friends. Before they all know that I am vegetarian, am I to be Banquo at their feasts, refusing not only the meat, but the anchovy-corrupted salad and the stock-made soup, inflicting on my hosts the embarrassment of having nothing to offer me but bread, potatoes, and a couple of bananas? Politeness and consideration would give me good reason to eat what was put in front of me and that would not count as greedy or self-indulgent. Should I not have telephoned them well beforehand to tell them that I have become a vegetarian? Well, sometimes yes; there would be circumstances in which it was either thoughtless or (supposing I had thought about it) cowardly, in a way, not to do so. I don't telephone, and I eat what is put in front of me, because I want to avoid the confrontation and the cries of 'Oh no, not you too! I thought you had more sense.' But, after all, I think I have sense on my side; in ducking the issue I merely manifest the fact that I lack the courage of my conviction.

Of course all my friends will have to know one day that I have become vegetarian, and most will change their menus accordingly, at least somewhat, when they have me to dinner. Some may choose to ignore it (this is less common than it used to be) and what then? Their doing so is hardly a mark of the quasi-virtue of friendship, but neither is my continuing to attend their dinner parties, bringing embarrassment and censure to the table every time I do. (Other guests will notice how little I am eating and ask why, or whether I am vegetarian; on learning that I am they will naturally ask, Did our hosts not know? I can't lie about it so I will say yes, they know, or imply by my smile or shrug that that is so.) So I could give up the friendship, or I could excuse myself from their invitations but continue to have them to my (vegetarian) dinner parties in the hope they will come round. Or I could initiate our talking about it—not about their becoming vegetarian, but about their being more conciliatory about my having done so.

So, with respect to vegetarianism, a virtue ethicist may reach roughly the same practical conclusions as Singer and, albeit to a lesser extent, Regan, though on different grounds. The practices that bring cheap meat to our tables are cruel, so we shouldn't be party to them.

3. Experiments on the Other Animals

Does virtue ethics run the same line of thought about using sentient animals in scientific experiments? To a limited extent, yes. In other ways, no—not, or at least not immediately, because of virtue ethics' 'human centredness' (of which more later) but, surprisingly, because of virtue ethics' extreme practicality.

Let me deal very briefly with the first, in part because it will allow me to clear up a common misconception of cruelty. Consider the use of the other animals to test cosmetics. A virtue ethicist should agree with Singer and Regan that this is wrong, for it is, in my view, quite certain that such experiments are cruel. However, this is not beyond question, since some philosophers, such as Regan, maintain that cruel actions are limited to the intentional causing (or allowing) another to suffer by an agent who either enjoys or is indifferent to it.

This claim enables Regan and those who follow him to reject the idea that the prohibition against cruelty will suffice to ground any robust negative duties to animals. For, they point out, it allows people to subject animals to suffering as long as they regret the necessity. However, the claim is quite false, as a quick look at a dictionary should remind us. The causing of pain or suffering can count as cruel even when it is unintentional; people can be found guilty of cruelty to children and animals without the prosecution having to establish intent. More commonly, a cruel action is intentional, but the agent's professed or manifest purpose is quite enough, and neither his pleasure, his indifference, nor his regret is required for the assessment of his action as cruel or not. All that is needed is that the action is the infliction of pain for a purpose that does not justify it. Some experimenters on animals have inflicted horrifying suffering on cats; their purpose was to discover how much pain cats can stand before it kills them. Such experiments can be rightly condemned as cruel simply on the grounds that the knowledge gained was far too insignificant to justify the experiments, without any consideration of the experimenters' feelings.

The same is true of experiments to test new cosmetics, for, as Singer so rightly remarks, we don't *need* any new cosmetics, and, as virtue ethicists mindful of the vices of vanity and self-indulgence could add, we don't actually need any cosmetics at all. Their use could be a harmless pleasure, but only if limited to the use of those produced by companies that do not test their products on the other animals.

So, as before, the three different approaches may reach the same practical conclusion regarding the use of animals to test cosmetics—that we should refrain from being party to these practices. A utilitarian shouldn't be party to the infliction of unnecessary suffering, a deontologist to the violation of rights, and a virtue ethicist to cruel practices.

However—moving on now to the ways in which a virtue ethicist cannot continue to pursue this line—this is action-guidance only if 'refraining from being party to such practices' can amount to something that I can *do*, something that people who are being party to them don't do. It is ironic that the critics of virtue ethics, claiming that it couldn't give an account of right or wrong action and *hence* couldn't provide action-guidance, failed to notice that, in many cases, for most of us, their establishing that an action type is wrong provided no action-guidance whatsoever. This is true for many people regarding experiments on animals to test cosmetics, and becomes striking when we turn to the field of medical experimentation.

It is here that the issue of moral standing is assumed to be crucial. Medical experimentation on the other animals is directed toward saving, and improving, the lives of human beings. If many of the other animals used have the same moral status as human beings, then either we should be using brain-damaged orphans instead, or we shouldn't be doing it at all; it is wrong. What could be more important than establishing whether or not this is so?

But why is it so important, practically speaking? Suppose I had accepted that Singer and Regan have, in their different ways, shown that most/all experiments on the other animals are wrong. How does that provide action-guidance? What does it tell me to do? Obviously, to refrain from performing such experiments. For most of us, that's not an issue. I'm not an experimental biologist or technician, I'm a philosopher. So is just continuing to be a philosopher all their arguments tell me to do? That's also what I would do if I had rejected their conclusions.

As we have just seen, for some people, for some of the experimental practices, what one should do is obvious enough. Women who regularly buy cosmetics, and the few men who buy them for themselves or their partners, should refrain from buying them from companies that test their products on animals because we shouldn't be party to that practice. This leaves those who have no reason to buy cosmetics unaddressed, and, more importantly, leaves us without any action-guidance with respect to the vast field of medical experimentation. What *is* it to refrain from being party to medical experimentation on animals? One might, if the choice were offered, refuse to save or prolong one's life by accepting a transplant of a vital organ from a nonhuman animal, but that is an issue for very few of us. And, short of refraining from *any* of the benefits modern medicine has to offer, there doesn't seem to be anything that most of us could do that would count as 'refraining from being party to the practice'.

If normative ethics is to be truly about action, finding things to do with respect to medical experimentation on animals is far, far more important for philosophers concerned about our treatment of the other animals than trying to work out whether or not human lives and suffering count in some way more than the lives and suffering of the animals used, or whether the rights of human beings outrank theirs. Whichever way the arguments fall out, for or against, the conclusions on their own won't say anything practical to most of us. They are philosophical exercises we engage in, but not to discover what each of us, individually, should do about medical experimentation on animals. Suppose I do reach the conclusion that experimenting on a nonhuman animal is every bit as wrong as experimenting on a brain-damaged orphan. 'So', I say to myself, 'I must...' Must what? Practically speaking, I am no better off than I would have been if I had concluded that it isn't as wrong, but still, in many cases, it may be very wrong, or quite wrong. Now, why is this?

Here we come to another piece of the structure imposed by the other two approaches that needs to be unpicked. I should note that I do not think the following mistake is intrinsic to the other two approaches, only that, in practice, their overly theoretic stance has resulted in its prevalence.

Suppose one begins doing normative theory by thinking in terms of providing a systematic account of why 'act X' or 'such and such an action' is right or wrong. The intentionally abstract phrases leave it unsettled whether one is talking about action types or action tokens, and, moreover, whether the action—type or token—is, or forms, part of a practice. Sometimes this doesn't matter. Given an act description such as 'lying', direct utilitarianism will tell you when a token is right and when it is wrong, and deontology will tell you that the action type is wrong and hence each token is (or that the action type lying-in-such-and-such-circumstances is wrong though the action type lying-in-so-and-so-circumstances is justifiable), and with the ascription of wrongness to a token, that is, an individual action, we have our general action-guidance.

The prevalent mistake lies in assuming that what goes for something like 'lying' goes for any other act description; that is, that getting 'is wrong' attached to it is going to provide general action-guidance by somehow hooking up with an action token. Lying is not a practice, but a type of individual action that any one of us might do on almost any occasion. When practices are what is at issue, it is much harder to get to individual actions that any one of us might do or refrain from doing.

Singer overlooked this problem in the first edition of *Practical Ethics*,[5] failing to notice that while the direct utilitarianism he had committed himself to might support the conclusion that farmers should stop meat production; it did not license his conclusion that I should not buy meat in supermarkets. He had argued that the *practices* of producing meat were wrong, that those who engaged in it were failing to give equal consideration to the interests of the animals involved. Yet when I turn up at the supermarket and follow his instruction 'to take account of the interests of all those sentient beings affected by my decision', I know that my individual action of buying meat is not going to affect the interests of any nonhuman animal, except, perhaps, my dog. His claim that I should not be party to these wrong practices needed the support of the indirect utilitarianism he introduced in the second edition.

---

[5] Peter Singer, *Practical Ethics* (Cambridge: Cambridge University Press, 1979). A second, expanded edition appeared in 1993.

Here again, it is a mistake to assume that what goes for one description of a practice goes for any other description; that is, that attaching 'is wrong' to it is always going to provide corresponding guidance to be derived from 'being party to the practice is wrong'. You have to look at the practice at issue and see what it is like.

Medical experimentation is, unlike lying, a practice. But, unlike meat production, it is not a practice that any one of us can readily, in our individual actions, refrain from being party to. What is it like?

It is a practice that is deeply entrenched in a powerful, and also well entrenched, set of institutions—not only medical schools training doctors, medical research centres, and corporate research centres and laboratories seeking drugs or treatments that will make money, but also universities training students who can then work in such places, some of whom will remain in the universities doing research that may feed back into the training of the doctors and medical and corporate research centres. This set of inter-locked institutions is something that most of us, individually, are utterly powerless to change.

That is why the debate over whether '*it*', or only *many*, or *some*, aspects of it, are wrong is not important, practically speaking. Settling that issue one way or the other will not make most of us one whit less powerless.

Conversely, making no more than the modest assumption, consistent with any outcome of the debate a philosopher might reach, that at least *some* of it is wrong, is enough to get us going, once we have it under that description—a practice entrenched in an interlocked and also entrenched set of institutions. We have to begin by thinking about what changes that sort of setup. Racism was like that, and although it still is to some extent, things have improved enough in the last forty years for us to be able to look back and learn something from the changes. What brought them about?

In part, as we know, the leadership of some great figures such as Martin Luther King and Nelson Mandela. In part, as we know, the courage and determination of a great number of black people. However, as we also know, in part the individually insignificant but collectively influential actions and reactions of a great number of white people. Some people were in a position to do more than others; for example, lawyers, journalists, writers, and teachers—and academics, being both writers and teachers. Some of them joined in the collective action and some of them didn't. A lot of what was done was, individually, very insignificant indeed. People signed petitions, joined pressure groups, went on perfectly safe marches, voted for politicians who spoke against racism. And, I suppose, argued and often broke off relations with their parents and some of their friends. These are not the sorts of things one can recount with justifiable pride when asked 'What did you do about racism in the sixties, Mummy?' but they were things that almost anybody white could do, they were worth doing, and again, not everybody did them.

We are, perhaps, inclined to think that 'What would a virtuous agent do in the circumstances?' has to be answered by the description of an action that merits praise. That certainly is not always true; it depends on the circumstances. When I do something as ordinary as tell the truth in response to the stranger's question 'How do I get to the station from here?' I do what is honest. When I leave a standard tip for the waiter who brought me my coffee I do what is just. Such actions are too minimally decent to call for praise, and since 'virtuous' is a term of praise, it is contrary to common usage to call them 'virtuous'. However, they are no less 'what a virtuous agent would do in the circumstances' just because they hardly call for virtue and are regularly done by a lot of people who doubtless fall far short of possessing it. In the circumstances imagined here, there isn't anything else for the virtuous agent to do, the doing of which would distinguish her from the nonvirtuous, either the merely conventional or the dishonest and unjust.

Now the white antiracists who signed petitions and so on did a bit better than that. Protesting against the prevailing convention, they did distinguish themselves from the merely conventional, and from the unjust racist and also from the cynics and those who despaired of bringing about change and were paralyzed by their individual powerlessness. If they hadn't, things would still be just as bad as they once were.

Much of this is directly transferable to the issue of medical experimentation. Any of us can sign petitions, support animal rights pressure groups, and vote for politicians who speak up on behalf of the other animals. In this context, the role that lawyers play in combating the racism entrenched in the legal systems will mostly have to be played by scientists within the set of institutions that enshrine the practice, but it is up to the rest of us, collectively, to make enough noise to get more of them concerned about bringing about changes.

Some people are in a position to do more than others. A growing number of science undergraduates now refuse to do animal dissections. I gather (without being quite sure) that some have just been kicked out of their classes and thereby forced to fail them, but I have also been told on good authority that, in some universities at least, the system has been changed to accommodate them. Some people can get onto the ethics committees that, in some institutions, now regulate, to some extent, the use of the other animals, and some can campaign to get such committees established.

Suppose one does get on such a committee, what should one do? Isn't this a situation in which one would have to make up one's mind one way or the other whether at least some of the other animals had the same moral status as human beings? In my view, no, because if you decide that they do, and argue and vote against every experiment that comes under scrutiny, you will just be thrown off the committee. Your only chance of staying on and achieving anything at all is to join forces with those who are arguing and voting against the experiments whose benefits to humans are (in Singer's words) 'either non-existent or very uncertain'. But suppose you really, truly believe it? Is it not a failure of integrity, or shameful hypocrisy, to allow any of the experiments to pass without protest, however fruitless? How could a virtuous agent do that?

Well, if you really believed in the equal moral status, for you the set of institutions in which medical experimentation is entrenched would, I think, be comparable to the set of institutions imposed by the Nazis. Yet most of the people we admire from that dreadful time concentrated on doing the very little that they could, 'allowing' many Jews to go to the death camps 'without protest', and we do not condemn them for hypocrisy or lack of integrity. Think of Schindler, jovially entertaining powerful members of the SS while he schemed to get more Jews into the protection of his factory.[6] How, situated as he was, could he have shown more virtue?

True, everyone who did anything to help the Jews in Germany or the occupied countries risked their lives, and so we admire them for their courage as well as their compassion, justice, and practical wisdom. Their virtue was, in Philippa Foot's words, 'severely tested' and passed the test.[7] It may be that some of those who are strongly committed to the cause of animal liberation yearn for some appropriately heroic expression of this strong commitment, something that would severely test their virtue, finding it intolerable that all they can find to do are such trifling things as sign petitions and join pressure groups.

There is no reason to suppose that, for many of us, there is any such expression. Think of racism again. There was very little most people living outside South Africa could do to express their commitment to ending apartheid beyond boycotting South African goods and the usual trifling things one hopes will, eventually, influence one's government to bring more pressure to bear. Aristotle does not give enough attention to the nameless virtue, which we might now call proper modesty, that consists in correctly assessing one's

---

[6] Thomas Keneally, *Schindler's Ark* (London: Hodder & Stoughton, 1982).
[7] Philippa Foot, *Virtues and Vices* (Oxford: Oxford University Press, 2002).

limited capacities to achieve great things, being more interested in its grand form, *megalopsuchia*. No doubt in such a tiny democracy as his Athens, the idea that change could be brought about only through years of collective endeavour made up of individually insignificant actions was unlikely to occur to him. However, that is how things are with us now. It is not heroic courage but unexciting virtues that call us to such actions—amongst them, hope, patience, and modesty.

You may complain that none of what I have said about our actions in relation to the other animals is exciting but all pretty obvious. I think myself that this is how it should be. Most of the results of applying virtue ethics *should* be pretty obvious, because, rather than constructing theoretical principles, virtue ethics just applies the everyday virtue and vice terms to our actions in the world as we find it. But what is there to be found, even right under our noses, is often not obvious until it is pointed out. We have to make sure we really are looking at the ways human beings are affecting the world and, if they are bad, that we ask ourselves 'What can I do?' instead of getting tied up in abstruse questions about moral status.

4. Human-Centredness

It will not have escaped the observant reader that much of the preceding discussion smacks more of consequentialism than of an absolutist rights-based position. Of course, virtue ethicists have always shared a form of anti-absolutism with consequentialists, agreeing with them that many act types—lying, killing, meat-eating—are right in some circumstances, wrong in others, adding 'depending on the circumstances' rather than 'on the consequences'.

This might lead a committed animal-rights advocate to protest—as Regan protests against Singer—that someone approaching the matter via the virtue ethical term 'cruel' has really missed the point. '[W]hat is fundamentally wrong', Regan says, 'isn't the pain, isn't the suffering...[though] [t]hese compound what's wrong. The fundamental wrong' is viewing animals 'as *our resources*'.[8] Hence his insistence that the other animals have inherent, rather than merely instrumental, value. Can virtue ethicists take some leaves from Regan's book too?

Well, we had better not do so by taking on the blanket ascription of inherent or intrinsic value, because that will take us straight back into moral status

---

[8] Tom Regan, 'The Case for Animal Rights', in Singer (ed.), *In Defense of Animals*, 13.

territory and the usual problems of whether Xs have the same value as, or less value than, non-Xs. We can recast talk about things having intrinsic value as talk about their being worth our pursuing or having or preserving (or bringing into being, protecting, maintaining, restoring, desiring, loving...) for their own sake, and there is no reason why virtue ethicists shouldn't agree with Regan that the good of the other animals is such a thing and thereby has intrinsic value in that sense.

Unconstrained by the need to assign moral status, and thereby to find a feature (such as being the experiencing subject of a life) that grounds it, there is no reason for us to stop there. The environmental ethics literature has compellingly reminded us that species, and the good of plants and ecosystems, also have 'intrinsic value'—that is, in our terms, they are also worth our pursuing or preserving, protecting, desiring, and so on for their own sake, not merely for our own.[9]

However, it is often supposed that virtue ethics (or at least, Aristotelian or eudaimonistic virtue ethics) has a peculiar problem in ascribing intrinsic value in *any* robust sense to the other animals, let alone to plants or ecosystems, because, it is thought, it counts *human* flourishing or the good *human* life (*eudaimonia*) or *human* virtue as 'the fundamental' or 'top' value. Thereby, it is thought, virtue ethics is objectionably 'human-centred', regarding the rest of nature as no better than a resource for us.[10]

This is a mistake (or set of mistakes) but it is hard to pin down how it arises. Let's begin by considering *eudaimonia*—i.e., human flourishing or the good human life—separately from virtue. At least part of the trouble arises from misunderstanding the role this plays in eudaimonistic virtue ethics and trying to identify that role in terms of its 'counting as the top value'.

According to ancient Greek ethics, my final, architectonic end—and everyone else's—is indeed *human* flourishing, living a good human life. But, as Julia Annas has frequently pointed out,[11] this is not, in itself, a form of egoism, nor, we may now add, does it in any way privilege the value of *human* flourishing or *human* life. It is not egoistic in virtue of its directing me to think about *my* flourishing, *my* good life. I am to think about how I should live *my* life, how to

---

[9] It is, I think, in the area of 'environmental', rather than 'animal' ethics—assuming that to be a currently comprehensible division of the academic literature—that discussion of wild animals belongs, though space does not permit it here.

[10] See, for example, Holmes Rolston III, 'Environmental Virtue Ethics: Half the Truth but Dangerous as a Whole', in Philip Cafaro and Ronald Sandler (eds), *Environmental Virtue Ethics* (Lanham, MD: Rowman & Littlefield, 2005), 61–74.

[11] In many places, but see *The Morality of Happiness* (Oxford: Oxford University Press, 1993), especially 127–8, 223, 322–5.

give it a shape, simply because it is only *my* life that I can live, not because I am to take it to be necessarily more worth preserving than yours. It is not chauvinistic in virtue of its saying that my end—and everyone else's—is human flourishing, living a good human life. This doesn't rank human life over other animals' lives and direct me to choose to live a human one because it is more valuable. I have no choice. Since I am a human being, there is no other kind of life I could live.

So far, the content of human *eudaimonia* has been left unspecified. Let us move on to (human) virtue. As Annas has also stressed,[12] ancient eudaimonism could, and did, take an egoistic form—when, that is, *eudaimonia* is taken to be the life of pleasure. No doubt someone who lived only for pleasure (of the egoistical sort) would indeed regard the rest of nature, as well as other human beings, as no better than resources, but things are very different when we take *eudaimonia* to be the life of virtue. Just as the exercise of virtues such as charity, generosity, justice, and the quasi virtue of friendship, necessarily involves *not* focusing on oneself and one's virtue but on the rights, interests, and good of other human beings, so the exercise of compassion and the avoidance of a number of vices, involves focusing on the good of the other animals as something worth pursuing, preserving, protecting, and so on.

It is a commonplace of our thoughts about virtue—not only philosophical virtue ethicists' thoughts, but everyday thoughts, reflected in common usage—that the exercise of virtues such as charity, friendship, courage, honesty, and justice may, if one is unlucky, turn out to involve laying down one's life. This not only makes it clear that one's individual virtuous actions are not aimed directly at either one's *eudaimonia* or one's personal virtue, but also that it is not virtue ethics, per se, which says that such self-sacrifice could not be required by virtue if what was at stake was 'only' another animal, or the survival of a species or an ecosystem. It is not virtue ethics that says such things are not worth dying for; it is our everyday use of 'worthwhile' and the virtue and vice terms.

Everyday usage of the virtue and vice vocabulary is indeed human-centred by and large (compassion and cruelty are the obvious exceptions) and we know why; namely, that centuries of Western ethical thought have been human-centred. Thereby, the same is true of our everyday use of such terms as 'duty', 'obligation', 'rights' and 'right' and 'wrong' applied to actions. The problem of traditional human-centredness is one that every philosopher who

---

[12] Ibid.

wants to change our attitudes toward the other animals and the rest of nature has to face, not one peculiar to virtue ethics.

Singer and Regan have become rightly famous for making it obvious to many of us that a great deal of gratuitous suffering is involved in our use of some of the other animals for food and experimental purposes. Once we have brought ourselves to recognize this fact, the ordinary usage of 'cruel' and 'compassionate' latches on to it quite unproblematically. However, as environmentalists constantly urge, we need a substantial change in our outlook to get any further—in virtue ethics' terms, a clearly seen and affective recognition of the fact that human beings, and thereby human lives, are not only interwoven with each other but with the rest of nature. Then, and only then, will we apply virtue ethics correctly to what we are doing.

References

Annas, J. 1993. *The Morality of Happiness*. Oxford: Oxford University Press.

Callicott, J. B. 1980. 'Animal Liberation: A Triangular Affair', *Environmental Ethics* 2: 311–38.

Foot, P. 2002. *Virtues and Vices*. Oxford: Oxford University Press.

Keneally, T. 1982. *Schindler's Ark*. London: Hodder & Stoughton.

Regan, T. 1985a. 'The Case for Animal Rights'. In P. Singer (ed.), *In Defense of Animals*. Oxford: Blackwell: 13–26.

Regan, T. 1985b. *The Case for Animal Rights*. Berkeley: University of California Press.

Rolston III, H. 1985. 'Environmental Virtue Ethics: Half the Truth but Dangerous as a Whole'. In P. Cafaro and R. Sandler (eds), *Environmental Virtue Ethics*. Lanham, MD: Rowman & Littlefield: 61–74.

Singer, P. 1979. *Practical Ethics*. Cambridge: Cambridge University Press (second, expanded edition 1993).

Singer, P. (ed.). 1985. *In Defense of Animals* Oxford: Blackwell.

Singer, P. 1990. *Animal Liberation*, revised edition. New York: Avon.

VanDeVeer, D. 1979. 'Interspecific Justice', *Inquiry* 22: 55–70.

Warren, M. A. 1987. 'Difficulties with the Strong Animal Rights Position', *Between the Species* 2: 163–73.

11
Environmental Virtue Ethics

Environmental ethics is concerned with the articulation and defence of what I shall call 'the green belief'—the belief, namely, that a fairly radical change in the way we engage with nature is imperative. Environmental virtue ethics, then, is concerned with articulating and defending the green belief in virtue ethics terms, rather than in the terms of its two rivals, utilitarianism and deontology. This chapter is about what an environmental virtue ethics might be like. I consider two significantly different versions. First, we might have an environmental virtue ethics that seeks to articulate and defend the green belief in terms of old and familiar virtues and vices that are given a new interpretation when applied to the new field of our relations with nature. The second version goes beyond the first by introducing one or two new virtues, explicitly concerned with our relations with nature. (Note, in the description of both versions, a stress on the 'new'. It is pretty much agreed ground amongst environmental ethicists that the truth of the green belief calls for 'a new ethic', but just how new, and new in just what way remains unclear and extremely tendentious.)

1. Old Virtues and Vices

I begin by illustrating (with necessary brevity) how much mileage I think can be got out of the old virtues and vices when they are used to articulate and defend the green belief.[1] One of the earliest modern philosophy books devoted to environmental issues was Passmore's *Man's Responsibility for Nature*. Without explicitly espousing virtue ethics, which barely existed at the time, Passmore argued in defence of the green belief in largely virtue and vice terms, claiming that it is primarily through the vices of greed, self-indulgence, and short-sightedness that we have brought about, and are continuing to bring

---

[1] I wrote the final version of this chapter before reading Louke van Wensveen's (2000) wonderful book, which shows that writers have found it quite natural to invoke over 170 old and familiar virtues in the context of environmental ethics.

about, ecological disasters and that what was needed to avert them was 'that old-fashioned procedure, thoughtful action' (1974: 194)—or, as virtue ethicists would say, the virtue of prudence or practical wisdom.

The point that greed, self-indulgence, and short-sightedness are very much to blame is not, I think, questioned by any environmentalist. It can, and frequently does, form an implicit part of the most straightforward 'human-centred' utilitarian defence of the green belief, and of green economists' and scientists' defences. That some of our practices are, or have been, just plain short-sighted as far as our own interests are concerned is the most straightforward position to defend. No one, no matter how indifferent to environmental issues in general, welcomes air pollution in their city, or the unavailability of uncontaminated shellfish, or being made sick by their water. True, most people believe that 'the government should do something about it' in a way that neither raises their taxes nor prohibits their doing any of the things they have become accustomed to doing, but this response, the defence will plausibly claim, is just short-sightedness all over again. There isn't a quick fix; there is not any way in which the pollution can be halted and turned around without our forgoing a number of practices and activities that we, at least in the 'developed' nations, think of as enjoyments that are part of ordinary pleasant life.

Is it greedy and self-indulgent of us to want to enjoy such things? This is a much less straightforward position to defend, but much of the literature in environmental ethics (by no means just the minute amount that argues in terms of virtue ethics) suggests that convincing others, and ourselves, of the far reaching truth of the green belief, will necessarily involve bringing us all to see that it is. At the moment, a very small number of people have come to see their previous enjoyment of a very small number of 'ordinary' things—the eating of meat and the wearing of fur coats, the acquisition of new mahogany furniture, the owning of several cars—as greedy and self-indulgent, and changed their practices.

However, such a shift in moral self-assessment clearly does not come about just through the recognition that our current practices are short-sighted, if at all. People usually convert to vegetarianism on moral, rather than health, grounds because of some sort of concern about the animals we standardly consume. A change in the many ways in which we use animals, particularly for food, can be defended, in virtue ethics terms, by reference not only to the vices of greed and self-indulgence, but also to that of cruelty and the corresponding lack of the virtue of compassion, without any attempt to defend the idea that animals have rights.[2] Few people nowadays are prepared to deny outright that a great deal of animal suffering is involved in the processes that bring cheap meat to our supermarket shelves. A surprising number still believe that the consumption of meat is necessary for human health, but once that ignorance is dispelled, the animal suffering is revealed to be quite gratuitous and our practices thereby cruel. The fact that I myself, as an ordinary deskbound city-dweller, am not actually out and about inflicting cruelty on chickens, sheep, cows, pigs, and so on, may preserve me from being rightly called 'cruel' but I do not merit being called compassionate, if, knowing about the cruel practices, I still enjoy their fruits, any more than I merit being called just if I knowingly enjoy the fruits of slave labour while congratulating myself on not actually being a slave owner.

It has long been recognized that, although the vices do not form a unity, some of them certainly aggravate others. The old, familiar, vices of pride and vanity make us unwilling to acknowledge our greed, self-indulgence, short-sightedness, and lack of compassion; dishonesty, exercised in the form of self-deception, enables us to blind ourselves to relevant facts and arguments and find excuses for continuing as we are (think of the people who are still pretending that global warming isn't happening); cowardice makes us unwilling to go out on a limb and risk the contempt of our peers by propounding unpopular views, and so on.

It seems clear that much of what is wrong about our current practices with regard to nature springs from these familiar and ancient human vices—played out, in environmental ethics, on an unfamiliar stage. And it may well be that if we could find a way of releasing many human beings from the grip of these familiar vices, the change in our current ways of going on would be so extraordinarily radical that it would indeed adequately set the scene for all the changes that environmentalists dream of. After all, no one suggests that we need a new ethic to deal with the human-centred moral problems of poverty, war, and, quite generally, 'man's inhumanity to man'. We suppose that if (and what a big 'if') we could somehow induce many more of ourselves to be truly compassionate, benevolent, unselfish, honest, unmaterialistic, long-sighted, just, patient—virtuous, in familiar ways, in short—the way human beings live would be radically different, and the entirely human-centred moral

---

[2] For a beautifully clear discussion of ancient Greek defences of animals that did not appeal to animal rights (even when maintaining that we owed justice to them) see Sorabji (1993), especially chapter 11.

problems that our own vices create would become things of the past. And if these hitherto intractable human-centred ones, why not the environmental ones as well?

This does not seem to be an unreasonable position, though it perhaps needs to be supplemented by the mention of one more virtue, which, although old, has become somewhat unfashionable in recent decades and thereby unfamiliar, namely humility, which has been emphasized by Thomas Hill Jr. (1983). (Hill calls the virtue 'proper humility' in order to distinguish it from those failings or vices that many people nowadays would find to be connoted by describing someone as 'humble'—obsequiousness, false modesty, wimpishness, and the like.)

Proper humility is the virtue traditionally opposed to the vice of arrogance, the undue assumption of dignity, authority, power, or knowledge, and a constantly recurring theme in environmental ethics—especially in writings that call for a new 'biocentric' approach—has been that we should, indeed, must, recognize and, in recognizing, perforce, abandon our undue assumption of dignity, authority, power, and knowledge—our arrogance in short—in relation to nature. Notwithstanding the surprisingly common belief that Darwinism shows that we are to be dignified as the top species, it gives us no reason to suppose that we are any such thing. As Stephen Clark, early on in environmental ethics, nicely put it, 'We sometimes speak of the dinosaurs as failures; there will be time enough for that judgement when we have lasted even one tenth as long' (1977: 112). The rationality that Western philosophical tradition has made the distinguishing mark of our superiority may well turn out to be, in evolutionary terms, a poor strategy. By the same token, our rationality, whether in its own right, or as the mark of our having been made in the image of God, gives us no especial authority. We do not have 'dominion' over nature; it is not true, as Aristotle claimed, that plants exist for the sake of animals and all other animals exist for the sake of human beings. We can—that is, it is possible for us to—make use of plants and animals and indeed minerals and other inanimate things, but the old idea that we can do so without restraint, and that bountiful nature would somehow make good our depredations has now been proved to be a fantasy. (It is a notable fact, which might strike one as enragingly arrogant, or heart-wrenchingly innocent, that Aristotle believed that no species could be destroyed.) Our power over nature, we have discovered, is much more limited than we supposed when we first got modern science going, mostly because, as we discovered rather recently, our knowledge and understanding of the biosphere is in its infancy. (I think it is correct to say that the undue assumption of our power over, and knowledge of, nature is comparatively recent. Prior to the dawn of modern science (whenever we might date that) we may have thought that we had superiority and authority, but I don't think we were under any illusion that we had much of the power over nature that knowledge brings until industrialization.)

In that paragraph on arrogance I crudely sum up an extensive body of environmental ethics literature. Most of the literature that emphasizes such points is, polemically, directed towards establishing the inherent or intrinsic worth or value of individual living things or biotic communities but, in the context of virtue ethics, it serves equally well as a convincing condemnation of our arrogance—and thereby as a call to the unfashionable virtue of humility.

It can be seen that defending the green belief in terms of the old virtues and vices involves a particular strategy. Each old virtue or vice mentioned is considered in the context of the new area of our relations with nature, and thereby acquires a new application or dimension. I have briefly alluded to the old virtues of prudence, practical wisdom, compassion, and proper humility, and the old vices of greed, self-indulgence, short-sightedness, cruelty, pride, vanity, dishonesty, and arrogance. We acquire a new perception, or understanding, of what is involved in being compassionate, or greedy or shortsighted or properly humble or arrogant; some of the old virtues and vices get reconfigured. And, we might well say, from the virtue ethics standpoint, this has been a standard strategy for ethical advance. (We might note a parallel strategy in much deontological environmental ethics; you take a familiar old moral rule or duty, such as the duty not to kill, or to harm, and you play it out on a different stage, thereby giving it a new interpretation.)

2. Still Human-Centred?

Is a virtue ethics thus reconfigured human-centred? Well, it is obviously still concerned with what sort of people we human beings should be and what we should do. But any normative ethics is concerned with the rightness or wrongness of human actions, with what we human beings should do and be and there is nothing in the environmental ethics literature that calls for a new ethic to suggest that there is anything wrong with that. However, there is more than a whiff of a much less widespread human-centredness in Hill which, having noted his views, we should pause to consider.

Hill argues that neither utilitarianism nor deontology can account for the wrongness of wantonly destroying a living thing such as a tree. But when he moves on to account for its wrongness in the virtue ethical terms of proper humility and arrogance, his discussion disconcertingly parallels Kant's account of the wrongness of inflicting gratuitous suffering on animals. And this is notoriously human-centred. Kant held that the animals' suffering was incidental. What is really wrong with cruelty to animals is that it leads to cruelty to one's fellow human beings. Hill, similarly, holds that what is wrong with lack of proper humility in regard to nature is its dangerous tendency to lead the agent to treat other persons disrespectfully.[3]

Most philosophers who deplore the way we use animals have long made two objections to Kant's account. One is that it is based on a false empirical premise. Notwithstanding their enjoyment of watching bullfights, the Spaniards are not notably crueller to each other than members of other European nations. The second, deeper, objection is that Kant's account simply misses the point. Of course the animals' suffering matters. That is why it is right to describe the gratuitous infliction of it as cruel and to deplore it thereby, regardless of whether or not it leads to cruelty to human beings. How manifestly perverse it would be to account for the wrongness of cruelty to small children not in terms of what it did to the children but in terms of how it led to cruelty to rational adults! And most environmental philosophers would want to make the same two objections to Hill. It is quite implausible to say that being humbled before nature promotes humility before persons, and, more importantly, the untoward death of living things matters. That is why it is right to describe me as acting arrogantly if I assume dominion and authority over the lives of non-rational living things, and act as though they were mine to dispose of at a whim, and to deplore my action thereby, regardless of whether or not I am likely to act arrogantly to other humans.

However, it is Hill's Kantian predilections that lead him down this path. He is thinking of virtue (vice) as a tendency to right (wrong) action independently specified, and his paradigms of right (wrong) action involve other human beings. But virtue ethics, as is well known, specifies right and wrong action in terms of the virtues and vices. If cruelty is a vice, then to recognize an act as one of cruelty to animals is thereby to recognize it as wrong, and no further account of wherein its wrongness consists is called for. Similarly, if arrogance is a vice, to recognize an act of wanton destruction of a living thing as arrogant is thereby to recognize it as wrong and no further account of wherein its wrongness consists is called for. So, in particular, no account in terms of its dangerous tendency to lead to the disrespectful treatment of humans is called

---

[3] '[T]hose who value such traits as humility, gratitude, and sensitivity *to others* have reason to promote the love of nature', 224, my italics.

for. So virtue ethics need not take on the excessive human-centredness of Hill's account.

It is true that neo-Aristotelian virtue ethics holds that the virtues benefit their possessor, that they are necessary and (with a bit of luck) sufficient for *eudaimonia*, for living well as a human being. Does this claim entail that human well-being is the only thing that really matters morally, or that it is the top value, ranked above any other (in an improperly human chauvinistic way)? Some environmentalist philosophers seem to suppose so, but it is unclear why. However, I do not want to dodge this issue, and I shall return to it at the end of the chapter.

Sometimes the disquiet seems to amount to no more than the thought that we should stop thinking about our virtues and vices—and thereby ourselves—and direct our attention to the natural world. And there may be a grain of practical truth in this thought. How, after all, is the reconfiguration of the familiar virtues and vices to be brought about except by a radical change in our ways of thinking and feeling about, and hence acting in relation to, the natural world? Is it not just this change that, for example, Aldo Leopold, Arne Naess, Paul W. Taylor, and Holmes Rolston III have attempted, with some success, to bring about? But a 'way of thinking, feeling and acting in relation to' some field or area of activity is, quite often, an ethical character trait, a virtue or a vice. If what is needed is or are a new way or ways, perhaps what is needed is at least one new virtue, explicitly concerned with our relations to nature.

This brings us to a consideration of the second version an environmental virtue ethics might take.

Before we embark on exploring this, we should note that the introduction—or discovery—of a new virtue is a formidable task. As an ethical character trait, a virtue, say, honesty, is far more than a mere disposition or tendency to go in for certain sorts of actions (say, honest ones). For a start, someone who is honest not only does what is honest but does so for certain reasons, not, for example, simply because they think honesty is the best policy. Further, virtue is also concerned with feelings or emotions; it also involves dispositions to certain sorts of emotional reactions, including finding certain things enjoyable and others painful or distressing. On the more intellectual side, it involves a certain perceptive capacity with regard to the area of the virtue in question (such as, in the case of honesty, an acute eye for occasions on which we are all about to connive unwittingly at dishonesty) and 'practical wisdom'—the capacity to reason correctly about what is to be done—which itself involves reasoning in relation to good ends. And all these apparently disparate elements can form a unity in human nature; that is, they can be recognized as a way a human being, given human psychology, could be.

And finally, if we are not to depart too radically from tradition, this way that we could be should have a recognizable preliminary version; a way that children can be that, although on the right track, still needs to be developed and expanded, and ultimately corrected, by practical wisdom.

Standardly, though by no means invariably, this complex and elusive concept of an ethical character trait is grasped through a noun which names the character trait (e.g. 'generosity'), with an associated adjective ('generous') that can apply to people and to acts—to people as possessing the character trait, to acts that, though not necessarily springing from the virtue, are typical of it. So the introduction or discovery of an unfamiliar, 'new', virtue would, on the face of it, need to involve the invention or coining of a new term or concept, which named a complex unity of dispositions to act and feel for certain sorts of reasons, and to see and respond to things in certain sorts of ways, which we had discovered, or realized, was a way human beings, given human psychology, could be. And this complex unity would have to be the sort of thing we could conceive of as being inculcated in children as part of their moral education—not totally against the grain, but expanding on and correcting some natural inclination(s) they have.

3. One New Virtue

Hill himself mentions two features that seem to be involved in being rightly relate to nature which proper humility does not capture—some sort of aesthetic appreciation of it and some sense of gratitude towards it—and it is noteworthy that finding beauty in nature, and feeling gratitude to it for, not only its beauty, but its abundance are emotional reactions that are perfectly consistent with proper humility but which rescue one from the proper humility's being crushing or dispiriting. (Could the reflection that human beings and all their works are but an insignificant and fleeting part of the great unfolding of the natural world fail to be crushing if it were not ameliorated by the joyous thought that we are part of something glorious?) The aesthetic appreciation of nature has, as a topic, its own extensive philosophical literature—in aesthetics—and it is not easy, in this area, to transfer aesthetics talk into ethics talk. However, there are certainly some suggestive lines of thought to be pursued. R. W. Hepburn (1984), an aesthetician, has at least two important essays which find many echoes in environmental ethics literature.

One explores 'the enjoyment of natural beauty as tending towards an ideal of oneness with nature or as leading to the disclosure of unity in nature' (1984: 17) and the other analyses the concept of an emotion, wonder, that, as he says, 'occupies in a paradigmatic way exactly that territory common to the aesthetic, moral and religious' (1984: 7).

Some of the points that Hepburn makes about wonder in relation to nature could well be taken over into an account of (proper) humility, to which he explicitly links it, but he also links it, surely rightly, to openness, to gratitude, and to delight. The interesting question for virtue ethics is whether the emotion of wonder might resemble the emotions of fear and anger in being one whose correct orientation amounts to a virtue. Being rightly disposed with respect to fear amounts to the virtue of courage. Being rightly disposed with respect to anger amounts to a virtue, nameless in Aristotle's time and to this very day. (Following Aristotle, in translation we call it 'patience', while recognizing that this, as he says, 'tends towards describing the deficiency' of not getting angry when one should.) Could being rightly disposed with respect to wonder—i.e. being disposed to feel wonder the right way, towards the right objects, for the right reasons, to the right degree, on the right occasions, in the right manner, and to act accordingly—count as a virtue, a character trait of the required complex sort? It may well be that it could.

There is, one might say, unrecognized by generations of philosophers and psychologists, a human emotion as familiar and everyday as fear and anger which is wonder, typically expressed (in English speakers) by the happy cry 'Oh isn't that wonderful!' (or nowadays, with unwitting appropriateness, 'awesome!') that children come up with spontaneously as soon as they have learnt to talk. (In fact it is not quite true that it has always been unrecognized. Descartes has it in the *Passions of the Soul*.) If Hepburn is right, this emotion can be felt in accordance with, or contrary to, reason just as fear and anger can. Some objects, for instance nature and its works, are proper objects of it; some, such as the merely novel or unfamiliar, are not. And getting this natural human emotion in harmony with reason really matters morally, just as getting the emotions of fear and anger in harmony with reason do. If we think and feel, not that nature is wondrous but that Disneyland or the Royal Family of Windsors are, that the other animals are not, but we are, that the seas are not but swimming pools on the twentieth floor of luxury hotels are, and act accordingly, then we will act wrongly, just as we do when we fear pain to ourselves but not to others, or are angered by justified criticism and not getting our own way but not angered by cruelty to animals or injustice to our fellow humans.

The putative virtue of being disposed to feel the emotion of wonder the right way, towards the right objects, for the right reasons, to the right degree, and so on is, I think, explicitly concerned with our relations to nature (who has written about wonder without talking about the wonders of nature?) and the exploration of this putative virtue, in that explicit connection, would probably form an instructive and inspiring part of an environmental virtue ethic. But it is not uniquely so concerned. Hepburn, after all, discusses it in relation to works of art, and it would be odd for a philosopher to deny that the works of the Great Dead Philosophers are proper objects of wonder. So we might look further, for a putative virtue that takes our relations with nature as its unique concern and incorporates just that part of right wondering which is concerned with recognizing the wonders of nature. (Compare the way the personal virtue of justice incorporates that part of 'patience' which is concerned with being angered by injustice to others.)

4. Another New Virtue

The existing literature suggests the possibility of a further new virtue, one which, unlike the putative virtue of being disposed to feel the emotion of wonder in the right way and so on, has actually acquired something in the way of a name—namely the term 'respect for nature'. The term was originally brought into environmental ethics by Paul W. Taylor, who used it to signify what he calls an 'ultimate moral attitude' rather than a virtuous character trait. However there are at least three, related, problems with Taylor's account, all of which are side-stepped or dissolved if we recognize his 'respect for nature' as a character trait rather than simply as an attitude (even an 'ultimate moral attitude') which I want to spend a little time discussing.

Before I do, I must stress how admirable I think Taylor's introduction and discussion of 'respect for nature' are. I do take him, along with Aldo Leopold, Arne Naess, and Holmes Rolston III, as amongst the really ground breaking, towering, figures in environmental ethics. They, as far as I am concerned, are the people who came up with the real practical wisdom about the subject, so I regard the following points as relatively speaking, mere philosophers' quibbles.

The first problem concerns how it can come about that someone has 'respect for nature' in Taylor's sense.

Taylor begins with the (actually very old Aristotelian) idea that any living thing has a *telos*—a good of its own—and the related claim that, as such, any living thing can be benefited (by that which enables it to achieve its *telos*) or harmed (by that which interferes with its doing so). He then adds the claim that any living thing possesses 'inherent worth', as a member of 'Earth's Community of Life'. This latter claim, he says, is not the sort of statement that can be proved; rather, to regard or conceive of living things as having 'inherent worth' is to adopt the attitude of respect for nature. And he makes his commitment to a Kantian theoretical framework explicit by drawing a parallel between this ultimate moral attitude and that of the attitude of respect for persons as persons. To regard persons as having inherent worth or 'dignity' is, in Kantian ethics, he says, to adopt the attitude of respect for persons as persons.

Taylor's construal of Kant (which I think is probably wrong) on respect for persons as persons is instructive, for he says 'When this is adopted as an ultimate moral attitude *it involves the disposition to treat every person as having inherent worth or human dignity*' (1981: 207, my italics). Twenty years ago, such a claim might well have passed without question, but the more recent, fruitful, exchanges between Kantians and virtue ethicists prompt several very awkward ones. The disposition in question is clearly supposed to be much more than a tendency of intention. It is supposed to be an efficacious tendency—a tendency to succeed in treating people as having inherent worth or human dignity. But how does adopting the attitude of respect for persons bring in its train the practical wisdom that enables one to know how to treat a person as having human dignity when, for example, their cultural or social expectations are different from yours and unknown to you? How indeed does it bring in its train the ability to recognize a member of a despised race or religion or sex as a person at all? How does it bring the perceptual capacities and emotional sensibilities needed to appreciate what is called for in particular situations when there appears to be a forced choice between treating one person as having human dignity and another as not having it? How does it bring with it either strength of will or a systematic reorientation of the emotions such that you standardly treat people as having human dignity ungrudgingly and without resentment and moreover with the right light in your eye?

No one gets to have all that just by 'adopting an attitude'. These dispositions and capacities have to be inculcated, from childhood, in the moral training of character.

Taylor always speaks of 'taking up' or 'adopting' the attitude of respect for nature, as though this were something one could do more or less overnight, through a rational process. But as people familiar with his writings will know, adopting the attitude of respect for nature turns out to involve acquiring a set of dispositions and capacities similar to those that would have to be involved in having the efficacious disposition to treat people as having human dignity. What he describes, and explores, brilliantly, is being rightly oriented to nature, through and through, in action, emotion, perception, sensibility, and understanding. What is involved in 'adopting' this attitude would, according to what he says about it, manifestly have to be a complete transformation of character. Really coming to see oneself as sharing 'a common bond' with all living things would involve a radical change in one's emotions and perceptions, one's whole way of perceiving and responding to the world, of one's reasons for action and thereby actions. And that is the sort of change that cannot (for the most part) come about just through, say, reading a philosophical book and deciding to change; it cannot (for the most part) simply be 'adopted' or 'taken up'.

So he has a problem. Can having 'respect for nature', as he describes it, not come about at all, given that it cannot simply be adopted or taken up? The problem is solved if we construe it as a virtue. You can't just decide to have a virtue; virtuous character traits cannot be acquired theoretically by attending lectures or reading books or articles and just deciding to be that way. But they can be acquired through moral habituation or training, beginning in childhood and continued through self-improvement.

The second problem with Taylor's account is his reliance on the contentious notion of 'inherent worth' which, *if introduced in a foundational premise*, notoriously brings standard problems with it. Does it or does it not admit of degrees? Either answer lands one in difficulties, as the ethical literature based on the foundational premise that the other animals share inherent or intrinsic worth or value with human beings illustrates. It seems impossible to allow that it admits of degree without claiming that human beings (or at least all the human beings who are persons) have the highest degree and thereby what promised to be a radical reformation of our old understanding of ourselves in relation to the other animals loses most of its revisionary character. But to the modern city-dwelling philosopher—and her readers—the alternative seems hopelessly impractical. The Jains may command our admiration but we do not go into print saying that that is how we all should live.

From the perspective of virtue ethics, Taylor's introduction of the contentious notion of inherent worth is superfluous. 'Regarding a living thing as having inherent worth' amounts to nothing more (though nothing less) in his account than regarding facts about whether a proposed course of action will benefit or harm a living thing as providing non-instrumental reasons for or against it, and it is his rich and insightful identification of this range of reasons which is significant. For, once they are identified, we can readily see how they might be used to inculcate a character trait—the virtue of 'respect for nature', or, as I would prefer to call it (given the restrictive connotations of 'respect'), 'being rightly oriented to nature'.

This range of reasons not only might be, but in fact *are*, given to children by adults who are beginning to inculcate in them at least the beginnings of a virtuous character trait oriented to nature. The child pokes or hits or tears at the living thing, and the parents say 'Don't do that, you'll harm it.' Or the child swats or slashes at a living thing and the parents say 'Don't do that, you'll kill it.' Or the child is taught how to look after a plant or animal—'You have to do this, because it needs water', 'She wants to go for a walk, take her out.' Or the child condemns some living thing's way of going on as 'stupid' and the parents say 'No, it's not stupid, it's brilliant; what it's doing is this' and then explain how what the living thing is doing results in its achieving its *telos*. And as nature-loving (not yet 'nature-respecting') parents and teachers know, one of the best ways to enable children to get over their disgust and fear, whether instinctive or learned, of various living things is to tell or show the child how the thing in question works—how it achieves its *telos*—and/or how this sort of thing, living in its sort of way, contributes to the life-processes of other sorts of things, including us. Whereupon the children start saying (in effect), 'How wonderful!' rather than 'Yuck!'

Such training begins to shape a particular way of perceiving, acting in relation to, feeling and thinking about, the natural world. We could well say, speaking colloquially, that such training involves teaching a child to recognize the inherent or intrinsic worth or value of at least some living things. (Only some, as things are at the moment, which is why I stressed 'nature-loving' as opposed to 'nature-respecting'.) But there is a very important theoretical difference at issue here. On the one hand, we may start, as virtue ethics does, with the training of children in reasons for action and emotional responses and the colloquial redescription of such training as teaching the child to recognize the inherent or intrinsic worth or value of living things. On the other hand, we may start, as Taylor and many other 'biocentric' deontological ethicists do, with foundational premises ascribing such worth or value to them.

One might bring out the difference as follows. Suppose it is agreed ground that bringing up children to be, at least partly, rightly oriented to nature in fact involves training them through the range of reasons suggested above. (This contrasts with the implausible claim that the training involves no more than 'Don't do this, do do that, look at this, be interested in that, because it has inherent worth.') Then the stance of those who seek foundational premises is that the unity of this practice must be underpinned or guided by something unconsciously or dimly apprehended by the parents and latched on to by the children, namely, the inherent worth of the living things in question, the property that they all share. And, granted the existence of such a property, it is clearly part of the philosopher's task to give an account of it, by working out what the 'worth/value-making characteristic' is that everything with this property has in common. But the stance of those who, following Wittgenstein, regard the search for such foundational premises as a philosophical mistake is that the unity of the practice so far described (insofar as it has a unity) need not be underpinned or guided by anything, let alone by any one thing such as inherent worth somehow apprehended by the parents.

The third problem with Taylor's account is this—he limits his ascription of inherent worth to individual living things (though it seems that these include species' populations and ecosystems). Hence what he has, officially, identified is not so much 'respect for nature' as 'respect for living nature'. According to him, things have inherent worth only because, or insofar as, they are 'members of the Earth's Community of Life'. And he identifies the characteristic outlook of someone with 'respect for nature' as follows:

> one sees one's membership in the Earth's Community of Life as providing a common bond with all the different species of animals and plants that have evolved over the ages. One becomes aware that, like all other living things on our planet, one's very existence depends on the fundamental soundness and integrity of the *biological* system of nature. When one looks at this domain of life in its totality, one sees it to be a complex and unified web of interdependent parts.   (1986: 44, my italics).

Now what does seem a little odd about that, read strictly, is the insertion of 'biological' before the words 'system of nature'. Do the sun, the moon, and the seas, the minerals in the earth, the ozone layer, have no role to play in maintaining the 'domain of life in its totality'? Is it not nature, animate *and* inanimate, that, in its totality, is seen to be a unified web? True, not much of the inanimate depends on the animate for its existence but why stress interdependence as the all-important feature of unification? Drawing a hard and fast distinction between the animate and the inanimate seems particularly inappropriate in the context of environmental ethics. Some years ago, when the rising of the seas and the consequent higher sea levels at high tide were recognized to be having an unmistakable deleterious impact, I remember reading that someone had brightly suggested we could solve the problem by blowing up the moon. And every environmentalist was (surely rightly) horrified, notwithstanding the inanimate nature of the moon. (Of course I know that the absence of the tides would kill a lot of plants and animals whose survival depends on their occurrence. My point is that many people's horror was, in fact, quite independent of those consequences of the proposed act of extra-terrestrial vandalism.)

Taylor is landed with this problem because of his attempt to provide a foundational premise about inherent worth. Things have inherent worth, when they do, because they share a common feature—being a member of the Earth's Community of Life. This gives the account a philosophically satisfying unity, and one can see that much of this would be lost if one tried to formulate a second feature, common to just the right inanimate things, and claimed that they had inherent worth because of it, yielding a disjunctive premise about what grounded inherent worth. But if we think of being 'rightly oriented to nature', not as an attitude founded on an adult's rational recognition of such a one-sentence premise but as a character trait arising from a childhood training that gives us particular reasons for action (and omission) in particular contexts, and shapes our emotional response of wonder, the hard and fast line he draws between the animate and the inanimate becomes insignificant. (That is why I implied above that the unity of the practice thus far described, which was of inculcating the beginnings of being rightly oriented towards living nature, wasn't much of a unity.)

Environmentally minded parents teach their children not only not to harm and kill the living but also not to despoil or destroy natural inanimate objects. Although a theory-obsessed parent might go to the lengths of teaching a child not to slash at a spider's web just because this might harm the spider, few nature-loving parents find it necessary to do so. The spider's web, notwithstanding its being inanimate, is reconstructed as an object of wonder—so delicate and light but so strong, so intricately patterned—and not to be wantonly destroyed simply because it is such an object. It fits into a spider's achieving its *telos* in such and such a way, and that is also part of what is wondrous about it, but in teaching this to children, who would look around to check that the web-maker was still alive and dependent upon it?

Spiders' webs, like ammonites and other fossils, make it impossible to draw Taylor's hard distinction between the animate and the inanimate. An ammonite is something else that is not to be wantonly destroyed but wondered at—once again so intricately patterned, and also so awesomely old. And, despite being inanimate, it is part of (not the present, or near present, but) the long past domain of life. 'Look', one says to the child, 'do you know what this is—and *was*?' And the child is thunderstruck. Nor do we find ourselves suddenly talking in distinctively new ways to our children when we come to the Grand Canyon, and similar rock formations. They are so intricately patterned, so old, and so huge, such proper objects of wonder, and have a connection with the domain of life insofar as the geological workings of our planet are inseparable from the workings of life on it, all being part of 'the system of nature', that 'unified web'.

As before, when we teach children not to slash mindlessly at spiders' webs, to look at fossils carefully and try to understand their shape, to be glad rather than sorry that the Grand Canyon is not rimmed with machines dispensing Coca-Cola, giving the reasons that we do, we could, colloquially, redescribe what we are doing as teaching them the inherent worth or intrinsic value of spiders' webs, fossils, and the Grand Canyon. But giving that colloquial redescription simply sidesteps the problem of advancing a foundational philosophical theory which has to start from some (indefinitely?) large set of premises to the effect that these things have such worth or value because or insofar as they are intricately patterned and/or delicate and light (or not delicate but incredibly hard and heavy) or fresh and new (or awesomely old) or tiny and yet still effective (the revelations of the microscope) or huge (the Grand Canyon again) or whatever.

The contrast here is between, on the one hand, trying to ground intrinsic/inherent value/worth/considerability in a few 'x-making characteristics' and, on the other, just starting with an indefinite range of reasons taught for responding, in the broadest sense, to nature, in certain ways. These include, at least, wondering at, looking hard at, finding out more about, rejoicing in, understanding why other people spend their whole lives studying, being anxious to preserve, not dismissing or ignoring or destroying or forgetting or assuming one can always put a price on . . . everything in the natural world.

At the moment, as I think we all know, none of us, however committed to environmentalism, has achieved any more than getting a few of our responses to a few of the things in the natural world right. Possession of the virtue of being rightly oriented to nature quite generally is still a long way off. But the green belief does, after all, call for a radical change in us, something rather more radical, one would suppose, than a change in a few theoretical beliefs about intrinsic worth that few people but philosophers are conscious of holding anyhow.

5. What to Do?

'But' it might be objected, 'what is the point of thinking of environmental ethics in virtue ethics' terms when it will manifestly fail to tell us what we should do? For whether we talk about reconfiguring the old virtues or recognizing a new one, we don't seem to get any answers to our pressing problems. All we get are some fairly obvious prohibitions against wanton, gratuitous, selfish, materialistic, and short-sighted consumption, harm, destruction, and despoliation.'

True enough. But suppose we turn to any other environmental ethics for guidance about what is morally required of us in detail in the way of actions and changes in life style starting, say, tomorrow. What will we find? Apart from the same fairly obvious prohibitions I think it must be admitted that the answer is 'Not much'.

I am not denying that Taylor, for example, offers principles intended to enable us to adjudicate between the competing claims of human beings and other living things. But the only things such principles clearly yield are the obvious prohibitions that even the palest green environmentalist is already living in accordance with. Has any one of my readers recently bought ivory or a caged tropical bird or hunted a rare wild mammal? One might interpret some of Taylor's principles as, more forcefully, yielding a prohibition against driving a car in, at least, all those circumstances in which one will inevitably kill a number of insects but not save any other lives, but Taylor himself does not construe them as doing so, speaking instead merely of the requirement to use anti-pollution devices on automobile exhausts. And not driving around in a car without an anti-pollution device seems another pretty obvious prohibition.

So if all we find are obvious prohibitions, but no guidance for further detailed changes, the questions arise 'Why not? What's still missing? Is the normative theory incomplete or what?' I don't know whether any non-virtue ethicist has ever answered these questions, but virtue ethics has a straightforward and, I think, extremely plausible answer.

Virtue ethicists seek answers to questions about what we should do and how we should live by considering what someone who really possessed virtue to a high degree would characteristically do, and how they would live. And we have little idea of the answers to such questions in the context of environmental ethics because we have so few exemplars of the relevant virtues, real or fictional, if any.

Suppose that being rightly oriented to nature is pre-eminently, the relevant virtue. (I think, at this stage, that little hangs on the distinction between reconfiguring the old virtues and recognizing this new one. Acquisition of the new would go along with reconfiguring the old, and anyone who had adequately reconfigured the old could be truly described as having acquired the new.) This virtue is not a character trait we see manifested by any academic philosophers who, inevitably, lead lives of standard Western, materialistic comfort, driving to shop at their supermarkets, buying new clothes, listening to opera on their CD players, dining in restaurants, writing their books and articles on computers, jetting to international conferences to present their views on environmental ethics, and teaching them to their students in large, land-occupying, buildings. (This does not mean that environmental philosophers are hypocritical, just that our sincerely held ethical beliefs still leave us far short of possessing virtue, in particular perhaps, the practical wisdom, permeating every virtue, that enables its possessor to know what to do in particular circumstances.)

It is possible, though this is contested, that we have glimpses of what it might have been like to live in accordance with the virtue of being rightly oriented to nature in the little we know of the lives of the Australian Aborigines and the Amerindians before European hegemony. But even if we knew a lot more about their lives and even if it were certain that they had possessed the virtue, this would not entail that that is how we should strive to live and be now. Human beings are, essentially, socially and historically situated beings and their virtuous character traits have to be situated likewise. A twenty-first-century city-dweller who possessed the virtue to some degree could hardly manifest it in just the same ways as Australian Aborigines and Amerindians perhaps used to when they lived as hunter-gatherers. What we need to know is what would count as living in accordance with it *now* or in the near future.

One pessimistic possibility is that nothing would count, and that perhaps nothing ever will, because we have already made such a mess of things that there is no virtuous way of sorting them out by human means. In virtue ethics, the (putative) virtue of 'being rightly oriented to nature' is but one virtue amongst many; what one can, morally, do in its name is restrained by other virtues such as justice. Although any environmentalist may well believe that growth is not what we want, justice, if nothing else, restrains what any of us might do to prevent growth while there are still so many people in poorer countries who disagree, because their—and their children's—lives depend on economic growth.

This seems the right juncture to return, as promised, to the question whether virtue ethics is committed to the claim that *eudaimonia* or human well-being is the 'top value', ranked above any other in an improperly human chauvinistic way. The answer is that it is not. If anything counts as the 'top value' in virtue ethics, it is acting virtuously, and the pessimistic possibility envisaged above is not that our choice lies between human well-being and (as it were) the 'well-being' of the natural world, but that our past and present folly has put human well-being beyond our grasp, perhaps forever.

Virtue is an ideal of human excellence, constitutive of *eudaimonia* or living well as a human being. But *eudaimonia* was never something that we could be confident was within our individual grasp. Right back in Aristotle, there is the recognition that it requires 'a complete life' (1101a15) but that there are things one must sooner die than do (1110a27–8) and that it is nonsense to call someone *eudaimōn*, however virtuous, if they are being broken on the wheel or surrounded by great disasters (1153b19–20). If I am living under the sway of evil tyrants, then *eudaimonia* may not be possible for me if, for example, they force on me the choice between action contrary to virtue and death by torture.[4]

Limited as this example is, it should suffice to remind us that whatever blocks virtuous activity blocks *eudaimonia*. It might be a few tyrants. It might be the nature of the society into which one was born, unwittingly, as a member of the privileged class whose past horrendous injustice is only just beginning to be righted. Perhaps I can live in accordance with the virtue of justice in such a society, in the vanguard with those bringing about the needed changes at considerable personal self-denial. But perhaps, given my family commitments or some disability which, in my society renders me helplessly dependent on others, I cannot; if I am to live at all, I am forced to live the life of the highly privileged dependent. And then *eudaimonia* is beyond my grasp, for willy-nilly, I shall, perforce, reap the rewards of injustice. Or it might be the nature of the world into which I was born, a world whose societies have become so predicated on despoiling nature that their very existence depends on continuing to do so. Perhaps I can live in accordance with the virtue of being rightly oriented to nature to some extent if I leave society. But then I will have cut myself off from the exercise of most of the other virtues. So *eudaimonia* is beyond my grasp.

---

[4] Cf. Philippa Foot on the 'Letter-Writers' who died because they refused to go along with the Nazis. She says of them that they were so placed that it was impossible for them to pursue happiness 'by just and honourable means....Happiness in life, they might have said, was not something possible for them.' See Foot (2001).

Virtue ethics is 'about' human beings living well, but it is not committed, in advance, to our living well being a realizable state of affairs regardless of how we, or many of us, are living or have lived up until now. It is possible that we have already made such a mess that we shall not be able to live well, as part of the natural world, for many generations to come, if ever.

More optimistically, the very next generation may start to show us the way. Concern about the environment, and proto-versions of the virtue of being rightly oriented to nature, are currently much more widespread amongst children than they are amongst adults. Many of them have received more training in it than any of us did, and are beginning to have their own ideas about how they and we should live. At the time I began working on this chapter, in 1999, it was reported that 135,000 German schoolchildren had decided to help reduce their communities' emissions of greenhouse gases by 10 per cent, and within seven months had more than reached their target—something that (I believe) no government has achieved in a comparable time. It may be that they will choose to live in ways rather different from our ways, and that their children will choose to live in very different ones. If the deeper green versions of the green belief are true, it is a radical change in human beings' ways of living in the natural world that is called for. If the virtue ethics approach is right, it is hardly surprising that we, currently lacking the relevant virtues, should be unable to imagine, in any concrete detail, how we should live, and we should expect change to come about not primarily through philosophical argument, and not overnight, but through the actions and practical reasoning of people in whom the relevant virtues have been inculcated. Our current task is, thereby, to do what we can to develop those virtues in ourselves and our children, and to adhere to the 'obvious prohibitions' in the hope that we may bequeath to them a world that is not irrevocably spoiled.

References

Aristotle. 2000. *Nicomachean Ethics*. Edited and translated by Roger Crisp. Cambridge: Cambridge University Press.

Clark, S. R. L. 1977. *The Moral Status of Animals*. Oxford: Clarendon Press.

Foot, P. 2001. *Natural Goodness*. Oxford: Clarendon Press.

Hepburn, R. W. 1984. *'Wonder' and Other Essays*. Edinburgh: Edinburgh University Press.

Hill, Jr., T. E. 1983. 'Ideals of Human Excellence and Preserving Natural Environments', *Environmental Ethics* 5: 211–24.

Leopold, A. 1949. *A Sand County Almanac*. Reissued Oxford: Oxford University Press, 2001.

Naess, A. 1989. *Economy, Community and Lifestyle*. Cambridge: Cambridge University Press.

Passmore, J. 1974. *Man's Responsibility for Nature*. London: Duckworth.

Rolston III, H. 1988. *Environmental Ethics*. Philadelphia: Temple University Press.

Sorabji, R. 1993. *Animal Minds and Human Morals*. New York: Cornell University Press.

Taylor, P. W. 1981. 'The Ethics of Respect for Nature', *Environmental Ethics* 1: 197–218.

Taylor, P. W. 1986. *Respect for Nature*. Princeton, NJ: Princeton University Press.

Van Wensveen, L. 2000. *Dirty Virtues*. Amherst, NY: Humanity Books.

PART III
ACTION THEORY, POLITICS, AND NATURALISM

12
Virtuous Action

In many contexts, the phrase 'virtuous action' is just virtue-ethics speak for 'right action'. In this use, it figures in debates within normative ethics about the relative merits of different virtue ethical accounts of right action and whether any of them is adequate. It is also used as a general phrase to apply to a smaller class than the phrase 'right action'—namely to actions which can be described using a virtue adjective: just actions, courageous actions, kind actions, honest actions. (When discretion is the better part of valour, the courageous (rather than foolhardy) agent may rightly run like mad, but his running isn't a courageous action.)

In either of these uses, 'virtuous action', like 'right action', allows for the possibility that an agent can do such an action without possessing virtue. Call this 'everyday virtuous action'. But, in the most interesting use of the term, a virtuous action has to come *from* virtue. Call this 'ideal virtuous action'. And, in the context of this volume, the concept of 'ideal virtuous action' is interesting not so much as the concept of morally ideal action (though it is that) but as the concept of ideal rational action (or 'acting for a reason' or 'from reason') *itself*, in some special sense—the upshot of an ideal practical rationality.

The concept is, of course, derived from Aristotle, though for some reason to do with Greek usage he rarely, if ever, uses the phrase whose literal translation would be 'virtuous/excellent action'. Instead he speaks of actions in accordance with virtue, or uses examples (just or temperate actions). All these phrases have the ambiguity of 'virtuous action' noted above, and Aristotle pinpoints the ambiguity in a famous passage of the *Nicomachean Ethics* (Aristotle 2000: 1105a30–b1).

Yes, we can perform everyday virtuous actions, actions that are in accordance with virtue in the sense of conforming to it; we can do what is just and temperate, and exactly what, in the circumstances, someone with the virtues of justice and temperance would do. Even quite small children can perform everyday virtuous actions. But we can do better than that, namely perform them *in the way* in which the just and temperate perform them, namely 'for their own sake', *from* virtue. In the later passage, where he repeats the point, Aristotle is more explicit about the difference between ideal and everyday virtuous action (ibid., 1144a14–20). Unlike the former, the latter might be done unwillingly, under compulsion (through fear of punishment perhaps) or 'for some other reason'—but not for its own sake.

That ideal virtuous actions are (for the most part) not done unwillingly flows immediately from the condition that they are done from virtue; and it is in this point that we find the most well-known difference between Aristotle and Kant in normative ethics. Virtues, in Aristotle, are settled dispositions to act *and* feel well (or excellently or virtuously). The distinction between the virtuous and the merely continent lies not in what they do, nor the reason(s) for which they do it—they both do the virtuous action for its own sake—but in how they feel about what they do. The merely continent execute the everyday virtuous actions because their reason 'urges them in the right direction', but their emotions or desires 'conflict with or resist it' (ibid., 1102b15ff.); so they do not take pleasure in what they do. The emotions of the virtuous agents, by contrast, are in harmony with their reason, so they do the everyday virtuous actions gladly or willingly, with no inner conflict, and thereby produce the morally ideal actions.

But what of the concept of the rationally ideal action? To grasp it, we need to begin with the special sense of 'action', or 'acting for a reason', which is at issue, for which I will use the capitalized terms 'Action', 'Act', and 'Acting' (in the phrase 'Acting for a reason'). Although my concern here is with Aristotle's account of Action, it is no accident that Korsgaard has written more influentially on this concept than any other modern philosopher; for, as will become clear, Action is as much a Kantian notion as an Aristotelian one.

Not every philosopher will agree that there is any sense to be made of the term Action (perhaps Hume would deny it), because the first thing we need to note about it is that children, at least young children, and the other animals don't Act. 'For we do not say that a child acts, or a brute either; only someone who is already doing things from reason' as Aristotle asserts in the *Eudemian Ethics* (1982: 1224a29). So Action isn't the same as intentional action, because children and some of the other animals certainly act intentionally and thereby, we might say, for a reason. One might want to insist that, although some of the other animals act 'for reasons' in a way—surely, the lioness chases off the marauding male *in order to* protect her cubs—there is another way in which they don't. Unlike us, they are not aware of their reasons as reasons. But in this respect they are also unlike children. Any child old enough to respond appropriately to Anscombe's question 'Why?' could be said to manifest awareness of his reasons as reasons in those responses and, further, in his responses to us when we give him reasons for doing one thing rather than another—as we can't do with the other animals. (I mean, by giving a child information such as 'You could make it stand up if you put it on the table instead of putting it on your knee'—not by coercion or by changing the circumstances.) So Action isn't the same as 'acting for a reason' in any ordinary sense of the phrase. It is acting *from* a sort of rational capacity that we think children and the other animals lack.

Philosophers may, naturally, be interested in giving an account of intentional action and/or of acting for a reason, but not in giving one of Action. But, given the premise that adult human beings can be rational agents in some sense in which children cannot, we would expect that their accounts, if adequate, should be able to generate a story about what changes as we move from acting as children to acting as rational adults do. (For example, does some set of things—say, beliefs, desires, intentions, plans—simply get bigger? Or get bigger by the addition of more complex things—say, desires about beliefs/desires—or more abstract or general ones? Or does something quite new happen?) The terminus of those changes, whatever they may be, would be Action, the concept of the fullest expression or development of our rational agency or practical reason.

In Aristotle, Acting is acting from rational choice—*prohairesis*. He introduces this idea in Book III of the *Nicomachean Ethics*, defining it simply as the outcome of deliberation, and deliberation is described as what we would now call instrumental reasoning (taking that to cover both means–end and part–whole reasoning): reasoning about what to do to achieve some end by working out ways and means to it. You consider means, and if the best, or only, means is not something you can bring about immediately, you consider by what further means it can be brought about, until you reach something you can do. Then you conclude that this is what you'll do—or you 'rationally choose' or 'decide' (another possible translation)—to do that.

But all that this gives us is 'acting for a reason' in the ordinary sense, which children and the clear-eyed akratic certainly do; and it remains a puzzle until Book VI why Aristotle denies that they act from rational choice (as he does in Book III). In Book VI, rational choice turns out to be (at least in the favoured cases) the outcome, not of any deliberation, but only of ultimate end-directed deliberation, which is reasoning related to the 'architectonic' end of *eudaimonia* ('happiness' or the good life, or living well). And thereby Acting for a reason emerges as acting for—or at least in the light of—not just an end, but that ultimate, 'architectonic', end.

Followers of Aristotle find it entirely plausible to make this the ideal of practical rationality (see Annas 1993: 27–46). Assuming that each of us wants our life to go well, is it not irrational—just folly—to make daily choices without having formed any conception of what we want our life to be like, given that so many choices, willy nilly, rule out future options? Practical reasoning is, after all, concerned with what to do quite generally, not just with some areas of action, and, as Aristotle implies, we shall be more likely to make the correct practical decisions if we have a target to aim at. But, even if the ideal is plausible, it does, surely, create the possibility that not only children and the other animals, but quite a few of 'us', don't Act.

However, if this is a problem for Aristotelians, it is a problem that other philosophers aiming to give an account of Action share. This is hardly surprising, since 'Action' is the concept of an ideal, and when we are considering such ideals in philosophy we have to make some decision about how high we think it plausible to set the threshold, and tailor our account correspondingly. Do we think that most ordinary rational adults reach a threshold of this ideal of rational agency, or only a few of them?

If we are following Aristotle or Kant, which way we go (for the many or the few) is partly determined by what we want to say about the prevalence of virtue or a goodwill, since both philosophers give accounts according to which, when the virtuous agent (or an agent with a goodwill) acts, she Acts. But, whichever way we go, we must not over-intellectualize Acting for a reason in such a way as to guarantee that only people who have studied academic philosophy can do it. So we can't demand conscious reflective endorsement of such-and-such a conception of *eudaimonia*, nor an articulated *de dicto* recognition of the categorical imperative or anything similar (such as a consciously articulated theory of oneself, rather than an implicit one, as in Velleman 2007). The modern challenge is to find a way to describe those features of adults' capacities we take to be sufficient for attributing to them some form of whatever it is that figures in our account of Action, and this is currently still proving very difficult.

But now, assuming the virtuous Act, we may ask, can the wicked Act too? For most Kantians, the answer is 'No' and there is an explanation of why not. Capital 'A' Acting is the outcome of a special sort of practical reasoning, which the wicked do not employ. But when Action is specified as the outcome of rational choice rather than reasoning in terms of the categorical imperative, things are more complicated. If the wicked can't Act, we need an answer as to why not; and if they can, what becomes of my initial claim that Aristotle's concept of ideal *virtuous* action is not only the concept of ideal rational action, but of ideal moral action as well?

In common with most moral philosophers, Aristotle does not say much about the wicked, and indeed seems to offer two competing pictures of them. We have, on the one hand, the view in Book IX of the *Nicomachean Ethics* of the wicked as psychological wrecks, torn, like the incontinent, by inner conflict. It is hard to conceive of the wicked, described as they are in this way, as Acting. How can they be acting from rational choice, unless we suppose that they take their ultimate end to be 'making myself miserable' or 'a ruined life'?

But, as we all know, one can't be confident that someone is not wicked on the grounds that they are not conflicted and miserable. And elsewhere (Book VII, chs 4 and 8) Aristotle presents a different view—one in which the intemperate (who do lots of wicked things in their pursuit of pleasure) are contrasted with the incontinent *and* the continent precisely insofar as they do not suffer from inner conflict. But, like the continent, they do act from rational choice, and hence Act.

Capital 'A' Acting for a reason is itself meeting some sort of norm of rational agency. So, if we can make out that, although the wicked do it, the virtuous do it better, then we can say that the practical rationality of the wicked falls short of the ideal—that their rational agency is indeed defective to some extent, and that the virtuous are ideally rational. But how can we say that?

According to Anscombe (1989), Aristotle offers a really neat account. She draws a tight analogy between the assessments of practical and theoretical reasoning. In the latter, as everyone learns in baby logic, we distinguish between sound and valid reasoning; the latter is good, but the former is better. The difference between them simply lies in their starting points or premises; sound reasoning proceeds from true premises; valid reasoning may not. Bearing the analogy firmly in mind makes it harder (though not impossible, of course) to accept the Humean idea that the exercise of practical reason can be critically assessed *only* in terms of the adequacy of the steps it takes to achieve the agent's ends. Although, when teaching philosophy, we always stress the importance of valid reasoning, and sometimes we recklessly say to our students 'I don't mind what conclusion you reach as long as you give a decent argument for it', we take that back if they avail themselves of a premise which, in context or quite generally, is just plain false; sound reasoning is better. The same holds for practical reasoning. There is both sound and valid practical reasoning; the former is better; and the difference between the two lies in their starting points. Sound practical reasoning proceeds from a true/right/correct starting point or premise, namely that such-and-such an end is good to pursue; valid practical reasoning may not.

On the Aristotelian picture, the virtuous employ the best practical reasoning because theirs proceeds from a true premise; *as* virtuous, they have the correct conception of the ultimate end—the life of virtuous activity. But the wicked have a different, and hence false, premise: for example that the ultimate end is the life of pleasure—so, even if their reasoning is valid, it will still fail to be sound.

Aristotle's stress is all on the 'major' premise ('*The* ultimate end is...') and on the impossibility of getting this right without the possession of virtue. But modern Aristotelians have laid as much stress on those among the 'particular' premises in practical reasoning which identify—correctly or incorrectly—the relevant features of the situation in which the agent is to act—and the impossibility, in many cases, of getting *these* right without the possession of virtue. And at this point the modern contrast between the fully virtuous and the merely continent comes to play a new role.

In its original role, as I noted above, this contrast figured in debates within normative ethics about what is formally required in order for one to be a morally excellent person. Can someone who always acts correctly but does not always feel correctly be as morally good a *person* (albeit, perhaps, not as good a human being, as people sometimes used to say) as someone who does both; or is she morally inferior? But, in its new role, we use the contrast to query whether that question is not based on a false assumption, namely that the merely continent agent *can* be supposed to reason soundly—and hence to reach correct practical conclusions and to act correctly—to the same extent as the virtuous agent does. ('To the same extent' rather than 'always', because even the ideal virtuous agent is not infallible and may, incorrectly but quite innocently, identify the poisoned chalice as containing life-saving water.) Given the ways our emotions shape our perceptions, will the merely continent not be liable to misread (the term used in McDowell 1998) or misdescribe (the term used in Murdoch 1970) some situations and, as a result, to plug in false particular premises about them? 'This person (isn't in need of help but just) needs to pull herself together', 'This person (isn't the victim of misfortune but) has brought this trouble on himself' or, indeed, 'This human being (being of such and such a race, gender, age) is not an autonomous agent and, for her own good, needs me to make this decision for her.' If that is so, then the merely continent agent will sometimes fail to do what she should do, and culpably so, unlike the virtuous.

Finally, the way the emotions sometimes prompt us to immediate action brings us to a new version of the problem of over-intellectualizing Acting. Suppose we think of Acting for a reason or 'from reason' as acting from a clockable period of prior, conscious, ultimate end-directed practical thought. There is, as we noted above, a persisting difficulty in finding a way to describe that thought without making it too overtly philosophical. Now, the problem is whether to allow some actions which are clearly not preceded by such thought at all to be Actions, and, if so, how?

For the Aristotelian, the obvious cases are many of the 'everyday' virtuous actions of the virtuous (and, though they are not our concern, many of the 'everyday' vicious actions of the vicious.) A nice child might spring forward immediately, 'without thought', to help someone who had fallen in front of them, but they, *ex hypothesi* do not Act when they do so. The mature virtuous agent might well do the same in the same circumstances. And there is nothing to be seen in the moment of acting which distinguishes what the virtuous agent does from what the child does, nor, necessarily, in what the agents can say afterwards in response to Anscombe's 'Why?' (A child raised in a pious household may well say sincerely that she did it because it was her duty, and an inarticulate virtuous agent, that he couldn't help it or 'just did it'.)

But, in the life of the virtuous agent, such spontaneous action is just what is to be expected from him, since everyday uncomplicated virtuous actions are just what such agents do from habituated virtue. If in these circumstances the agent does not act immediately, spontaneously, 'without thinking', his failure calls for explanation ('Did he not see?' 'Is he ill?' 'What was it about the situation that made him pause?'). And we have already assumed that, when the virtuous act, they Act. So when the virtuous agent springs forward, he Acts.

How can this be so? At this point we might insist that, though it may be unseen, there is something in the moment (roughly speaking) of acting which distinguishes what the virtuous agent does from what the nice child does. It is, obviously, what it was said to be before, namely that the virtuous agent's action, unlike the child's, comes from rational choice and thereby prior ultimate end-directed deliberation—it is just that, in these cases, the deliberation is split-second and unconscious. And then we try to give some further account of that.

Alternatively, we may stick with saying that, in these cases—of the child and of the virtuous agent—there is nothing in the moment of acting, or in its proximate antecedents, which distinguishes between the two. Instead we reconsider what we mean by Acting 'for a reason', abandoning the idea that it has to involve prior reflection, conscious or unconscious, regarding the action done. We may take our lead from Anscombe on acting for a reason— that is, on intentional action quite generally—of which she says:

> We do not add anything attaching to the action at the time it is done by describing it as intentional. To call it intentional is to assign it to the class of intentional actions [...]. (1963: 28).

As a particular 'Eureka!' moment constitutes understanding in a subject with a certain past and a certain future, so a spontaneous virtuous action constitutes an Action, an operation of the ideal practical rationality of the agent, in the setting of a virtuous life. To call it 'Acting for a reason' is to assign it to the class of actions which manifest such a rationality, not to say that anything extra was going on in the agent at the time when it was done.

This would fit well with the one place in the *Nicomachean Ethics* where Aristotle mentions spontaneous virtuous actions, since there he apparently claims that the rational choice of such actions comes directly from the agent's character—his virtue—rather than from deliberation (Aristotle 2000: 1117a17–22).

He thus leaves unquestioned his claim that deliberation takes time, but he suggests that the activity of the ideal practical reason of the virtuous agent is not limited to such time-occupying thought. Her practical reason is hardly having to work hard when she does what the nice child does; but it is still at work, informing what she does.

References

Annas, J. 1993. *The Morality of Happiness*. Oxford: Oxford University Press.

Anscombe, G. E. M. 1963. *Intention*, 2nd edn. Oxford: Blackwell.

Anscombe, G. E. M. 1989. 'Von Wright on Practical Inference'. In P. A. Schilpp (ed.), *The Philosophy of Georg Henrik von Wright*. LaSalle, IL: Open Court: 377–404. Reprinted as: 'Practical Inference' 1995, in R. Hursthouse, G. Lawrence, and W. Quinn (eds), *Virtues and Reasons*. Oxford: Oxford University Press: 1–34.

Aristotle. 1982. *The Eudemian Ethics*. Translated by M. Woods. Oxford: Clarendon Press.

Aristotle. 2000. *Nicomachean Ethics*. Edited and translated by Roger Crisp. Cambridge: Cambridge University Press.

McDowell, J. 1998. *Mind, Value, and Reality*. Cambridge, MA: Harvard University Press.

Murdoch, I. 1970. *The Sovereignty of Good*. London: Routledge.

Velleman, D. J. 2007. *Practical Reflection*, new edn. Stanford, CA: Center for the Study of Language and Information.

13
Arational Actions

It is often said that there is some special irrationality involved in wreaking damage or violence on inanimate objects that have angered one, and, correspondingly, something rational about striking people or animals in anger. The explanation of this seems obvious, for the first surely manifests the irrational belief that inanimate things are animate and can be punished, whereas the second has no such flaw. But behind this seemingly innocuous observation lies, as I shall argue, a false account of action explanation and a false semantic theory. According to the standard account of actions and their explanations, intentional actions are actions done because the agent has a certain desire/belief pair that explains the action by rationalizing it. Any explanation of intentional action in terms of an appetite or occurrent emotion (which might appear to be an explanation solely in terms of desire) is hence assumed to be elliptical, implicitly appealing to some appropriate belief.[1] In this paper, I challenge this assumption with respect to the 'arational' actions of my title—a significant subset of the set of intentional actions explained by occurrent emotion. These actions threaten the standard account, not only by forming a recalcitrant set of counterexamples to it, but also, as we shall see, by undercutting the false semantic theory that holds that account in place.

I define these actions ostensively by means of a list of examples, and then define them explicitly, thereby making it obvious why I call them 'arational' actions (rather than 'irrational', on the model of the distinction between 'amoral' and 'immoral'). I cluster the examples around the emotion (or emotions) that would, usually, explain the actions; the explanation would, usually, be of the form 'I φ-ed because I was so frightened (or happy, excited, ashamed...so overwhelmed by hatred or affection or...) that I just wanted to, or felt I had to.' Arational actions:

---

[1] So, for instance, Donald Davidson has said in lectures that 'She fled out of fear' (or 'because she was frightened') and 'She killed him out of hatred' are to be construed in terms of the actions' being caused by appropriate beliefs and desires.

(a) explained by a wave of love, affection, or tenderness—kissing or lightly touching in passing, seizing and tossing up in the air, rumpling the hair of, or generally messing up the person or animal one loves; talking to her photograph as one passes, kissing it;

(b) explained by anger, hatred, and sometimes jealousy—violently destroying or damaging anything remotely connected with the person (or animal, or institution) one's emotion is directed toward, e.g., her picture, letters or presents from her, awards from her, books or poems about her; the chair she was wont to sit in, locks of her hair, recordings or 'our' song, etc.;

(c) explained by anger with inanimate objects—doing things that might make sense if the things were animate, e.g., shouting at them, throwing an 'uncooperative' tin opener on the ground or out of the window, kicking doors that refuse to shut and cars that refuse to start, tying towels that keep falling off a slippery towel rail on to it very tightly and then consolidating the knots with water; muttering vindictively 'I'll show *you*', or 'You *would* would you';

(d) explained by excitement—jumping up and down, running, shouting, pounding the table or one's knees, hugging oneself or other people, throwing things;

(e) explained by joy—running, jumping, leaping up reaching for leaves on trees, whistling or humming tunelessly, clapping one's hands;

(f) explained by grief—tearing one's hair or clothes, caressing, clutching, even rolling in, anything suitable associated with the person or thing that is the object of grief, e.g., pictures, clothes, presents from her (cf. anger above). (The example of rolling in comes from a novel in which a man takes his dead wife's clothes out of the wardrobe, puts them on the bed and rolls in them, burying his face in them and rubbing them against his cheeks);

(g) explained by shame—covering one's face *in the dark*, or when one is alone; washing with violent attention to scrubbing and scouring;

(h) explained by horror—covering one's eyes when they are already shut;

(i) explained by fear—hiding one's face, burrowing under the bed clothes;

(j) explained by feeling proud, or self-satisfied, or pleased with oneself—talking to or posturing to oneself in the mirror.

I maintain, with respect to these examples, that on very many (though *not* necessarily all) occasions on which such actions were performed, it would be true to say the following of them: (i) that the action was intentional; (ii) that the agent did not do it for a reason in the sense that there is a true description of action of the form 'X did it (in order) to...' or 'X was trying to...' which will 'reveal the favourable light in which the agent saw what he did',[2] and hence involve, or imply, the ascription of a suitable *belief*; and (iii) that the agent would not have done the action if she had not been in the grip of whatever emotion it was, and the mere fact that she was in its grip explains the action as much as anything else does.

I shall say that when and only when these three conditions hold of an action it is, by definition, an *arational action*, and appropriate to the emotion or emotions that explain it. The examples are of action types, most of whose tokens would be arational actions, but, as noted above, I am not insisting that they always would be. Many of them, for instance, might be done on occasion without the agent's being aware of what she was doing, thus violating condition (i), and many might be done, on occasion, in order to..., thus violating condition (ii). On such occasions, the actions are not, as performed, arational actions; whether or not an agent has performed an arational action on some occasion is determined by whether the three conditions obtain.

I have encountered great resistance, both explicitly in discussion and implicitly in philosophy-of-action literature, to the very idea of arational actions as defined. What people want to do is deny that when condition (i) obtains, condition (ii) *can* obtain. 'If an action is intentional', they say, 'it *must* be done for a reason, i.e., because of an appropriate desire and belief'—for this is, indeed, the standard account. Now I do not want to quarrel about senses of 'done for a reason'; the central point at issue is certain belief ascriptions to agents performing intentional actions of the sort described above. I am just using 'not done for a reason' here to capture my claim that these actions are explained solely by reference to desire—'I was so angry/delighted, etc., I just wanted to' not to an appropriate belief.

To get quite clear about what is at issue, let us consider as an example, Jane, who, in a wave of hatred for Joan, tears at Joan's photo with her nails, and gouges holes in the eyes. I can agree that Jane does this because, hating Joan, she wants to scratch her face, and gouge out her eyes; I can agree that she would not have torn at the photo if she had not believed that it was a photo of Joan; and if someone wants to say, 'So those are the reasons for the action', I do not want to quarrel, for these 'reasons' do *not* form the appropriate

---

[2] 'Explanations of action in terms of reasons work by revealing the favourable light in which the agent saw what he did (or at least what he attempted)'—John McDowell, 'Reason and Action', *Philosophical Investigations* 5(4) (1982): 301–305.

desire-belief pair assumed by the standard account. On the standard account, if the explanatory desire in this case is the desire to scratch Joan's face, then the appropriate belief has to be something absurd, such as the belief that the photo of Joan *is* Joan, or that scratching the photo will be causally efficacious in defacing its original. And my disagreement is with adherents of the standard account, who must think that some non-absurd candidates for appropriate beliefs to ascribe to agents performing arational actions are available.

An exhaustively detailed rebuttal of the various candidates that may be offered cannot be given, of course, but I now review the most plausible.

When one attempts to think of appropriate beliefs, it becomes clear quite rapidly that there is no point in trying to find them piecemeal, token by token—beliefs such as the belief that by harming a photo one harms the original. Viewed abstractly, the desires to perform arational actions when in the grip of an emotion provide, apparently, a rich fund of those cases which Gary Watson neatly characterized as those in which 'one in no way values what one desires',[3] and what is needed to show this is mere appearance, is a belief, ascribable to the agent in every case, about the value of what she is doing. My claim was that these actions are not done in order to φ; the counterclaim, coming from the standard account, should be that they *are* done in order to φ, where the agent always wants to φ and where the appropriate belief, showing in what way the agent values the action, would be of the form 'and the agent believes that doing this (gouging out the eyes on the photo or whatever it is) is φ-ing'.

We seem to find the promise of a candidate in the thought that tokens of the types in question are done *in order to express the emotion*, to relieve it, or vent it, or make it known. This, it is said, reveals the standard desire-belief reason for which arational actions are done: the agent desires to express her emotion, and believes that whatever she is doing *is* expressing it.

But quite generally, what is wrong with this suggestion once again is that it involves ascribing a belief to the agent which should not be ascribed. If I φ in order to express or relieve my emotion, I do so in the belief that my φ-ing will indeed have (or is likely to have) this upshot. And in such cases, there is the possibility that I am not setting about fulfilling my intention in the right way; that I am open to correction. But arational actions would not usually admit of any possibility of mistake in this way; they are not the sort of action an agent would usually do in the (possibly erroneous) belief that they would achieve this effect. Nor should we accept it as obvious that in every case the agent has the

---

[3] 'Free Agency', *Journal of Philosophy* 72(8) (1975): 205–20 (205).

desire to *express this emotion*, a desire whose content is distinct from that of the desire to, say, throw the tin opener violently on the floor. The ascription of this extra desire requires an extra justification.

Of course, I grant that, on some particular occasion, such a justification may be available; as before, I am not insisting that *no* token of an arational action type is ever done in order to express an emotion. I might indeed, on occasion, break up the furniture in the belief that this is expressing my rage and wanting to express it, because my psychotherapist has convinced me that I have hitherto suppressed my emotions too much, that it is better to express them than to bottle them up. Here, my decision to follow the therapist's advice provides the justification for ascribing to me the extra desire *to express this emotion*—and, significantly, it also introduces the possibility of my being open to correction. 'You're not really expressing your rage', knowledgeable onlookers may say, 'Why don't you really *scream*!'

Similarly, I might tousle someone's hair in the belief that this will make it known to them that I am feeling a wave of affection for them, and that they would like to know this. Or I might deliberately try to get my corrosive hatred for Joan out of my system and tear at her photo in the belief that doing so will bring me this relief. In such cases, the information that my belief is false, that I am not going to succeed in making known or relieving my emotion, or that my expressing it in this way on this occasion is not a good idea would be seen by me as a reason for stopping what I am doing. Granted, this can happen on occasion. But on most occasions, this is not how things are; usually the agent will not be *trying* (successfully or unsuccessfully) to express her emotion, in the belief that this is a good idea, at all.

Notwithstanding this, there seems to be something right about the idea that arational actions are done 'to express the emotion' that has not yet been brought out. Let us consider the claim, not that the agent does the action *in order to* express the emotion, but rather *qua* expression of emotion.

What does this mean? If it is saying that arational actions *are* 'expressions of emotion' or 'expressive of emotion', this is, I think, obviously true, but it adds nothing to the claim that arational actions are as defined—i.e., intentional actions appropriate to certain emotions, whose only explanation is that, in the grip of the relevant emotion, the agent just felt like doing them. Indeed, it is less explicit than the definition, for both unintentional actions (such as unknowingly gnashing one's teeth) and intentional actions done for further reasons (such as tearing at someone's eyes in order to hurt them) also count as expressions of emotions. But if the 'done *qua* expression' turn of phrase is intended to capture something more explicit, what could this be?

Given the obvious fact that in some sense the agent does arational actions '(just) because she wants to', or 'for their own sake', prompted by the occurrent desire, it is natural to compare arational actions with actions prompted by appetite, and to look to Stephen Schiffer's[4] account of actions prompted by 'reason-providing desires', such as eating a piece of chocolate because I am seized by a desire for chocolate. These, according to Schiffer, are done 'for pleasure'—not in quite the same sense in which one goes to the ballet 'for pleasure', where I desire to go to the ballet because I believe I shall enjoy it, but still in the sense that they are done *in the belief* that satisfying the desire will yield pleasure. This being so, the obvious cases of actions prompted by Schifferian reason-providing desires can be given a standard belief-desire reason explanation; the agent desires physical pleasure, and believes that acting in accordance with the currently aroused appetite will yield this, and so acts. And similarly, it might be said, in the case of arational actions; the agent desires pleasure, and the appropriate belief, ascribable in every case, is that acting in accordance with the occurrent desire to do whatever it is—tear up the photo, cover one's eyes, throw the tin opener out of the window—will yield this.

But the difficulty with extending Schiffer's account in this way is that the ascription of the relevant belief is plausible only with respect to the standard bodily appetites. It is indeed 'almost always' true, as he says, that the bodily appetites, once aroused, are pleasurable to satisfy, which is why we talk of the pleasures of food and drink and sex, why we have the concept of *physical* pleasure, and why actions prompted by appetite can so often be described as done 'for pleasure'. The belief that we shall get physical pleasure from actions done to satisfy such appetites may plausibly be ascribed to any one of us. But the ascription is either implausible or vacuous in other cases.

Suppose I am seized by a sudden desire to lick something furry, and do so because of that desire. Do I do so *in the belief* that doing so will yield me pleasure? A philosopher could indeed, parodying Thomas Nagel,[5] introduce the notion of a motivated belief; the description of an agent as doing something 'because she wants to do it' simply entails that the agent believed that doing whatever it is would 'give her pleasure'. This 'motivated belief' could then be ascribed to the person who licks something furry 'because she wants to'; but in such a case the ascription is clearly vacuous. There are no grounds on which she could believe it will give her *physical* pleasure—quite the

---

[4] 'A Paradox of Desire', *American Philosophical Quarterly* 13(3) (1976): 195–203.
[5] *The Possibility of Altruism* (New York: Oxford University Press, 1970), 29–30.

contrary, in fact. She does not necessarily believe she will enjoy it—indeed, if one were seized by such an odd desire, one might well act on it because one was curious to find out whether doing so was enjoyable or not. The only 'pleasure' the agent believes in is 'the "pleasure" of desire-satisfaction', and this is an entirely formal and empty concept of pleasure.

Now, the desires to perform arational actions (unlike the aroused bodily appetites but like the desire to lick something furry) are not generally known as being pleasurable to satisfy; on the contrary, we know of some of the cases that acting in accordance with the desires makes one feel terrible, and of others that acting in accordance with them is neither pleasant nor unpleasant. To ascribe to the agent of an arational action, in every case, the belief that satisfying this desire now will yield pleasure is hence, implausibly, to ascribe an absurd belief—one for which the agent has no grounds, and which she knows is probably false. Or it is the vacuous ascription of a 'motivated' belief.

Actions prompted by odd physical cravings are, I claim, genuine examples of cases in which 'one in no way values what one desires' and are thereby counterexamples to the standard account of intentional action, albeit so odd and rare that they might be dismissed as fringe cases. Arational actions, however, are not, in the same way, odd or rare; if they do indeed resist appropriate belief ascription, as I have maintained, then the standard account is shown to be fundamentally flawed.[6]

For not only do arational actions provide a large set of counterexamples, but they also, once their resistance to belief ascription is acknowledged, justify our looking with a sceptical eye at actions done in the grip of an emotion to which the full rational panoply of belief, desire, and 'intention with which' is usually ascribed. It is generally said, for example, that, if someone flees in terror from a lion, she is doing so in order to get to safety and preserve death; she desires self-preservation and believes that flight is the best way in the circumstances to get it. And, it is said, if someone strikes a person with whom she is angry, or says cruel things to him, she does so in order to hurt, or even to punish him; once again, an appropriate desire-belief pair is ascribed.

Anyone who confidently holds the view that these ascriptions of reasons or 'intention with which' must apply in such cases is committed to seeing a great disanalogy between them and cases such as feeling frightened of burglars,

---

[6] I am not, of course, unaware of further variations on the appropriate belief which might be tried, but only space prevents me from showing that they fail, too. The belief that in performing the arational action one will eliminate discomfort or agitation (rather than achieve actual pleasure) does not turn the trick; nor does the fascinatingly symbolic nature of many of the examples of arational actions yield anything helpful, as many people are initially tempted to suppose.

ghosts, or thunder and burrowing under the bed clothes (to safety?), feeling angry and kicking furniture (to hurt it?), and muttering imprecations under one's breath (for whose ears?), or to making them analogous by ascribing quite lunatic beliefs to the agent.

If there really is a great disanalogy, the account of the 'rational' cases provides us with no clue about the account to be given of the arational ones, which must then seem utterly mysterious. Nor is the problem they present solved—not at least for anyone interested in giving a systematic account of action—by denying that arational actions are intentional. For they are clearly not unintentional, and to say they form a significant class of actions that are neither intentional nor unintentional is to admit that, within the standard account, they present a formidable problem.

If, on the other hand, they are accepted as analogous and the lunatic beliefs are ascribed, these will show up nowhere else in behaviour, be sincerely and vigorously repudiated by the agent, and that agent's momentary acquisition of them will, in turn, be utterly mysterious.

A deep problem is found here by anyone who holds that whether or not an action is intentional or was done for a reason (because of a desire and a belief), whether or not an emotion [*sic.* action?] was motivated by emotion e, and whether or not an agent believes that p must be all-or-nothing matters. And this view is held by people in the grip of the false semantic theory according to which predicates such as 'intentional', 'for a reason', 'motivated by emotion e', and 'believes that p' have clearly determinate, necessary and sufficient satisfaction conditions. On this theory, an action must be intentional or not, done for a reason or not, motivated by an occurrent emotion or not; an agent must believe that p or not. And then we find these mysteries.

The new 'solution' to this problem is to say that, if the world proves thus recalcitrant to our attempts to carve it up with our predicates, this shows that there is something wrong with the predicates and the concepts they express; that, under the pressure of the facts about human behaviour, they 'fragment' or 'come apart'. So 'intentional' and 'belief' (for example) must be abandoned, and replaced by more accurate concepts derived from neurophysiology.[7]

But suppose we abandoned this false semantic theory, and instead said the following. Actions done because one is in the grip of an emotion do not form discrete groups, but a range. In the grip of an emotion, we do some things quite involuntarily, such as sweating, trembling, and colouring up. These are

---

[7] Cf. Patricia and Paul Churchland's and Stephen Stich's writings, *passim*; e.g., Patricia Churchland, *Neurophilosophy: Toward a Unified Science of the Mind/Brain* (Cambridge, MA: MIT Press, 1986), 382.

things over which, as things are, I have no direct control at all. There are other doings over which I can exercise direct control but can also do involuntarily, without realizing that I am doing them. I can clench or unclench my fists at will, smile or frown, but these are also things I can easily do unawares. I may begin to do some things, e.g., scream or cry or run without realizing that I am doing so, and once started, find it easier to go on than to stop; here perhaps I may be said to refrain intentionally from stopping. Other actions I do intentionally because, in the grip of the emotion, I just want to do them, though I do not do them in the belief that there is anything good about them at all (arational actions). Then there are actions that I do, momentarily believing that there is something good about them, though, looking back, I may not be able to understand how I could have (some cases of *akrasia*); and finally there are actions I do for a reason, in order to do or achieve something I believe to be good or desirable. Although there are clear cases in each of these groups, some of the actions that are clearly done 'because the agent is in the grip of an emotion' will have features in common with some two adjacent groups, and there will be nothing that does or could settle to which group it 'really' belongs.

Fleeing in terror might well be a case in point. It may be, on occasion, that one has a reason for fleeing—that it will get one out of danger—and flees, but it still may be that one did not flee, on that occasion, in order to get out of danger. Perhaps, after all, it is simply the case that one of the desires we are seized by when seized by fear is the desire to run or hide—such a desire would have good survival value—and that sometimes we act on it as impulsively, and with as little thought, as we act on the desire to scream or jump for joy.

Now, if this is indeed how things are with us, what are the consequences for the roles of reason and emotion in action? Well, let us go back to the thought with which I started—the contrast between the supposed irrationality of striking inanimate objects in anger and the supposed rationality of striking animate ones. If what I have argued is correct, then both sides of this contrast may be false. It may be that neither is irrational nor rational, but rather that both are arational, in the sense of being done without reason.

Moreover, insofar as one can see the potential for rationality or irrationality in either, the ascription goes the other way. I have deliberately stayed away from the murky waters of the topic of *akrasia* or weakness of will, but it is, I take it, perfectly obvious, and consistent with all I have said, that on some occasions an arational action may be irrational in the standard akratic way, i.e., contrary to some practical judgement about the good or necessity of refraining from it. If I throw the only tin opener out of the window, I certainly shall not be able to open the tin and may have to go hungry to bed; if I wreak violence on someone else's valuable antique furniture, I violate her rights. So, assaulting inanimate objects in anger may be irrational in the sense of being akratic. But it is surely the case that assaulting animate ones is much more likely to be so. Reason may well have nothing to say against assaulting the inanimate, but the fact that the animate can be hurt and harmed always stands as a potential reason against assaulting them.

In highlighting this point, I do not mean to ally myself with those who see emotion as opposed, in some important sense, to reason (or Reason) or who think that the practical rationality manifested in moral action must be somehow independent of the desiderative faculty. On the contrary, I stand firmly on the Aristotelian side of the Aristotelian-Kantian debate. But those of us who follow Aristotle should not, I think, push our luck too far, and I want to conclude by showing how the existence of arational actions creates something in the way of a problem even for us.

An important fact about human beings, stressed in neo-Aristotelian virtue-based ethics, is that we are creatures such that our appetites and passions may prompt us where reason would also have led. In this fact lies the sense in which we are 'constituted by nature to receive the virtues',[8] the possibility of harmony between our desiderative and rational faculties, of the virtuous person's grasp of 'truth in agreement with right desire' (*Nicomachean Ethics*, 1139a31). Aristotle maintains, (and Dennis Stampe[9] has recently reiterated) that desire is for the seeming (or apparent) good (or pleasant); when what seems good in the faculty of desire is truly good, then the desire is right, and the true judgement of reason about what is good will be in agreement with it.

Now, the apparent pleasures to which the bodily appetites prompt us may indeed be judged truly good and pleasant by reason. In relation to the bodily appetites, Watson rightly emphasizes the fact that we may 'judge that to cease to have such appetites is to lose something of worth'[10] and thereby both desire *and* value (some of) the actions to which the appetites prompt us. A human being *can* be seen 'in his role as Rational Animal'[11] while eating, drinking, and making love (if it is in the right way, on the right occasions, and so on), odd as that may initially seem, not because he is, necessarily, acting 'for a reason' of the standard sort, but because these are activities that can properly form part of a flourishing human life; reason may correctly judge that such actions are good and endorse them.

[8] *Nicomachean Ethics*, 1103a24–6.
[9] 'The Authority of Desire', *Philosophical Review* 96(3) (1987): 335–81.
[10] Gary Watson, 'Free Agency', *Journal of Philosophy*, 72(8), 205–20, 213.
[11] Donald Davidson, 'Actions, Reasons, and Causes', *Journal of Philosophy* 60 (1963): 685–700.

The same is true of most of the emotions. Reason may judge truly that to cease to have many of the emotions to which we are subject would be to lose something of worth, thereby conferring value on many of the actions to which they prompt us which it would endorse. Once again, a human being can be seen in her role as a rational animal when she flees the dangerous, honours the dead, repels aggressors, punishes wrongdoers, makes recompense for her own wrongdoing, cherishes her children, celebrates joyful occasions, and so on. Reason may correctly judge that such actions are good.

The only sense in which Reason and emotion are opposed, according to Aristotelian ethics, is that (except, perhaps, in people who have 'natural virtue') the untrained passions tend to represent things as good and pleasant (or bad and unpleasant) which are not truly so. We have to be trained to fear dishonour more than death, to desire sexual intercourse as an expression of love within a lifelong partnership rather than as simply fun or the exercise of power, to be angered by injustice rather than deserved criticism. Unless they are properly trained, the passions will prompt us to action contrary to reason, or, even worse, corrupt our reason so that we judge things to be good and pleasant falsely. But, properly trained, most of them—it has been said, all[12]—will be in agreement with rational judgement.

But can the same be said about the arational actions to which our emotions prompt us? It seems to me that, by and large, it cannot, though we might make out a plausible case for some of the actions appropriate to a wave of affection or tenderness. Reason can find good in touching and caressing the people and animals one loves (in the right way on the right occasions, etc.); it forms and endorses loving bonds, is found innocently pleasurable, reassuring, or endearing by the recipients, may speak louder than words, especially to the pre- or non-linguistic, and so on. Although we usually do not rumple our children's hair for these excellent reasons, we could. But I do not see how one could even begin to make out a case for finding any good in any of the others; they are arational not merely in the sense that one is prompted to them only by desire and not by reason (which is equally true of actions prompted solely by appetite) but further, in the sense that they cannot be *made* rational; reason cannot endorse them.

---

[12] In 'Aristotle's Doctrine of the Mean', *American Philosophical Quarterly* 10 (1973): 223–30, J. O. Urmson maintained that, according to Aristotle, there is no emotion that one should never exhibit. In 'Plato on the Emotions', *Proceedings of the Aristotelian Society*, Supplementary volume 58(1) (1984): 81–96, I argue, following Aquinas (*Sum. Theo.* la2ae Q24 a.4.), that, on the contrary, some passions may be bad in themselves, insofar as they involve an attachment to the truly bad or an aversion to the truly good, for example, envy and *accidie*. But the intrinsically bad emotions are few.

We might still think, however, that our lives would not, quite generally, be better if emotion never prompted us to act in these ways, or if we always resisted the prompting. We might well find something rather touching or endearing about people's performing many of the arational actions;[13] even the disturbingly violent ones seem to evoke some sort of bond of sympathy. When I have read this paper to discussion groups, I have found that the list of the examples at the beginning always provokes instant delighted recognition; everyone knows what it is like to act in some of these ways, and is somehow pleased to hear it acknowledged and described. Now, someone might maintain that this is just a case of the weak and fallible taking (improper) pleasure in having company. But to me it suggests that we value ourselves and each other as emotional creatures—not as *rational*-emotional in the way pinpointed by Aristotle, but as just plain emotional—and do not believe that the perfect human being would never act arationally.

The importance of this fact, if it is a fact, should not be overemphasized. It leaves general claims about the connections between human perfection, moral agency, and practical *rationality* intact, if it is remembered that we make these claims in the area where things are, as Aristotle says, not true of necessity but 'for the most part'.

Acknowledgements

Earlier versions of this paper have been read at philosophy colloquia at UCLA, UC/Irvine, and, most recently, at a conference on *Reason and Moral Judgment* at Santa Clara in 1989. I am grateful to the many people who contributed to the discussion on these various occasions, and also to Anne Jaap Jacobson, Christine Swanton, and Gary Watson for detailed comments on earlier drafts.

References

Aristotle. 2000. *Nicomachean Ethics*. Edited and translated by Roger Crisp. Cambridge: Cambridge University Press.

Churchland, P. 1986. *Neurophilosophy: Toward a Unified Science of the Mind/Brain*. Cambridge, MA: MIT Press.

Davidson, D. 1963. 'Actions, Reasons, and Causes', *Journal of Philosophy* 60: 685–700.

---

[13] I owe this point to Watson in discussion.

Hursthouse, R. 1973. 'Aristotle's Doctrine of the Mean', *American Philosophical Quarterly* 10: 223–30.

Hursthouse, R. 1984. 'Plato on the Emotions', *Proceedings of the Aristotelian Society*, Supplementary volume 58(1): 81–96.

McDowell, J. 1982. 'Reason and Action', *Philosophical Investigations* 5(4): 301–5.

Nagel, T. 1970. *The Possibility of Altruism*. New York: Oxford University Press.

Schiffer, S. 1976. 'A Paradox of Desire', *American Philosophical Quarterly* 13(3): 195–203.

Stampe, D. 1987. 'The Authority of Desire', *Philosophical Review* 96(3): 335–81.

Urmson, J. O. 1973. 'Aristotle's Doctrine of the Mean', *American Philosophical Quarterly* 10 (1973): 223–30.

Watson, G. 1975. 'Free Agency', *Journal of Philosophy* 72(8): 205–20.

14
Hume on Justice

1. Introduction

As everyone knows, Hume begins his discussion of justice in the *Treatise* by claiming 'that no action can be virtuous or morally good, unless there be in human nature some motive to produce it, distinct from the sense of its morality' (T, 3.2.1.7/479). He recognizes that this makes for a 'great difficulty' because, in the case of just actions, it seems that my motive for them is my regard for justice, which is *not* distinct from my sense of their morality, their justice.

Why does he think that this seems to be so? Well, he might simply take it as obvious; a number of other people have done so. After all, when we try to think of a reason for doing something that is just other than the (putative) fact that it is, we seem to get stuck. Bernard Williams, for instance, discussing what Aristotle can mean by saying that the virtuous agent chooses virtuous actions 'for their own sake', considers whether 'A V person chooses V acts *qua* V acts' and rejects it (taken in a *de dicto* sense) as largely false. 'Courageous people' he says, 'rarely choose acts as courageous, and modest people never choose modest behaviour as modest' (Williams 1995: 16). But, he adds casually in passing, '[j]ustice is about the only case in which it clearly holds'—that is, just people choose just acts because they are just.

What other reason or motive could they, after all, have? As Hume points out, the obvious candidate—with regard to the public interest—won't do, and in some contexts, especially perhaps the contexts in which we are trying to think in Humean terms, nothing else seems to come to mind.

But shouldn't we be able to think of another candidate? After all, hundreds of philosophers are currently writing, confidently, about respecting others' autonomy as rational agents and what we owe to each other. Does nothing they say suggest a reason or motive for doing what is just beyond the putative fact that it is?

We might say it suggests the following: what motivates the just agent to do what is just is regard for another's rights. Do I hear you cry, scornfully, 'But talk about the regard for others' rights is simply talk about justice in different terms!' True, but I might reply 'So what?' What motivates the benevolent or charitable agent is regard for another's good or well-being, but talk about regard for others' good or well-being is simply talk about benevolence or charity in different terms. Yet Hume clearly holds that the regard for another's good is a motive to produce benevolent acts that is distinct from a sense of their benevolence. So what is the difference?

'Well', one might say, 'intuitively, rights are very different from wellbeing.' Yes indeed. And that, I shall contend, is Hume's point. (I return to this intuition below.)

My general contention is that Hume's discussion of justice is in fact an attack on that concept of rights we think of as having motivated the American and French revolutions, a concept that is still (deplorably in my view) prevalent. I think the very fact that it is so prevalent and so sanctified by its position in the American Constitution has blinded most readers to the power and plausibility of Hume's attack, which I shall try to defend.

On the face of it, linking Hume on justice with the American and French revolutionary talk about rights must seem odd, because, as we all know, the latter is concerned with natural, or as we now say, human rights, whereas Hume concentrates exclusively on *property*. Surprisingly, few commentators say anything about this but surely it cries out for comment. After all, it is beyond belief that Hume could have been ignorant of the 'natural rights' talk that was going on before and around him—Locke is full of it, discussing not only the right to property but also the rights to life and liberty; Grotius and Pufendorf discuss these three and more, and they are in the *Encyclopédie*. We *have* to suppose that it is common talk at least among the educated. So how can Hume argue for the 'artificiality' of justice solely on the basis of property rights and leave himself wide open to any critic to attack his *general* claim simply by appealing to the other 'natural' rights, as Thomas Reid was quick to do?

Reid claims that there are six branches of justice, four that pertain to certain natural or innate rights, viz. 'an innocent man has a right to the safety of his person and family, a right to his liberty and his reputation' (Reid 1977: 425) and two others, one regarding goods or property, and the other, contracts. And he says that, when we read Hume 'it appears evident, that he had in his eye only two particular branches of justice. No part of his reasoning applies to the other four. He seems, I know not why, to have taken up a confined notion of justice, and to have restricted it to property and fidelity in contracts' (Reid 1977: 427).

So there is the question—why *would* Hume, knowingly, take up such a 'confined' notion of justice? A theoretically possible answer is that he was too stupid to see the objection coming. But that too is beyond belief. So we are left with only one possibility. He thought that his reasoning concerning property applied equally well to the other putative natural rights and, moreover, that this was so obviously the case that he need not bother to mention it. This may seem beyond belief too, so I will try to show that it is not.

2. Hume on Private Property

Let us start with the example in Section I of 'Of Justice and Injustice':

> I suppose a person to have lent me a sum of money, on condition that it be restor'd in a few days; and also suppose, that after the expiration of the term agreed on, he demands the sum: I ask *What reason or motive have I to restore the money?* (T, 3.2.1.9/479).

We might observe that, to anyone with the virtue of justice, the answers come readily enough: the money must be restored because it is his *property*, he has a *right* to it, it is *his*, I am under an *obligation* to restore it to him, I *owe* it to him. And Hume would be happy with the idea that such answers are intelligible to human beings in their 'civilised state, and when train'd up according to a certain discipline and education' (T, 3.2.1.9/479). But, he wants to say, if we imagine ourselves in our 'rude and more *natural* condition', namely before we have united into society and entered into the convention to abstain from the possessions of others, the answers would be 'perfectly unintelligible'. I might just as well say, unintelligibly, 'the money (of course there wouldn't be *money* in the rude and natural condition either, but let that pass) must be restored because it is his *cloperty*, he has a *smight* to it, I am under a *gobligation* to restore it to him, I *powe* it to him'.

What turns cloperty into property? The existence of laws of society. 'Our property is nothing but those goods, whose constant possession is establish'd by the laws of society; that is' (as Hume perhaps too quickly remarks) 'by the laws of justice' (T, 3.2.1.11/491). These laws turn cloperty into property and simultaneously turn smights-to-money into rights, gobligations-to-restore money into obligations and powing into owing.

Now let us return to Hume's claim, let us call it—

(C) That 'no action can be virtuous... unless there be in human nature some motive to produce it, distinct from the sense of its morality'.

How does he arrive at it? His basis for it is an earlier conclusion:

> [T]hat the first virtuous motive, which bestows a merit on any action, can never be a regard to the virtue of that action, but must be some other natural motive or principle.   (T, 3.2.1.4/478).

And he gets to that from the premise that

> '[t]is evident, that when we praise any actions, we regard only the motives that produced them, and consider the actions as signs or indications of certain principles in the mind and temper. The external performance has no merit... all virtuous actions derive their merit only from virtuous motives, and are consider'd merely as signs of those motives.
> (T, 3.2.1.2, 4/477–8).

So let us begin with that premise.

We should, I think, be struck by the fact that, at first sight, the premise sounds much more like Kant than like Bentham or Mill. It is the utilitarians who say that an action is right—has merit or is praiseworthy in that sense—if and only if it has the right consequences, but Kant who says that, although an action that aids others may be right, it has no genuinely moral worth—lacks merit in that sense—unless it is done from a sense of duty. And this is very odd, given that Hume is going to move from this premise to the claim that seems so obviously un-Kantian, namely claim (C). How does the move come about? I take it that the premise has to be read carefully, as an aspect of his virtue ethics. It is a premise about actions as *virtuous*—that is, benevolent, just, courageous, kind, honest, etc.—rather than as *right*.

It is not invariably true that an action cannot be given a virtue description (benevolent, courageous, kind, grateful, friendly, generous, etc.) if it was not prompted by the motive proper to the virtue in question, but it is certainly true enough to make Hume's premise quite plausible—certainly much less tendentious than it would be if we construed it as being about actions that are right and had to read him as prefiguring Kant. If I do what appears to be benevolent or generous for ulterior motives, then, I think, I do not do what is benevolent or generous at all; and if I face danger through fear of punishment I do not do what is courageous. If my apparently honest action of telling you the truth is intended to deceive you long term, it does not count as honest and so on. So the correct reading of the premise does not make it about the necessary conditions for morally worthy action in the Kantian way, but about the grounds for praising actions by describing them in virtue terms. If my action regarding you is to count as genuinely benevolent, my motive must be a concern for your well-being.

What about the intermediate conclusion he derives from this—'that the *first* virtuous motive, which bestows a merit on any action, can never be a regard to the virtue of that action, but must be some other natural motive or principle' (my italics)?

What would be examples of virtuous motives? He gives us a parent's concern for her child; a concern for the well-being of others—both of which, we may note, are passions that occur in us naturally. But what about a regard to the virtue of the action? Well, suppose I want to do a benevolent action because it is benevolent, that is, virtuous. As Hume notes (in a very Kantian passage), this may happen (T, 3.2.1.8/479). Feeling my heart devoid of concern for the well-being of others, I may hate myself on that account and perform the action 'from a certain sense of duty'. But although this may happen on occasion, it could not always happen among human beings in general. The very reason I hate myself when I find my heart thus devoid *is* that the benevolent motive, though lacking in me is 'common in human nature', and grounds the praise given to benevolent actions. For benevolent actions are so-called, and merit bestowed on them thereby, because they are taken as signs of a benevolent motive, the naturally occurring concern for the well-being of others. If there were no such concern in human beings, common in human nature, but only a 'concern to do (as it were) benevolent actions' there would not *be* any benevolent actions, and hence the 'concern' to do them would lack an object. (Cf. Wittgenstein 1953 §337: 'If the technique of the game of chess did not exist, I could not intend to play a game of chess.')

So, before—logically 'before'—there can be a concern to do *benevolent* actions as such, there must first be a natural concern for the well-being of others. That concern is logically prior to benevolent actions—the 'first' virtuous motive as far as benevolent actions are concerned.

Hence (C). Quite generally, no action can be virtuous unless, somewhere in human nature—not necessarily operative in the moment of action, but somewhere—there is some motive (or motives or 'distinct principles') capable of producing it.

But there is not, and could not be, a natural concern, common in human nature, to abstain from others' *property*, or respect others' property *rights*, or honour one's *obligations* regarding others' property any more than there could be a natural concern to play chess. Before there can be that concern, there has to be chess, with its rules, which is something that human beings invent or contrive—an artifice. And before there can be property, property rights, and obligations, there has to be a society with laws governing the stability and transference of external goods, which is something else human beings invent or contrive. The artifice or convention of the laws of justice, which establishes which acts in relation to possessions are just, comes 'first'. So just actions with regard to property are logically prior to the motive(s) proper to them. *They come first.*

So there *is* something wrong with saying that what motivates the just agent to do what is just (that is, restore the money), is regard for another's right to his property and that this is parallel to saying that what motivates the benevolent agent to do what is benevolent is regard for another's good or well-being. The intuition above was at least partially correct; well-being is *indeed* different from property and property rights.

I turn now to the question of whether property and property rights are significantly different, in the context of Hume's discussion, from other, 'natural' rights, such as the right to life or the right one has over one's own body, and argue that they are not.

3. Grotius, Pufendorf, Locke, and Hume on Property

The first point I want to make is that 'property rights' would have been for Locke, and I think is still for Hume, a pleonasm. In Locke's day, saying that something was one's property *was* a way of saying that it was something you had a right to or in. Hence his claim, in the *Essay*:

> 'Where there is no property there is no injustice' is a proposition as certain as any demonstration in Euclid: for the idea of property being a right to anything, and the idea to which the name injustice is given being the invasion or violation of that right; it is evident that these ideas being thus established.... I can as certainly know this proposition to be true as that a triangle has three angles equal to two right ones.   (4.3.18/549)

So saying you have a 'property right' would have to be saying something like 'you have a right to or in something you have a right to or in'. We can see this in *Two Treatises of Government*, where Locke discusses rights concerning life, limbs, body and actions all under the heading of 'property'. When he says there that 'the chief end of civil society is the preservation of property' (Locke 1970: 2.4/85), this is not the claim it became in the mouths of anti-socialists who thought that nationalization was going to bring about the downfall of civilization. The preservation of a man's 'property', in Locke, is the preservation of not only his private property but also his life and liberty: 'to preserve his property—*that* is, his life, liberty and estate, against the injuries and attempts of other men' (1970: 2.4/87, my italics).

We find this very odd nowadays, because for us 'property' by and large covers only what Hume refers to as 'external goods'—my house, my car, my money, those external goods that are mine. But that use of 'my' and 'mine' gives us the clue that can take us back to understanding the seventeenth- and eighteenth-century use of 'property'. The very word 'property' is derived from *propria*—that which belongs to someone, is 'of him' or 'his' (*suum*)—and in Grotius and Pufendorf, in Locke and Filmer and Hooker, the debates and arguments about 'property' are debates about *rights*—not particularly property rights, but rights to what is one's own (*suum*) such as one's life, limbs, body, liberty, actions, virtue and reputation.

So let us just use 'my' and 'mine' (yours, his) for the moment and look at Hume on private property just in those terms. Here we are, let us suppose, in our rude and more natural condition before we have united into society. Wandering around one day, I come upon a rather nice horse and take it home with me. The horse and I get on very well for several months—I feed it, it pulls my plough and gets me from A to B, everything's fine, and then one day someone passing by says 'Hey! That horse is *mine*.' What can he possibly mean? That he was ploughing with it and riding it at some earlier time and wants to again? But so what? So shall I say that it is not his but *mine*? But what can I mean by that? That I have been ploughing with it and so on recently and want to go on doing so? We can both shout and fight about what we have been doing with the horse and what we want, but clearly, in the absence of any laws, neither of us can claim that the horse is our *property* and that we have a *right* to it. If a third person, considerably stronger than either of us, comes along and says, 'I fancy that horse, I'll take it' and does so, he has not violated the property right of either of us because, as Hume says, in this 'state of nature', 'there was no such thing as property'. (I note here, because I shall want to come back to it, that the fuller quotation is 'tho I assert, that in the state of nature, ... there be neither justice nor injustice, yet I assert *not*, that it was allowable, in such a state, to violate the property of others. I only maintain that there was no such thing as property' (T, 3.2.2.28/501, my italics).)

This seems obvious enough in the case of private property where, as Hume nicely puts it in the *Enquiry* 'uninstructed Nature' surely never made any such distinction as that between *mine* and *yours*. But, we might say, nature surely has drawn a distinction between *my* life, limbs, body, and actions, and *yours*. Even in the rude state before we unite into society, surely my life is *mine*, my *property*, I have a *right* to it, and, thereby, if you take *my* life or injure *my* body, you have failed to abstain from what is another's and thereby violated my rights and hence done me an injustice.

But, enlightened by Hume, we can deny that in the rude state you have done me an injustice by violating a right of mine by, for example, killing me. For we can plausibly maintain that the obvious or natural sense in which my life or body is mine is not and could not be the *meum* and *suum*, 'anything I have a right to or in', sense, that is, the Lockean property sense. This is simply shown by the fact that a life (limbs, body, actions) may be mine or another's in one sense but not in the other.

My life, limbs, body, and actions are, in the natural sense, necessarily mine, inalienable. There is nothing I, or anyone else can do, to make them *not* mine. But in the *meum-suum* sense they are not. We should recall that the slave trade was still thriving in Hume's day and that, in the context of slavery, it made clear sense (I can't bring myself to say 'perfect' sense) to claim that someone else's life, limbs, body, and actions were *mine*—naturally his, indeed, but *my* property, what I had a right to and in because he was *my* slave. (Recall that when Locke claims that something becomes *mine* when I have mixed *my* labour with it, he is actually talking about the labour that someone else has done at my behest, for which I have paid some (notional) amount and thereby made it *mine*.) Perhaps some of the rationalist moral philosophers against whom Hume waxes so sarcastic attempted to argue that what was wrong with slavery could be discerned by pure reason, namely that it embodied a contradiction—how could *his* life be *mine*! But it would have been a bad argument and moreover contrary to the common acceptance of the contemporary view that my life isn't actually mine in the *meum-suum* sense but God's.

Those of us who do not believe that my life is God's in the *meum-suum* sense tend to recognize an obvious way in which I can make what is naturally my life not mine in the *meum-suum* sense. I do it by explicitly waiving my right to life. What is naturally my life then ceases to be mine in the sense of something I have a right regarding, and so (given some other restrictions) you can kill me without violating any right of mine or doing me an injustice, as in cases of voluntary (but not involuntary) euthanasia. Similarly I can give you one of my kidneys (I don't know that it is yet possible for me to give you one of my limbs, but no matter). In the natural sense, it will always be mine, but once I have given it to you, it is yours in the *meum-suum* sense; you are the one who has rights regarding it.

Or consider an example that was also of interest to Hume's predecessors. In the natural sense of the possessives, a man's semen is his, a woman's ovum is hers, and any child a woman bears as a result of intercourse with a man, hers, his, and theirs. But in the *meum-suum* sense, none of these are necessarily so. Many societies have made sense of the idea that it is the begetter of a child who has rights regarding it, not its mother; the child is *his*, not hers nor theirs. And the ancient phenomenon of adoption has always allowed the people who brought up a child to say that it is *theirs* in the *meum-suum* sense without claiming that it is naturally so.

And so, contrary to first impressions, we see that uninstructed nature can no more draw a distinction between what is *mine*—life, body, limbs, actions, child, say—and *yours* in the *meum-suum* sense than it can between my piece of private property and yours. The very idea of *mine* and *yours* in this sense can arise only after we have united into society and established laws that fix their content.

Does this mean, you may cry in scandalized tones, that, according to Hume there would be nothing wrong with your killing or raping me in the state of nature? No indeed, for remember I quoted him as saying 'tho I assert, that in the state of nature,... there be neither justice nor injustice, yet I assert *not*, that it was allowable, in such a state, to violate the property of others. I only maintain that there was no such thing as property.' Of course murder and rape are not 'allowable' in the state of nature because they are ruled out by *benevolence*. The natural motive of benefiting, or not harming others is all that is needed. We are so accustomed to thinking of murder and rape as violations of rights that I constantly find myself having to reiterate Foot's point that killing someone when their life is a good to them—as it normally is—is as contrary to charity as it is to justice. And hence Hume's oft-repeated claim that if our benevolence were not limited, if 'cordial affection, compassion, sympathy, were the only movements with which the human mind was... acquainted' (T, 3.2.2.15/494), 'if every man had a tender regard for another' (T, 3.2.2.16/494), there would be no need for justice. (In fact, I think he is wrong about that. He is right that strong universal benevolence or charity would stop us from murdering and raping and enslaving each other, and from meanly depriving another of something he would feel the lack of, all with no need for justice. But living together in perfect benevolence, we might still find the need for some justice to protect each of us from the well-intentioned efforts of others to benefit us where we saw no benefit. That, after all, is Foot's point in 'Euthanasia' (Foot 1977). If I am absolutely convinced that you would be better off dead, charity or benevolence bids me kill you, regardless of your firmly expressed wish to be left alive. It is only justice—the fact that your life is yours in the *meum-suum* sense and thereby that you have the right to decide whether you live or die, not me—that stays my hand.)

So my right to life, my right to determine what happens to my body, my right to my child, all these rights are as 'artificial', in Hume's sense, as my right to my car. But Hume's sense is not, I want to argue, a sense that excludes the common intuition that my right to life, at least, is a 'natural' or human right whereas my right to my car is not. To do this I have to backtrack.

4. Hume on Natural Law and Natural Rights

Earlier, considering the question 'What turns cloperty into property?'—or, as we now might say, the natural 'mine' into the *meum* 'mine'—I gave Hume's answer as 'The laws of society'; and noted that 'perhaps too quickly' he adds 'that is, the laws of justice' (T, 3.2.2.12/491). Given that, in illustration of the fact that the natural 'mine' and the *meum* 'mine' have clearly distinguishable uses, I have alluded to societies whose laws were far from being laws of justice, such as those allowing slavery, I can hardly leave this casual move of Hume's unexamined. Why—*how*—can he possibly say 'the laws of society, *that* is, the laws of justice'?

On the strength of this remark, and many others, and his claim that justice is not a natural but an artificial virtue, some people take Hume to be a conventionalist or 'positivist' about law (and thereby rights) as Hobbes was ('No law can be unjust', Hobbes says). But this is surely a mistake. Hume is perfectly aware of the fact that we have no difficulty in annexing the idea of injustice to that of an actual civil law, and moreover has firm views about what can justify our doing so. He has no objection to the contrast between civil (or actual or conventional) law and so-called natural law understood, that is, *as* a set of just laws.

Hume's assumption that we are talking, not about any particular legal code—some civil law—but about civil law as it should be, that is as enshrining laws of *justice*—is perfectly comprehensible when we keep to the forefront of our minds the fact that he is talking about the *virtue* of justice, that thing we *approve* of. And everyone knows what it is to approve of some actual law in one's society and to disapprove of another because, say, it serves the interest of some members of the society, but not all. So his search for the origins of justice is a search for the origins of something to which we give moral approbation, and he already has in place his views about the sort of mechanisms that can generate this rather special thing. I think myself, that in the *Treatise*, his detailed attempts to describe its aetiology lead him into ascribing a power to indoctrination which, though rightly ascribed, threatens at times to put him back in the conventionalist camp, but however far he strays in that direction, he never fails to return to his fundamental view that justice—real or 'natural' justice, not conventional or civil or legal justice—is approved of because it is *useful*—'absolutely requisite to the well-being of mankind and existence of society' as he says in the second *Enquiry* (EPM, 3.2.159/199).

It was, and is, a commonplace in natural jurisprudence that the natural laws, being just, are the criterion against which civil laws are to be judged. The way you work out whether a particular civil law is just is by working out whether or not it coincides with a law in the ideal code of natural law. And, if Hume is right, the way in which you work *that* out is by working out whether or not the particular civil law is useful—whether it is 'requisite to the public interest, and to that of every individual' (T, 3.2.2.20/496).

Now what does Hume's view contrast with? Well, one might say, with at least the following line or lines of thought.

Suppose someone were to say 'Justice is a constant and perpetual will of giving every one his due' (T, 3.2.6.2/526) or, as we might say nowadays, 'of giving everyone what one owes to him' or 'of giving everyone his rights'. Those suggest that, in order to find out what is just, we must first determine what is due to everyone, what we *do* owe to each other, what *are* our rights. So we come up with some supposedly incontestable premises about our rights, say that we have rights to life and liberty, and then infer 'and so a just law protects/enshrines these rights'.

This way of arguing encapsulates the concept of rights that I referred to at the outset as the one Hume is attacking and, in my view, rightly. For, as he remarks of the first ('Justice is giving every one his due') and might equally well remark concerning the others, 'In this definition 'tis suppos'd, that there are such things as right and property [*meum* and *suum*] independent of justice and antecedent to it; and that they wou'd have subsisted tho' men had never dreamt of practising such a virtue' (T, 3.2.6.2/526–7). For Hume, trying to get to just laws from such premises is a logical howler and has things back to front. If you want to claim that we have a right to life or liberty, you have to argue for that *from* a claim about just laws, not from it *to* what the just laws would be or are. You argue for it by arguing that laws protecting or enshrining those rights are or would be just laws, and then you have to argue that the laws are or would be just because they are or would be *useful*, not because they enshrine rights. No wonder Bentham and Mill claimed him as a utilitarian, and no wonder Bentham, taking himself to be following Hume, said that talk about rights was nonsense and talk about natural rights nonsense on stilts. In the absence of talk about *useful* laws, actual or hypothetical, established in society, both of them are nonsense, just as talk about owing someone $5 is nonsense in the absence of talk about currency.

So talk about Humean rights and natural rights *does* make sense in the context of talk about useful laws, but I think it is worth noting (given the prevalence of the nonsensical concept) that the talk about rights has to change in certain respects—all of which, I might say, I regard as distinct improvements. Here are some examples.

The question 'What are my/your/Māori's, (real) rights?' is a way of asking 'What laws establishing certain rights ought New Zealand to have?' and *that* is a way of asking 'What laws establishing certain rights would be useful in New Zealand society?' The question 'What are my, or the, natural rights?' is a way of asking 'What laws establishing certain rights ought to be part of any society's legal system?' and *that* is a way of asking 'What laws establishing certain rights are or would be useful to any society?'

The question 'Who (or what) are the bearers of rights?' is a way of asking 'With respect to whom (or what) would useful laws establish rights?' 'Do men and women have equal rights?' is a way of asking 'Are there any useful laws (for our society or many or any) which would establish different rights for men and women?' And faced with the question 'Do you believe we have a right to autonomy?' anyone who has accepted Humean rights will sensibly say, 'I haven't a clue. Give me some examples of laws that you think would establish such a right and I'll tell you when I have worked out whether or not I think they would be useful.' And none of these ways of talking is quite what we are accustomed to in discussions of rights.

How are rights established in law? Hume illustrates with some glee the ways in which 'those rules, by which property, right and obligation are determin'd, have in them no marks of a natural origin, but many of artifice and contrivance' (T, 3.2.6.6/528), describing 'the variations, which all the rules of property receive from the finer turns and connexions of the imagination, and from the subtilties and abstractions of law-topics and reasonings' (EPM, 3.2.161/203). In determining 'what is a man's property' (what he has a right to or in) we have 'recourse to statutes, customs, precedents, analogies and a hundred other circumstances; some of which are constant and inflexible, some variable and arbitrary' (EPM, 3.2.158/197).

This brings out two significant features of the Humean concept of rights. One is that what 'having a (real) right to or in x' consists in, may be relative to a particular society at a particular time. Customs and precedents vary between societies with different histories. Some circumstances (for instance the local weather, the concentration of population) vary; given different cultures, what people find 'analogous' varies. So different societies may formulate different laws determining different rights and there may be *no question* as to which society has secured the 'real' rights. For *if* the different laws that different societies come up with are equally useful to their members, then the laws are equally just, and the real rights of the members of each society will be determined by those laws, despite being different. And that does not seem to me quite how we tend to talk nowadays about real (as opposed to 'merely conventional') rights.

The second feature is that what 'having a right to or in x' consists in may be made up of a mass of details—a whole set of useful laws. A Humean concept of natural rights makes sense on the supposition that there are some useful laws—say a law prohibiting murder—which (a) establish a right and (b) are 'constant and inflexible'; that is, such that they would be useful to any society no matter what its history, culture, circumstances or whatever. But no society (as far as I know) ever has a *single* short sentence law establishing the right to life. It has, say, laws forbidding different sorts of murder, laws or statutes about killing in self-defence and/or through recklessness or through letting die, and/or about capital punishment, infanticide, suicide, euthanasia, abortion and so on—a whole set of (perhaps) useful laws.

When we talk about rights nowadays we do not, I think, tend to talk about them as things you can have to some degree, especially where the natural rights are concerned. I have the right to life or I don't; a foetus has a right to life or it doesn't; there's not much room for saying, well I have more of the right to life than a foetus does. But when we think of 'having a right to x' as supervening on a fair number of useful laws, (and remember that, in order to *be* useful, laws have to be consistent with other laws so that they are all applicable, *and* that they have to be applicable in the ordinary life of human beings) the idea does not seem so strange. As Hume says, 'Half rights and obligations... seem so natural in common life' (T, 3.2.6.8/531). (Notwithstanding that quote, I must confess that I am going against Hume on this point. *He* maintains that 'abstract reasoning, and the general maxims of philosophy and law' *do* establish that 'property, and right, and obligation admit not of degrees' and that it is in our 'common and *negligent* way of thinking' that we think otherwise; this is yet another of his arguments which purports to show that justice is artificial not natural. But the argument looks to me like a confused attempt to argue against Grotius' distinction between perfect and imperfect rights.)

Finally—and briefly—in what sense, according to Hume, is justice useful? Useful to what end? It is clear in Hume that the end is human well-being. What is nothing like as clear is where Hume stands on human well-being—with, at one extreme, the hedonistic Bentham or, at the other extreme with Aristotle, the Epicureans and Mill in *On Liberty*—and *consequently* it is unclear what he means by 'useful'. I have argued elsewhere (Hursthouse 1999) that he is not consistent on this, but that he tends strongly towards the latter, eudaimonistic account; here, I will close with just one point in its favour.

Hume claims in the *Enquiry*, 'Examine the writers on the laws of nature [he means on "natural law"]; and you will always find, that, whatever principles they set out with, they are sure to terminate here at last, and to assign, as the ultimate reason for every rule which they establish, the convenience and necessities of mankind' (EPM, 3.2.156/195).

From the little I know of the natural law theorists, that seems to me true. But the human well-being that they all thought natural law served or preserved—as Hume must have known—was, of course, the *sort* of human well-being that the God of Christianity intended when He laid down natural law; not the sort that consists in mere animal pleasure or the satisfaction of desires, but the eudaimonistic sort that is found only in virtue. So we must surely take it that this moralized conception of 'the convenience and necessities of mankind' is what Hume is talking about here.

And, insofar as that is true, we have the final Humean nail in the coffin of the modern concept of rights, *insofar* as that is predicated on the Rawlsian assumption that ethics is not prior to politics and that we can limn the laws of a just society without committing ourselves to any substantive ethical views on the good for human beings. This is far from being the Humean picture of rights.

References

Foot, P. 1977. 'Euthanasia', *Philosophy & Public Affairs* 6(2): 85–112.

Hume, D. 1975. *A Treatise of Human Nature*. Edited by L. A. Selby-Bigge, revised by P. Nidditch. Oxford: Clarendon Press.

Hume, D. 1975. *Enquiries concerning Human Understanding and concerning the Principles of Morals*. Edited by L. A. Selby-Bigge, revised by P. Nidditch. Oxford: Clarendon Press.

Hursthouse, R. 1999. 'Virtue Ethics and Human Nature', *Hume Studies*, 25(1–2): 67–82.

Locke, J. 1975. *An Essay Concerning Human Understanding*. Edited by L. A. Selby-Bigge. Oxford: Oxford University Press.

Reid, T. 1977. *Essays on the Active Powers of Man*. New York: Garland.

Williams, B. 1995. 'Acting as the Virtuous Person Acts'. In R. Heinaman (ed.), *Aristotle and Moral Realism*. Boulder, CO: Westview Press: 13–23.

Wittgenstein, L. W. 1953. *Philosophical Investigations*. Edited by G. E. M. Anscombe and R. Rhees, translated by G. E. M. Anscombe. Oxford: Blackwell.

15
After Hume's Justice

Hume's attack on that concept of rights enshrined in the constitutions of the American and French revolutions, and his rival account, has, I believe, been unjustly neglected. Those of us who agree with Aristotle that ethical science precedes and is continuous with political science,[1] and who hence are inclined to reject the 'priority of the Right' made famous by Rawls, may find hints in Hume of the bridge we need between Aristotle's discussion of justice and post-Enlightenment thought. It would be anachronistic to look for the liberal concept of rights in Aristotle; and yet many of us are unwilling to declare shamelessly that we want no truck with liberalism and to follow MacIntyre in espousing traditionalist authoritarianism.

In this paper I explore a concept of rights inspired by some of Anscombe's papers on Hume, locating it within an Aristotelian framework; in the first part I describe the concept and in the second I consider some of its most striking features.

At first sight, Hume may seem hardly more use than Aristotle on rights, because the oddest feature of his writings on justice is that he gives such limited account of it. Though well acquainted with the writings of such 'natural rights' proponents as Pufendorf and Locke, Hume makes no mention of the rights they, and we, think of as central, such as those to life or to liberty, concentrating instead exclusively on *property*. This appears to leave him in a weak position. Since he has argued his case only for property rights, it is open to any critic to attack his general claims about justice simply by appealing to the other 'natural' rights, as Thomas Reid was quick to do.[2]

We could blandly ignore this obvious problem, as most commentators do, or assume that Hume is simply open to any Reid-type criticism. More interestingly, we could allow ourselves to wonder whether there is more in Hume's account than immediately meets the eye.

---

[1] *Nicomachean Ethics*, II.2.1094a22–28.
[2] *Essays on the Active Powers of the Human Mind*, Essay V. Chap. v, 'Whether Justice be a Natural or an Artificial Virtue'.

As far as I know, the only philosopher to have done so is Anscombe in her series of papers on rules, rights, and promises.[3] Anscombe points out that Hume has not just one but 'two theses about promises: one, that a promise is "naturally unintelligible", and the other that even if (*per impossibile*) it were "naturally intelligible" it could not *naturally* give rise to any obligation'. She claims that his discovery of *natural unintelligibility* is 'a great one' and that it is 'of wider application than he gave it'.[4] The wider application she gives to it is to rules and rights. 'A right is not a natural phenomenon that can be discerned and named as a feature found in some class of creatures by, say, a taxonomist. It is in this respect like a rule and a promise; that "natural unintelligibility" which Hume attributed to promises is found in all three things.'[5]

Anscombe's papers all take off from Hume's account of promises. But they might inspire us to consider the question of whether some aspects of what he says about the right to private property might be fruitfully applied *mutatis mutandis* to other rights, such as the right to life, and thereby supply a more general account of rights and justice. I shall follow Anscombe in looking to Hume for insights, not making claims about his actual account. I also follow her in emphasizing the thesis that certain concepts are 'naturally unintelligible', and put to one side, as incidental (albeit, closely connected) the thesis that certain motives, such as the motive to acts of justice, are not 'natural'.

Despite the fact that I put the question of the naturalness of the motive to justice to one side, I begin with Book III, Part II, Section I of the *Treatise*, where Hume asks 'What reason or motive have I to restore the money?' (p. 479).[6] For anyone who has the virtue of justice, the answer to this question comes readily enough: 'The money must be restored because it is his *property*; it is *his*, not *mine*; I am under an *obligation* to restore it to him; he has a *right* to it.' Such reasons are 'sufficient' and the answers 'satisfactory' against a background of civil (not merely familial) society in which people have been 'train'd up' (p. 479) in certain ways, namely to respect certain laws and conventions. *But*, the claim is, the answers would be 'unintelligible' (pp. 479–80) without that background. This does not mean merely 'They would be unintelligible as reasons' but, strongly, 'They would be unintelligible, make no sense.'

---

[3] Rules, Rights and Promises', and 'On the Source of the Authority of the State', reprinted in *Ethics, Religion and Politics*; 'The Question of Linguistic Idealism', reprinted in *From Parmenides to Wittgenstein*; Vols. III and I respectively of *The Collected Papers of G. E. M. Anscombe* (Minneapolis: University of Minnesota Press, 1981).
[4] *Ethics, Religion, and Politics*, 97.   [5] Ibid., 138.
[6] All page references to the *Treatise* are to the edition of L. A. Selby-Bigge, revised P. H. Nidditch, (Oxford: Clarendon Press, 1975).

They would be unintelligible against a 'natural' (as opposed to civil, cf. p. 475n) background because it is only in virtue of the fact that we unite into civil society, are trained up regarding its laws and conventions, and respond to that training in certain ways, that such things as *property*, the distinction between *his* property and *mine*, his *right* to what is his, and my consequent *obligation* regarding it, come to be. So a property right is 'naturally unintelligible' in the sense that it is a necessary condition of having the concept of a property right that we first have the concept of that 'non-natural' phenomenon, a law or convention.

Let us suppose for the moment (I will return to an objection below) that Hume is correct about *property* and property *rights*; that they are 'naturally unintelligible'. Can the same be said about other rights? It is instructive, in considering this question, to begin by noting the Lockean sense of 'property' according to which it covers not only external goods, but anything which is one's own (*suum*) and which one has a *right* to or in. Grotius and Pufendorf discuss life, limbs, body, and actions under the term *suum* and, continuing this tradition, Locke includes these under 'property' in the *Two Treatises of Civil Government*.[7] So we could rephrase the question as: could what Hume says about private property be extended to cover Lockean property?

At first sight, it seems that the answer must be 'No'. With respect to private property we may well agree with Hume that 'uninstructed nature' (E, 156)[8] could make no distinction between your horse and my horse. This horse is my *property*, I have a *right* to it and you an *obligation* to abstain from taking it, only because we live in a civil society with certain laws, and it is possible that there should be no civil society and laws, and, thereby, no such property and no such right. If, in such a 'natural' non-civil state, you take a horse I have been feeding and using, you have not taken my *property* and have not violated a *right* of mine nor done me an *injustice*.

But nature surely has drawn a distinction between my life, limbs, body, and actions and yours and, on natural law theory, this seems enough to ground the natural rights. Even in the 'natural' state my life is my own, my property, I have a right to it and if, in the natural, non-civil state, you take *my* life or injure *my* body or imprison me and hence restrict *my* actions, you have failed

---

[7] For an authoritative and illuminating discussion of Locke on 'property' and his debts to, amongst others, Grotius and Pufendorf, see James Tully, *A Discourse on Property* (Cambridge: Cambridge University Press, 1980).

[8] All references to *An Enquiry Concerning the Principles of Morals* within the text are given by E, followed by a figure which cites not a page, but the number of a marginal section.

to abstain from what is *another's*, violated my *rights* and hence done me an *injustice*.

But, following Hume, we could deny that in the natural state you could have done me an injustice by violating a *right* of mine by, for example, taking my life. For we can plausibly maintain that the obvious or natural sense in which my life or body is mine is not, and could not be, the *meum* and *suum*, Lockean property, 'anything I have a right to or in' sense. This is readily shown by the fact that a life may be mine or another's in one sense but not in the other.

To illustrate this we may exploit an example Hume uses elsewhere (p. 467); there is, in nature, a distinction between my life and that of an oak tree (uninstructed nature has drawn *that* distinction), but if I kill it, thereby taking what, in this natural sense is not mine but its, I have not violated a *right* of the oak tree's, nor done it an *injustice*, and hence its life cannot have been *its* in the property sense.

Further, my life, body, and actions are, in the natural sense, necessarily mine, inalienable, but in the *meum-suum*, Lockean property sense, they are not. Even if we allowed theological premises to support the view that I cannot make my life *your* property, this would not suffice to show that I cannot make it not *my* property. I may choose to waive my right to life; then my life ceases to be *mine* in the Lockean property sense, for you can kill me without violating any right of mine, or doing me an injustice, as in cases of voluntary euthanasia. Similarly, you can confine me, or take out one of my kidneys without violating any right of mine, and doing me an injustice if I have consented. So that which is mine in nature, in the obvious sense, is not the same as what is *mine* in the Lockean property sense. So it is still open to us to claim that something—even my life—can only be *mine* in the Lockean property sense in a civil society governed by laws; that Lockean property—what I have a right to or in—is as 'naturally unintelligible' as private property.

I promised above to return to an objection to Hume's limited account of justice and property rights. According to this objection, the account is hopelessly wrong-headed, because Hume regards 'laws of justice' as synonymous with 'actual civil laws'. Having overlooked the ideas of equality and fairness that are so essentially tied up with justice, he has committed himself to the absurd view that if the law sanctions a distribution of property in which a few are rich and many starve this will be a *just* (since legal) distribution.

If Hume were indeed committed to this sort of conventionalism, it would be obvious that his account could not be extended to cover the personal or natural rights—obvious at least to anyone who takes it as a premise that there are some rights such as the right to life or the right not to be tortured, and that laws, in securing or ignoring these rights can be just or unjust. But there is more than one way of being a conventionalist about rights.

Consider Hume's definitions of property: 'Our property is nothing but those goods whose constant possession is establish'd by the *laws* of society; that is by the laws of justice' (p. 491) and 'What is a man's property? Anything which it is *lawful* for him and him alone to use' (E, 158) (my italics). There are two ways of interpreting 'laws' and 'lawful' in these sentences. Firstly, we can take them as meaning 'actual laws' and 'in accordance with actually exiting laws'. And then we read the first definition as specifying not only what *property* is, but also what the laws of justice are—they simply are the actual laws of (some? any?) civil society. This is the extreme conventionalist interpretation according to which it is impossible to raise the question of whether actual laws are just or unjust.

Secondly, we can take 'laws of society' as meaning 'laws of a *well* or *properly* functioning society', that is, 'laws of a society which is functioning as a society is supposed to function'. 'Laws of society' taken in this sense can be identified with 'the laws of justice' without a commitment to extreme conventionalism. It may well be that no actual society is functioning properly; if so, at least some of the actual laws may not be laws of justice, and are open to criticism on those grounds.

As I said above, I am not primarily concerned with Humean exegesis, so I shall not argue here that Hume's definitions of property should be interpreted this second way.[9] I am concerned with the question 'Could a limited claim about the "natural unintelligibility" of private property be plausibly made about "natural rights" or "Lockean property"?' If the question 'Is my life *mine*? Do I have a *right* to or in it?' must, on a Hume-inspired account be answered by saying 'Look at what the laws of actual civil societies determine. Where they establish your life as *yours* then you do have such a right; where they do not, you do not', then it would be obvious that the limited claim could not be extended.

But suppose the answer, on a Hume-inspired account, can be 'Look at what the laws of a society *which is functioning properly* are or would be. If they do, or would, establish that your life is *yours* then it is, and you do have such a right.

---

[9] However I would if I had more space; it is, I think, crystal clear in the *Enquiry* and fairly unambiguous in the *Treatise*, that Hume is well aware of the distinction between (as we might describe it) civil or legal justice on the one hand and 'natural' justice on the other; between actual law and just law. Inevitably, given his concern in the *Treatise* to show that justice is an 'artificial' and not a 'natural' virtue, he does not use the terms 'natural justice' or 'natural law' there. But in the *Enquiry* he has abandoned the 'artificial/natural' vocabulary and is happy to talk in terms of natural justice and law in contrast to civil. See, for example, E, 157 and 158, especially the big footnote.

If they do not, or would not, then it is not, and you do not.' Then the strong conviction that we do have a right to life would be based, within the framework of this account, on the conviction that there could not be a 'properly functioning society' which did not have, for example, a law prohibiting murder.

'But', a liberal might say, 'what can a "properly functioning society" be but a *just* society? And what can a *just* society be but a society whose laws protect and enshrine certain rights? Surely we *begin* with the premise that we have certain rights e.g. a right to life, or liberty, define justice in terms of rights, and then define a "properly functioning" society as a just one.' Such a line of thought assumes that the way to figure out what constitutes a just society is to begin by figuring out what rights we have, and *then* derive the specification of a just society as one that protects and enshrines those rights. This is the assumption that lies behind the constitutions of the American and French revolutions (and is still to be found in e.g. Rawls and Nozick).

But according to an account inspired by Hume and Anscombe, this gets things the wrong way round. The logically prior concept is that of a *properly functioning society*; *justice* is then specified as the virtue or excellence of such a society, and the laws of justice as those which are in place in such a society; and *rights* come last, as those things which such laws establish as *mine* and *thine* (and *ours* and *theirs*.) This is the point of saying that a right is 'naturally unintelligible'; it is intelligible (only) *via* the concept of a law or convention (*nomos*).

In order to answer the question 'What is a properly functioning society?' without appealing to the concept of rights, we turn to the philosopher who thinks in terms of functions, namely Aristotle. According to him, the function of a society is to enable its members to achieve *eudaimonia*; society that is fulfilling that function well is functioning properly and is thereby just.

So the logically basic concept is that of *eudaimonia*, the concept which is the concern of that ethical science which, according to Aristotle, is the necessary preliminary to political science. (This is not the place for a lengthy discussion of *eudaimonia* but we should emphasize here that it is (what we would call) an explicitly moral concept. We have (*ex hypothesi*) made it clear in our preliminary ethical study, that it is impossible without virtuous activity.)

So, putting the above three paragraphs together, we have a concept of rights with the following features. It is, ultimately, based on the concept of *eudaimonia*; hence, on this account, ethics is prior to politics. It is, moreover, claimed to depend on the concept of a law or convention within a just, that is, a properly functioning, society; and in that sense can be described as a societal or institutional concept as opposed to an individualistic one.

It is worth noting that the opening claims made by my hypothetical liberal above, are preserved in this *eudaimonia*-based account. Yes indeed, a 'properly functioning society' can be nothing but a just society. Yes indeed, a just society protects and enshrines rights. These claims, which in part determine the concepts of *properly functioning society, justice,* and *rights,* are not in dispute. What is in dispute is the logical priority of those concepts, and hence where argument about the truth of sentences employing at least one of them must start. Do we argue from previously identified rights to the conclusion that a society cannot be just unless it protects them? Or do we argue from premises about what any just society—a society whose members are to be enabled to achieve *eudaimonia*—must be like, to the conclusion that its laws would establish certain things as mine and thine, and hence that we have a right to them?

When the logical priority of concepts is in dispute, it is often hard to discern the difference between two accounts. The easiest way to make the difference clear is to find a claim, in this case about rights, over which the two disagree. But this is not easy to do. Not only is there much detailed disagreement between liberals themselves, but further, there is no reason to believe that a *eudaimonia*-based account of rights and justice would wind up denying the existence of many of the rights dear to their hearts.[10] So in what follows, rather than attempting to identify disagreements, I shall highlight some features of a *eudaimonia*-based approach which drop out fairly readily and which, let us say, *may* represent differences between that approach and a liberal one.

Let me begin by considering the question 'Who (or what) are the bearers of rights?' Within an Aristotelian framework, this question is not answered in advance, by e.g. 'rational adults' but case by case.

A *eudaimonia*-based account of rights does not need to consider whether babies or children are potential persons, or rational in some required sense; it finds nothing paradoxical in the idea that human beings might have certain rights at some stage of their life which they lose later. It asks 'Must a society which functions as a society should, have rules which determine some things

---

[10] For an interesting discussion of how *eudaimonia*-based and liberal accounts might tend towards convergence on liberty, see Douglas B. Rasmussen, 'Liberalism and Natural End Ethics', *American Philosophical Quarterly* 27 (1990): 153–61.

as the "property" of babies and children; as *theirs*?' If the answer to that is 'Yes', it simply follows that babies and children have rights to those things.[11]

Indeed, given Aristotle's emphasis on the importance (for achieving *eudaimonia*) of being trained from infancy, it is to be expected that a *eudaimonia*-based account of rights will give unusual prominence to the rights of babies and children, and that it is likely to introduce some rights that do not usually figure in the literature of political morality. Discussing Aristotle's view that certain things are instrumentally necessary for human beings if they are to have even a chance of achieving *eudaimonia*, Nussbaum cites 'food, clean water, family love, above all an education'.[12] If this were correct, then a just society, whose purpose is the *eudaimonia* of its members, would have laws or rules securing these goods insofar as it is possible to do so. And the content of such rules would, on the Hume-Anscombe inspired account of rights, determine (some of) our rights. Though food, clean water and an education are not unfamiliar examples, family love may strike one as so odd as to discredit the account. Is it not a *reductio ad absurdum* of a *eudaimonia*-based account that it entails (if Nussbaum is correct) that each child has a *right* to family love?

I do not myself find any obvious absurdity in saying that every human being has a right to family love, but, be that as it may, the assertion of such a right does not follow simply from the hypothesis that it is necessary for *eudaimonia*. For the next step in the argument has to be 'So a just society has rules to secure this *insofar as it is possible to do so*', and it is those rules which determine our rights. What might such rules be like? A rule which determined a straightforward right to family love would have to be something of the form 'Every baby and child is to have a loving family which is *hers*' (where the 'hers' is the *meum-suum* possessive which signifies Lockean property). Now such a rule would probably be impossible to implement, and, if so, not a rule that a just society must have.

But it might well be possible to implement a *set* of rules whose upshot approached this ideal. Such a set would not determine a straightforward right to family love, but a range of rights-under-certain-conditions which pertained to children enjoying the benefit of family love. The current laws in Britain concerning family membership and adoption (who counts as a member of *my*

---

[11] Note too that if a properly functioning society, enabling us to achieve *eudaimonia*, must have laws constraining our actions regarding animals (as I believe it must—see my *Beginning Lives* (Oxford: Blackwell, 1987), Chapter 6, §3), some of these may be of the form that confer rights on animals. For example, a law creating a nature reserve might be of the form 'This piece of land belongs to the animals currently living on it and their descendants; it is *theirs*.'

[12] Martha Nussbaum, 'Recoiling from Reason', her review of MacIntyre's *Whose Justice? Which Rationality?* in *The New York Review of Books*, 7 December 1989.

family in the Lockean sense of 'mine') and the circumstances under which children may, or must, be taken into care, may indeed be seen as such a set (albeit still a rather unsatisfactory one). If the example of 'a right to family love' strikes us as odd, the fault may lie with the political theorists who ignore such familiar laws, rather than with an account which expects to find them in a just society.

The fact that most societies have laws (or conventions) establishing family membership in the above Lockean sense, and that these vary to a certain extent, serves to remind us of another feature of Humean-Anscombean rights. Hume illustrates with some glee the ways in which '[T]hose rules, by which properties, rights, and obligations are determin'd, have in them no marks of a natural origin, but many of artifice and contrivance' (p. 528), describing 'the variations which all the rules of property receive from the finer turns and connexions of the imagination, and from the subtilties and abstractions of law-topics and reasonings' (E, 161). In determining 'What is a man's property' (what he has a right to or in), we have 'recourse to statutes, customs, precedents, analogies, and a hundred other circumstances; *some of which are constant and inflexible, some variable and arbitrary*' (E, 158, my italics).

Now some customs and precedents vary between societies with different histories (and between the 'same' society at different periods of its history). Some circumstances (for instance the local weather, the concentration of population) vary; given different cultures, what people find 'analogous' varies. So different societies may formulate different laws, (and the same society change its laws over time), determining different rights, and *there may be no question as to which society has secured the real rights*. For *if* the laws different societies come up with enable the members of those societies to achieve *eudaimonia* equally well, each society will be just, the laws will be laws of justice, and the 'real' rights of the members of each society will be determined by those laws, despite being different.

This is not vulgar 'anything goes' cultural relativism, for the concept of *eudaimonia* is not relativistic. It presupposes that human beings have a common nature, thereby denying that their 'nature' is *simply* a product of their society; insofar as this is true, some of the laws and consequent rights of just societies will be 'constant and inflexible'. But it formally allows the possibility that, for example, two societies with rather different family structures might have different rules which determined whose child was whose, and (though both might be thereby unjust, and though one might thereby be just and the other unjust) both might be just.

At this point we should recall again the point of saying that a right is 'naturally unintelligible'. In the natural sense of the possessives, a man's semen is his, a woman's ovum is hers, and any child a woman bears as a result of intercourse with a certain man, hers, his, and theirs. But, according to the arguments considered earlier, this natural sense of the possessives is not the same as the Lockean property 'what one has a right to or in' sense; what is *hers*, *his*, and *theirs* in this sense is determined by the laws of a just society. To believe, within this framework, that a society in which the child a woman had conceived and borne was not *hers*, not a child she had a right to or in, must be unjust, would be to believe that any society which is to function well must contain a law along the lines of 'Any child a woman has conceived and borne is *hers*'. The grounds for such a belief would be beliefs about human nature, such as that human offspring cannot in general thrive without their natural mothers, and that human females cannot in general thrive if deprived of their natural offspring.[13]

The preceding discussion illustrates two important points that arise from the fact that the Hume-Anscombe inspired account of rights is, in the sense described, conventionalistic. One point is that what 'having a right to x' consists in may be made up of a mass of details (a whole set of laws); the second is that what it consists in may be relative to a particular society at a particular time. It also illustrates the way in which the account is not conventionalistic. In being *eudaimonia*-based, it is based on human nature; premises about what human beings need, given their nature, if they are to have any hope of achieving *eudaimonia*, provide the grounds for such laws as must be 'constant and inflexible' amongst just societies, and hence for conclusions about what might naturally be described as 'natural' rights. To admit that it is hard to know what is part of human nature is to admit, within this framework, that it is hard to work out which rights are 'natural' rights.

This freely acknowledged difficulty of the question about human nature brings me to the related problems of paternalism and pluralism, which may be thought to constitute the major stumbling block for a *eudaimonia*-based account of rights. The current split between the Right and the Good in liberal theories of justice aims, as I understand it, to avoid the vices of authoritarianism by embracing pluralism. There is, amongst members of society at least nowadays, a plurality of views about our duties, about what constitutes

---

[13] Such claims about human nature are, of course, of the odd sort that Aristotle describes as being true 'for the most part' (*hōs epi to polu*), not to be falsified by, for example, the phenomenon of successful adoption.

eudaimonia, or living well and (often the source of such disagreements) about human nature. Our past is replete with examples of morally iniquitous societies that attempted to impose, by means of their laws, a favoured conception of our duties, or of what living well consists in, or of human nature. The only way to avoid such iniquity is to specify a just society in a way that guarantees that such a society can accommodate widely differing moral views.

The first point that should be noted is that a *eudaimonia*-based account of rights is not committed to authoritarian state intervention which rides roughshod over the views of many, or any, of its members. We must recall two points. The first concerns what is contained in the concept of *eudaimonia*; the second concerns what such intervention necessarily involves.

Recall firstly, that we said above that *eudaimonia* is an explicitly moral concept; it is, in particular, the concept of something that is impossible without virtuous activity, and which excludes vicious activity. Now consider, secondly, what is involved in implementing a law which rides roughshod over the passionately held views of many of its members. It would require a great deal of vicious action in the way of violence, cruelty, callousness, dishonesty, disloyalty, and indeed injustice, all of which would be most detrimental to *eudaimonia*. A *eudaimonia*-based account of rights, is, unlike utilitarianism, not a doctrine according to which 'the end justifies the means'.

It is not clear who should be blamed for the now prevalent, but absurd, idea that Aristotelianism, or 'virtue ethics', should be lumped together with utilitarianism as a 'teleological' theory, defined as that in which 'the good is defined independently from the right and then the right is defined as that which maximises the good. More precisely, those institutions and acts are right which of the available alternatives produce the most good...'.[14] I am inclined to blame Rawls, on the basis of the publication date, context, and famous location, of the passage just cited. Rawls cites W. K. Frankena's definition of teleological theories as the inspiration of his definition but Frankena does not make the mistake of putting Aristotelianism under the heading of teleological theories, noting rather that, insofar as Aristotle can be classified, he 'suggests' the theory of 'extreme act-deontology'. It is Rawls who, appropriately introducing the definition under the section-heading 'Classical Utilitarianism', continues the discussion *under that heading* by citing Aristotle as an exemplar of 'perfectionism', a form, according to the index, of 'teleological' theory.

The very idea that Aristotelianism is a 'teleological' (or 'goal-based', in Dworkin's terminology) theory *as defined* is so perverse that a whole paper

[14] John Rawls, *A Theory of Justice* (Oxford: Clarendon Press, 1972), 24.

would hardly suffice to show what was wrong with it. I confine myself to three bald assertions. (1) Insofar as 'the good' is defined within Aristotelianism, it is 'defined' as 'the object of right desire or wish' or 'that which the virtuous agent desires/wishes for', which forges a conceptual link between *good* and *virtue* rather than encapsulating a reductive definition. (2) 'Right act' is defined not as 'that which maximises the good' but as 'that act which, in the circumstances, a virtuous agent would, characteristically, choose to do'. (3) 'Right institution' is not defined as such; institutions can be just or unjust (according to whether they enable or prevent members of society from achieving *eudaimonia*) or, more broadly (I suppose) good or bad or neither, where, reverting to (1), a good institution is an institution which a virtuous agent wishes for, not necessarily because it is just, but perhaps for some other reason such as its efficiency.

Of course it would be just as perverse to deny that Aristotelianism was a 'teleological' doctrine in any ordinary sense of the term; one might well say that Aristotle *invented* teleology. But there is then nothing perverse in rejecting Rawls' definition of a 'teleological' theory, within political theory or without it.

So, pending further argument, I maintain that we have no reason to suppose that embracing a *eudaimonia*-based account of rights commits us to the paternalistic faults of utilitarianism. The thought that motivates regarding utilitarianism as a threat is the thought that wrong or wicked acts regarding particular individuals can be 'justified' when they maximize the good of happiness, because they are not really *wicked* or wrong. The rightness and wrongness of acts are reductively defined in terms of their consequences regarding maximizing happiness. But a *eudaimonia*-based account gives no such reductive account of wicked or wrong acts. If a just law, determining a right, cannot, as things stand, be implemented in a particular society, without necessitating that some members of the society act wickedly or wrongly, then it *cannot*, as things stand, be implemented. The society, as things stand, is irremediably unjust, and this injustice cannot be changed by changing the law, but only by some other process—which might well not be within the control of legislation. If, for example, the agent with the erring conscience cannot act rightly, as Aquinas plausibly maintains, then it may well be that the state cannot always legislate rightly concerning such agents; the agent will act wrongly, and the state will remain unjust in some way or ways, until such agents change or die out.

I shall conclude by directing what I take to be a disconcerting question at the upholders of pluralism, viz. 'Can a just society be a wicked one?' Let us note initially that from within an Aristotelian framework the answer to this question is 'Of course not'. Justice is but one virtue amongst many; the function of the state is not merely to foster justice in its members, but all the virtues since they are all necessary for *eudaimonia*.

If the point of liberalism is that it should be able to accommodate, within a *just* society, widely differing moral views, and if this is to have any bite, the just liberal society must surely accommodate the differing views of the virtuous and nonvirtuous. I believe that this is thought of as unproblematic because the possibility is not considered in sufficient abstraction. A society made up of mostly quite decent people, with, moreover, a history in which the state has concerned itself, directly or indirectly, with its members' virtues as well as their (liberal) rights, will not contain many examples of startlingly different moral views. Indeed, it is notable that on the rare occasions on which 'differing moral views' are discussed in the literature, it is nearly always different religious views that are mentioned, where what is common to the differing views is that they share a deep concern with *virtue* and its connection with *eudaimonia*.

But rather than thinking of our society as mostly made up of rather decent people, with, at the worst, differing views about religion, let us suppose that it were to be mostly made up of people who, while not actually psychopathic are, characteristically, rather cruel, callous, selfish, hedonistic, irresponsible, dishonest, materialistic, and light-minded. Then the society that secures the liberals' rights (and is thereby just according to liberal theory) will undoubtedly curb some of the worst excesses of these vices, but if it is to refrain from importing substantive moral views into political theory, it will not be able to do more. And then the society will be, I take it, a just but wicked one according to liberal theory.

People differ not only in their religious views but over, for instance, whether we have any moral obligations to people in other societies. So it would seem to be no part of a just society, conceived in the liberal way, that it necessarily ruled out the most callous and ruthless, even unjust, exploitation of other societies. I can imagine that people might well envisage extending the liberal theory to cover international justice, so I shall not insist on this example. But others, I think, come readily to hand. People have different moral views about our treatment of animals, so it would seem to be no part of a just society that it necessarily ruled out the torture of animals as an engaging public spectacle; or, supposing a just society can have the death penalty (which I leave as an open question) the execution of human beings. No doubt a plausible case can be made for ruling out some physical cruelty to members of the society, but what of the mental cruelty that unloving, callous, selfish, and hedonistic people inflict on their children, spouses, and parents, thinking that the recipients have unreasonable expectations? If their views are to be accommodated, society must exert no pressure on them to behave otherwise. People differ over the age below which sexual experience is psychologically harmful to children, so a just society, accommodating such differences, need not rule out paedophilia except where it involves actual physical damage.

If all such activities are ruled out by the liberals' rights, then it seems that the liberal theory is nothing like as morally neutral as it professed to be. If they are not thus ruled out, then, on the liberal conception, a just society can be a wicked one. (I am, of course, simply taking it as a premise that a society which allowed such practices would be a wicked one.)

I do not regard this as a *reductio ad absurdum* of the liberal conception. It is open to its defenders to abandon the thought that a just society is *ipso facto* a good one, and to say instead that although being just (securing liberals' rights) is a necessary condition of being a good society, it is far from being sufficient. They might, for example, say that another necessary condition of being a good society is that art and education thrive in it, or that it be efficient. Or indeed that it enables its members to achieve *eudaimonia*. But an explicit acknowledgement of the possibility that a just society can be a wicked one would certainly effect a startling change in much of the current discussion.

Actually, I believe that there is much in some rights-based theories to suggest that, as a matter of fact, the question 'What rights must be secured by a society if its members are to be enabled to achieve *eudaimonia*?' is covertly guiding the discussion, and hence that we might reasonably expect much agreement between *eudaimonia*-based and those rights-based accounts.[15] Even if I am wrong about this covert influence, there is still, as I said above, no reason to believe that a *eudaimonia*-based account of rights would wind up denying the existence of many of the rights dear to the hearts of contemporary liberals. In many cases, the differences between the upshots of the two approaches might well be in matters of emphasis, argument, and detail rather than in substantial disagreements about what our rights are. (Similarly, the differences between deontological and virtue ethics tend to be

---

[15] For example, Rawls' and Dworkin's, but notably, not Nozick's. Charles Taylor in 'Atomism' (in A. Kontos (ed.), *Powers, Possessions and Freedom: Essays in Honour of C. B. MacPherson* (Toronto: University of Toronto Press, 1979)) argues convincingly that 'the doctrine of the primacy of rights is not as independent as its proponents want to claim from considerations about human nature and the human social condition'. The sorts of 'considerations about human nature' he discusses include the idea of 'the properly human' capacities which have 'moral worth' and which ought to be *developed* (not merely 'not interfered with') and he charges Nozick with 'normative incoherence'. However, the grounds on which he does so would quite possibly not apply to Rawls and Dworkin (whom he does not discuss).

in such areas, rather than lying in substantial disagreements over what ought and ought not to be done, where proponents of the two different approaches are often united in their opposition to utilitarianism.) But such differences may still be significant and important, not least in the attitudes they tend to foster. Rights-based theories avowedly attempt to draw a sharp line between political and moral philosophy, to allow for a pluralism in society of widely differing 'comprehensive' moral views; this tends to foster the idea that we can get a just society—a properly functioning one—without concerning ourselves either about the correctness of our own comprehensive moral views, or about the comprehensive moral education of the up and coming generation. But a *eudaimonia*-based account draws no such line, seeing the investigation of ethics and political science as continuous; it should foster the idea that nothing in our individual lives is more important than acquiring a correct grasp of what *eudaimonia* consists in, and nothing in our communal life more important than the moral education of our children.

Acknowledgements

An embryonic version of this paper was read at the Hume Society Conference in Iceland in 1984. I am grateful to Christine Swanton for discussion of a later version, and to Anne Jaap Jacobson for suggestions which resulted in this final version.

References

Anscombe, G. E. M. 1981. 'Rules, Rights and Promises', and 'On the Source of the Authority of the State', reprinted in *Ethics, Religion and Politics*; 'The Question of Linguistic Idealism', reprinted in *From Parmenides to Wittgenstein*; Vols. III and I respectively of *The Collected Papers of G. E. M. Anscombe*. Minneapolis: University of Minnesota Press.

Aristotle. 2000. *Nicomachean Ethics*. Edited and translated by Roger Crisp. Cambridge: Cambridge University Press.

Hume, D. 1975. *A Treatise of Human Nature*. Edited by L. A. Selby-Bigge, revised by P. Nidditch. Oxford: Clarendon Press.

Hursthouse, R. 1987. *Beginning Lives*. Oxford: Blackwell.

Nussbaum, M. 1989. 'Recoiling from Reason', review of Alasdair MacIntyre's *Whose Justice? Which Rationality?*, *The New York Review of Books*, 7 December.

Rasmussen, D. B. 1990. 'Liberalism and Natural End Ethics', *American Philosophical Quarterly* 27: 153–61.

Rawls, J. 1972. *A Theory of Justice*. Oxford: Clarendon Press.

Reid, T. 1977. *Essays on the Active Powers of Man*. New York: Garland.

Taylor, C. 1979. 'Atomism'. In A. Kontos (ed.), *Powers, Possessions and Freedom: Essays in Honour of C. B. MacPherson*. Toronto: University of Toronto Press.

Tully, J. 1980. *A Discourse on Property*. Cambridge: Cambridge University Press.

16
The Good and Bad Family

1. Stage-Setting

Social philosophy is by definition about social issues, but it is not thereby coextensive with political philosophy. It is, for example, quite possible for a philosopher to discuss the rights and wrongs of abortion or euthanasia without committing herself to a single explicit thesis about what a, or any, just or good society would enact, endorse, enforce, promote, prohibit, or permit (Foot 1977; Hursthouse 1987: ch. 1). A discussion of the nature of the family, and what would count as a good family, can be similarly noncommittal, and in this chapter I aim to provide such a discussion. But given that the current philosophical literature on the family is overwhelmingly situated in political theory, I must make some preliminary remarks about why I have chosen to distance myself from it.

It used to be maintained that, in a pluralistic age rife with moral disagreements, the only respectable 'liberal' position in political theory was moral neutrality. It was assumed that 'we' were all in favour of a just society, but that the spelling out of what it would enact, endorse, etc. could proceed without presupposing any further 'substantial' agreement about moral values.

But there is more to moral disagreement than disagreement about values. Such disagreements frequently arise because people see the world, especially the social world, in different ways, and hence are forcibly struck by different facts. Generations of political philosophers, mostly, though not invariably, male, have been struck by the fact that society is constructed and, in some sense, maintained by autonomous, rational individuals. But others, most notably in recent years Sue Moller Okin (1989), have noticed, rather, that society is maintained, in a different sense, by the production, nurturing, and socialization of children within the family.

Another rich source of disagreement is the interpretation of facts. How might the one just mentioned—about the social significance of children and the family—be interpreted? Here is one way: it highlights a necessary burden that traditionally has been imposed on autonomous, rational individuals who happen to be female, in violation of their rights, and is hence, given the requirements of justice, up for redistribution. This, I take it, is more or less the way Okin interprets it. Here is another: it highlights a very desirable (fulfilling, satisfying, enriching) form of life that traditionally has been enjoyed by large numbers of autonomous rational individuals but denied to some others and is hence, given the requirements of justice, up for being made available to the latter.

And here is another—the way I am inclined to interpret it. It highlights the fact that any remotely plausible political theorizing about the family must rely on a concept of the good family, where that involves the good nurturing and socialization of children. For if the next generation is not nurtured and socialized at least fairly well, society will fall apart. Reliance on the concept may be unconscious and writers may disavow their commitment to any such substantial moral value, but I think it must be there. For consider this. Suppose a discussion is couched solely in terms of a 'theory of family justice' and concerned with the rights of rational autonomous adults to, for example, form a family and raise children. Any argument toward the conclusion that, for example, gay couples have a right to do both, and that a just society must recognize and enshrine such a right, is surely shaped by the background assumption that gay couples are as likely as heterosexual couples to raise children well, to form, with their child or children, a good family. It is true that we tend to think of justice as, in some rather unclear way, overriding considerations of welfare. 'Let justice be done though the heavens fall', the saying goes, but I doubt that anyone would commit themselves explicitly to the following view: 'A good/just society should permit gay couples to marry and raise children notwithstanding the fact that they are less likely than heterosexual couples to raise their children well.' And if someone did, they would thereby render their view so implausible as to defeat their liberal purposes; no gay couples would thank them for putting it forward.

The unconscious reliance on a concept of the good family seems to me both dangerous and philosophically inept; that is one reason why I want to distance myself from much of the contemporary philosophical literature. The other reason is that such literature on the family tends to be not only in political philosophy but also, if written in English, to be written by American citizens. The combination of the two tendencies has an unfortunate upshot. Given the first, the discussion is usually couched in terms of what the state should do or the law should be. Given the second, the discussion is usually—albeit, again, often unconsciously—about what should be done in the USA, through policy or legal enactment, and addressed to an American audience.

This makes it difficult for citizens of other countries to join in; we start from different places and we have different concerns. For instance, my own country, New Zealand, is like many others (including the US) in having laws, institutions, and conventions relating to family life that developed out of a prevailing European Christianity. However, New Zealand is unlike the US, though like the UK and many other European countries, in having many laws, etc. that were shaped, in the nineteenth and twentieth centuries, by explicitly welfarist and socialist policies more than by considerations of rights, and in not having a powerful 'moral majority' that strongly influences state policies. And it is unlike any other country on earth in having an indigenous non-European population, the Māori, whose culture was not completely devastated by colonization and in being committed, as a matter of governmental policy, to the preservation and encouragement of that living culture as part of our national, communal life. For some of us, the successful working through of that policy (sometimes described as 'honouring the Treaty of Waitangi') is of central concern. And, unsurprisingly, the Māori concept of the family (*whānau*) is very different from the European (and hence American) one. The term is regularly used to describe both small and extended kin groups, which may include well more than 100 members.

I do not intend to discuss this concept here, but it is my consciousness of it that makes me want to step back from the prevailing literature and to seek an account of the good family that is not geared to producing conclusions about what American society should be like, but which aims to be more noncommittal. So I will begin with some etymology.

2. The Concept of 'Family'

It is clear from the *Oxford English Dictionary* that the concept of a family has been what Wittgenstein called a 'family resemblance concept' in English (and some other European languages) for centuries.[1] From at least the fifteenth century (according to the *OED*'s quotations) it had two strands, which are both still operative today.

---

[1] '[I]f you look at [what we call "families"] you will not see something that is common to *all*, but similarities, relationships, and a whole series of them at that...we see a complicated network of similarities overlapping and criss-crossing:...I can think of no better expression to characterize these similarities than "family resemblances"; for the various resemblances between members of a family: build, features, colour of eyes, gait, temperament, etc. overlap and criss-cross in the same way' (Wittgenstein 1953: sections 66–7).

One derives more directly than the other from the meaning of the Latin *familia*, 'household', which was formed from *famulus*, 'servant'. This yielded at least one use in English in which 'family' had nothing to do with marriage, intergenerational relations, sexual relations, or kinship in general, and did not even connote a body of people living together. In this use, very few of us would count as having a family, because we do not have a retinue of servants. A monarch or nobleman who did have such a retinue thereby had a 'family', but was not, of course, part of it. Moreover, such a 'family' could be very large (500 or more according to a 1641 quotation) and, far from living in one house, be scattered widely across one or several estates. However, one can readily see how 'household' would get applied to less grand establishments in which the servants all live with their master or mistress, and so, from at least the sixteenth century, we get a use in which a 'family' is a body of people living in one house.

This still does not connote any kinship amongst any of the members of the family. But side by side with the family-as-a-retinue-of-servants use ran the one that forms the second strand in our current concept of the family, namely family as kindred—'those descended' (as the *OED* puts it) 'from a common ancestor'—and hence as interchangeable with 'clan' or 'tribe'.

Now this use does not connote anything about people living together. All it picks out is a set of people with a common feature and thereby it generated a scientific use which even lost the connection with ancestry. (A seventeenth-century quotation is about the 'family' of sulphurous as opposed to mercurial things.) But one can see how easily the two different strands will interweave. For one thing, so many European households would have consisted of groups of people many of whom were blood-related. Not only did the sort of people who had servants intermarry a lot, but generations of servants served in the same household and themselves intermarried.

The two strands are further woven together by a third. Which group of people who live in one house would have associated closely with each other and formed strong ties? Perhaps the servants 'under the stairs', but also the group consisting of the head of the household and those related to (mostly) him by blood and marriage. What else, apart from living together, makes for strong ties? Well, blood—kinship—itself. From early on, we get a third use of 'family'—as a group of people united by strong ties—that can apply to groups of people who neither live together nor are related by blood (a religious sect called themselves 'the family of love' in 1579) but will also tend to be appropriate to either.

But all along it is the same word, and when it is used to apply to a group of people, say 'the family next door', who (a) live together, (b) are related by blood (with some qualifications I am about to mention), and (c) are united by strong ties, as it so often could be, and can be used to this day, there may well be no answer to the question, 'Which one, or two, of those three—(a), (b), and (c)—is it singling out in this context?' Nor will it do to say that the word 'family' now means all three, and that these give the necessary and sufficient conditions for a group's being a family. The concept is much more flexible than that and is constantly, and correctly, applied to groups which do not, strictly, satisfy the three conditions.

Most obviously, (b), when used in conjunction with (a) and (c), never did hold, strictly. We may be sure that, from the earliest uses of the English word 'family' in the kinship sense, women who had 'married in' somehow counted as their husband's kin thereby, notwithstanding the fact that they were usually not blood-related to their husbands. Although there is the usage of 'my wife's/mother's (side of the) family', 'the family' with no qualification, recorded for instance in 'the family tree' or 'the family bible', is the group related by blood through the male line or through marriage into it.

We should also note our talk about 'the family of swallows under the roof' and 'the family of wolves in the cave', something that, in the infuriating way of dictionaries, the *OED* neglects to mention. It does record an early nineteenth-century specification of a family as 'a group consisting of a Father and Mother and Children', without mentioning marriage, and perhaps our talk of family groups amongst the other animals arrived at about the same time. But, whenever it arose, the use is clearly established now, and weaves another strand into the rope: sexual relations will do instead of marriage in (b).

We also have the 'extended family'—a fairly new use brought in to correct unthinking expectations that a family is bound to be a nuclear one—but it is not only 'extended families' who do not strictly satisfy condition (a). Even the standard 'nuclear' family may have a father who in fact spends most of his time at sea, and when the children of a nuclear family grow up and leave home, the friends of the parents will still inquire about how 'the family' is doing, expecting to hear news of the children and of their children. The sailor and his family, the grownup children and the parents may not share a roof, but if they still share a life, that's enough.

Moreover, as is characteristic of family resemblance concepts, the lack of one feature is not enough to make the concept inapplicable. I cannot offhand think of a way in which a group of people could be (b), related by blood or marriage-or-sexual-relations, and (c), united by strong ties, without having (a) at least to the extent of sharing a life, but the three features can certainly break apart in the other ways. A group of people may share a house and a life and be united by strong ties without being related by blood or marriage-or-sexual-relations—(a) and (c) without (b); and they may share a house, and in some sense a life, be related by blood or marriage-or-sexual-relations, and horribly disunited—(a) and (b) without (c); and it would be foolish to deny that such groups may correctly be described as forming a family.

So we should recognize that many different sorts of groups form a family, and that any such group has social significance. However, it is clearly no mere accident that some version of (a) and (b) and (c) have, for centuries, tended to occur together in many societies and allowed the English word 'family' to apply to intergenerational groups which exhibit all three features (in some version) simultaneously. Any species of animal that reproduces by producing offspring that need nurture for the early stages of their existence to survive is bound to be a species in which at least one parent provides such nurture in some way, and with the (sole?) exception of the cuckoo, does so by propinquity. All the social animals provide that nurture within their social group and socialize the offspring thereby. Unlike the other social animals, at some stage human beings started building themselves shelters in which sub-groups of the social group lived, so (a) and some version of (b) started to coincide. And it seems to be a feature of human psychology (though not unique to our species) that we tend to form strong emotional bonds of love and attachment with those with whom we share a life, hence some version of (c).

Strong emotional bonds are not the only way in which groups of humans, perhaps uniquely, are united by strong ties. As moral agents and language-using creatures, we create such ties within our families by recognizing special responsibilities and/or duties for and to each other and by participating in what Searle has nicely described as 'collective intentionality' (Searle 1995). We, my family, do, go in for, support, certain things where the claims about what we, the Hursthouses, do, go in for, etc. are not reducible to claims about what each member of the family in conjunction does. *We* are a unit.

It is not, I hope, tendentious to claim that when we speak of 'the family' as the fundamental or foundational social unit, we are thinking of human intergenerational groups which exhibit all three features (in some version) simultaneously. Their non-accidental coinciding is what maintains society in the sense that it produces the next generation of society's members. So I am, in what follows, going to concentrate on the cases in which 'the family' has all three features. (Note that this still encompasses a wide range, from single parent/one child families to very extended ones.)

3. The Good Family

Our word for bad families—families that are the opposite of good ones—is 'dysfunctional', and appropriately so, according to a perspective derived from Aristotle. Many sorts of things, according to Aristotle, have an *ergon* or 'function', and this, he claims, determines 'the good and the well' in relation to that sort of thing (*NE* 1097b25–8). There are platitudinous cases; the *ergon* of a flute-player is playing the flute, whereby a good flute-player is one who plays the flute well. More interesting cases emerge when we translate *ergon* (as we may) as 'characteristic activity' or even 'business'. For many sorts of things—hearts, eyes, human beings, Xs—there is an answer to the question 'What do Xs, as such, (characteristically, or *qua* Xs) do?' (or, in the case of artefacts that are functional objects, 'What are Xs, as such, used to do?') which reveals something about what Xs essentially are. Largely ignorant of American football, I learn what quarterbacks are from being told what they characteristically do—throw in the ball—and immediately acquire some idea of what makes for being a good quarterback, namely someone who regularly throws the ball in well, for example (I plausibly suppose), in such a way that his teammates rather than the opposing side can get it.

The Aristotelian idea is easily extended to examples such as quarterbacks, less easily to other concepts such as that of the family. But it is instructive to try.

So what is the *ergon* of a (human) family? Some people are inclined to say that it just is the production, nurturing, and socialization of children or the next generation, but that is not adequate if finding out what something's *ergon* is is a way of coming to understand what that thing is, of grasping the concept. We couldn't teach alien anthropologists our concept of 'family' just by telling them that a 'family' characteristically produced, nurtured, and socialized the next generation, even if they were already familiar with the concepts of 'next generation', 'socialization', etc. 'Oh yes', they might say, 'we have families too.' But then we discover that they live like the people in Huxley's *Brave New World* and are taking 'family' to refer to a state institution in which the next generation is produced in test-tubes and nurtured and socialized by a varying succession of part-time state employees.

If we are to teach them our concept, we will have to bring in more of the characteristic activity of families that relates to the three features outlined above. We might say the following. 'The members of a family characteristically live together (or at least share a life), for at least a period roughly determined by the time it takes to produce, nurture, and socialize its younger members; at least some of the older members characteristically do, or share, the producing, nurturing, and socializing; in this process, they form strong emotional bonds with each other and the younger members and the latter form strong emotional bonds with them (and with each other if there is more than one) and recognize special responsibilities and duties to and for each other...'

If the psychology and biology of the alien anthropologists were very alien, that might still leave them rather confused. Suppose that they go through two major phases during their natural life span. They begin as social animals like us, during which time they grow up in and then form families and bring up the next generation in just the way we do. But they are biologically and psychologically set up to become solitary animals halfway through their natural life span, at which point the other members of their former family become unrecognizable and uninteresting to them. (No doubt they will have evolved means of coping with late families, or perhaps their biology limits both sexes to reproducing while they are themselves young.) So in a way they would understand about the strong emotional bonds, and the special responsibilities and duties, but in another way they would not, because they would not anticipate how such ties, in us, affect the *continuance* of a family. The above description has left implicit the point that a family characteristically goes through certain changes as members come and go. The younger ones grow up and most will go to live elsewhere and become part of a different family, but the older members do not automatically then disperse, nor do they and the younger ones who have become part of a different family automatically cease to share a life, and some of the older and younger ones may indeed come to live together again after a period of living apart.

But taking that as read, I think the above gives us enough of an account of the characteristic activity of a 'family' to generate at least the beginnings of an account of a good family, as follows:

> The members of a good family live together well, for at least a period roughly determined by the time it takes to produce, nurture, and socialize its younger members; at least some of the older members do, or share, the producing, nurturing, and socializing well; in this process, they form strong emotional bonds with each other (if there is more than one) and the younger members well, and the latter form strong emotional bonds with them (and with each other if there is more than one) well; they recognize special responsibilities and duties to and for each other well.

No doubt some readers will be inclined to dismiss the use of 'well' in the above paragraph as a 'merely' evaluative term which anyone can fill in any way they like. This is not the place to argue against such a view, so I shall just make it an explicit premise that this is not the case. There is room for a fair amount of disagreement but only within agreed limits. And the areas of agreement in this account of what a good family is underpin, I claim, our agreed-upon use of 'the dysfunctional family'. Families in which any of the children are abused or neglected or allowed to run wild, for whatever reason, are dysfunctional. Families in which the older members fight like cat and dog all the time are dysfunctional. Families in which one member wreaks violence on one or more other members of the family are dysfunctional. Families in which there is no love are dysfunctional. All of these commonplaces arise directly from the fact that such families are not doing well what a family characteristically does.

We should note that a family can be dysfunctional without any member's being at moral fault. One reads tragic accounts of nuclear, and even more extended, families that have been torn to tatters by the extreme mental or physical disability of one of their members. It is no one's fault that the extremely disabled member and the others can't live well together, no one's fault that the disabled one has to take up so much time and energy and emotional commitment at the expense of other members, no one's fault if the youngest members can't understand and are frightened or repelled or resentful. Sometimes it just happens, and the family is or becomes dysfunctional, and sometimes cannot recover. We should note further that poverty may make it impossible for older members to nurture the younger members well, and may even destroy families by making it impossible for a group to live together or even share a life.

This account can also extend our use of 'dysfunctional family'. Okin does not describe a nuclear family in which the woman does all the domestic work and all the nurturing of the children as a bad family, but I assume she thinks that it is, and why should we not say, on the above account, that it is dysfunctional? Given her premises, the man and woman are not living well together, because they are not living in accordance with justice; the man is not nurturing the children well because he is not nurturing them at all; and neither of them is socializing the children well because they are socializing them into the continuance of this unjust, patriarchal set up. In a later article, Okin (1996) hints at a further point that I would want to add. In entirely forgoing the early nurturance in the way that used to be common in many European and English-speaking societies, the man is not living well with the children, at least during the period when they are young, but merely inhabiting the same house, and in so doing he is not forming strong emotional bonds with them well, nor they with him. (Looking forward to the gender-free society she endorses, Okin says 'Most men would be—and would be expected to be—as capable of nurturance as most women' (1996: 32). It may be that she meant no more than, 'as capable as most women of changing nappies, getting up at all hours to feed babies, and mopping up vomit', but since she goes on to say that such a society would be 'liberating to many people', I infer that she is assuming that most men would find it fulfilling to cherish their children from birth, in sickness and in health (as most women always have when not over-burdened)—which indeed seems to be proving to be the case amongst the 'new' men in Western society.)

The account may also serve to draw our attention to elitist biases in our use of 'dysfunctional family'. Unless they are hotbeds of drugs or violence or alcoholism or involved in public bitter disputes, rich upper-class families are rarely described as dysfunctional. But at least some of the families in England, and others like them, who barely knew their children and left their upbringing to servants and other employees, should count as such, because none of the older members of the family was doing the nurturing and socializing. (One might think that such families would count as dysfunctional simply because there was no love in them, but, when I read autobiographical accounts of them, that does not seem to be always so. It seems that the parents and children may indeed love each other, estranged as they are; what was missing was the parents doing the nurturing and socializing.)

4. The Good Family and Political Theory

What follows from the above account of 'the good family' about what a (or any) good society would enact, endorse, enforce, promote, prohibit, or permit? Absolutely nothing, without the addition of extra premises. Here is a possible starter:

> Premise: A good society has policies, laws, and institutions which, within it, promote, preserve, sustain, and encourage good families. It eschews policies, laws, and institutions which, within it, would tend to create dysfunctional families or turn good ones into dysfunctional ones.

This looks pretty obvious. Would anyone want to assert that a society could be a good one even if many of its families were dysfunctional and, far from vigorously attempting to correct this state of affairs, it was committed to policies, etc. which exacerbated it? As I noted at the outset, my suspicion is that political theorizing about the family always does presuppose, albeit often unconsciously, some such premise. But the nature of much of the literature would surely change if it were always made explicit. Bring it out into the open as a starting point for thinking about social policy regarding the family, and we have to give up the standard claim of 'liberal' neutrality, namely that state action and policy ought to be neutral amongst values or ends, for the above premise commits us to aiming for more good families and fewer bad ones as values or ends, quite possibly at the cost of infringing some individual liberties.

Many US communitarian philosophers have indeed called for recognition of the value of 'the family' in the context of criticizing contract-/rights-based liberalism for its excessive individualism and its consequent emphasis on rights at the expense of responsibilities. But in their anxiety to combat individualistic liberalism, they have remained in its territory, concentrating on adults (those with the responsibilities) rather than addressing the practical issue of how their country might aim to have more good families and fewer bad ones head on, in any considered detail. (The communitarian sociologist Amitai Etzioni (1993) seems to be an exception.) Hence there is a great deal about same-sex marriages, but nothing about *families* which have same-sex, partnered, older members; a great deal about divorce, but nothing like as much about how to prevent a *family's* becoming dysfunctional when a marriage breaks up.

There is a major difference between talk about rights or responsibilities and talk about achieving a specified end. The former too easily turns to addressing the question 'What does justice or morality require?' while the latter has to address 'How can we bring about such and such?' The former too easily remains abstract or utopian; the latter has to address details and be practicable. Of course, this is not to say that the latter ignores the constraints of justice and morality; in this context, the latter presupposes that the premise above has given us what justice or morality require—more good families and fewer dysfunctional ones. It is to say, in this context, that, unless anyone wants to deny that premise, philosophical debates about social policy regarding the family should turn to considering 'How can we bring that about?'

Even those who do not want to deny the premise outright might still be worried about the consequentialist, anti-liberal flavour of committing themselves to bringing about more good families and fewer dysfunctional ones. Surely, in many societies there is radical disagreement about what constitutes a good family (which the account given above has explicitly allowed for) in particular because there is room for much disagreement about what counts as nurturing and socializing children well. In the terms of the above account, this can be seen as the disagreement that generated the famous *Wisconsin v. Yoder* (1972) case, although it was fought on different grounds. The Amish parents believed that, in taking their children out of school after the 8th grade, they were nurturing and socializing them well, and indeed that they would be prevented from nurturing and socializing them really well if they were forced to expose them to the corrupting influence of high school and prevented from preparing them for life as Amish adults. Those that agreed with Wisconsin's case thought that the Amish parents were, at the least, not nurturing the children as well as they could because they were depriving them of autonomy, and not socializing them at least as well as they could because they were preparing them only for life as Amish adults, not for adult life more broadly conceived. Another familiar source of disagreement exists between those who believe that children can't be nurtured and socialized well by only one parent, or by two adults of the same sex, because they will grow up without valuing marriage, or without adequate role models of the other sex, or something of the sort, and those who think they can. How, in many countries, can social policy be geared toward the end of more good families without privileging a model about which there is such disagreement and riding roughshod over the views and values of many of its citizens?

This is a legitimate worry, reinforced by the point that (as far as I know) legislation and policy aimed at promoting good families narrowly conceived has, in a number of countries, a bad track record. The persisting difficulty seems to lie in formulating the laws or policies in such a way as to avoid their making less than ideal (according to the model) families much worse by tearing them apart. But it suggests not that we should give up on aiming at the end of more good families and fewer dysfunctional ones, but that we should devote more thought to how it might be broken down into subsidiary ends.

Are there any indisputable preconditions for good families, ones that do not privilege any particular model? On the open-ended account I have given above, one condition for being a good family is that 'the members of a good family live together well, for at least a period roughly determined by the time it takes to produce, nurture, and socialize its younger members.' A precondition of that is that children are produced, but, although some countries are worried about their declining birth rates, aiming to encourage more people to have children seems a rather oblique (and uncertain) way of achieving the end of more good families. But it is also a precondition that the children produced survive long enough for nurturing and socialization to take place. However long that may be, it is surely longer than a year. And hence an appropriate subsidiary end which would promote the end of more good families is 'reduce infant mortality', something which I have not seen mentioned in philosophical literature on the family.

How can we bring that about? In relation to such a specific end, it is obvious that an adequate answer to the question must address empirical details and be practicable. We can find the answer only by finding the causes of infant mortality in whatever country we are talking about and doing something about them. And here we see how essential it is that answers to this practical question be based on sound empirical premises supporting claims that a certain policy will be effective in achieving a specified end, and how one country might learn from another. How interesting it is that Japan, Sweden, Iceland, Singapore, Finland, Andorra, and Germany (in that order) have the lowest infant mortality rates in the world (*CIA World Factbook*, 2003 data). Do such a diverse range of societies and cultures have something in common which explains it? If so, could we develop or do whatever it is in our own country? Or do varied factors somehow achieve the same effect? If so, which of the countries is most like our own and could we bring about their successful factors?

Even more obviously, if it is a condition for being a good family that the family members live together well (albeit in a broad sense of 'living together'), it is a precondition for being a good family that the members manage to live together. Hence another appropriate subsidiary end which would promote the end of more good families is, 'ensure accommodation for homeless families'. It is important to specify the end in that way rather than as, 'reduce the number of homeless families'. Victorian England was quite good at reducing the number of homeless families; it did it by breaking them up and putting the women in one workhouse, the men in another, and the children in a third, all widely separated.

As well as looking for indisputable preconditions for good families, we might also look to reducing the number of dysfunctional families—not, of course, on the Victorian model, but by aiming for the subsidiary end of helping them to become less dysfunctional. This would further both the end of fewer dysfunctional families and the end of more good ones, but, for two reasons, without the dangerous implications of aiming at the second directly. One is that there is much more agreement about what counts as a dysfunctional family than there is about what counts as a (really) good one. (Though some people do think the Amish parents are not nurturing and socializing their children as well as they could and should, I have not read anyone who claims that Amish families are, characteristically, downright bad and dysfunctional.) The second, related, reason is that the subsidiary end of helping dysfunctional families to be less dysfunctional is modest rather than utopian. One foreseeable consequence of achieving such an end is that, in fact, at least a few more families that are splendid by anyone's lights will result; another is that rather more families that are good by many people's standards will result, but the end can be aimed at without the intention to secure these results, and thereby aimed at in such a way that it does not privilege any particular model of the good family.

Social and political philosophers tend to go for ideals rather than modest aims. It is exciting to discuss the nature of the ideal family and argue for one's favoured detailed specification of what is involved in nurturing and socializing the next generation really well, less exciting to garner the sad and sometimes sordid facts about dysfunctional families and think about the nitty-gritty details of how they might be helped in a modest way. Quite generally, it is more exciting, and much grander, to talk about what justice or morality require of a good society, upholding that as an ideal, than to pursue the mundane question of how we can bring about more good families and fewer dysfunctional ones in our own society, right now, or in the foreseeable future.

I would not want to deny that the upholding and promulgation of ideals is part of the philosopher's duty. But disagreement about the ideally good family is as common amongst philosophers as it is at the grass-roots level, and although it is no doubt also part of our duty to foster critically informed debate, one might hope that, in social philosophy, we could do more for our society than that. The suggestion of this chapter is that we could—by coming up with practicable proposals, soundly based, which would bypass most disagreements about the nature of the good family. Many of us would have to do it to get our voices heard, and getting the details right would take some time, as we learnt from each other's writings, but it would be a fine endeavour to be part of.

References

Aristotle. 1985. *Nicomachean Ethics*. Translated by Terence Irwin. Indianapolis: Hackett Publishing Company.

Etzioni, A. 1993. *The Spirit of Community*. New York: Crown.

Foot, P. 1977. 'Euthanasia', *Philosophy & Public Affairs* 6(2): 85–112. Reprinted in *Virtues and Vices and Other Essays in Moral Philosophy*. Oxford: Clarendon Press, 2002.

Hursthouse, R. 1987. *Beginning Lives*. Oxford: Blackwell.

Okin, S. M. 1989. *Justice, Gender and the Family*. New York: Basic Books.

Okin, S. M. 1996. 'Sexual Orientation, Gender and Families: Dichotomizing Differences', *Hypatia* 11: 30–48.

Searle, J. 1995. *The Construction of Social Reality*. New York: The Free Press.

Wittgenstein, L. W. 1953. *Philosophical Investigations*. Edited by G. E. M. Anscombe and R. Rhees, translated by G. E. M. Anscombe. Oxford: Blackwell.

Editorial note:
Though not cited in the body of the paper, Hursthouse included the following items in her bibliography. We have preserved them for those interested in the scholarship that informed her thinking on this topic.

Galston, W. 1991. *Liberal Purposes*. Cambridge: Cambridge University Press.

Midgley, M. 1991. 'Rights-Talk Will Not Sort Out Child-abuse: Comment on Archard on Parental Rights', *Journal of Applied Philosophy* 8, 103–14.

17
On the Grounding of the Virtues in Human Nature

In this paper I want to outline and defend a form of neo-Aristotelian naturalism. It is Aristotelian insofar as it takes over from Aristotle at least the following two, connected, claims:

(1) that the virtues are those character traits that human beings, given their nature, need for *eudaimonia*, to flourish or live well as human beings, whereby
(2) considerations of human nature provide, in some sense, a rational foundation for ethics.

It is neo-Aristotelian insofar as it is distinctively modern; it incorporates elements not to be found in Aristotle and addresses issues with which he was not concerned. Indeed, one might well say that he was not *concerned* with providing a rational foundation for ethics; the project of trying to show how we are to get ethical judgements validated by considerations of human nature is itself a distinctively modern one. Nevertheless the second claim is currently thought of as embodying what is called Aristotelian, rather than neo-Aristotelian, naturalism and I shall assume the label is correct.

The modern naturalism project has been got going by Philippa Foot, who, in several papers,[1] has been defending the idea that whether or not someone is a good human being is 'determined by facts about the nature of human beings and the life of our own species',[2] just as whether or not a particular wolf or bee is a good wolf or bee is determined by facts about their nature and the life of their species. She argues that 'the behaviour of an unjust person (is) defective... for the same reason, broadly speaking, as is the behaviour of a free-riding non-dancing dancing bee, or a lioness who does not teach her cubs to hunt'[3]

---

[1] Foot (1994, 1995). Note that this paper was written before those articles were developed and supplanted in Foot (2001).
[2] Foot (1995: 14).   [3] Foot (1994: 211).

and says, that she is 'quite seriously, likening the basis of moral evaluation to that of the evaluation of behaviour in animals'.[4] Her idea is that, just as 'there is something wrong with a free-riding wolf who eats but does not take part in the hunt (and) with a member of the species of dancing bees who finds a source of nectar but does not let other bees know where it is',[5] there is something wrong with a human being who lacks, for example, charity and justice.

Although a wolf who didn't join in the hunt (because, say, it had been brought up by humans) might be a jolly good companion, and a good watch dog and a good all sorts of other things, it cannot be a good member of its species, a good *wolf*, because wolves are social creatures whose characteristic way of getting nourishment is to hunt together; a wolf that doesn't join in the hunt is, in at least that respect, a defective wolf, not a good one. A worker bee that lacked a sting would be a good survivor as worker bees go, and no doubt a good bee to have trapped in your car on the motorway, but it cannot be a good member of its species (or subspecies), because hive bees' survival collectively depends on their having stings. And the naturalistic claim is, analogously, that a human being that lacks a virtue might be a good gangster, or a good survivor, or a good-getter-of-what-they-want, but they cannot be a good member of their species, an ethically good human being.

Our defective wolf or bee might, in virtue of their defects, live longer than more perfect specimens of their kind, and, in the case of the wolf, live a life with less injury and pain in it. But they would both still fail to live well as a wolf or a bee; they would not live good wolf or bee lives. Analogously, an ethically defective human being, one who lacks the virtues, might live a long and very enjoyable life, but he would still fail to live well as a human being, to live a good human life. And so there is the standard Aristotelian claim about the criterion for a character trait's being a virtue: The virtues make their possessor a good human being, one who is excellent rather than deficient; thereby human beings need the virtues in order to live well as human beings, to live a good characteristically human life, the sort of life we call *eudaimōn*.

A fundamental doubt about the modern project has been well described by Gary Watson. Many of our suspicions, he says, 'can be put in the form of a dilemma. Either the theory's pivotal account of human nature (or characteristic human life) will be morally indeterminate or it will not be objectively well-founded... and far from grounding moral judgement, merely express it.'[6] Bernard Williams, who in his many discussions of Aristotelian naturalism is undoubtedly its most subtle and penetrating critic, has pinpointed basically

---

[4] Foot (1995: 9).   [5] Ibid.   [6] Watson (1997: 67).

the same dilemma. If 'good human being', as it figures in the modern naturalism project is, like 'good wolf', a biological/ethological/scientific concept, then it is objective all right, but it won't yield anything much in the way of ethics; it will be largely morally indeterminate (I think he says somewhere that it would probably yield you some prohibitions on homicide but not much else). A concept of human nature formed within our ethical outlook may yield us quite a rich hoard—but then, of course, the rich hoard will not be objectively well-founded but the mere reiteration of the views involved in the ethical outlook.

In fact there is another doubt about the whole project too, which identifies the first horn of the dilemma differently. When we think of trying to get even utilitarianism let alone all of ethics out of nothing more than the supposedly stunning discovery that human beings are not, by nature, entirely selfish but have altruism built into them by their genes, we may agree with Watson and Williams that a scientific account of human nature is bound to be morally indeterminate. But when we think of the recent suggestions of evolutionary psychologists, the idea that 'good human being' is 'determined by facts about the nature of human beings and the life of our own species' may seem to threaten far too much moral determinacy. Does it not reaffirm the dangerous old idea that what is natural is good, committing us to resting far too content with nature as we find it, and is this not just what feminists rightly objected to when they denied essentialism? It is guaranteed to be true of the female members of any other species that has male and female that a female x that does not go in for reproduction is, in that respect, defective; she is bound to be a bad x in at least that respect. Is the hair-raising suggestion of naturalism that we should go back to saying that and similar things, about us!

So the naturalism project looks like a non-starter, faced, as it is, with a trilemma. Either it will provide an objective grounding for ethics which delivers conclusions we reject in advance, or it provides something objective but fails to deliver anything substantial or it does not provide anything objective at all.

At this point we need to turn to the writings of John McDowell, who claims that, in rejecting the first two uncomfortable positions, we are not forced to accept the third. Disputing Williams' interpretation of Aristotle, he has maintained[7] that Aristotelian naturalism is not to be regarded as, in Williams'

---

[7] McDowell has argued this point in many places, but perhaps most illuminatingly in McDowell (1995).

words, 'a top down derivation of ethical conclusions from a scientifically respectable account of human beings'.[8]

For one thing, the establishing of ethical conclusions, like the establishment of scientific ones, is not a matter of top-down *derivation* from a few independently established premises; in ethics, as in science, the validation of our conceptual scheme is Neurathian. We proceed from within it, scrutinizing it, validating or changing it, bit by bit, plank by plank. For another, the account of human beings in question has no pretensions to being scientific in our modern sense; to suppose otherwise, in Aristotle's case, is an anachronism. The conceptual scheme we proceed from within in the naturalism project is a conceptual scheme that embraces our ethical outlook, and lays no claim to being the 'view from nowhere'.

How does this show that the naturalism project is not a non-starter, but can be objective without being scientifically based? Well, with all due respect to McDowell, I do not think that what he says does show this. I think he shows, rather, that it is a possibility. Once you have the 'There's no basing things on an *independent* foundation', Neurathian, image firmly in mind, you can see the possibility of radical ethical reflection, the critical scrutiny of one's ethical views which can be genuinely radical and not merely a reiteration of an acquired ethical outlook despite proceeding from within it. (Neurath's boat might, after all, over many years, become like Theseus's ship, without a single plank of the original remaining.) He creates a space, we might say, within which an enterprise of ethical naturalism could proceed, unhampered by a false scientism. But the existence of a space is no guarantee that there is anything to fill it, nor, in particular, that it can be filled by something that is recognizably *ethical naturalism*.

Now I myself do not believe that that is the sort of thing that can be shown, or ruled out, by the sort of abstract argument McDowell gives. We just have to look at detailed attempts to occupy the space and see. Since the modern naturalism project is only just getting going, and would, in practice, have to be a very long term one, I regard the question of whether McDowell's space can be filled by it as still open. For all he has said, it is still possible that the project may yield only disappointingly sparse results, or that, at the other extreme, it yields too many horrific ones to count as ethics or that, in our attempts to get richer results, or avoid the horrific ones, we find ourselves too clearly just reiterating the very things we are trying to validate. But, in the space available, I want to look at a few possible details which suggest to me, at

[8] Williams (1995: 200).

least, that it looks well worth having a go, and which may dispel some doubts—and indeed hopes—about it by removing misunderstanding.

The first detail I want to mention relates to not raising false hopes. The sort of ethical naturalism I, and I think Foot, espouse and which (I take it) McDowell defends (though he does not say so) is not going to yield crisp conclusions about the rightness or wrongness of, say, abortion, euthanasia, vegetarianism, or homosexual activity. If it can work, its work will largely consist in providing grounds, based on human nature, for believing that, e.g. charity, justice, honesty, courage, temperance etc. are virtues, and, as both proponents and critics of virtue ethics agree, there is no straightforward deductive step from the premise that e.g. honesty is a virtue to the conclusion that e.g. lying is always wrong. Nor, virtue ethicists standardly claim, is there even some very elaborate set of steps that will take you from that premise to a complicated but still statable version of a comprehensive moral rule or principle against lying. All that the premise 'honesty is a virtue' yields straightforwardly is that acting honestly is right and acting dishonestly is wrong, and, with respect to some particular cases of lying or other forms of deception, a great deal of thought, casuistry, and *phronēsis* has to go into determining whether *this* case, with all its local details, counts as acting dishonestly or not—if indeed that can be done, which may not always be so. The naturalism, *ex hypothesi*, grounds the starting premise that honesty is a virtue; but from then on, any debate about a particular case will be as messy and indeterminate and reliant on the notion of the *phronēsis* of the virtuous, as the critics of virtue ethics despise it for being.

So you should neither hope that naturalism might validate your belief that abortion or homosexual activity is permissible, nor fear that it might validate the belief that both, or either, are or is, impermissible. It just doesn't work that way. So I will acknowledge straight out that, from the perspective of some philosophers, with a certain view on what an adequate ethical theory is supposed to be like, the naturalism project I want to defend is, notwithstanding the space McDowell makes for it, doomed to failure: in limiting itself to aiming to validate some character traits rather than others as the virtues, instead of validating Real Moral Rules, it has impaled itself on the horn of moral indeterminacy. It may yield us a bit, but nothing like enough.

Since I'm a virtue ethicist, and thereby don't believe in these Real Moral Rules, I am unmoved by this objection. Having identified it as, fundamentally, the familiar debate about virtue ethics vs. deontology or utilitarianism, I acknowledge the existence of that ongoing debate and turn to the question of whether the project looks remotely feasible (and thereby worth pursuing) if it just has that—from the perspective of some—limited aim of merely validating the familiar list of the virtues.

Well, it is hard to form any opinion about that if you don't know what the arguments within the project are supposed to look like, so I'll tell you what I think they're supposed to look like. (This is the point at which I depart from Foot.) To cut a long story short, I think that as we trace our evaluation of living things as good or defective specimens of their kind from plants through to the higher social animals, we find a developing structure in that evaluation. By the time we get to the higher social animals, it looks like this:

A good sophisticated social animal is one that is well fitted or endowed with respect to its (i) parts, (ii) operations, (iii) actions, and (iv) desires and emotions. Whether it is thus well fitted or endowed is determined by whether these four aspects well serve (1) its individual survival through its natural life span, (2) the continuance of the species, (3) its characteristic freedom from pain and its characteristic enjoyments, and (4) the good functioning of its social group—in the ways characteristic of the species.

Now if Foot is right, our ethical evaluations of ourselves as rational social animals ought to exhibit at least a recognizably similar structure. And I think they do. Once again, cutting the story rather short, we find, I claim, that as far as our ethical evaluations are concerned, that

(a) the ethically relevant aspects we evaluate are neatly encapsulated in the concept of a virtue, for to possess a virtue—a character trait—just is to be well-endowed with respect to actions, emotions, and desires.

and

(b) that whether a human being is thus well endowed is determined by whether the character trait in question well serves the four ends appropriate to a higher social animal.

Two things that I think make this look feasible are that it promises to validate the most familiar list of the virtues and in not unfamiliar terms. Is it not plausible to say, for example, that courage plays much the same sort of role in human life as its analogue does in that of, say, wolves? Good wolves defend themselves and their cubs and each other, and risk life and limb as the pack attacks the prey, thereby fostering their individual survival, the continuance of the species, and the characteristic way the members of the social group cooperate in order to secure food for the group and protect themselves from predators. Human beings who are good insofar as they are courageous defend themselves, and their young, and each other and risk life and limb to defend and preserve worthwhile things in and about their group, thereby fostering their individual survival, the continuance of the species, their own and others' enjoyment of various good things and the good functioning of the social group.

I have read that, amongst the social animals, both wolves and elephants have patterns of action that resemble our charitable or benevolent acts, and, again, it seems plausible to say that the patterns play similar roles in the different forms of life. Charity directed to the young and helpless particularly serves the continuance of the species; directed more widely, it serves the good functioning of the social group by fostering the individual survival, freedom from pain, and enjoyment of its members, and also by fostering its cohesion. Charity, unlike courage, does not serve the end of individual survival directly but, like worker bees' stings, indirectly. An individual worker bee's functioning sting, unlike a wolf's sharp teeth, is not a good part because it fosters its individual survival; when a worker bee uses its sting, it promptly dies. But given that bees have stings, predators learn to avoid bees because they sting, and that fosters the survival of each individual bee. Charity does not, by and large, foster the individual survival of its possessor (though it may do), but given that members of a human group have charity, they can often live longer, avoid some suffering, enjoy more, because others help them.

Other virtues that perhaps have no analogue amongst the other animals still serve some of the four ends (without being inimical to the others.) Without honesty, generosity, and loyalty we would miss out on one of our greatest characteristic sources of joy, namely loving relationships; without honesty we would be unable to cooperate or to acquire knowledge and pass it on to the next generation to build on. And it has long been a commonplace that justice and fidelity to promises enable us to function as a social, cooperating group, something that, unlike the other social animals, we cannot do by instinct alone.

All this seems to me not only plausible but also not entirely unfamiliar. It is not so far removed from Hume's claim that the virtues are those characteristics that are useful and/or agreeable to their possessor and/or to others, nor from modern attempts to evaluate actions or principles of action as right in the light of their tendency to promote the greatest happiness and freedom from suffering, or as necessary for our living together in society. True, modern discussions, being mostly by non-virtue ethicists, tend not to mention the virtues or good human beings; but most accept the point that good human beings are those who have the virtues as a truism, and specify the virtues as those character traits that tend to produce, or be in accordance with, what they identify as right actions or principles.

And although the ends of individual survival and the continuance of the species do not look as familiar as the other two, I believe one can usually discern their influence too. Accounts that turn out to require widespread self-sacrifice or the fatal turning of the other cheek are criticized on that score and usually amended accordingly, so that good human beings—the ones who tend to produce right actions—have a reasonable expectation of individual survival. The continuance of the species is a much trickier issue as far as reproduction is concerned, but insofar as it involves the nurturing and education of our children (like the lioness suckling her cubs and then teaching them to hunt) I would say that, though rarely mentioned, it is almost universally presupposed. No moral philosopher knowingly attempts to validate actions or principles of action which foster general happiness, or 'persons' living together in society, at the expense of the nurturing and education of the children. We can see that most moral philosophers we read are obviously assuming that the existing babies are going to survive and become adults like them and their readers in the future, even if they have overlooked how much deliberate human activity has to go into ensuring that this happens. So I think there is enough similarity for us to suppose that, if this naturalistic project were to be pursued, it is unlikely that it would yield a bizarre characterization of a good human being.

And of course, that is important. If, as soon as we embarked on the naturalism project, it looked as though the character traits of charity, justice, courage, honesty, etc. were not going to turn out to be good-making characteristics of human beings then, I would say, we had better give up on naturalism entirely. That is why I said at the outset that McDowell's creating a space for it is no guarantee that it is not a non-starter; we have to look at some details and see.

Brief as these illustrations are, they will have to suffice. I now move on to making a few more general points. The *first* is that this form of neo-Aristotelian naturalism does not require that, in order to be a good human being and live well, we all have to live the same sort of life. True, it insists that a good human being must live a life in accordance with the virtues, but such a life can take a great variety of forms, even including those in which the exercise of one virtue figures much more largely and even at the expense of others. And one thing I find quite thrilling about this naturalism, is that we find this possibility of variation in evaluation anticipated even at the level of plants.

An individual specimen of a certain species might be rather poorly endowed in one aspect but compensatingly particularly well-endowed with respect to another and thereby count as a good x overall. Nor should we suppose—as is often supposed—that every virtue is something that a human being must possess or be, in that respect, defective. Once again, even at the level of the evaluation of plants, and much more so at the level of the other animals, we find that good x's do not necessarily all have the same characteristics. In evaluating an individual member of a species as good or defective, sometimes we stick at the species level, but sometimes we have to go through a more specific move, assessing the individual as, say good or defective leader-of-the-pack wolf or next-leader-of-the-pack wolf before we can get back to good or defective wolf *tout court*. For human beings, there is indeed a much greater diversity of roles or lives than we find in any other animals, but, given that *is* how we are, there is nothing in this naturalism which suggests that considerations of human nature are going to yield a conception of *good human being* that is even more rigid than that of good wolf or good bee. If being the sort of person who is a good parent, or a good leader, or a good academic or even a good artist are virtues, they are virtues that a human being could lack entirely without thereby failing to be a good human being, if, that is, they lacked them because they were not a parent or a leader or an academic at all.

The *second* general point is that naturalism locates some—by no means all but some—of our ethical disagreements exactly where, in my view, they should be located—in disagreements about human nature. One of Hume's most instructive mistakes is his conviction that he can dismiss 'celibacy, fasting and the other monkish virtues' without making any assumptions about the end of man, and whether he is created for this life or for the next. Of course he cannot; he can dismiss them only if he assumes that human nature is as conceived by atheists and that thereby the end, or rather ends of man are given by naturalism rather than supernaturalism. The monkish virtues (supposing them, as Hume does, to be agreeable neither to their possessor nor to others) are not obviously useless *tout court*, as Hume also supposes, for they are traditionally recommended as being 'useful' for bringing one closer to God and as preparing one's soul for the life hereafter. If human beings are no more than rational social animals, then, quite possibly, the so-called monkish virtues are not virtues at all. But if you believe that human beings are animals endowed with an immortal soul, then the four ends appropriate to social animals in the light of which we evaluate ourselves are clearly not enough; one would need to add at least a fifth end, say the preparation of our souls for the life hereafter, and then, as we know from Aquinas, the list of standard virtues gets extended a bit.

In more familiar territory, it is surely the case that many of the ethical disagreements we would have with our sexist and racist forebears spring from disagreements about human nature. They saw the ethical aspects of female and male, or different races, as much more distinct, and much more determined *by* nature than we now have reason to believe they are.

Now beliefs in, for example, the existence of the God of Christianity, or fundamental differences between women and men, or different races, surely count as part of the believer's ethical outlook, just as their opposites do, and it is worth noting that in none of these cases, I think, do we believe that the basic disagreement about human nature, which can give rise to so many other ethical disagreements, is anything other than a disagreement about fairly straightforward facts—supernatural or metaphysical facts perhaps, in the case of the existence of God, but facts nonetheless.

But in other cases, that is not so clear. In common with most if not all other moral philosophers, I have no detailed personal knowledge of how the mind of anyone really wicked works, but, speaking from the same position of ignorance as the rest, I find it ludicrous to imagine that many of them hold, even implicitly, general views about the rationality of egoism. My bet is that most of them are totally indifferent to the goodness or badness of human beings and what it consists in, and to ethical judgement in general; they just aim for what they want and do what they want to do because they want it.

But it may be that some of the so-called 'immoralist' philosophers, such as Plato's Thrasymachus, Nietzsche, and Ayn Rand, can be read as the philosophical articulation of the views of at least some wicked people. We might regard them as saying that, rather like hive bees, human beings fall into two distinct groups, the weak and the strong, or (to adapt R. M. Hare's unlovely distinction) the proles and the clever Dicks, whose members must be evaluated differently, as worker bees and drones, or worker bees and the queens are. Good weak human beings or proles might, perhaps, have the virtues as we know them and live well in a way appropriate to them, but good strong clever human beings need something quite different, appropriate to their different nature.

Can grounds drawn from facts 'about human beings and the life of our species' be given for rejecting such views? I believe that the answer to that question is 'Yes', but that the 'facts' are of a very odd sort, hitherto, as far as I know, unrecognized in philosophy.

In an instructive passage in his book *Moral Thinking* Hare sets himself the task of refuting the immoralist, on the following grounds.[9] Human beings are for the most part, he says, incapable of getting away with being immoral; exceptional talent is needed to do it. Successful crime, he says, is, for nearly everyone, an impossibly difficult game and not worth the candle. He claims that money does not on the whole bring happiness to people who amass large fortunes in dodgy business careers and that 'by far the easiest way of seeming upright is to be upright'.[10] Referring (we may suppose) to virtues such as charity, generosity, loyalty, honesty, and justice as 'the dispositions which make possible mutual co-operation and affection', he says that without them 'all our endeavours would miscarry and all joy and warmth in life would disappear. Those who do not love their fellow men are less successful in living happily among them.'[11]

With these claims I basically agree. But he describes all of them as 'empirical' claims about the way human life works ('the way the world goes'), regarding them as providing reasons 'of a non-moral sort' for not choosing to be an immoralist 'from the point of view of an egoist',[12] and I do not agree with him that they have this status. When Hare makes these claims he is not, it seems to me, speaking from a neutral point of view he might share with an egoist, but from the point of view of the humane high principled man that he is—the man who (as he reveals) regards Albert Schweitzer and Mother Teresa as 'very saintly' (rather than as cranks or deluded fools who wasted their lives) and Oxfam as doing 'wonders' (rather than as tipping good money down the drain).[13]

The trouble with supposing (as Hare appears to do) that these claims about human nature and the way our life goes are 'empirical' and thereby recognizable by anyone is that we can all so readily imagine the immoralist disagreeing with them. He denies that exceptional talent is called for—just a reasonable amount of *nous* which he, of course, has. Valuing wealth and power as he does, he denies that successful crime is not worth the candle; not only does Hare overestimate the risks, but the really big rewards justify a high risk strategy anyhow. Of *course* large amounts of money 'for the most part' bring people happiness he says, though it is true that some people are foolish enough to throw this happiness away by getting too involved with some of their fellow human beings instead of sensibly making sure that the ones you associate with are always in your control. There is nothing particularly difficult about

[9] Hare (1981: ch. 11, 188 ff.).   [10] Ibid., 196.   [11] Ibid., 197.   [12] Ibid., 205.
[13] Ibid., 200, 202.

seeming upright when it is necessary. You can fool most of the people most of the time and so on.

Now our picture of empirical facts is that they are facts accessible from the neutral point of view. Those who subscribe to a form of moral realism can also form a picture of 'evaluative' or 'moral' facts that are only accessible from within a well-formed ethical outlook but are facts nonetheless—such as that, in these circumstances it is rational to do so and so because it is virtuous. (Those who reject this picture of evaluative or moral facts can still produce an analogue of it in terms of evaluative beliefs or projected attitudes.) But the putative facts and beliefs about whether you can fool most of the people most of the time, or whether they can be easily manipulated, about what can be discerned to be a pattern in human life (i.e. what is to be attributed to good or bad luck and what is 'just to be expected'), about, in short, human nature and the way human life goes—do not fall tidily under either classification.

Neither side believes what they believe about how life works on the basis of even local, let alone worldwide, observation or statistical analysis. The beliefs are part and parcel of their ethical (or immoralist) outlook, and the (imagined) disagreements surely count as ethical disagreements. But they are far from being *obviously* part of an ethical outlook and far from being obvious candidates for 'evaluative beliefs'. It is hardly surprising that Hare *took* his to be empirical and non-moral, for very few of them can be regarded as being about values.

For want of anything better, I suppose we could classify them as 'ethical but non-evaluative beliefs about human nature and how human life goes' and describe their corresponding facts in the same way. This is why I said above that the 'facts' we would draw on, within the form of naturalism I am defending, to reject immoralism are of a very odd sort, hitherto, as far as I know, unrecognized in philosophy. I draw them to your attention both for their intrinsic interest and also as a detailed illustration of some of what might be called the limitations of the proposed naturalistic project.

And this brings me to my final point, one with which I hope, probably vainly, to forestall a lot of pointless discussion. It is that this form of naturalism is *not*, absolutely *not*, intended to produce motivating reasons for mafioso drug barons or any other wicked or morally sceptical people. Of course such people will be unmoved by any argument that purported to show, on naturalistic grounds, that e.g. charity and justice are virtues—if one can imagine their bothering to listen and follow it. (As Aristotle so rightly remarks, anyone like that would not listen to an argument to dissuade him from leading the kind of life he leads, nor understand it if he did.) Of course they will say that they are not interested in being a good human being.

I think that there are, indeed, contexts in which naturalistic arguments play a role in producing motivating reasons, most notably in the moral education of children. When we are trying to inculcate the familiar virtues in them, indicating the important role that charity, justice, honesty etc. play in human life is, I suspect, an indispensable part of that training. I might, too, reflect on the naturalistic arguments to beef up my own motivation if I thought it was getting a bit slack. But the basic context for naturalism—its natural home we might say—is the rather arcane context of finding a rational justification for one's ethical beliefs, something that by and large, only moral philosophers go in for. Being fairly virtuous, I am not in need of motivating reasons for acting honestly, charitably, justly, generously and so on; I've got them already. But being a moral philosopher, I find myself in need of something to ground my conviction that honesty, charity, justice, generosity etc. are virtues, to give me some reason to believe that, although my conviction is the result of my upbringing and culture, it is not merely that. And I think neo-Aristotelian naturalism will provide it.

References

Foot, P. 1994. 'Rationality and Virtue'. In H. Pauer-Studer (ed.), *Norms, Values and Society*. Dordrecht: Kluwer: 205–216.

Foot, P. 1995. 'Does Moral Subjectivism Rest on a Mistake?', *Oxford Journal of Legal Studies* 15: 1–14.

Foot, P. 2001. *Natural Goodness*. Oxford: Oxford University Press.

Hare, R. M. 1981. *Moral Thinking*. Oxford: Oxford University Press.

McDowell, J. 1995. 'Two Sorts of Naturalism'. In R. Hursthouse, G. Lawrence, and V. Quinn (eds), *Virtues and Reasons*. Oxford: Clarendon Press: 149–79.

Watson, G. 1997. 'On the Primacy of Character'. Reprinted in D. Statman (ed.), *Virtue Ethics*. Edinburgh: Edinburgh University Press: 56–81.

Williams, B. 1995. 'Replies'. In J. E. J. Altham and S. Harrison (eds), *World, Mind and Ethics*. Cambridge: Cambridge University Press: 185–224.

18
Human Nature and Aristotelian Virtue Ethics

Given that it relies on claims about human nature, has Aristotelian virtue ethics (henceforth AVE) been undermined by evolutionary biology? There are at least four objections which are offered in support of the claim that this is so, and I argue that they all fail.[1] The first two (Part 1) maintain that contemporary AVE relies on a concept of human nature which evolutionary biology has undercut and I show this is not so. In Part 2, I try to make it clear that Foot's Aristotelian ethical naturalism, often construed as purporting to provide virtue ethics with a foundation, is not foundationalist and is not attempting to derive ethics from biology. In Part 3, I consider the other two objections. These do not make a misguided assumption about Aristotelian ethical naturalism's foundational aspirations, nor question AVE's use of the concept of human nature, but maintain that some of AVE's empirical assumptions about human nature may well be false, given the facts of our evolution. With respect to these, I argue that, as attempts to undermine AVE specifically, they fail, though they raise significant challenges to our ethical thought quite generally.

1. Two Failing Objections

First Objection: No Human Essence

What is the Aristotelian connection between the virtues and human nature? We could locate it in the following claim (henceforth 'the Aristotelian claim about the virtues').

---

[1] One of the objections comes from Bernard Williams. The other three are ones I have heard made at conferences over the last ten years or so, and occur in articles too numerous to be cited.

(The) virtues arise in us neither (i) by nature nor (ii) contrary to nature, but (iii) nature gives us the capacity to acquire them and completion comes through habituation.[2]

No significance should be attached to 'nature gives us'. An equally authoritative translation runs—'neither by nature nor contrary to nature but because we are naturally able to receive them'.[3] AVE accepts this claim, and the first objection consists of saying that it relies on the discredited concept of a human essence. Does it?

I accept that, although Aristotle was not the essentialist that Plato was, he certainly did believe some things about species essences which evolutionary biology undercuts. So he is, doubtless, alluding to such a human essence in the above claim. But we might just say, 'So what? Who cares?' The nineteenth-century marine biologists had no difficulty in assessing Aristotle's observations in that field and (so I have read) finding most of them to be true; no one said then, and no one says now, post Darwin, 'Oh well, they have *all* been undercut by modern biology because we now know that there are no such things as the species essences that he assumed there were.' They just took the observations as being about the creatures they were obviously about and assessed them as true or false or worth exploring or whatever.

And we can do the same with his claim about the virtues. Modern Aristotelian virtue ethicists can take it as obviously about us, us humans, in the same way as human physiology is about us humans, and human psychology is about us humans and the human genome project is about us humans.

What is the claim saying? We can get a handle on it by thinking of a parallel claim to be made about human nature and language. The claim above is made up of three bits, and, in the case of language it goes (i) language does not arise in us by nature; each of us has to be taught to talk. But (ii) it does not arise in us contrary to nature either—our children lap up the teaching, Helen Keller thirsted for it—what could be more natural to human beings than language? And (iii) we suppose that, far from being blank slates as far as language acquisition is concerned, we are naturally able to receive language/have a natural capacity to learn a first language—any first human language—through initial training, and to complete the process ourselves. Given a training by our elders in our early years, we babble away, and after a time, we've got it.

---

[2] Aristotle, *Nicomachean Ethics*, trans. Crisp (2000: II.1.1103a14–26).
[3] Aristotle, *Nicomachean Ethics*, trans. Rowe (2002).

Someone might want to say that the third bit regarding language—or indeed virtue—is very speculative or they might want to say that the claim about language is more plausible than the claim about the virtues—but surely no one would want to say that the claim about language must be false or nonsensical because—as we have now realized, given evolutionary theory—there is no such thing as a human essence. So the same goes for the Aristotelian claim about the virtues. It may be false, but if so, this is not because there is no such thing as 'essential' human nature, rather that at least one of the three claims about us that make it up is false (the form of objection that will be considered in Part 3).

So, my conclusion regarding this objection is that Aristotelian virtue ethics is not undercut just because there is no such thing as a human essence, only (at the moment and for a few millennia back and for maybe not much longer in the future) the human species, or humans, or us.

Second Objection: No Concept of Health

Now we come to another, closely related, objection. The Aristotelian ethical naturalism which modern proponents of AVE promote relies heavily on the concept of health, claiming to find an analogy between the evaluations of members of other species as good, that is, healthy, members of their kind or defective in some way, and our ethical evaluations of ourselves. But modern biology, it is claimed, not only rejects the concept of an essential human (or any species') nature; it also, and perhaps thereby, rejects the concept of health (and related concepts such as those of defect and malfunction and abnormality).

That may well be true of evolutionary biology, but that is, after all, but one amongst many of the biological sciences, and it seems pointlessly foolish to deny that many of them do employ the concept of species-related health (and thereby the related ones of defect etc.). For, obviously, medicine, and veterinary science do.

In response, it may be pointed out that medicine and veterinary science are both primarily practical and professional rather than theoretical subjects, and hence a reflection of our interests and desires. They are aimed at being put into practice, at getting things in the world to go the way we want them to. So the concepts of human health, and domestic cat health pick out ways we want to be, or want our cats to be; they do not carve the world at the joints.

But then, one might say, what about human and animal physiology, with which the two practical/professional schools of study are so closely entwined?

Medical and veterinary science are taught in universities as a mixture of both practical and theoretical, the list of the participating academics' research subjects is a mixture of both. True, medicine is distinct as an academic subject from human physiology, and veterinary science from animal physiology, because the former are primarily practical whereas human and animal physiology are not; they are not aimed at getting things in the world to go the way we want them to go, but to identify and explain the things there are. Nevertheless, physiology is primarily focused on studying normal body function, where 'normal' is *not* just a statistical notion and human physiology gets defined as the science of the mechanical, physical, and biochemical functions of humans in good health, their organs, and the cells of which they are composed.

It may well be that human physiology first got going as an object of study only because of our interests in, or our valuing of, our living in certain ways; perhaps animal physiology got going for the same reason plus widespread prohibitions on human vivisection. Or perhaps we initially became interested in animal physiology because we valued domestic animals with certain properties—long life, large size, large reproduction (for their kind), resistance to external factors that inhibited any of these etc. And perhaps we first became interested in plant physiology because of our interest in agriculture.

Who knows. And again, who cares, because whether the just so story says that, or claims that the disciplines all began because we were struck with wonder about the world and wanted to know how all these bits of it worked—which was certainly what motivated Aristotle's marine biology—we wind up in the same place, with 'modern biology' as we have it now. Goodness knows how it evolved, but evolved 'it' certainly has, so that now we refer to 'it' as 'the biological sciences', using the plural to encompass its multiple branches, subdisciplines and developments, which are quite beyond the ordering of a hierarchical taxonomy. We can classify the areas of study in different ways and I suppose two of the ways we could do so would be according to the extent to which they contributed to medical science or employed the 'evaluative' concept of health. But either grouping would have fuzzy edges.

The point of the above is not to try to set up the biological sciences as providing a suitably 'value-laden' foundation for ethics, but rather to draw attention to the fact that the ones that might be called value-laden or value-informed or to contain evaluations are not to be clearly distinguished from those that are not. We could regard medicine as applied biology but this is not to say that the other biological sciences are all value-neutral or non-evaluative and that values suddenly appear on the scene only when we do medicine. If evolutionary biology is indeed quite value-neutral, and has no use for concepts such as *health* or *malfunction* or *normal* (in its non-statistical sense) this presumably does not cut if off from the biological sciences of which that is not true—it gets material from at least some of them, and some of them get material from it. It is, as I said, but one biological science amongst many and not in any privileged position.[4]

So that evolutionary biology has no truck with the concept of health—or defect or malfunction or abnormality—has no bearing whatsoever on the fact that Aristotelian virtue ethics relies on those concepts.

To what extent does it indeed rely on them? Well, not to the point that some critics suppose, which brings me to the second part of the paper, which is a brief interlude on foundationalism and the Aristotelian biological analogy.

2. Aristotelian Ethical Naturalism Is Not Foundationalist

A number of critics go to great lengths to illustrate why virtue ethics cannot be derived from evolutionary biology, or why evolutionary biology cannot provide it with a foundation. I am not going to discuss this form of objection because it is, simply, misplaced, but I will say something briefly about why it is misplaced, and what role the Aristotelian naturalism is playing if it is not a foundational one.

As we have just seen, it would be foolish to think that evolutionary biology would provide virtue ethics with its foundation; if any biological sciences did, it would be some of the other ones—the ones that provide medical science with its foundation—and ethology.

I take it that some of the biological sciences do provide medical science with a foundation in an obvious sense. They—and sometimes perhaps when one is talking about, say, pacemakers or laser surgery not only they but also some of the physical sciences—explain and justify a large number of medical claims. Where we still do not know how to do what we want to do (prevent cancer say, or cure chronic fatigue syndrome) because we do not know enough about how our bodies work, we are expecting that the biological sciences will tell us. Moreover, where we can justify but not explain, we are expecting the biological sciences to come up with the explanations. For example, we know (I think)

---

[4] Sterelny and Griffiths note that 'The contrast between polymorphic and monomorphic traits is standard in biology', defining monomorphic traits as traits that 'exist in the same form in every "normal" individual. Leg number is monomorphic in humans.' Sterelny and Griffiths (1999: 346).

that at least some acupuncture works—the sort that allows for open heart surgery on conscious patients—and it is very mysterious, but we expect some day Western science will be able to explain it.

Now in this obvious sense in which biology provides medical science with a foundation, no Aristotelian ethical naturalist—including Aristotle on some authoritative interpretations—has ever supposed that it similarly provided a foundation for ethics. I certainly do not know of any modern virtue ethicist's work in which it is implied, let alone asserted, that ethics can be expected to become a branch of applied biology, as we might say medicine is, and I cannot think of any ethical claim of which any of us might want to say, 'Well we know that so and so is the case, and it's very mysterious why, but I expect one day biology will be able to explain it', the way we want to claim that about acupuncture and indeed hypnotism. Everyone who is taking the Aristotelian naturalist line takes it as obvious that they are not pretending to derive ethical evaluations of human beings from an ethically neutral human biology, but are already thinking about human beings in an ethically structured way.[5]

Perhaps thereby we divide ourselves from some of the proponents of the other sorts of normative ethical theories. Perhaps, amongst those proponents, there are still some stalwarts who believe they are, or who aspire to be, in the business of justifying their moral beliefs in some rational but ethically (and culturally) neutral way, whereas we virtue ethicists know we are not and are not even trying to be.

If we did think it was possible, we would surely avail ourselves of what was on offer. After all, it is obvious enough that, as far as justifying the claim that such and such a character trait is a virtue is concerned, there is no reason why virtue ethicists shouldn't make the same sorts of moves that proponents of the other normative theories make. We could spin the story that it is a character trait such that everyone's possessing it would have the best consequences; or the story that I can rationally will everyone's possessing it to be a universal law. If we thought one of these sorts of stories could provide a rational but ethically neutral foundation for virtue ethics—which biology clearly cannot—of course we would go for it. But, characteristically, we do not think that. So we think we would fare no better telling any of those sorts of stories.

'Well then', it might be said, 'if Aristotelian naturalism isn't seeking to provide ethics with a foundation in biology, what is it doing?' I think Bernard Williams came to give a good description.

---

[5] Arnhart (1998).

Williams originally objected[6] to what he took Aristotelian naturalism to be, but he eventually conceded to Nussbaum[7] that there was a better way to read Aristotle, and he acknowledged (generous and honest man that he was) that most of his animadversions against it had been misplaced. (He retained one, which I shall consider in Part 3.) 'I grant', he said, 'that the Aristotelian enterprise may be seen in coherentist or hermeneutical terms.'[8] And, as far as the modern version is concerned, that seems a good description—it is offering a sort of coherentism—but a coherentism with a certain hermeneutical agenda.

Foot's Ethical Naturalism

After all, what you bring to a programme of achieving reflective equilibrium or coherence amongst your beliefs in a certain area is going to shape where you wind up, not least because it will affect what you take as relevant in that area. When Foot first began having her naturalistic thoughts, hardly anyone but her thought that they should work on getting their ethical and meta-ethical beliefs to cohere with a whole lot of other beliefs they had about good roots, good eyes, good cacti and so on, because they assumed those were irrelevant.

Taking Foot as the most influential ethical naturalist, it seems to me perfectly clear that what she takes herself to be doing is most certainly not putting forward a foundation for ethics. She is a Wittgensteinian through and through, and hence anti-foundationalist, and she is doing what Wittgenstein says is the work of the philosopher namely assembling reminders for a particular purpose.[9] The general Wittgensteinian purpose is always to '*command a clear view* of our use of words';[10] the particular purpose in Foot's case has always been to get clearer about our use of words when we are expressing or talking about our moral beliefs. When we evaluate someone as a good person, their action as right or wrong, their character as good or bad, what are we doing, what other uses of these words are these moral uses like?

When Foot first began objecting to the fact/value dichotomy, her opponents were quite sure they knew what the moral uses of 'good' and 'right' in assertions were like. They were like expressions of enthusiasm or disgust (the old boo hurrah stuff, remember). Or they were like commands—we saw more clearly what we were doing when we asserted 'John is a good man' when

---

[6] Williams (1972: 69–76) and Williams (1985: chapter 3).   [7] Nussbaum (1995).
[8] Williams (1995b).   [9] Wittgenstein (1953: §127).   [10] Ibid., §122.

we saw our doing so as akin to our saying 'Be like John.' Or they were like self-addressed exhortations, 'Let me be like John!' And they were *not* like, were utterly unlike, 'John is a good thief' for example, because that was, obviously, a purely factual statement, as was 'That tree has good roots', and a different use of 'good' entirely.

Against these prevailing views, early Foot made at least two moves, just about the adjective 'good'. One was the old point that it is, at least for the most part, attributive, the way 'large' and 'small' are, and colour words, for the most part, are not. What that means is that, with a non-attributive adjective such as 'pink', you can say truly that something is pink without worrying about how you otherwise categorize the pink thing. It doesn't matter, for instance, whether you say it's a mouse or an animal, as long as it is, indeed, pink. But you can't do the same with 'large', because whether it's true that something being identified is large does depend on whether we categorize it as, for example, a mouse or an animal—one and the same thing is both a large mouse and a small animal. And so for 'good'; the good thief is the bad man, the good lover may, alas, be the bad husband, and so on.

Her second point was suggested by those examples. The adjective 'good' has a wide range of (as philosophers say) non-moral uses as well as moral ones. But we do not have any reason—such as a distinction drawn in a language other than English, or a satisfactory philosophical account—to suppose that this philosophical distinction between the moral and non-moral uses can always be made.

Regarding Foot's early work, I think one could say that the programme was simply coherentist, intended to show the crude subjectivists around her the error of their ways—hence her readiness to discuss 'good' in relation to inanimate functional objects such as pens and knives. And one could say too, that the programme was successful, generating the vastly more sophisticated forms of subjectivism we have nowadays.

But what began as the assembling of many, varied, examples of the use of 'good' with the purpose of undermining the fact/value dichotomy, became, in her culminating work, the assembling of a narrower set, with a much more specific purpose—to show a likeness, an analogy, between our evaluation of aspects of the other animals and our ethical evaluations of ourselves. She was, she said, 'quite seriously likening the basis of moral evaluation to that of the evaluation of behaviour in animals'.[11]

---

[11] Foot (2001: 16).

The claim that there is a likeness or an analogy between two areas of talk distinguished by their subject matter (us and other animals that is) really is a pretty mild and one would think innocuous claim. If I stress that that is Foot's naturalist position—and mine, and I think MacIntyre's—not that there is a foundation, not that there is any sort of primacy about the biological evaluations of the other animals, just that there is a likeness—it might be said, 'Well if that's all there is to it, what is all the fuss about?' That seems to me to be a good question. Why are people making such a fuss, trying to wipe virtue ethics right off the board?

It looks as though it really is Foot's analogy itself that is upsetting people, because they go on wanting to attack it even after we have belaboured the point that it is *not* an attempted foundation, for virtue ethics in particular, that the other theories would lack, but just an analogy. My suspicion is that, deep down, people don't like the analogy because, quite simply, it does not make human beings special enough as ethical agents; it does not keep us and our ethical thought and talk about ourselves properly insulated from any nonethical thought and talk we have about the other animals. They want the difference in subject matter to make for lots of other differences, not to be told by Foot that they should be looking for similarities.

Why go for the animal or biological analogy, they say, encouraging us to think of our ethical evaluations as being species-relative, when our ethical thought and talk about ourselves is about us as these very special beings, *persons*, which isn't a species-concept at all?

The response is—we go for the analogy in part to curtail our hubristic tendency to think of ourselves in that inflated way. The analogy puts us firmly in our place as something distinctly less than that special.

This does *not* rule out the significance of the fact that most of us are persons, that is, that we have a special sort of rationality. That would be odd, would it not, given that Foot's naturalism is Aristotelian and Aristotle is hardly an exemplar of a philosopher who downplays the point that our rationality distinguishes us from the other animals. That significant fact is present—it is us we are talking about after all—but in a species-relative way. Acquiring the rationality that makes us moral agents or persons fairly early in our development, and, if we are lucky, keeping it until we die, just is normal, healthy, human development. But, note, it is a stage in *human* development. The rationality and 'personhood' in question are human rationality and human personhood; the two concepts apply only to human beings, and thereby only to beings with certain biological properties, each of whom is, moreover, culturally and historically situated. We are not a whole different order of beings just because we spend most of our human lives being persons, and there is no reason to suppose, in advance of our encountering some promising candidates, that the concepts could also be applied, by family resemblance, to aliens or divine beings.

So one reason for heeding the analogy is that it helps us to shake off a bit more unwarranted Enlightenment optimism about what the Age of Reason will bring. Another reason is that we learn some interesting things about our ethical thought when we heed it.

Here is a little example of the sort of difference taking heed of the analogy can make. When, talking ethics, we are talking about good people and good lives, somewhere along the line we will probably come up against the problem presented by very different sorts of people and lives, all of which we are strongly inclined to say are good. Some of us incline to saying that there must always be an answer to which is best, it can't be indeterminate, and so search for some theoretical justification for ranking one over the other. Others find at least some of these attempts manifestly unsatisfactory, and accept the indeterminacy, saying that it reflects the Incommensurability of Values. We intend the capitals here, because we think of the incommensurability as being a significant feature of *moral* values, related to various features of us as Rational Beings—more capital letters—such as our autonomy, our integrity, the fact that we have personal values and so on.

However, if we follow Foot, we can recognize, agreeing with the second group, that the indeterminacy is certainly there, but not interpret the fact of its existence in such capitalized terms. Seen in the light of the analogy with the evaluation of other living things and how they are faring, all we are looking at is the sort of indeterminacy and 'incommensurability of values'—very much lower case—that we find right down at the level of plants, not something peculiar to ethics and our talk about ourselves as rational agents.

Here is a specimen of a particular sort of plant strikingly well-endowed in some respects, mildly defective in others, pretty good and healthy over all, and doing well in the way one would expect, given where it is growing. Here is another specimen, not as well-endowed in any respect, but without any corresponding defects; it is a good one too and also doing well. Is one better than another? Well, not according to any general criterion or standard. We might use a further criterion for a particular purpose; the showy well-endowed one may obviously be better for the village flower show competition. And we might invent a new criterion and make it general. But what would be the point when obviously the best description of the set up is to follow Aristotle and say that each is 'good with qualification'. The first is good despite-having-a-few-defects; the second is good though-with-nothing-outstanding-about-it.

A more general sort of difference that heeding the analogy can make is to encourage us to think about what empirical assumptions we make about ourselves as a kind of animal with a contingent nature when we talk about ethics and thereby to consider what would happen to that ethical thought and talk if the assumptions proved to be false.

In the remaining part of the paper I am going to do just that, through considering the second pair of objections.

3. Two Failing but Thought-Provoking Objections

The objections considered in Part 1 took it that we Aristotelian virtue ethicists were talking old fashioned nonsense about the human essence. But a different set of critics have interpreted us rather more sensibly, allowing that we are, as I claimed in Part 1, talking about human nature in just the same way as, for instance, sociobiologists such as Wilson do when they say that human nature is ultimately selfish and philosophers of science such as Philip Kitcher do when they say no it isn't.[12]

Indeed, these critics want us to be talking sense about human nature, to be making straightforward empirical claims, because they think that evolutionary biology shows—well, no, not actually shows, but suggests—that some of these empirical claims are false; that the facts about human nature are, we may speculate, otherwise.

I will discuss two problematic putative facts about human nature allegedly suggested by evolutionary biology. I do not dispute that each of them, if it were a fact, would undermine one of the three bits of the Aristotelian claim about the virtues I cited at the outset. Nor do I dispute that they may well be suggested by evolutionary biology. My strategy will be to argue that, insofar as they are problematic for virtue ethicists, they are no more so than they are for most people who want to engage in ethical thought and talk.

Let us go back to the Aristotelian claim about the virtues. (The) virtues arise in us (i) neither by nature nor (ii) contrary to nature, but (iii) nature gives us the capacity to acquire them and completion comes through habituation.

It looks, does it not, as though it is not far off the obvious modern resolution of the nature/nurture debate; we become what we are because of the interaction of what we are 'born' with (saying 'conceived with' sounds too odd) and the environment. Take the first bit. It is obvious that we are not all born good,

---

[12] Kitcher (2006).

that virtue does not arise in us by nature, just as it is obvious that (contrary to Wilson) we are not all born selfish. (Of course, some people say that evolutionary biology shows that we are all born selfish, but this, if a fact, would so obviously be a problem for any ethical theory that I am not going to discuss it.)

But now take the third bit. It claims that there is a way in which we are born different from the other animals. Unlike them we can become virtuous because we are born with the capacities or propensities to acquire the virtues through habituation. The other animals cannot acquire *virtues*, which involve the recognition of certain considerations as *reasons* for acting because they do not, in the ethically relevant sense, recognize reasons *as* reasons at all. What 'habituation' covers in Aristotle is a lot. It begins in early childhood with an 'environment' which consists in being trained to behave in certain ways and gradually becomes something self-sustaining, i.e. you continue to act in those ways for reasons that you have made your own.

So there is one fairly straightforward empirical claim. We human beings are (for the most part) born with the capacities to acquire the virtues in this way.

Aristotle has also, in the second bit, made a point of saying that we do not acquire the virtues 'contrary to nature'. What is that claim doing? In part, it is just the denial of a picture that Plato, in his darker moments, draws. We would have the virtues contrary to nature if we were, psychologically, a battlefield for the irreconcilable forces of Reason and Passion (or Desire). We would acquire the virtues if (and only if) Reason wins, but at a hefty price, our natural passions or desires destroyed, crippled, deformed, enslaved. And, according to the second bit, we are not like that. But this unfolds into much more.

Aristotle, and Plato more often than not, think that the passions are not insulated from reason, deaf to its suggestions. Insofar as we are born with the capacities to experience, (Aristotle's examples) appetite, anger, fear, envy, joy, love, hate, longing, emulation, and pity, we are born with the capacities to have these passions shaped by our upbringing and early experiences and later, by ourselves, by what we make of further experience and our reflections. Moreover, they think that, when the passions are shaped the right way by reason, they can come to be in perfect harmony with it.

Hence the famous Aristotelian distinction between virtue and mere continence which modern virtue ethicists sling at Kantians. If you tell the truth or pay your debts or help other people against inclination, because you think you should, that is mere continence and not good enough. You have more work to do on getting your passions into harmony with your reason. And when you have, you will find that, by and large, you enjoy doing what is virtuous; you will do it gladly; virtuous action—for the most part—gives pleasure to the virtuous.

(In the terms of contemporary causal theories of action, your virtuous actions are overdetermined, caused both by the desire to do whatever it is and also by the belief that doing whatever it is is right plus the second order desire to do what is right.)

So there is a second empirical claim. We are all (pretty much) born to be such that we can bring our passions/desires into harmony with our reason and live happily and harmoniously together.

So we have two substantial empirical claims about human nature, about what (for the most part) is true of human beings.

(i) We are all pretty much born the same as far as those capacities or propensities that pertain to ethics—cognitive, affective, desiderative— are concerned. (I'll call them 'the ethically relevant capacities'.)
(ii) All (pretty much) of these ethically relevant capacities have a further feature; they can all be developed together, not at each other's expense.

So Aristotle's claim about the virtues, embodying as it does these two empirical claims, is up for refutation. So now let us look at the two obvious ways in which it can be false. They are the following two Putatively Problematic Facts, which are brought as the two further objections I shall now discuss.

PPF1 is that as far as the ethically relevant capacities are concerned, yes we are all born pretty much the same, but we are born a mess—the capacities cannot be developed together.

PPF2 is that as far as the ethically relevant capacities are concerned, we are not born pretty much the same but significantly varied.

Third Objection: We Are an Ill-Assorted Bricolage

That PP1 may well be a fact, and that this is suggested by evolutionary theory, is an objection to Aristotelian naturalism that has been pressed by Williams (I noted above that he had retained one of his objections to it). We may well be, as he has memorably put it, 'an ill-assorted bricolage of powers and instincts'.[13]

Indeed, he thinks that evolutionary theory suggests that we are born as just such an ill-assorted mess. 'The most plausible stories now available about (our) evolution, including its very recent date...suggest that human beings

[13] Williams (1995b: 199).

are to some degree a mess, and that the rapid and immense development of symbolic and cultural capacities has left humans as beings for whom no form of life is likely to prove entirely satisfactory either individually or socially.'[14] We might note that this second quote is tentative—human beings are 'to some degree' a mess; they are beings for whom no form of life is 'likely' to prove 'entirely' satisfactory. But if we take that tentativeness seriously, the claim, as something aimed at Aristotelian naturalism, is just too weak to touch it, and hence not interesting. None of us thinks—do we?—that democracy, as a social form of life, is entirely satisfactory. After all, it brought in Hitler and, after a fashion, Bush. But we think it's the best practicable one. And that's good enough; it gives us something to aim at socially, in the global village. *Eudaimonia*, or a flourishing life, the life of virtuous activity, which is what Aristotle thinks we can each individually live when we get our passions into harmony with our reason, does not have to be thought of as entirely satisfactory. In fact, Aristotle himself rather suggests that it is, in a way a kind of second best—our rational aspect ('the divine element within us') would be better satisfied if we lived the divine life of reflective activity. But it is the best practicable option for us, because we are human not divine. (I'm not endorsing any of that of course—it's the funny stuff from Book 10. I'm just mentioning it to make it clear that even for Aristotle, let alone a modern virtue ethicist, 'the good life' for human beings doesn't have to be roses all the way.) And that's good enough; it gives us something to aim at individually.

So to make the objection interesting, I think we have to take it as something rather stronger. Then it appears as, basically, an old idea—old enough to be present, at least to some extent, in Plato, as I noted earlier—namely that our unique combination of some set of affective/desiderative capacities not very different from those of some of the other animals plus a set of tricksy cognitive capacities unique to us (as a set) in the animal kingdom, makes us seriously at odds with ourselves—to the extent indeed that there is no likelihood that living *this* way, say, ethically, will be more satisfying or fulfilling or make us happier than living some other way. On the contrary, it is unlikely that any one of us will live a satisfying life, fulfilling our nature, given each of us is a mess, and if it turns out that some of us actually do, this will just be luck, no indication that anyone would be well-advised to take us as a model in the hope of winding up in the same happy state.

As the Platonic parallel to this gloomy picture reminds us, there corresponds to this old version of the idea, an old way to deal with it, namely aim at

[14] Williams (1995a: 109).

the life hereafter. Yes, it is agreed, the combination of the spirit and the fleshly desires is most unfortunate, the two never to be reconciled, so the only thing worth doing is preparing your spirit for its release in either the Western or the Eastern ways. Less familiar is another Eastern way of dealing with the problem which recommends dismantling or reshaping (according to one's favoured interpretation) one's cognitive and cultural powers to return to the state or condition of small children.

What should be noted about these ways of responding to the idea that we human beings are a mess is that they are responding in *the only practical way*, that is, by finding something substantial and long term for practical reason to aim at. Because that's the problem that the speculation presents us with which has to be addressed. And it is a problem not just for virtue ethicists, but *everyone*.

If there is no such thing as a predictable form of *eudaimonia*, or happiness or well-being for us humans, if any individual who winds up leading a satisfying life does so just by chance—then how can we make rational long term decisions about what to do? What is there for practical reason to do? I rely on being able to take the well-being of others as an end whether I am a virtue ethicist, a Kantian or a consequentialist.

Moreover, even if I am an egoist, I rely on being able to take my own well-being as an end. If it is not a practicable end, I could exercise my practical rationality in keeping alive (just in case I might be one of the lucky few) and in securing short term enjoyments and freedom from pain, but as for any more long term goals, I might just as well flip a coin to decide whether or not to go for them, and if so how. For, like everyone else, I am a mess of irreconcilable powers and instincts and there is no form of life that is at all likely to be satisfying to me.

So, I would say, the idea that Aristotle's more optimistic view is completely misplaced, and that we are all just a mess is, indeed, a very disturbing idea, but it is no more disturbing to Aristotelian virtue ethics than it is to any other position, including egoism. As I have noted, it is hardly a new idea, and why the facts of our evolution should be thought to give it a new plausibility is unclear to me, but I think we should all cross our fingers and hope that this is not so or we are all in trouble.

Fourth Objection: We Are Not Born Pretty Much the Same, But Varied

There are at least two ways in which we are not *all* born *exactly* the same which were (perhaps) recognized by Aristotle and which should be distinguished from the second Problematic Putative Fact that evolutionary biology is claimed to suggest.

One is very obvious; he classifies some people as 'brutish', noting that brutishness can arise 'through disease and disability' and asserting that such people possess neither virtue nor vice. On a charitable reading (ignoring some typically dreadful remarks about the condition being mostly found amongst non-Greeks) he is noting a familiar variation in human cognitive abilities, namely that some humans are born severely 'mentally handicapped' as we say. And he is excluding them from the category of people who are up for ethical assessment, as we all do today.

Many people find the second way he seems to recognize variation more disconcerting. In a tantalizingly brief passage in Book VI, he apparently introduces the idea of natural virtue, what you are born with, in contrast to full virtue, which is the set of character traits you wind up with after many years of dedicated habituation and the acquisition of practical wisdom. On one way of reading the passage, in saying we are born with natural virtue, he is just saying again what he said in the claim I began with—that we are all (pretty much) born naturally able to acquire the virtues. But on another way of reading it, he is noting what might well have seemed to him to be a fact, as it may to us, namely that some of us—only some of us—are lucky enough to be born much more able to acquire the virtues than others. After all, it often looks as though some babies are just born happy, amenable, and sweet-tempered and that, as toddlers, they display vestigial courage and self-control long before any training has had a chance to kick in, whereas others are born unhappy, cranky, difficult, and timorous.

All right, so let us suppose, with Aristotle interpreted this way, that this is a fact. It entails that, as far as becoming good people is concerned, we do not start on a level playing field; some of us are likely to find it easier than others. Is that problematic for virtue ethicists? Well, it doesn't seem to bother Aristotle and I do not see it as a problem for any of us moderns. It is not a major qualification on the claim that we are all (for the most part) naturally able to acquire virtue. When we recognize virtue as a threshold concept, all we need is that, born with natural virtue or without, we are all, for the most part, born naturally able to reach the threshold. That some of us are bound to find it easier than others and get there more quickly, that within life's short span, some of those born without natural virtue can never get to be as good as some of those who started with that natural advantage, is just how things are. There are greater and lesser grades of virtue which are not in any way under the control of their possessors, just as there are greater and lesser grades of intelligence similarly beyond their possessors' control.

So this particular way in which there may be variation in the human population does not seem to be problematic for virtue ethics at all. I think myself that one advantage of going back as far as Plato and Aristotle for one's philosophical ethics is that one goes back to something so manifestly un-Christian, so untouched by the idea that a just and loving god creates us all equal, with an equal chance of becoming good. Aristotle's view of natural virtue, and Plato's serene assumption in the *Republic* that we are born as guardians or not are clearly untouched by it, as is their taking as obvious the enormous effect of nurture on whether we turn out good or bad.

It does not seem to me so obvious that proponents of the other ethical theories, if they incline to some sort of equality we all have as persons, can shrug off this sort of unfairness in life so readily. Maybe they can, because, after all, everyone nowadays accepts that being born into a certain sort of family and/or social milieu gives you a substantially greater or lesser chance of becoming good than being born into a different sort. But one still sometimes encounters an unwillingness to admit that A is a better person than B, notwithstanding some rather nasty emotional reactions that B has carried over from her unfortunate upbringing and that A is virtuously without, when B has, *ex hypothesi*, done 'everything she could' to extirpate them.

Be that as it may, the modest amount of variation perhaps implied by Aristotle's idea of natural virtue is not, as I said, a problem for Aristotelian virtue ethicists. But that we are able to accommodate some such inequality does not show we can tolerate a lot more, and it is, theoretically, on the cards, that we are born much more varied than Aristotle's sketchy idea of natural virtue allows.

This brings me to what, I take it, those who appeal to evolution are really after. Sterelny and Griffiths say

> [So] no general biological principle suggests that human moral feelings, mental abilities, or fundamental desires should be any more uniform than human blood type or eye color. On the contrary, human cognitive evolution seems likely to have involved an evolutionary mechanism that produces variation within a population...[15]

---

[15] Sterelny and Griffiths (1999: 8).

I take it their thought is that, as far as the ethically relevant capacities are concerned, we are varied in really serious ways.

Since we have no idea whether or not this is so, thinking about it involves a thought experiment and the obvious one that springs to mind is: What if it turned out to be the case that about 10 per cent of the population, say, were born psychopathic. (Insofar as I have grasped the distinction between that and sociopathy, I really do mean psychopathy.) Given we are not quite clear about what psychopathy is, we have to make the story up as we go along, but what I am imagining—and the people I have found bringing this objection forward are clearly imagining—is that, assuming some of us are born this way, there would be something biologically identifiable very early on with fairly clear cut edges. I mean something which, although there are very occasionally borderline cases, is otherwise an all or nothing matter. And given that it is psychopathy that we are imagining, what we are also imagining is that the presence of this identifiable whatsit is a very reliable, though certainly not infallible indicator of seriously immoral behaviour in adulthood. (Fill in for yourself whatever you take to be the prime examples of immoral behaviours to be.)

This sort of example tends to be brought up to frighten virtue ethicists, but it seems to me that it ought to frighten the living daylights out of anyone who is serious about ethics, or at least that we should all find it very problematic. Again, it is not a new threat or a new idea. It is just the old idea that some significant group of us are born irredeemably (for the most part yet again) wicked or amoral—or rather, predisposed to become wicked or amoral. You might think that the modern pseudo-scientific version gives an especially threatening twist to the idea by introducing the point that, *ex hypothesi*, we would be able to identify these people, when or even before they are born, but that really is not so—that is part of the old idea too. We have a lamentable history of some group of us believing that another group of us is born irredeemably wicked; it is mostly a history of the assumption that the bad sort can be spotted before or at birth because mostly it is simply the history of racism (well, and sexism too of course).

No doubt because of that history, our modern sensibilities are not at all attuned to taking this idea on board in our ethical thought. If we really did discover such a thing, what on earth would we do and how would we justify whatever we did in ethical terms, *whichever* normative theory we appealed to? I can imagine that some particularly hardline act utilitarians, and some of the redneck fundamentalists might cheerfully say oh well we'll kill 'em off at birth, and justify this in their usual ways, but I would say the rest of us are in real trouble.

So this is another speculation with respect to which I think we all, not just the virtue ethicists, had better cross our fingers and hope it is not so. That is as far as I have got in my exploration of the idea that our being varied, rather than pretty much the same as far as ethically relevant capacities are concerned, would present a serious problem for virtue ethics. And so far my conclusion is, in some versions it would not present any problem (though in the case of 'natural virtue' it might be awkward for some egalitarians or people who believe in fairness) and in the some-of-us-might-be-born-psychopathic version, it would present a serious problem for any of us, whatever normative ethical theory we espouse.

4. Conclusion

Overall my conclusion is that, pending further efforts, neither evolutionary biology nor armchair speculations about what it suggests might yet be revealed about human nature pose any threat to virtue ethics as such, though the two speculations I have discussed above would indeed be problematic for ethics as we know it.

References

Aristotle. 2000. *Nicomachean Ethics*. Edited and translated by Roger Crisp. Cambridge: Cambridge University Press.

Aristotle. 2002. *Nicomachean Ethics*. Translated by Christopher Rowe, introduction and commentary by Sarah Broadie. Oxford: Oxford University Press.

Arnhart, L. 1998. *Darwinian Natural Right*. New York: SUNY Press.

Foot, P. 2001. *Natural Goodness*. Oxford: Clarendon Press.

Kitcher, P. 2006. 'Comment'. In F. de Waal, *Primates and Philosophers*. Princeton, NJ and Oxford: Princeton University Press.

Nussbaum, M. 1995. 'Aristotle on Human Nature and the Foundations of Ethics'. In J. E. J. Altham and R. Harrison (eds), *World, Mind, and Ethics*. Cambridge: Cambridge University Press: 86–131.

Sterelny, K. and P. A. Griffiths. 1999. *Sex and Death: An Introduction to Philosophy of Biology*. Chicago: University of Chicago Press.

Williams, B. 1972. *Morality*. Cambridge: Cambridge University Press.

Williams, B. 1985. *Ethics and the Limits of Philosophy*. Cambridge, MA: Harvard University Press.

Williams, B. 1995a. *Making Sense of Humanity*. Cambridge: Cambridge University Press.

Williams, B. 1995b. 'Replies'. In J. E. J. Altham and S. Harrison (eds), *World, Mind and Ethics*. Cambridge: Cambridge University Press: 185–224.

Wittgenstein, L. W. 1953. *Philosophical Investigations*. Edited by G. E. M. Anscombe and R. Rhees, translated by G. E. M. Anscombe. Oxford: Blackwell.

19
The Grammar of Goodness in Foot's Ethical Naturalism

Not a lot of people know that Foot's original title for her book *Natural Goodness*, was actually 'The Grammar of Goodness'. With hindsight, it seems that this would have been a better title, making it clear that the book really doesn't have much to do with the natural, biological sciences but is about the logical grammar of moral judgements.

It also seems that not many people know why this was *bound* to be so, namely the fact that, from her earliest years as a philosopher, under the guiding hand of Anscombe, Foot was always a Wittgensteinian, through and through. Hence she was anti-foundationalist and antireductionist on principle, and the most unlikely philosopher in the world to think that any of the natural sciences had any bearing on the philosopher's task, let alone if that were moral philosophy. What she has always been doing is what Wittgenstein says is the work of the philosopher namely assembling reminders for a particular purpose (§127). The *general* Wittgensteinian purpose is always to '*command a clear view* of our use of words' (§122); the particular purpose in Foot's case has always been to get clearer about our use of words when we are making moral judgements. When we evaluate someone as a good person, their action as right or wrong, their character as good or bad, what are we doing, what grounds do we typically give for our judgements, what do we expect from someone who has said it, what other uses of these words are these uses in moral judgements like, what background do these uses presuppose, what is the standard role or function of their use, and so on.

Looking back much further, to her earliest philosophical work, we can also see that such an account of the nature of moral judgements was what she had been looking for right from the very beginning, but found only very late in her philosophical career.

In her preface to the first edition of *Virtues and Vices* (1978a [= VV]), which collected most of what she had written in the previous twenty years, Foot described the last eight essays as representing 'the development of a certain line of thought on the theory of moral judgement' and also as ones in which she was making 'a painfully slow journey...away from theories that located the special character of evaluations in each speaker's attitudes or feelings, or recognition of reason for acting' (VV xvi). But, given what was in that collection that seems to be inaccurate on both counts. There was nothing *slow* about her journey away from the contemporary subjectivist theories of moral judgement that appealed to the speaker's attitudes or feelings or motivating reasons. She was dead against them right from the word go, as is clear in the earliest of the essays reprinted—the 'Moral Arguments' paper in which she discussed the use of the word 'rude'. But, on the other hand, we do not find her developing her own 'line of thought on the theory of moral judgement' until the two papers 'Rationality and Virtue' (1994) and 'Does Moral Subjectivism Rest on a Mistake?' (1995) which prefigure *Natural Goodness* [= NG].

By her own account (in two of the three post-*Natural Goodness* interviews I have read), her opposition to subjectivism was born of her reaction to the films of the concentration camps that came out after the war. According to Hare and other non-cognitivists, it could not be an objective moral *fact* that what the Nazis had done was wrong; the judgement that it was merely expressed the speaker's personal attitude to what had been done, and the Nazis' attitude was presumably different. And, Foot tells us, she thought this *had* to be bad philosophy, and that there *must* be grounds for moral judgements (*The Harvard Review* [= THR], 34–5). So she set out immediately on the task of chipping away at the bad philosophy, but it took her a long time to find what she thought should supplant it.[1]

Now actually, she had the germ of the idea of what she would eventually produce *very* early on, right back in that 1958 'Moral Arguments' paper. For already there she is defending the idea that moral judgments had to be connected to human benefit and harm *somehow*.

Why then, it might be wondered, did she not go for utilitarianism as Hare wound up doing? To my regret, I never asked her what her earliest reactions to utilitarianism were, and I have never heard anyone reporting anything she said about it. But if we remember that Anscombe's 'Modern Moral Philosophy' also came out in 1958, and that, by then, Foot and Anscombe had been talking philosophy almost daily, at least on weekdays, for over ten years, we shall not be surprised that it was the relation between the *virtues* and human benefit and harm that she is already thinking of in this early article, rather than act consequentialism.

---

[1] Baggini and Stangroom (2007).

In one of the post-*Natural Goodness* interviews, she says a very interesting thing about how (it seemed to her with hindsight) she had been thinking back then. She had (following Anscombe's advice) been reading Aquinas on the individual virtues and vices and was struck by the fact 'that there were always good reasons' for saying of one of them that it *was* a virtue or a vice, and with this, she says:

> [T]he whole subject of moral philosophy *thickened up* in my mind. Before that, I had simply thought "there must be objective grounds for moral judgement," without being able to say much except that they would have to be connected to human welfare or something like that. But *looking in detail*, as Aquinas made me do, made me see that a virtue-vice point of view provided an excellent way to make an idea of objectivity in moral judgement *concrete*. If one only considered a proposition such as "this act is wrong" it didn't lead one on to *particular* reasons or judgements in the way "such and such is a vice" did. (THR 35–6)

Notice all the emphases on the non-general—the thickening up and looking in *detail*, making the objectivity *concrete*, the being lead on to *particular* reasons.

Here's the way she described 'the progression of her thought' later in that interview: 'from thinking subjectivism must be wrong to thinking that *when we look at the individual virtues and vices* we can actually begin to see an objective basis for particular moral judgements and on from there' (THR 36).

But, as in her preface to *Virtues and Vices*, that's not quite accurate. Again, she got from 'thinking subjectivism must be wrong to thinking that when we look at the individual virtues and vices we can begin to see an objective basis for moral judgement' almost immediately. Right after she wrote the 'Moral Arguments' paper, she wrote 'Moral Beliefs' in 1958; there she takes a position influenced by Plato and Aristotle, arguing that, given 'the facts of human existence . . . any man has reason to aim at virtue and avoid vice' because the virtues are what we need, rather as everyone has reason to avoid injury because an injury, by its very nature, disables one (VV 123). And in that she is, albeit very briefly, sketching the Thomistic details peculiar to the individual virtues, citing *particular* facts about human existence—such as the fact that anyone of us may need to face something fearful for the sake of some good on the one hand, and the fact that anyone of us may need to resist the temptation of pleasure when there is harm involved on the other as the grounds for courage and temperance respectively being virtues (VV 123–4). That is, in *general* it's the virtues that we need, there is that general connection with human welfare, but there are these *particular* reasons why we need courage and these other ones for why we need temperance, and they concern different facts about human existence or human life. So *there* she is in 1958.

But, as we know, she didn't just go '*on* from *there*' for *there* is pretty much where she wound up in *Natural Goodness* over 40 years later. As we know, rather than *going* on from there back in the 60s, she stalled almost immediately, because of the conclusion she reached when working on the relation between 'Goodness and Choice' (published in 1961). There she concludes that 'we may not be able to give a reply' to someone who demands a reason for choosing to be a good daughter or good friend, these being attributive uses of 'good' which, unlike for example, 'good knife' and 'good rider' are attached to what, she says 'should be called moral terms' (VV 138). Notably, she does not go so far as to say that this suggests we may find ourselves similarly helpless when someone demands a reason for choosing to be a good—that is a virtuous person—but that is obviously the way her thought is tending, abandoning that confident 'Moral Beliefs' claim that *anyone* of us has reason to aim at virtue.

And then she didn't do *anything* on her theory of moral judgement for ten years, at the end of which she devastated all her objectivist followers by coming out with 'Morality as a System of Hypothetical Imperatives' whose whole point, one might say, is to assert explicitly that we can't give anyone a reason to be a virtuous person unless they have virtuous ends or desires.

Why did she arrive at this view? When we look back at 'Goodness and Choice', we can see a couple of significant things she overlooked, which, I believe, lead her astray. In this paper, she is just looking at our use of the word 'good'. She begins with words such as 'knife' and 'pen', 'functional words', which name things in respect of their function or 'ergon', in Aristotle speak, and, more or less in passing, she goes on to mention some other words, 'roots' and 'claws', 'lungs', 'eyes', and so on, which also name things in respect of their function. In Aristotle's terms, we would say the same of the third batch of examples she then went on to, namely 'farmer', 'rider', 'teacher', 'tailor', though, in keeping with ordinary usage, she denies that they too are 'functional' words. And she discussed a whole lot of others, including, as I just mentioned 'good daughter', father, and friend. The *general* point she wanted to make about all these words was, contrary to Hare, that a connection with the choices of the speaker was neither necessary nor sufficient for the use of the word 'good' in combination with them; since 'good' was an attributive adjective, the criteria for goodness in every case was determined or at least strongly constrained by the meaning of the noun (or noun phrase as in 'good Cruft's show spaniel' or, indeed 'good *x for my purposes*') that followed it.

However she was not maintaining that choice was irrelevant. She spent some time exploring the many ways in which we (and hence speakers) *do* choose a good A (and would normally choose it, and choose it if such and such is the case), and showing how they are relevant. In the course of doing so, she encountered an anomaly, though she did not recognize it as such at the time. Indeed, if anything she hailed it as the final endorsement of her objections to Hare.

The anomaly was the goodness of features of organism such as good roots and claws. Of these she truly—and triumphantly—remarks that in these cases:

> [T]he A that is called good may be one that *no one* has reason to choose. We say, in a straightforward way, that a tree has good roots meaning by this that they are well suited to the performance of their function [...]. Our interests are not involved, and only someone in the grip of a theory would insist that when we speak of a good root we commit ourselves in some way to choosing a root like that. (VV 145).

So she has spotted that the good roots and claws form a terrific set of counterexamples to the prevailing crude forms of subjectivism. The goodness of these sorts of things just has nothing to do with *us*, our interests, desires, choices, attitudes, whatever, *at all*. But then, that's just what makes these anomalous examples. In all the other cases she discusses, we—what *we* want or *we* use or *we* need or *we* take an interest in—*are* forming the necessary background to the evaluative judgements somehow.

When the roots and claws examples strike us as anomalous in this respect, we can notice something else which is peculiar to them that she also overlooked. She says 'Good roots are like good eyes, good pens and many other things that are good, in being of the kind to perform their function well', passing smoothly from the natural examples to the manufactured ones (VV 145). But just before that she says '*Because* the root plays a part in the *life* of the organism we can say "it has a function", relating what it does to the *welfare* of the plant' and what she overlooked is that you can say the same sort of thing about other parts of living organisms and indeed their behaviour or 'operations' as she came to use the term in *Natural Goodness*, but you can't say anything *remotely* like it about pens or knives, not even about their parts. As she will come to recognize through Michael Thompson, the evaluations of the parts and 'operations' of living things, not only, except in special contexts, have nothing to do with us, but moreover, and uniquely, they all *do* have to do with the *life*, or life-form of the organism, and to do with its *welfare*. They really are in a *sui generis* category.

But not having noticed these things, she got stuck. She was in search of an account of moral judgement—in particular, our moral evaluations of *ourselves*. I don't suppose for a moment that she set off to write 'Goodness and Choice' purely with a view to doing down Hare; she did it because she expected that if she could get clearer about why he was wrong about goodness and choice, she would thereby get clearer about what the right account of moral judgements would be. So she argues that there isn't a special, isolable *moral*, or *peculiarly* evaluative use of the adjective 'good'. It's always doing the same job, just sitting there in front of its noun or noun phrase, waiting for that to determine the criteria for goodness in question. But what, now, can she say about our moral evaluations of ourselves? What can she say about (as she continued to express it for many years) the judgement 'X is a good man' or (as she at last got round to saying in *Natural Goodness*) 'a good person'? It cannot have escaped her attention that although, in one sense, there isn't a special moral use of 'good', in another sense there is; when we attach it to the word 'person', we are usually bound to be making a moral judgement. 'Person' or 'man', like 'daughter' and 'father' is a 'moral term'.

I'm just not sure *what* she thought about 'good person' at the time she was writing 'Goodness and Choice'; however I am sure that she was taking it as obvious that a good person had the virtues, and that whether or not someone had the virtues was a matter of fact, and hence that whether or not someone was a good person was a matter of fact.

So, even if 'good man' didn't quite fit into the 'Goodness and Choice' picture, one might say, she had got 'good' judgements all sorted out as objective. But now what about 'ought'? There is a bit in her reply to Frankena where she makes it clear that she *was* thinking of the moral judgement 'x is a good man' as belonging with good doctors, good friends, good citizens, 'and the rest', that *they* are all equally unproblematic as far as their objectivity is concerned, but that the 'true gap' between is and ought 'comes within what has been called evaluation'—that is, quite generally in the case of all these judgements of the form 'good F' (VV 178). It seemed clear enough—and quite unproblematic—that someone *ought* to choose a good pen, tailor, novel, whatever IF (but only if) they were selecting the whatever for the usual reasons. But if what they want is to make blots, or an ill-fitting suit, or trashy chick-lit book to read on the beach then they have no reason to choose such things; that is just what she had argued. And, as noted above, she thought that it was obviously true that not everyone had a reason to be good friend and good daughter. So it seemed that the same would have to be true of 'good man'. We can establish that Hitler was a thoroughly bad person, a wicked man, that, indeed, he acted badly, but we cannot move from that to 'He had reason to choose to do other than he did.'

And she knew that wasn't what she wanted. So in effect, she stalls for ten years. She does a bit on abortion, she does 'Morality and Art' (which she was so dissatisfied with that she wouldn't have it in the original *Virtues and Vices* collection) and in 1963 she produces a paper on Hume on moral judgement. Perhaps she went back to look at him in the hope of nailing something wrong in him that would show her the way round her problem. But all she finds there is the familiar mistake about the fact/value dichotomy she is confident she has sorted out all mixed up with the is–ought gap that is the very thing that is bothering her. And then it looks as though she turns to Kant hoping to find something there. But, far from finding a solution in the categorical imperative, she becomes even more convinced that 'Goodness and Choice' was right; and armed with the famous example of etiquette, she now turns the thought 'has no reason to' into 'can't be convicted of irrationality if he doesn't' and produces the swingeing 'Morality as a System of Hypothetical Imperatives' (1972).

And then she stalls again. She goes back to the virtues and vices in the new paper for the collection (1978) but by then is so lost that she actually gives up the tight conceptual connection between possession of the virtues and being a good person, allowing herself the idea that a villain may be courageous (though perhaps courage is not a virtue 'in him' whatever that is supposed to mean) and that similarly that someone might be too temperate, or too hopeful or too prudent. She doesn't consider the possibility that someone might be too charitable or too just, but, consistently with what she says, she could well have done so. And then, for the next ten years, she turns to other issues—quite a bit in applied ethics and her two deservedly famous papers on utilitarianism. But somewhere in the mid-1980s (I have a draft of hers dated March 1987), perhaps as the result of conversations with Michael Thompson, by then a graduate student of hers at UCLA, the significant points in 'Goodness and Choice' she hadn't appreciated before came back to her, and she started on the *Natural Goodness* work.

I said that these points were, firstly, that the roots and claws examples were anomalous because they just didn't have anything to do with us—our desires, interests choices, attitudes, whatever, *at all*. In all her other cases she discusses, *we*—what *we* want or *we* use or *we* need or *we* take an interest in, what *our* lives are like—*are* forming the necessary background to the evaluative judgements somehow. The second point was that they *do* all have to do with the *life*, or life-form of the organism, and to do with its *welfare*.

And there was a third, which I have not yet mentioned. Once again truly—and triumphantly—she had taken Hare to task for implying that someone can set up his own criteria for whether or not something is a *good cactus*. She complained that 'There is no reference to the fact that a cactus is a living organism, which can *therefore* be called healthy or unhealthy and a good or bad specimen of its kind' and that without this it is unclear 'how the criteria could be criteria of *goodness* at all' (VV 141). Quite true—but she overlooked the fact that *nowhere* else in the article did she say *anything* about the evaluations of living things as good or bad specimens of their kind; she didn't have anything but the evaluations of their *parts*—the roots and claws.

And one might say the new dazzling thought she got from talking to Thompson was: when we evaluate ourselves we're evaluating *living things* which can *therefore* be called healthy or unhealthy or a good or bad specimen of their kind or, as she might well have added, good or excellent or *defective* specimens of their kind. And of course, to her ear, trained as it was in ancient philosophy and by Anscombe, this was not going to sound like a thought that was limited to medical evaluations. We drop the 'healthy' and 'unhealthy', and the use of 'specimen' but, keeping the terminology of excellence and defect, we find, when talking about ourselves in this way, that we are back with talk about the virtues and vices.

So, back to the Wittgensteinian technique of 'assembling reminders' or examples, for the purpose of understanding our moral judgements. She now sees that 'Goodness and Choice' told us damn all about 'the grammar of goodness' in living things, and that what we need are lots of examples of judgements of that sort, rather than all the others. And she found these in Thompson's 'The Representation of Life'.[2] I don't want to spend much time talking about Thompson rather than Foot, but, on the other hand, I don't want to leave what follows unintelligible to those of you who haven't read him, so I'll try to say just enough to keep the discussion of Foot afloat.

According to Thompson, there are many judgements which are (a) indisputably part of *some* (n.b.) of the biological sciences and (b) are normative. These are, typically, what Thompson called 'Aristotelian Categoricals' which take the form 'The S is (or has or does) F', or 'Ss are (or have or do) F'; doesn't matter which (2008: 65). These say, of a species or 'life-form' of living thing, the S, that 'it' has certain characteristics or features (is four legged, has a long

[2] Thompson (1995).

curved beak, has a tap root) or that it 'operates' or behaves in a certain way (sees in the dark, hunts in packs, self-pollinates, curls up its leaves when it's short of water). The class of Aristotelian Categoricals also contains slightly more specific judgements such as 'The female S (or "the mature female S") has/does F', 'The larval stage of the S, the immature S, the young S has/does F', and these also count as being about 'the S'. And it also, importantly, contains more complicated judgements of the form 'The S has/does F in order to...' A set of Aristotelian Categoricals about the S itemizes the Fs that, in the life of the S, have the function of achieving what is needed for development, self-maintenance, and reproduction, and thereby, of what an individual S needs in order for its life, the S life, to go well. Hence they are not merely statistical. They supply a standard—a 'natural norm' in Foot's terminology—for evaluating individual Ss. If it is true that 'The S is F', then an individual S which is not F is defective in that respect—not 'as it should be' or 'as it is supposed to be'. But if it *is* F then it is, in that respect at least, a good F—it has, again in Foot's terminology, 'natural goodness'. Hence they supply the norms we use to evaluate individual Ss as strong or weak, healthy or diseased, good or defective, Ss, or specimens of the kind S.

Critics often say that the use of the Aristotelian Categoricals relies on a notion of function and/or species—which *is* indeed Aristotelian and has thus been refuted by post-Darwinian biology. But Thompson, and following him Foot explicitly disavow any intention to use the terms 'function' or 'species' in the technical senses of evolutionary biology. In fact I think it is a pity that Thompson didn't stick with 'life-form' or 'kind of living thing', because everything he, and Foot, want to say, can be expressed in those obviously non-Darwinian terms. The claim is only that this strange, but immensely useful, form of judgement is alive and well in *some* of the biological sciences, whose researchers, we may presume, are proceeding in full knowledge of the post-Aristotelian insights of evolutionary theory. These biologists know that the concept of species is theoretically problematic; they know that the feature they identify as serving a certain function in the current life of the Ss they are interested in may be a spandrel, but, concentrating on, say, the threatened indigenous New Zealand kokako, and the failure of two of the males to feed their mates while she is incubating, they put this knowledge to one side as not affecting their research, for which the everyday concepts serve their purposes.

In making this claim about some judgements in some of the many biological sciences, Foot's ethical naturalism becomes involved in a current debate in philosophy of biology, basically the debate about whether the concept of function and, relatedly, teleological explanation, have a place in the post-Darwinian biological sciences, and, if so, whether or not they can be 'naturalized', that is, made value-free. So that is a major issue that seems to arise. But, as I shall say below, this really is a red herring. Unlike 'biological ethical naturalists', as we may call them, such as Casebeer and Arnhart,[3] Foot's ethical naturalism is not aiming to provide ethics with an explanatory biological foundation, so she does not need to deny that some analysis of the Aristotelian Categoricals about plants and the other animals might show that they can be interpreted in such a way as to be value-free in some sense. All they need is that they obviously can be interpreted as both evaluative or normative and fact-stating, and that, when they are, their truth has nothing to do with our desires or pro-attitudes.

So, supposing that the Aristotelian Categoricals are normative, and leaving it open whether they might in some way be naturalized, what follows? Well, it certainly does not *follow* that our moral evaluations of ourselves share, in Foot's words, 'a conceptual structure with evaluations... of other living things' but *that* they do is her distinctive ethical naturalists' claim—her new dazzling thought (NG 1).

On the face of it, especially when we remember that the claim includes our evaluations of plants, it seems this cannot be right. Only human beings have virtues and vices (good/excellent or bad/defective character traits), only human beings act 'for reasons' in the sense relevant to moral evaluations, and plants do not act at all.

But note, the claim is about an abstract 'conceptual structure', not about details of similarity between moral evaluations and evaluations of other living things. With respect to the latter, we evaluate their characteristics or properties, their behaviour or operations (even plants 'do', and fail to do, things— they set seed, curl up their leaves to conserve moisture); when we evaluate ourselves, the relevant characteristics include our character traits and the relevant behaviour pre-eminently includes our acting for reasons.

On Thompson's picture, we have a cluster of concepts, combined with a special way of talking, that apply to all, but *only*, living things, and our talk of good—and defective—roots and claws is to be located in this 'way of talking', which has, she says, a 'special "grammar"' (NG 26).

On Thompson's picture, we make factual judgements about how particular kinds of living things, say owls, get on in their lives, such as 'Owls see in the dark and hunt at night.' These tell us what owls need in order to live well as owls. The peculiarity of such judgements is that, combined with the judgement

---

[3] Casebeer (2003) and Arnhart (1998).

that a particular owl can or cannot see in the dark, or does or doesn't hunt at night, they yield an evaluation of that owl. If it can and does then, in those respects, it is a good specimen of its kind, a good owl; if it cannot or does not, it is, in those respects, a defective one. And Foot's thought is that our moral judgements have the same 'conceptual structure' (NG 5). There are true judgements to be made about what human beings need in order to live well as human beings, and in these we will find the objective grounds for maintaining that, for example, justice and kindness are virtues, or forms of 'natural goodness'. A just human is, in that respect, a good human being—or person as, colloquially, we say when making moral judgements.

This gives her the new version of her original position on the fact/value dichotomy with respect to good, that is, virtuous human being. Those 'facts about human existence'—different facts and details for the different virtues—which figured in 'Moral Beliefs' as the grounds for saying that everyone had a self-interested reason for aiming at virtue—are now fitted into this very general structure, with no insistence on self-interest or the 'profitability' of justice.

But what of the is–ought gap? Her new approach to this involves, firstly, abandoning the idea that reasons for action must be related to the agent's interests or desires. To this extent, she agrees with Kant and accepts 'externalism' about reasons. But, for Foot, there are no such things as the principles of *pure* practical reason; practical reason, as we know it, is not a feature of rational beings or rational agents as such, but simply a feature of us—terrestrial hominids.

But of *course*, we are a special sort of living thing. She is not denying the significance of the fact that most of us are persons, that is, that we are moral agents, and have a special sort of rationality. That would be odd, would it not, given that Foot's naturalism is Aristotelian and Aristotle is hardly an exemplar of a philosopher who downplays the point that our rationality distinguishes us from the other animals. That significant fact is present—it is us we are talking about after all—but in a relative-to-the-kind-of-living-thing-that-we-are way. Acquiring the rationality that makes *us* moral agents or persons fairly early in our development, and, if we are lucky, keeping it until we die, just is normal, healthy *human* development. But it is a stage in *human* development. The rationality and 'personhood' in question are human rationality and human personhood; the two concepts apply only to human beings, and thereby only to beings with certain biological and consequent psychological properties, each of whom is, moreover, culturally and historically situated. We are not a whole different order of beings just because we spend most of our human lives being persons, and there is no reason to suppose, in advance of our encountering some promising candidates, that the concepts could also be applied, by family resemblance, to aliens or divine beings.

This *human* practical rationality is conceptually inseparable from the *human* virtues, since anyone with a virtue is necessarily someone for whom certain considerations are reasons for action. And thereby she gets the version of 'the rationality of morality' that she wants. To establish, within the Thompson structure, that a certain character trait is a virtue, is also to establish that a human being who does not recognize certain considerations as reasons for acting is thereby defective in practical rationality. As she recognizes, common usage doesn't really allow describing the actions of the Great Train Robbers as 'irrational' (NG 14)—which was what bothered her so much in 'Morality as a System of Hypothetical Imperatives', but she can now express the point she wanted in terms of defect, and she is happy to say that what they did was 'contrary to reason', or that in saying truly that what they did was dishonest and callous we *would* be giving them reason to do other than they did, regardless of whether they recognize it.

So I think she achieved what she had always been aiming at—a theory of moral judgement. Throughout the book, she emphasizes the fact that she is outlining a 'conceptual structure' and I now want to turn to saying some more about what *goes into* that conceptual structure when our topic is the moral evaluation of ourselves. Given that we are talking about the goodness of this special sort of living thing, rational agents, we fit into the Thompsonian structure in a special way; it undergoes, as she wonderfully puts it, a 'sea change' (NG 52)— a remark that few of her critics have noted. Perhaps not many people know where the expression 'sea change' comes from. Foot knew all right, and I have no doubt that she used the term advisedly. It comes from Shakespeare's Tempest:

> Full fathom five thy father lies;
> Of his bones are coral made;
> Those are pearls that were his eyes:
> Nothing of him that doth fade,
> But doth suffer a sea change
> Into something rich and strange.
>
> (*Tempest* 1.2.560–5).

Now, as we learn from the extraordinary nature programmes now available, the Aristotelian Categoricals that describe how many of the other animals live are breathtakingly wondrous, but wondrous, strange, and in the case of the higher animals rich as they may be, ours, so Foot assumes, is *incomparably* so, for we, unlike any of the others *are* rational agents. So it is a bad mistake, I think, to suppose that the Aristotelian Categoricals that figure in the conceptual structure when we are morally evaluating ourselves are all supposed to be, like the biological ones which Thompson discusses, the sort of natural facts with which the natural sciences deal. That's why I said above that debates about whether the biological ones can or cannot be made 'value free' is just a red herring.

Many of Foot's critics take McDowell's 'Two Sorts of Naturalism',[4] to deal a fatal blow to Foot's naturalism. In this, you may remember, he invokes the rational wolf, who stands back from his fellow wolves joining in the hunt and says to himself 'Yes, indeed, wolves hunt in packs, they cooperate, they need to pool their energies if their style of hunting is to be effective, but why should I—what reason do I have?—to pull my weight?' But in my view, far from intending to undermine the sort of naturalism he knew, at the time of writing the paper, she was developing (this was in the late 1980s, before she had published anything on it, but she had been doing versions of it in lectures in the US and he, like Gary Watson, has heard them) nothing could be further from the truth; his paper is intended to *pave the way to it*. I mean look at the title!—*Two* Sorts of Naturalism. In the very opening paragraph, he makes it clear that his topic is ethical naturalism, and that he is going to argue that there are two sorts, one of which is 'the radical and satisfying alternative to subjectivism and supernaturalist rationalism' in ethics, and the other of which is, to put it mildly, a 'less satisfying variety' (McDowell 1995: 149). Well, in a paper for Foot's *Festschrift*, offered, as he explicitly says, as 'an appropriate token of friendship and *admiration*', why on earth would he be supposing that it is the *less* satisfying variety of ethical naturalism that she is espousing! Of *course* he thinks she is shaping up to producing the *other* sort—'the radical and satisfying alternative to subjectivism and supernaturalist rationalism' in ethics.

But alas, the paper by and large, didn't work because so many of Foot's, and McDowell's, readers are so gripped by the picture of nature, or reality, that he rejects. That is the 'natural-scientific' conception of nature, the view that anything that can rightly be called a 'natural fact' *must* be the sort of fact that the natural sciences discover—the sort that (in theory) everyone can recognize from the neutral point of view. No. The structure remains the same; the sea change occurs in what goes into it.

---

[4] McDowell (1995).

By way of illustration, I want to look at 'survival and reproduction' as they figure in the Aristotelian Categoricals that are pertinent to moral judgement, i.e., the ones that pertain to us as human rational agents.

Foot says that the 'natural goodness and defectiveness' of the features (e.g., eyes) and operations (e.g., hunting at night) of all the other living things is conceptually determined by the relation, for that sort of thing, of that feature or operation, to survival and reproduction. Actually, she hardly ever talks about *survival* and reproduction (in fact I think only twice, on pages 42 and 43 in *Natural Goodness*); instead she talks about development and self-maintenance and reproduction.

Now the obviously Darwinian ring of that phrase is undoubtedly one of the things—like her use of 'species'—that mislead people into expecting something much more 'scientific' to go into our Aristotelian Categoricals than she is offering; they forget about the sea change.

This brings with it two distinct upshots. One is that she claims that there is an *enormous* amount more to 'the human good', that is, the life that is the human's good to live, than there is in the life that is any other animal's good to live. For all of them, their life just *is* the life of survival and reproduction; our sort of life contains many goods which have nothing to do with either, and the human good is 'deep happiness'. That's one sea change, and a big topic on its own in Foot that I can't go into here.

But the other, which I do want to look at, is that what goes into survival and reproduction *themselves*, in *our* lives as rational agents, also undergoes a sea change.

Whatever the life that is the human's good to live may be, individual survival is bound to be significant, since one has to survive to live. And the first way the significance of individual survival fits in when we are thinking of ourselves as human rational agents is in terms of the sorts of considerations we need to recognize as reasons for action. 'That might well kill me' is a consideration that *we need* to recognize as a reason for action, and as a reason of a certain weight, frequently compelling, in order to live well/live the good human life, because we need to recognize it in order to live at all (NG 12). But note that nothing immediately follows from this about action or, in the term she uses for the animal's 'operations'. It is about the recognition of reasons and it is among the grounds *not* for saying that we are defective if we don't kill aggressors, but for saying that we are defective without *prudence*. The virtue of prudence involves recognizing (amongst other things) exactly that—'It may well kill me' as a frequently—but certainly not always compelling, reason for action; so we need prudence (NG 24). Hence also the need for courage *as opposed to* recklessness which involves the same recognition. Moreover, hence the need for courage *as opposed to* timidity or cowardice which also involves it; if fear prevents me from seeing clearly that it is running away rather than standing still, or *not* going to the doctor with the lump I have discovered rather than going that might well kill me then I am not well equipped for survival.

And also perhaps the need for temperance? Perhaps only in the modern days of AIDS and really dangerous drugs do we need to recognize 'that may well kill me' as a compellingly good reason for not choosing *that* way to get pleasure, but 'that may well shorten my life or undermine my physical health so I die before my time' must have been pertinent for a good way back.

So even keeping 'survival' at the rock bottom—merely 'biological'—level, it hasn't departed from the scene; it's still in the conceptual structure.

And there is much more to be said. As she notes 'the good of survival itself is something more complex for human beings than for animals' and mentions memory (NG 42–3). She might also have mentioned the retention of the other multiple capacities that go into our being rational agents, and 'the *same* rational agent' (or 'same person' as we would say if we *weren't* talking philosophy). It is so reasonable to fear Alzheimer's if one of the things it can do to you is make you mistrust and hate the very people you used to love—which I gather it does—and undo your painstakingly acquired virtue of 'mildness' so that you become aggressive and irritable. As everyone around you will say, alas, she is not the person she was, for all that her memory isn't so bad. If there were a drug that brought an Alzheimer's sort of condition on while prolonging biological survival, then one would be ill fitted for *survival as the same rational agent* if one didn't recognize 'That will be death to *me*' as an almost certainly compelling reason for refusing it.

Note that qualification of 'almost certainly compelling'. The very reason why we don't get anything straightforward about action when we are talking about *our* 'strategies' (if someone wants to insist on the term) for individual survival, is that they are the strategies of rational agents and hence involve reason recognition. But, in particular circumstances which call for action, reasons compete with other reasons. Not only 'That may well kill me' but also 'That will *certainly* kill me' or 'will be the death of me' is a consideration that, in certain circumstances, may well not be a compelling reason, that is, decisive, but give way to others, such as 'That is the only way to save or preserve my fellows.'

Foot notes the important point that, while we are still using the plant and animal Aristotelian Categoricals, what goes into the Ss' features and operations regarding 'reproduction' does not *merely* cover the bringing into existence of more Ss. As we understand better after Darwin, though I bet it's in Aristotle too, 'reproduction' covers bringing into existence Ss that will *have* a life, not just *begin* one, that is, at the very least, have enough of a life to reproduce in turn. So most non-defective plants produce thousands of seeds and the mayfly lays thousands of eggs (as I remember) in order that there will be some that survive to have a life. If an individual one only produces a few, it's defective; that's a failure in their reproductive operation regardless of whether the few they produce all miraculously survive. And as we move up the ladder of nature to the more complex living things, 'reproduction' comes to cover yet more, in particular, as she rightly notes 'defence' and 'rearing' (NG 33). For many Ss, part of the Ss' reproductive strategy is defending the few offspring produced, in order that they survive to have a life.

Now 'rearing', when we think about it, covers quite a variety of things. For a start, in (I think) all birds, and certainly in all mammals, it covers *feeding* the young (or making arrangements for feeding as in the case of the cuckoo) and moreover feeding them the right food, without which they won't *develop* as they should. Now as I noted above, rather than talking about survival, Foot mostly talks about development and self-maintenance, but as soon as we get to the stage where a failure to develop the S way can be attributed to a defect in the 'operations' of the parent rather than a defect in the offspring, we can see that 'development' *also* comes under 'reproduction' with respect to the 'rearing' of young. If a baby elephant doesn't suckle, and hence doesn't develop, despite being offered the opportunity, it is defective; it lacks a feature it needs to survive. But if the mother elephant won't let it, and it hence fails to develop, the defect lies with her; elephants reproduce by suckling their young until the young are able to feed themselves, and she lacks a feature she needs to 'reproduce'.

Now under 'rearing' in the biological Aristotelian Categoricals, Foot also includes, where relevant, teaching, and I want to add a bit to what she says that I think she missed. Her favourite example of teaching as part of the rearing of the young, is the lioness teaching her cubs to hunt, but this is, I think, a misleading example in two ways. One is that it is so blindingly obviously related to teaching the cubs what they need to learn simply in order to survive—to maintain themselves. In that respect, it's just like the suckling. But that it has this terribly obvious feature makes it easy to overlook a more pertinently detailed description, namely that she is teaching them the *lion's* way of hunting (which, according to Midgley, is quite different from the tiger's way of hunting; Midgley 1983: 106) that is, she is teaching them, in this respect, *how to live the lion life*.

The second reason the example can be misleading is that, the big cats being pretty sophisticated animals, what the lioness does really *can* be called teaching. There is a pattern of action—her taking them somewhere suitable, her not hunting down the prey herself but hanging back while they chase it around, her heading it off back towards them when they have lost it—which we can see as intentional. But although there are many cases in which the animal Ss' ways of rearing their young—that is, providing the wherewithal for their proper development, involves what we might call *teaching* there are others which might better be described as 'providing opportunities for learning'.

When ducks hang out with their ducklings, and hens hang out with their chicks, we don't see any pattern like that in the lioness's behaviour that we could call teaching. Nevertheless, the ducklings and chicks learn *from* the adults around them just going on in their ordinary way, how to live the duck or chicken life. I don't know whether there is any case in which this applies to *hunting*, but I think it certainly applies to some cases of *foraging* for food. And Midgley says that 'a solitary duck reared among chickens' will never get the clues it needs to perform many of its central behaviour patterns. And, she says 'It is therefore a deprived duck' unable to live the *duck* life (1983: 106). And of course it can't live the hen life either, because it wants to swim and mess about in the water with other ducks.

So I would say that what goes into being reared, and hence 'reproduction', for a whole lot of birds and animals, is learning, from the ones that are doing the rearing, *how to live the S life*, the life that it is *that* sort of bird or animal's good to live. I think there must be a lot of biological ACs which are roughly of the form 'The young Ss learn from the adults around them to avoid such and such and go for so and so and do this not that' though I don't know of any.

So bearing all that in mind what happens when we look at 'reproduction' after the sea change and come to consider the ACs that pertain to us as rational agents? Well, *now* what goes into 'the rearing of the young', i.e., providing for their appropriate development, is providing for their development *into human rational agents*.

And I might say, given the way *we* live, that the catch phrase 'it takes a village to rear a child' is basically true. Given the way *we* live, children's acquisition of reason recognition is far from being solely in the hands of their parents; what they come to recognize as reasons for action, for well or ill has all sorts of inputs. So—I suspect that as part of filling the conceptual structure in with the ACs that are relevant to our moral evaluations of ourselves, we would need lots of ACs about children's development. As what I take to be a very obvious candidate, consider 'Human children need attentive love and security', and note that whether it is to be classified as a 'natural fact' under the natural-scientific conception is at best unclear. I take it to be obvious that there is a lot of work to be done in finding the relevant descriptions of how human life goes—the Aristotelian Categoricals that are to parallel 'Owls see in the dark and hunt at night.' And I think it is perfectly clear from what she says that they may include many that are not biological at all, but such things, perhaps, as 'Humans can derive an enormous satisfaction from what they think of as a good job well done' and 'Humans do not need lots of material possessions to be happy' and 'The human being risks life and limb, even lays down her own life, for the sake of something she sees as good' and 'Human beings can acquire a second nature which enables them to enjoy virtuous activity', and 'Human beings form life-long loving relationships' and 'human beings pursue theoretical knowledge for its own sake' and... well, 'that sort of thing'.

I also think that doing this work is going to be a most rewarding and enlightening task.

References

Anscombe, G. E. M. 1958. 'Modern Moral Philosophy'. *Philosophy* 33(124): 1–16.

Arnhart, L. 1998. *Darwinian Natural Right*. New York: SUNY Press.

Baggini, J. and J. Stangroom (eds). 2007. *What More Philosophers Think*. London: Continuum.

Casebeer, W. 2003. *Natural Ethical Facts: Evolution, Connectionism, and Moral Cognition*. Cambridge, MA: MIT Press.

Foot, P. 1963. 'Hume on Moral Judgments'. In D. Pears (ed.), *Hume: A Symposium*. London: Macmillan: 67–76.

Foot, P. 1972. 'Morality as a System of Hypothetical Imperatives', *The Philosophical Review* 81(3): 305–16.

Foot, P. 1978a. *Virtues and Vices: Collected Papers*. Berkeley and Los Angeles: University of California Press.

Foot, P. 1978b. 'Goodness and Choice'. In *Virtues and Vices: Collected Papers*, ed. Philippa Foot. Berkeley and Los Angeles: University of California Press: 132–47 [orig. pub. 1961].

Foot, P. 1978c. 'Moral Beliefs'. In *Virtues and Vices: Collected Papers*, ed. Philippa Foot. Berkeley and Los Angeles: University of California Press: 110–31 [orig. pub. 1958–1959].

Foot, P. 1978d. 'Moral Arguments'. In *Virtues and Vices: Collected Papers*, ed. Philippa Foot. Berkeley and Los Angeles: University of California Press: 96–109 [orig. pub. 1958].

Foot, P. 1995. 'Does Moral Subjectivism Rest on a Mistake?' In *Moral Dilemmas*. Oxford: Oxford University Press: 189–208 [orig. pub. 1995].

Foot, P. 2001. *Natural Goodness*. Oxford: Clarendon Press.

Foot, P. 2002. 'Rationality and Virtue'. In *Moral Dilemmas*. Oxford: Oxford University Press: 159–74 [orig. pub. 1994].

The Harvard Review of Philosophy. 2003. 'The Grammar of Goodness: An Interview with Philippa Foot'. *The Harvard Review of Philosophy* 11: 32–44. ISSN 1062 6239. http://www.hcs.harvard.edu/hrp/issues/2003/Foot.pdf.

McDowell, J. 1995. 'Two Sorts of Naturalism'. In R. Hursthouse, G. Lawrence, and W. Quinn (eds), *Virtues and Reasons: Philippa Foot and Moral Theory*. Oxford: Clarendon Press, 149–80.

Midgley, M. 1983. *Animals and Why They Matter*. Athens: University of Georgia Press.

Thompson, M. 1995. 'The Representation of Life'. In R. Hursthouse, G. Lawrence, and W. Quinn (eds), *Virtues and Reasons: Philippa Foot and Moral Theory*. Oxford: Clarendon Press, 247–296.

Thompson, M. 2008. *Life and Action: Elementary Structures of Practice and Practical Thought*. Cambridge, MA: Harvard University Press.

Index

For the benefit of digital users, indexed terms that span two pages (e.g., 52–53) may, on occasion, appear on only one of those pages.

Annas, Julia 15n.27, 39, 100n.8, 115n.17, 116, 147, 207–8, 235–6, 270
Anscombe, G.E.M. 2–4, 7–8, 54–5, 79, 98, 98n.4, 162–5, 162n.1, 164n.8, 171–2, 234–5, 237, 239, 269, 274, 277, 333, 335, 340
Aquinas, Thomas 64, 251, 280, 335–6
Aristotle 1–4, 7–9, 11–13, 15, 23–43, 45–84, 86–97, 121, 125, 128, 145, 147, 150, 152, 157–8, 162–3, 167, 181, 205–7, 213–20, 228, 233–40, 250–2, 267, 269, 274, 276, 279–80, 291, 300–1, 303, 307–8, 311–31, 335–6, 343–4
Aristotelian categoricals 10–11, 340–2, 344–50

Benevolence, *see* Charity
Brewer, Talbot 86–7, 86nn.1,3, 90–3
Brown, Lesley 31–3

Character 9, 11n.16, 27–8, 34–5, 45–7, 48n.4, 49, 51n.7, 55n.11, 62, 62n.19, 86–7, 89n.11, 90–3, 93n.13, 123–6, 125n.4, 128–9, 134–5, 139, 141–2, 147–8, 150–1, 153, 159, 162–3, 197, 216–22, 224, 227, 240, 300–1, 304–7, 318–19, 328, 333–4, 342, 344
Charity 14, 14n.24, 54–5, 64, 125–7, 130–1, 131n.8, 147–52, 166, 208, 254–5, 262–3, 300–1, 306–7, 310–12
Chrysippus 94, 99, 102–8, 111–14, 116
Cicero 98n.7, 99–102, 100n.8
Codifiability 66–84
Consequentialism 70, 121–2, 141–2, 144–6, 154–5, 164–8, 176, 178–80, 185, 194, 200, 202, 206, 210–11, 214–15, 257, 264–5, 279–80, 295–6, 304–5, 318, 327, 330, 334
Curzer, H. 25–6, 34, 36, 38

Darwinism, Darwinian 99–100, 213–14, 341–2, 346
Deontology 121–3, 125–7, 144–6, 154–5, 158, 165, 167–8, 176, 178–80, 185, 194, 200, 202, 210, 214–15, 300
Dilemmas 7, 7n.9, 8n.11, 48–9, 52–3, 59–60, 162–91
Driver, Julia 147–52, 156–7, 159

Emotions 2–3, 70, 116, 133–5, 137, 139, 147–8, 156–7, 162–3, 170–1, 216–22, 224, 234, 238–9, 241–52, 290–4, 305, 329
Environment, the 210–29
Eudaimonia 9, 11–13, 45–6, 55, 73, 86–7, 123–4, 124n.2, 125n.4, 137, 145, 157–8, 207–8, 216, 228, 235–6, 274–83, 300, 325–7
Evolution 313, 315, 317, 323–7, 331, 341

Family 285–98
Flourishing 9, 10, 13, 15, 123–4, 125n.4, 137, 157, 207, 208, 250, 326
Foot, Philippa 2–3, 5, 9–12, 12n.17, 63–4, 64n.22, 159–60, 162–3, 163n.4, 205, 228n.4, 262–3, 285, 300–1, 305, 319–22, 333–50
Friendship 86–93

Galen 97–9, 103–4, 106–7
Generics (*see* Aristotelian Categoricals)
Goodwill 86–93

Habituation 41, 47–8, 80–1, 221, 314, 323–4, 328
Happiness, *see* Eudaimonia
Hare, R.M. 24, 166, 309–11, 334, 337–8, 340

354 INDEX

Human nature 300–31
Hume, David 13, 15, 54–6, 168, 179, 188, 234–5, 237, 254–67, 269–83, 306–9, 339

Intrinsic worth 214, 221–5
Irwin, T 64, 69–71, 69n.2, 74–5, 81, 83

Justice 13–15, 49, 77–8, 104, 125–6, 128–31, 131n.8, 132n.10, 150–1, 163, 188–91, 205, 208, 212n.2, 219, 227–8, 233–4, 254–67, 269–83, 285–6, 293–5, 298, 300–1, 304, 306–7, 310–12, 342–3

Kant, Immanuel 95, 146, 156, 162–3, 194–5, 214–16, 219–20, 234, 236, 250, 257–8, 318, 324–5, 327, 339, 343

Legal ethics 173–91, 276–7
Locke, John 259–60, 269, 271–3, 276
Lying, Lies 50, 53–4, 79, 128–9, 151–4, 163–4, 167, 169, 173, 176–8, 187, 199, 202–3, 206, 304

McDowell, John 8n.10, 12–13, 46n.2, 51, 60n.17, 67, 74n.4, 78n.9, 80n.12, 124n.2, 162–3, 238, 302–4, 307, 345
MacIntyre, Alasdair 13, 162–3, 269, 321
Mean, doctrine of the 3–4, 23–43, 45–6
Moral Status 132–4, 193–7, 200–1, 205–7

Naturalism 9–13, 15, 147, 300–31, 341–5
Nussbaum, Martha 8n.11, 56–7, 67, 69–71, 69n.2, 74n.4, 276, 319

Okin, Susan Moller 15–16, 285–6, 293–4

Particularism 45–84
Phronēsis 7–9, 41, 45–84, 100, 149–50, 152–3, 158, 304–5
Phronimos, see phronēsis
Plato 23–4, 30–2, 38–9, 132n.11, 162–3, 167, 309, 314, 324–6, 329, 335–6
Posidonius 97–9, 106–7

Practical Wisdom (see also Phronēsis) 7–8, 45–84, 149–50, 152–3, 165, 175, 181, 183, 193, 205, 210–11, 214, 216–17, 219–20, 328
Professional ethics 173–91

Rationality 11–12, 94–117, 122–4, 150–1, 166–7, 213–14, 233–7, 240–52, 309, 318, 321–2, 327, 343–4
Rawls, John 14–16, 14n.25, 145–6, 155, 267, 269, 274, 279, 282n.15
Right action 1, 4, 121–30, 152–60, 167–91, 233
Rights 13–15, 130–2, 134, 137, 139–40, 194, 200, 201, 204, 206, 211–12, 254–67, 269–83, 285–7, 295

Stoicism 15n.27, 94–117
Swanton, Christine 9, 147, 151, 160

Thompson, Michael 9–10, 10n.12, 337–44
Tragic choice 157–8, 178

Unity of virtues 77–8, 151–2, 216–17
Urmson, J 25–6
Utilitarianism, see Consequentialism

Virtues Project TM 41–3, 154
V-rules 5, 74–7, 124–5, 127–8, 153–60, 162, 193–4

Watson, Gary 244, 250, 252, 301–2, 301n.6, 345
Williams, Bernard 125n.3, 127n.5, 181n.7, 254, 301–3, 303n.8, 313n.1, 318–19, 319nn.6,8, 325, 325n.13, 326n.14
Wittgenstein, Ludwig 2, 4, 9–10, 12–13, 56, 56n.12, 80–1, 258, 287, 287n.1, 319, 333, 340
Wonder 217–18
Woods, Michael 29–30, 49–50, 51n.7, 60n.18

Zagzebski, Linda 9